Once Upon a Time in War

C&C

CAMPAIGNS & COMMANDERS

GREGORY J. W. URWIN, SERIES EDITOR

Campaigns and Commanders

GENERAL EDITOR

Gregory J. W. Urwin, Temple University, Philadelphia, Pennsylvania

ADVISORY BOARD

Once Upon a Time in War

THE 99TH DIVISION IN WORLD WAR II

*To Bruce, Mike's friend. I hope
you enjoy this narrative history
of ordinary young guys who
defended the United States in
World War II.*

Robert E. Humphrey

Robert E. Humphrey

UNIVERSITY OF OKLAHOMA PRESS : NORMAN

Library of Congress Cataloging-in-Publication Data

Humphrey, Robert E.
    Once upon a time in war : the 99th division in World War II / Robert E.
Humphrey.
        p.   cm. — (Campaigns and commanders ; v. 18)
    Includes bibliographical references and index.
    ISBN 978-0-8061-3946-3 (hbk. : alk. paper)
    1. United States. Army. Infantry Division, 99th. 2. World War, 1939–1945—Regi-
mental histories—United States. 3. World War, 1939–1945—Campaigns—Western
Front. I. Title.
    D769.399th .H86 2008
    940.54'1273—dc22

                              2008010524

Once Upon a Time in War: The 99th Division in World War II is Volume 18 in the Campaigns and Commanders series.

The paper in this book meets the guidelines for permanence and durability of the
Committee on Production Guidelines for Book Longevity of the Council on Library
Resources, Inc. ∞

1 2 3 4 5 6 7 8 9 10

To all those who served in the 99th Infantry Division

"I love the infantry because they are the underdogs. They are the mud-rain-frost-and-wind boys. They have no comforts, and they even learn to live without the necessities. And in the end they are the guys that wars can't be won without."

Ernie Pyle, World War II correspondent, May 1, 1943

Contents

Illustrations

FIGURES

Maps

Preface

War came suddenly and violently to the United States in 1941. Inadequately prepared for a global conflict, the government needed to build up a huge military force quickly to combat formidable enemies who represented a serious military and political threat. Eventually the army created eighty-seven active divisions (forty-two served in Northern Europe). The 99th became one of the many new infantry divisions that comprised the emergency army of the United States, distinguishing it from the small number of regular army divisions and eighteen National Guard divisions. Also called the Checkerboard Division, with its identifying left shoulder patch of blue and white squares superimposed on a five-sided black shield, the 99th came into existence in November 1942.[1]

At full strength of 14,208 men, the 99th Infantry Division followed the World War II triangular organization of three infantry regiments, in this case the 393rd, the 394th, and the 395th. The regiments were divided into three battalions (first, second, and third) with 860 men in each and subdivided into four companies identified by letters of the alphabet running consecutively. Thus the 1st battalion contained A, B, and C rifle companies (each consisting of 187 enlisted men) and D, a heavy weapons company, 166 men, with eight .30-caliber water-cooled machine guns and six 81mm mortars. The second battalion consisted of E, F, and G rifle companies, and H, the heavy weapons company; the third battalion included I, K, and L rifle companies and M, the heavy weapons company. The alphabet letters stood for radio code names: Able, Baker, Charlie, Dog, Easy, Fox, George, How, Item, King, Love, and Mike. In addition, a cannon company for each regiment could fire six 105mm howitzers, two rocket launchers, and three .50-caliber machine guns.

A rifle company had three rifle platoons and one weapons platoon. Each rifle platoon consisted of forty-one men, while the weapons platoon had an officer, a platoon sergeant, and thirty-three enlisted men. The weapons platoon contained two squads of light machine guns (.30-caliber, air-cooled) and three squads of 60mm mortars. Finally, each rifle platoon was made up of three twelve-man squads; in each squad eleven men carried a .30-caliber, semi-automatic M-1 Garand rifle (weighing 9 lb., 5 oz.), and one soldier lugged the 22-lb. fully automatic Browning Automatic Rifle (BAR). While no one fighting in the division could be assured of complete safety, those 3,240 GIs in the twenty-seven rifle companies served offensively as the spear tip and defensively as the shield; therefore, they suffered the highest casualties.

The 99th Division first assembled and trained at Camp Van Dorn in southwestern Mississippi. Following combat maneuvers in Mississippi and Louisiana, the division relocated to a training facility at Camp Maxey in northeastern Texas. When the army transferred three thousand enlisted men from the 99th to the 85th and 88th Infantry Divisions, replacements came from the Army Specialized Training Program (ASTP), which had placed bright GIs in colleges and universities to produce engineers, doctors, dentists, and language specialists. Disappointed and unhappy about the program's cancellation, ASTPers lost an opportunity to complete a free college education; worse yet they became privates in an infantry division. Most thought their abilities and skills could be better utilized than as cannon fodder.

After weeks of basic and advanced infantry training, the 99th Division left Camp Maxey for the Port of Embarkation, Boston Harbor, departing on September 29, 1944, for Great Britain and, ultimately, the Continent. In early November they rode in trucks from the destroyed harbor of Le Havre, France, to forested front lines in the Ardennes (Belgium), at the time a quiet sector where wintry weather conditions and difficult terrain would, it was thought, guarantee limited combat. For a month this prognostication proved accurate, and some believed the war would end by Christmas.

Everything changed on December 16, 1944, when the *Wehrmacht* launched a massive counterattack that came to be known as the Battle of the Bulge, the largest battle involving American forces in World War II. Greatly outnumbered with limited tank and fighter support, many companies of the 99th incurred serious losses. After putting up a stout fight, they withdrew to the high, barren ground of Elsenborn Ridge and established defensive lines that stopped elements of the German Army from breaking through in their sector. During the six weeks that followed, infantry soldiers of the 99th endured three infantry attacks, artillery bombardment, sniper fire, and unrelenting cold and snow without stoves, adequate clothing, or warm, waterproof boots.

At the end of January 1945, the 99th became engaged in mopping-up operations over territory lost during the battle. After a brief respite behind the lines, the division moved across the Cologne Plain, reaching the Rhine River near Düsseldorf in early March 1945. Almost immediately the 99th rushed southward after the capture of the Ludendorff Bridge, crossed the Rhine at Remagen, and advanced east and then north, where they participated in the encirclement and capture of German forces in the Ruhr pocket. With barely a day's rest, 99ers piled onto trucks and joined George Patton's Third Army near Bamberg. From there they proceeded past Nuremberg and advanced to the Danube River, which the troops crossed on the 27th of April. A few days later, on May 8, 1945, the war came to an official end, six months after the division's initial combat, and the victorious Checkerboarders relocated to northern Bavaria and settled into postwar occupation of Germany. They accomplished their mission at a cost of 1,134 killed, 3,954 wounded, and 6,103 nonbattle casualties.[2]

The 99th Infantry Division, part of a giant war machine, helped defeat the German Army. Composed of young men from all parts of the country, they served out of a sense of duty and patriotism, not unlike millions of other GI Joes. This narrative history focuses on the physical and psychological hardships these men endured and how they coped with stress, fear, killing, capture, death, and the miserable conditions of infantry combat.

• • •

I first learned of the 99th Infantry Division in early 2001 when I read in the *Sacramento Bee* that a local 99th veteran had written a book about his army training and the initial fighting during the Battle of the Bulge. Growing up, I had been interested in World War II, so a few weeks later I called George Neill, the author. As it happened, Neill was taking a class at Sacramento State University, where I teach, and he stopped by and chatted. Neill gave me the names of three other veterans who had served in the 99th. For reasons known only to my subconscious, I placed long-distance calls to these three former GIs, who were friendly, candid, modest, and pleased someone was interested in their army service. From them I discovered the 99th Division had a veterans association with its own newspaper, the *Checkerboard,* which published an annual list of current members and their addresses. Using that database, I began talking with other 99ers, a process that would continue for more than five years, until I had interviewed either by phone or in person some 350 veterans of the division. What began as an interesting study became a personal mission to tell their tale, even as they and the rest of their generation recede from memory.

In June 2001, I attended my first 99th Division reunion at Fort Mitchell, Kentucky, where ex-GIs met old comrades and renewed relationships begun decades earlier. I heard talk about the Battle of the Bulge, particularly a long winter spent on bitterly cold Elsenborn Ridge in eastern Belgium. Their stories so piqued my curiosity that I decided to see the place for myself. I flew to Europe, where Jean Louis Seel, an experienced Belgian guide, escorted me onto the ridge (today a Belgian Army camp) and through various villages and roadways in eastern Belgium where fierce fighting occurred during the winter of 1944–1945. (In 2004, I returned to the Bulge battlefield and then followed the route of the division from Belgium to southern Germany.) I wrote a few essays for the *Checkerboard,* but not with the intention of producing a book. Eventually, at the urging of veterans I decided to expand my research and trace the history of the division, focusing on the thoughts, feelings, actions, and experiences of the men involved in infantry warfare.

As I talked to these veterans, men in their late seventies and early eighties, I learned they had revealed little or nothing to their families (parents, spouses, children, grandchildren) regarding what had happened during the war. Most 99ers have gone to their graves without sharing what they endured. But those with whom I spoke related experiences that had been seared and sealed into their memory banks. During these interviews a few men displayed distressful emotions recalling painful events they had kept bottled up for so many years, not wanting to relive incidents that produced horror and sorrow. Many interviewees told me I was the first person to ask them directly about their harrowing trials in combat.

Interviews lasted several hours, and I often reconnected (by e-mail, letter, and telephone) with the men to ask additional questions. My sample was neither systematic nor random, but it was weighted toward frontline infantrymen because the most stressful and dangerous conditions existed at the front, where no one wanted to be. I have relied on 99ers' personal memories and written memoirs of events that happened years earlier (a few men wrote short accounts at the war's conclusion), and these recollections could be influenced by subsequent conversations, readings, and the passage of time. Some veterans possess fantastic memories, able to recall minute details of certain episodes; others could remember only a few incidents and conversations that stuck in their minds. Normally many of us cannot recall much of what occurred last week or last month. But most of us can remember past events that produced great joy, sadness, or pain. In World War II a lifetime of terror, suffering, and loss were crammed into seconds, minutes, hours, and days of combat.

I was quite taken by these men, not only for their participation in a world-shaping event, but also because they experienced life-threatening situations they chose not to avoid. Youthful and patriotic, these men thought the United States was in great danger, and it was their duty to defend their country. As World War II and these American soldiers fade from our collective memory, we might honor them by learning and remembering what they did, fighting for a cause they believed in. We are indebted to these men, especially those who did not return.

Acknowledgments

I would like to thank the 350 veterans of the 99th Infantry Division who gave me their time and memories, without which this book could not have been written. Sadly many of these gentlemen soldiers have passed on without seeing how their words provided the basis for a history of the division. Although not all interviewees are identified in the text, they and their families should know that each veteran provided valuable information in my attempt to recapture what happened.

I am especially indebted to a few veterans who repeatedly answered my questions, provided helpful comments, and offered encouragement along the way to completion. They include: Howard Bowers D/394, Radford Carroll E/393, William Galegar G/395, Fred Kampmier I/394, James Langford I/394, James Larkey I/394, Ernest McDaniel F/393, Robert Mitsch L/394, Louis Pedrotti L/394, David Reagler I/394, Byron Reburn L/394, Ken Reed E/395, Joseph Thimm K/395, Rex Whitehead H/394, Byron Wilkins K/393, and most importantly, Harold F. Schaefer G/394, who saved me from committing numerous factual errors.

I am also grateful for the services of Jack Smith and Dan Restaino of Sacramento State University library and Mary Ilario in the still photograph section of the National Archives.

I would like to thank Steven Weingartner, copyeditor; Charles Rankin, editor-in-chief; Jay Dew, my editor; and the staff of the University of Oklahoma Press for helping to produce this book.

Finally, my biggest debt is to my daughter Bridget and my wife Beverly, without whom life would not be worth living.

Once Upon a Time in War

CHAPTER 1

The Coming of War

The Japanese attack on Pearl Harbor on December 7, 1941, struck like a lightning bolt, igniting a firestorm of patriotism that engulfed America. Before that unexpected assault the country was divided, with large segments of the public adamantly opposed to involvement in another foreign war. Uncertain as to Pearl Harbor's location, most Americans nonetheless knew something horrible had occurred when radio announcers interrupted regular programming to broadcast news of the Sunday-morning bombing in Hawaii. At 2:31 P.M. Eastern Time, CBS radio correspondent John Daly informed his listening audience that Japanese forces had struck American bases. In Westerville, Ohio, sixteen-year-old Warren Thomas and his father heard the shocking bulletin as they sat in the front room. Like everyone else listening to a radio that day, they stayed glued to their set in anticipation of additional bulletins. Francis Iglehart and his classmates at St. Paul's Prep School near Concord, New Hampshire, received the news from a dormitory supervisor and excitedly began to discuss which branch of service they would join, though the impetus, he confessed, was as much an escape from school as an expression of patriotism. That Sunday afternoon James Larkey's uncle took the whole family to the Polo Grounds to watch the New York Football Giants play the Brooklyn Football Dodgers. During the game, the loudspeaker system kept summoning military officers to report immediately to their unit headquarters. At dinner that evening they learned the reason for the urgent departures.[1]

Grant Yager was working at his dad's little store in Sandusky, Michigan, when the news broke. The next day he took a bus to Detroit and tried unsuccessfully to enlist in the Marines. In Marshfield, Wisconsin, sixteen-year-old Raymond Wenzel was sitting in his grandparents' house waiting for the Green Bay Packer football game to start when the announcement came over the radio. Not knowing where Pearl Harbor was, he wondered if the Japanese would bomb his family too. Robert Mitsch, a sophomore at the College of St. Thomas in St. Paul, Minnesota, heard the news on a tiny crystal set in his bedroom and hoped the American forces would "take it" to the Japanese. A senior at Catholic Central High in Detroit, Joseph Thimm sat in his best friend's car while they discussed the future, which they guessed would mean either enlisting or waiting to be drafted: "At this point the war became the focus of our lives." Robert Maclin, a freshman at Texas A&M University, was watching a polo match when the swing music playing on the radio of a convertible parked nearby was suddenly interrupted by a report of the war-triggering event, which soon "brought a more serious and sober mood to the campus." Carefree days had come to an end for Maclin and young men across the nation.[2]

Upon hearing what had happened, Ken Reed, a high school student in Astoria, Oregon, near the mouth of the Columbia River, worried that the coastal state might be invaded or bombed. Eager to do his part, Reed immediately tried to volunteer. When Homer Kissinger of Ottawa, Kansas, came home late in the afternoon, his mother, thinking Pearl Harbor was located somewhere in northern California, gave him an incoherent and frightening account of an attack on San Francisco in which hundreds had been killed.[3]

The seriousness of the situation was confirmed on Monday, December 8, when President Franklin Roosevelt asked Congress for a declaration of war in a six-minute speech broadcast live to the nation. Throughout the country, high school principals organized special assemblies for their students. At Riverton High School in southeast Kansas, the entire school, including Howard Bowers, gathered to hear the president's address. William Galegar, a farm boy from rural Oklahoma, and his Avant High School classmates, one hundred strong, listened quietly to the sober message that would dramatically impact their lives. Working as an historical aide for the National Park Service in Washington, D.C., Charles Roland initially didn't believe the news; he thought "those funny-looking, little Japs wouldn't dare attack our great naval base." But after learning the truth, "shock, disbelief, patriotic anger, excitement, and anxiety overcame" him and everyone else. Within days isolationism virtually disappeared as Americans realized, especially after Germany also declared war on December 11, the two oceans no longer functioned as an attack-proof barrier against foreign aggression.[4]

Upon learning of the war's beginning, B. O. Wilkins and his ROTC classmates at Louisiana State University marched to the university president's house and asked him what they should do to defend the country. Deep in the heart of Louisiana, they stood ready to fight. Sam Lombardo, a sergeant in the regular army, and his outfit were bivouacked near Lynchburg, Virginia, when they learned of the Japanese air attack. He later recalled, "No one slept much that night" because "everyone was uncertain about what was going to happen next." When John Hendricks attended class the next day at General Motors Technical College, the machine shop teacher, who thought Japan could only produce cheap, shoddy goods, confidently predicted the United States would defeat Japanese forces in "just a few weeks."[5]

Although draft calls were speeded up, thousands entered the services voluntarily. Glenn Bronson recalled students in advanced ROTC leaving college and joining up. Likewise, James Bussen remembered many of his high school classmates in St. Paul, Minnesota, quit school and registered for the draft. James Larkey, a freshman at the University of Pennsylvania, canceled his registration at semester break and volunteered for the army because "I wanted to see what I was made of." Having enjoyed "a pampered life," Larkey wanted "to try hardship and prove myself." Rocco Razzano, twenty-six-years old with a wife and child, volunteered because he felt the "army needed me." Nicholas Gianopoulos' parents, poor Greek immigrants proud of their adopted country, told him the United States was a great country, and Nick should do his duty.

While parents accepted the necessity of service to the country, they did not eagerly embrace the idea of putting their sons in harm's way. When Edwin Stoch departed, he insisted his mother not accompany him to the train station in downtown Cleveland because he knew she would break down. Upon reaching the terminal, Stoch observed hundreds of draftees accompanied by their parents, all of whom were openly crying: "It was not a happy day." Although his father remained silent as he left, Stoch learned afterwards that he hardly spoke to other workers in the factory during his son's absence.

After receiving his draft notice, Steve Kallas of Cleveland, Ohio, boarded a train bound for an induction center, "curious as a cat to find out what army life was all about." Lyell Thompson, a farm boy in the drought-stricken dust bowl of central Oklahoma, heard the news on a battery-operated radio and worried that the "darn war would be over before I get in." Returning to the University of Washington after Christmas break, David Thompson was also "concerned the war would end before I had a chance to get involved." Having seen newsreels of Hitler and the havoc the Germans wreaked on Poland and France, Thompson felt they must be stopped.[6]

Some inducement came from a sense of patriotic duty; the country was in peril and in the mythic tradition of the revolutionary Minute Men, good patriots ought to come to the aid of the nation if they cared about its survival. Young men who stayed out lacked the character to make sacrifices and the courage to put their lives on the line. They were acting selfishly, not heroically, at a time when the whole nation was pitching in to save democracy from militarism. The war appeared to be an apocalyptic struggle between the forces of good and evil, and civilization would surely defeat barbarism if Americans pulled together.

After a decade of unemployment, poverty, social dislocation, labor unrest, and class conflict, the war offered an opportunity for the country to come together and unite in a selfless, idealistic crusade. Self-confidence and optimism replaced doubt and pessimism. America would stand up to authoritarianism and save the world for democracy. Given the lofty goals and values at stake, no one could ignore the seriousness of the struggle and the dire consequences of losing.

• • •

Frederick Feigenoff wanted to volunteer but his parents were opposed because his older brother had been wounded at Pearl Harbor. Instead, he went to work for a defense subcontractor where he could have used a deferment for the duration, but "thought I am no better than anyone else." So he requested the local draft board in New Jersey remove his deferment, and subsequently he was drafted. There existed, Feigenoff admitted, social pressure to serve. Strangers and neighbors "gave you dirty looks" with the unspoken question, "What are you doing here when other young men are fighting?" The Service Flag with a blue star (indicating a son in the armed forces) in a family's window testified to a household's sacrifice and patriotism, while silently pressuring those eligible but not serving.[7]

Edgar Henson, married and the father of a baby girl, might have avoided the draft because he worked for the Army Corps of Engineers. He decided, however, to volunteer because "his country was in need." Thor Ronningen, a twelfth-grader, felt "like a slacker" after his older brother was drafted and he couldn't join him. "It would have broke [sic] my heart," J. C. Jones commented, "if I hadn't gone. All the boys in Benton, Kentucky, were in; I thought it would be exciting." Francis Chesnick's two brothers were already serving, so he was keen to join the war effort, which promised to be "a great adventure" and a chance to see the country and the "world beyond the oceans." Joseph Hineman did not mind being drafted; he wanted to be like his father who had served in the First World War. Radford Carroll decided to go because "all the other people of my age group were going," except for the "physically or mentally defective," and he didn't want to be identified with those groups.[8]

John Barton, the son of a Montana rancher, could have used a deferment to avoid the military, but "my world was pretty small and limited mostly to the county line, and there were things out there I wanted to see." Earle Slyder was serving as an army air force x-ray technician but decided he "didn't want to fight the war taking x-rays." Charles Swann, happy to be drafted into the infantry, "wanted to be where I could fight. I wanted to be a big hero." Maltie Anderson's three older brothers and his cousins were already in the service; "every one was going," and it "would have been inappropriate not to go." Charles Katlic preferred to avoid the infantry, but he wanted to "fight the Japs." B. C. Henderson, who worked on his father's ranch, went to the draft board in Lubbock, Texas, and told them to remove his deferment: "I felt I wasn't contributing enough. I wasn't doing as much as others were. I felt I ought to be doing more." After induction the doctors discovered Hubert Moody had a hernia and advised he could be discharged honorably. Moody asked them to please operate, which they did, and he stayed. Idealism, innocence, social pressure, patriotism, a desire for adventure, anger at the evil aggressors, and the chance to prove one's manhood motivated men to serve. Everyone sensed, if only vaguely, this decisive event would affect the course of history, and few wanted to miss out on something so momentous.[9]

• • •

The tremendous upsurge in patriotic feelings roused by the onset of war did not subside until war's end. As each class (1942, 1943, 1944) of high school students reached eighteen and headed for their draft boards, the same sentiments persisted. Howard Stein, a student at Swarthmore College, became upset when others in the Enlisted Reserve Corps (or ERC, begun in April 1942) were drafted but he wasn't. Stein wrote a letter to the adjutant general of the army, asking why he wasn't taken—he soon was. Called up in July 1943, Mel Richmond was happy but worried (like his friends) he "might flunk the physical" and not be inducted. David Perlman would have been "crushed" if he had been rejected as 4-F. Apprehensive that poor eyesight might disqualify him, Perlman did his best to memorize the eye chart, and he passed. Similarly "gung-ho," Ralph Miller volunteered for the draft but was turned away because of a heart murmur and high blood pressure. Two weeks later, to his delight, the army drafted him and the doctors pronounced him fit for service. Radford Carroll was "uneasy" that he might be found "physically defective" and be rejected. James Langford tried to join the navy when he turned seventeen but was turned down because he wore glasses and had bad teeth. At eighteen, however, the army thought he would do fine. Since Donald Wallace had suffered a stroke as a baby, his right hand was useless. Nevertheless, by hiding that hand in a pocket and using his two hands together, he passed the physical. Wallace did not see himself as handicapped, so it was important he not be rejected; thankfully "the army was not too careful when it came to amassing cannon fodder."[10]

Patriotism was not the only motivation for enlisting. By the time Tony Pellegrino finished high school, his brother and his friends had already left for the service; consequently, he decided, since he had "nothing to do," he would join up. Drafted in 1942, Isadore Rosen looked forward to escaping the pressures of running a wholesale butcher business. Ralph Shivone volunteered because he had a chance to become an officer and send some money home to his widowed mother.[11]

Most recruits did not relish the prospect of serving in the infantry. The army air force scored high on the glamour scale. Even the navy was considered more desirable than the army; after all, the air force and navy had first rights on volunteers, and those who scored highest on the Army General Classification Test (150 multiple-choice questions in forty minutes) were more likely to be selected by the air force.

Young men already in college hoped they might finish their education. Many were told that if they joined the Enlisted Reserve Corps (ERC) they could complete their degrees while preparing to become officers in the army. Robert Mitsch delayed active duty for six months in ERC, but the extra time prompted "rumblings in the neighborhood as to why I was not in service, whereas others were." When finally ordered to report, Mitsch was glad to "get the monkey off my back." Occidental College student Louis Pedrotti explained that no one wanted to be sent directly to the front lines as a private in the infantry: "Even though we all felt that we were 'doing something' in a just cause, there was still the personal desire to get the best possible 'deal' in the service of our country." James McIlroy joined the ERC at Texas A&M for the same reason: "I wanted to be in the service because it was not popular at that time to be a draft dodger. I just didn't want to be in the infantry." Robert Maclin remembered being told by the army that enlisted reservists would not be ordered to active duty until after graduation, at which time they would receive commissions as second lieutenants. But all the enlisted reservists received a rude shock, for soon they were called to active duty—and not as officers-to-be. It was the first of many promises the army broke.[12]

INDUCTION AND BASIC TRAINING

When the volunteers and draftees received "greetings" from the Selective Service, they reported to local draft boards and were later transported to induction centers. There, young men, stripped naked, moved along what amounted to a human assembly line where physicians, dentists, and psychiatrists examined their suitability for military service. Prudery and privacy came under assault, which lasted for the duration of their service. Those who passed (and many did not, especially in the beginning) felt an affirmation of their fitness and manhood. They were fingerprinted, required to sign induction papers, and given an army serial number (ASN) to be memorized. Decades later Louis Pedrotti could recite his number instantly, almost as if it "were engraved permanently across the inner surface of my cranium."

In a short time the inductee reported to a reception center where he received immunization shots, clothing, shoes, and two sets of "dog tags," a self-mocking, sarcastic term coined by American soldiers, equating their status to a domestic pet. This all-important medallion (embossed with the soldier's name, serial number, year of tetanus shot, blood type, and religion) provided surgeons and grave registrars with vital information about the wounded and the deceased; for Jewish soldiers captured by the Germans, the "H" (Hebrew) stamped on their tags proved to be a source of anxiety and danger.[13]

A military bureaucracy, which hastily produced a huge army totaling eighty-seven divisions, required a serial number for each soldier to organize and track masses of men. The men were called GIs, for "government issue," a mass-produced, military commodity, like jeeps, tanks, and M-1 rifles. Soldiers may not have consciously reflected on the implications, but aware or not, the term acknowledged they had become numbered cogs in a gigantic war machine. The entire induction process systematically deprived recruits of their individuality, as they were assigned to units, camps, and occupations with some attention paid to their skills and interests, but many ended up as infantrymen. Military uniforms replaced civilian clothes, and individual tastes in grooming and appearance gave way to homogeneity, even in the matter of haircuts. The recruit could not at first fully grasp the nature and extent of his transformation, for he retained his name and a sense of being distinct. But after weeks of standardized training, the resulting change was visible. When Radford Carroll marched with his company during basic training in Tyler, Texas, a woman standing on the sidewalk gasped, "Why, they all look just alike!" An Army sergeant replied to her, "They are supposed to look all alike."[14]

• • •

Anticipating U.S. involvement in the conflict, the War Department had launched a crash program of camp construction even before December 1941. From the fall of 1940 through the summer of 1942, forty-six new training camps sprang up, many of them scattered throughout southern states. Established training centers were also expanded to accommodate the flood of new recruits. In some cases living quarters consisted of tarpaper shacks, cold and drafty in the winter, hot and muggy during the summer. At Camp Maxey, Texas, the basic training facility, separated from the base's main barracks, consisted of a fenced-in compound of small, olive-drab plywood shacks originally erected to house expected Japanese prisoners, hence its popular name the "Jap Trap." Trainees slept on canvas cots with straw-filled mattresses covered by two woolen blankets unneeded in the blistering heat of a Texas summer. Sanitary conditions included galvanized garbage cans that served as urinals and smelly outdoor two-holers that attracted swarms of flies. Surrounded by barbed wire fences and wooden guard towers, the recruits (college boys from the ERC) felt more like prisoners than soldiers.[15]

Basic training consisted of performing close-order drilling, learning army regulations and the manual of arms, cleaning and firing light infantry weapons, running the detested obstacle course, listening to lectures, doing calisthenics, scrubbing barrack floors and windows, "policing" or combing the grounds for paper scraps and cigarette butts, saluting commissioned officers, and marching on ten-mile (one twenty-five mile) hikes with full pack. Unrefined instructors introduced recruits to the tightly regimented world of infantry training. According to Robert Mitsch, noncommissioned officers, or "non-coms,"—sergeants, identified by stripes on their sleeves, as opposed to the single brass bar commissioned lieutenants wore on their shirt collars—could humiliate you just by their "rough talk and being picky, picky, about how your tie was tied, your bed was made, the foot locker's neatness, etc." Learning to gulp tasteless food was another army requirement; fussy eating habits were abandoned, for the choice was "take it" or go hungry. To Radford Carroll, basic training at Camp Fannin, Texas, represented the "nearest thing to hell that the Army [could] devise."[16]

The army emphasized conditioning, which required physical endurance and psychological toughness. Each young guy felt enormous pressure to measure up and overcome every obstacle and challenge thrown his way. It was considered humiliating to drop out of a march and return to camp in an ambulance. Not completing these tests reflected badly on one's manhood and self-esteem. Joseph Thimm asserted, "I had a responsibility to do my best. I was going to work as hard as I could to be the best soldier I could." These young guys knew they were "on trial," and they wanted, according to James Bishop, to show they "were worthy" and "could take it."[17]

Robert Walter thought noncoms were "sadistic" at Camp Wood, near Waco, Texas. After training all day, cleaning up, and having dinner, a sergeant would burst into the barrack and order everything be removed and the floors, latrines, and walls scrubbed down, even though the living quarters were clean. There seemed to be no purpose to this tiresome, petty harassment except to demean the recruits; moreover, some officers told the enlisted men they would never measure up as real soldiers. Once, when trying to escape camp life, Walter and a buddy attempted to rent a room in a Waco hotel but were informed nothing was available. As they were leaving, a lieutenant approached the front desk and was immediately given a room. The message in the army and in civilian life was the same; privates represented a lower form of being.[18]

Most recruits completed the thirteen-week, grueling trial, even those especially challenged by the rigors of infantry training. That they persevered despite handicaps testified to their determination and fear of failure. Stewart Fischer confessed his parents "would have been mortified and profoundly ashamed of me and of themselves if I had left the army." A few recruits did not share such patriotic sentiments or judge themselves by existing definitions of manliness, and they devised ways to be discharged. During basic training at Camp Wolters, Texas, Robert Mitsch observed tiny, bespectacled Wally Cox ("Mr. Peepers" on an early, popular television show) put on a uniform with full pack and pick flowers on Sundays—Cox was soon gone. At Camp Maxey, Howard Harris recalled "a sad sack character" in his platoon who took his rifle into the shower where he washed and oiled it. This and other bizarre behavior (getting lost on field exercises) convinced the men he did not belong. Much to their relief, he disappeared, never to be seen again.[19]

• • •

The close-order drill, an antiquated infantry battle tactic, accustomed recruits to obey instantly commands given by a noncom. John McCoy was told at Camp Fannin in Tyler, Texas, "The government is not paying you to think, just do what an officer tells you." Superiors would give orders, and novices need only act without questioning the reason or wisdom of the commands. Authoritarianism and conformity replaced self-direction and independence, for discipline served a critical function in the modern army. Lieutenant Robert Bass viewed his citizen soldiers as being superior to "the German, who has spent the better part of his life pursuing military training." The mythology surrounding Revolutionary War farmers besting trained British soldiers and mercenary Hessians persisted in the twentieth century.[20]

Privates (draftees and volunteers) quickly ascertained they were peasants in a class system where rank determined authority, privilege, and pay. Possessing considerable power, drill instructors and officers could punish and humiliate their charges to condition them to be obedient soldiers. Praise, a tonic for self-esteem and morale, went missing from the army's vocabulary. The most a recruit could hope for might be the absence of criticism.

The mandatory saluting of commissioned officers (except indoors) annoyingly reminded GIs of their inferiority. In civilian life differences in power and status existed, but inequality was not constantly and brusquely thrust upon subordinates, as was the case in the army. Those wearing stripes, bars, and eagles demanded overt respect for rank, even though some might not deserve it, if measured in terms of competent leadership. Many noncommissioned and even commissioned officers had attained their positions because they had joined the service in the Great Depression of the 1930s or had been members of the National Guard. As in many other organizations, length of service could lead to advancement.

Recruits arrived from all sections of the country: crowded streets of New York, coal mines of Pennsylvania, cornfields of Iowa, hills of West Virginia, and sunny locales of southern California. The army assembled this human mishmash and shaped it into a cohesive fighting unit. It happened, partly because of the training and partly because of the trainees' support for each other. Detached from home, family, friends, and familiar surroundings, recruits looked to their buddies for sustenance and companionship.

Younger recruits, especially those who had never been away from home, suffered homesickness. John McCoy's discomfort began at the reception center where he became "lonesome, dejected, and frightened of the future. I was close to tears." A recruit needed to make friends as a survival or coping mechanism. The army didn't care whether friendships developed, but it did want members of a squad or platoon to look out for one another as a means of promoting unit cohesion and combat effectiveness. Joseph Thimm found camaraderie often developed quickly: "You lined up for roll in order by squads, and your bunks were arranged the same way, so you got to know your immediate neighbors and the guys in your squad very well." If fortunate enough to be placed in a group with similar interests and background, the recruit's process of adjustment eased considerably.[21]

Educational levels and geography created lines of demarcation not easily broken. In the early 1940s only four out of ten white men (two out of ten black men) finished high school, and one-third had no education beyond grade school. Having a high school diploma or attending college reflected and produced different attitudes and values. A college education (though most hadn't finished their degrees) conferred prestige, carried the promise of a better-paying occupation, and perhaps signaled higher intelligence. The educated therefore considered themselves superior to the uneducated. By the same token, those with limited schooling perceived a certain arrogance on the part of so-called college boys. Some noncommissioned officers resented and feared their better educated trainees and accordingly could make their lives uncomfortable. It was a clash of culture and class.[22]

• • •

Northern boys, actually anyone from outside the old Confederacy, discovered southern recruits, calling themselves "rebels," identified strongly with southern values and attitudes. One GI recounted that if you ventured into a barrack dominated by southerners, you had to sing "Dixie" or suffer the consequences. Southern boys prided themselves on their ability to cope with the heat and humidity, in contrast to northern recruits who suffered mightily from such hellish weather. Moreover, "rebels" knew how to fight off chiggers—tiny, six-legged mites that burrowed into the skin, causing severe itching and scratching, which could lead to infections. Harold Mann of LaGrange, Georgia, claimed, "Rebs knew you sprinkled yourself with smelly sulfur to discourage these horrible vermin, but northerners were slow to learn." Hershel Kennedy, a Louisiana farm boy, understood one applied bleach or Dr. Tichner's Antiseptic to tick and chigger bites. Differences in language and dialects clearly identified and separated the two regions, as did overt southern prejudice toward black people. Joseph Thimm contended "an underlying hostility" existed between the two groups of soldiers because of different attitudes and beliefs. Thimm and other northerners could not accept southern racist attitudes and the frequent use of "nigger" and "coon" in referring to blacks. Soldiering and combat would eventually override but not completely reconcile these differences.[23]

Racial segregation appalled northern soldiers. Fred Ratowsky of Brooklyn was shocked by the impoverishment and servility of southern blacks. They seemed "beaten down, nearly invisible" and, if any climbed aboard a bus, "they put their heads down and headed right for the back of the bus." Tony Pellegrino, who hailed from Norristown, Pennsylvania, boarded a bus to Fort Worth and absentmindedly sat down in a seat toward the rear. Other white riders shouted sharply at him: "Those seats are for niggers!" Pellegrino was bothered by the use of that word and stunned to discover that segregation extended to seating arrangements on a bus. He decided to stay put, whereupon the bus driver came back and told him to move forward. Pellegrino replied indignantly: "I'll sit where I want to." With that, the driver kicked him off the bus.[24]

• • •

Leaving home meant being thrust into the harsh world of army life that included a shocking introduction to taboo subjects that many families rarely discussed. Like everyone else Howard Bowers had to attend personal hygiene lectures and films to learn about "horrible venereal diseases that I had never heard of back in Kansas." Louis Pedrotti saw filmic images of men with festering, ulcerated genitalia, victims blinded by syphilis, and others unable to speak because of larynxes diseased by oral activity. He quickly concluded that the dangers of the battlefield were nothing compared to the menace of the bedroom. At Camp Fannin, John McCoy discovered the first two toilets in the latrine were labeled, "for VD cases only." "Wow! Most of us wouldn't even look at the signs as we passed them."

Besides the rigorous training, recruits had to adjust to an utter lack of privacy. Platoon members showered, ate, and drilled together. They relieved themselves in open stalls and in slit trenches while on marches. An individual could almost never enjoy the pleasure of solitude. It meant recruits came to know one another quite well and sometimes close friendships developed out of these associations. It also meant that a trainee had to adjust to and deal with individuals he would normally not have encountered in civilian life for any sustained length of time.[25]

The army fostered a new ideal, namely, the group came before the individual, and each soldier had a responsibility to perform his job and look out for his buddies. Competition between platoons in marching, obstacle course runs, and shooting was encouraged. A few officers taunted the recruits for not measuring up to the accomplishments of other platoons. One captain made a company empty their canteens and march in the blistering Texas heat, while he rode away in his jeep with an ample supply of water. This macho attitude, that "real" men, especially subordinates, can and should endure any amount of physical deprivation, typified a long-standing American definition of masculinity.

Even though trainees were taught to think and act in concert, as part of a group, pre-army attitudes about competition and individual achievement persisted. Individual shooting scores on the rifle range reflected a recruit's proficiency. Soldiers were encouraged to become the most accurate shooters; the levels from top to bottom included "Expert," "Sharpshooter," and "Marksman." Robert Mitsch confessed the thought had crossed his mind that if he deliberately missed the targets, the army might pull him out of the infantry. But competitive juices and self-respect wouldn't allow him to perform poorly, and he attained "Expert" standing.[26]

Joseph Thimm, who stood 6' 2" and weighed 185 pounds (the average soldier in World War II measured 5' 8" in height and weighed 140 pounds), ran into a few guys who were bigger, stronger, and faster. "You tested yourself against them, determined to stay up." At Camp Maxey, Thimm met Harry Threlkeld, Jr. from Memphis, who was "strong, smart, and could do the Queen Anne Salute [a complicated rifle exercise]. I admired Harry and competed against him even in the boxing ring. Harry set a standard and a lot of us

wanted to be like him." Despite the army's emphasis on group solidarity, competitiveness and individualism were not extinguished;
rather, they were redirected toward army goals and values. Shooting
proficiency, obstacle course times, and team sports competition
emphasized a contribution to the group. The individual had a responsibility to perform well because it reflected on the platoon, company,
regiment, and ultimately the division.[27]

Young men who grew up on farms or engaged in manual labor
generally adapted more quickly to infantry training. Playing football,
basketball, and baseball or having athletic ability better prepared
the recruit for the physical demands of soldiering. Those who had
participated in the Boy Scouts had experienced living outdoors;
guys who took ROTC in high school or in college already knew
close-order drills and the manual of arms. Those who had hunted for
small game as kids excelled at target shooting. Size was an advantage
in carrying heavy weapons (the BAR, machine gun, and the mortar)
and full field packs weighing sixty pounds. Height favored the tallest
as they marched in front (for aesthetic reasons) with longer strides,
while shorter fellows inhaled dust and took extra steps to keep pace.

Youths with artistic and intellectual interests felt ill prepared for the
tough, dirty work of infantry training. The clumsy and the uncoordi-
nated struggled with demands imposed by impatient drill instructors
who shouted out commands. Loners, non-conformists, the undisci-
plined, and those who hated authority had difficulty obeying the rigid
(sometimes seemingly senseless) army regulations. Ridiculed and
punished, these individuals were forced to work long hours in the
kitchen (KP or "kitchen police"), clean latrines, dig foxholes, and
forgo weekend passes to leave the base and thus escape extra duty and
petty harassment, popularly known as "chicken shit" by the troops.

Recruits from churchgoing families were reared to respect authority
and act like gentlemen. Once in the army, however, these young men
encountered a rough, lower-class lifestyle in which swearing was an
accepted form of expression. Louis Pedrotti believed sergeants "deliberately brutalized our sensitivities" with a language he and his friends
called "shit/piss/fuck," though it "came out something like 'shipissfuk'."
Vulgar language demonstrated one's toughness and virility, and thereafter, to prove their masculinity and achieve inclusion, the new men
quickly embraced the army's profane vernacular.[28]

The trainees also learned soldier slang. Sleeping bags became "fart sacks," recruits ate in "the mess hall," "SNAFU" [situation normal, all fucked up] denoted an administrative or operational problem; an ambulance became "the meat wagon," and "the eagle shits," meant payday. The use of vulgar words expressed a vocabulary free of the restraints and gloss of polite society. Many took pleasure in acting out this rebellion. Referring to the dying, wounded, or injured in the ambulance as "slabs of meat" transformed an emotionally disturbing situation into gallows humor, thereby allowing soldiers to protect themselves from feeling and thinking about the awful condition that potentially awaited them. This raw candor contrasted sharply with the romanticized depictions of army life and combat in magazines, newspapers, advertisements, and movies.

Smoking cigarettes, cheap and plentiful in the Army, also signified manhood. Some had taken up smoking as teenagers, but many others became hooked on cigarettes during their stint in the military. Officers assumed everyone smoked and allowed smoke breaks during marches. Overseas on the front lines with its attendant dangers and tension, smoking became understandably even more necessary. Although tobacco companies encouraged and abetted the habit of chewing tobacco and smoking cigarettes, with disastrous consequences for health, Fielding Pope defended it as "one of the few pleasures left to GIs."[29]

While not legally permitted off the base in dry southern counties, beer was served to enlisted men at the Post Exchange or PX. Drinking alcohol, another mark of manliness, was looked upon favorably by noncommissioned officers. It offered refreshment to men dehydrated by long marches in the broiling sun and a means of relaxation. Sometimes it also led to excess and fistfights, both on and off the base.

Another temptation readily available to recruits was sex with prostitutes, who flocked to towns near military bases. Joseph Thimm, an upstanding Catholic boy, became aware that some men were "more worldly than I was." They visited "a nest of whores in Mineral Wells" and returned to Camp Wolters "bragging about getting laid." They urged him to accompany them and "get a piece too," but Thimm declined. One day William Galegar and two buddies met three friendly, young ladies willing to share a taxi ride to the amusement park in

Dallas. Along the way the GIs discovered, much to their chagrin, the women "were the type of ladies that our mothers stated we should avoid." When one guy began to lecture them on how such behavior was ruining their lives, the unimpressed women exited the taxi. Similarly one young recruit was shocked when his seaman brother, visiting him in Paris, Texas, called the front desk and ordered up a prostitute while staying at a local hotel.

The army automatically assumed soldiers would have sex with undesirable women and issued condoms to the troops. For many, this was their first exposure to "rubbers"; however, they were not emboldened but instead embarrassed by the implications. Ernest McDaniel and his friends were amused by army policy, for they "had little or no sexual experience, and the thought that the government actually expected us good Presbyterian boys to go out and have sex was one more indication that the powers that be were out of touch with reality." Still, having a condom in one's wallet might indicate sexual prowess, and for some, losing one's virginity signaled the attainment of manhood. Living in an all-male environment away from family, neighborhood, and respectable supervision offered young men the opportunity to break rules and conventions. Some took advantage of the possibilities; others adhered to standards ingrained from family, church, and school.[30]

Having survived the rigors of basic training, the recruits believed they had become soldiers. Those with high scores on the army's intelligence test (above 115) were offered a chance to resume or begin college, for the army (like the navy) had created a special program that would educate bright young men to become engineers, doctors, dentists, and language specialists. The Army Specialized Training Program or ASTP siphoned off 140,000 recruits to colleges and universities throughout the country. Most recruits who completed basic training in Texas were sent to the University of Texas, East Texas State, Louisiana State University, the University of Arkansas, Sam Houston State Teachers College, Oklahoma A&M, or John Tarleton Agricultural College in Stephenville, Texas. The army promised the inductees they would earn college degrees in an accelerated program and afterwards become commissioned officers. Escaping drudgery, harassment, and boredom for college life seemed like a dream come true. And for a time it was.[31]

ARMY SPECIALIZED TRAINING PROGRAM (ASTP)

Recruits who landed on college campuses rejoiced at this wonderful turn of events, which would save "the cream of the country's youth" from being slaughtered. Previously the army assured college students who joined the Enlisted Reserve Program they could finish their degrees before being called to active duty. That proved to be a false promise. The ASTP seemed to be the army's way of making amends. Everyone's spirits rose, for these GIs in college were working toward their futures while serving the country. Officers told them they were "special" and "should expect something great from [the] training." They could pursue college degrees at government expense, something many of them could not have afforded as civilians. The $50-a-month salary, with deductions for a $10,000 life insurance policy ($6.50 per month) and patriotic war bonds at $18.75 (to mature in ten years for $25) did not leave much spending money; nevertheless, it was more than they had earned previously.[32]

After a rough, strenuous interlude in basic training, these GIs had returned to civilized living and surroundings. For Radford Carroll, seeing the "green" of Louisiana State University in Baton Rouge "hurt my eyes." Instead of a "drab, dirty" army camp, he beheld a "clean, beautiful campus filled with shrubbery." The ASTPers lived in nice dormitories, two or four to a room, often with adjacent showers and toilets. They ate in college cafeterias, and, according to Robert Maclin, at East Texas Teachers College in Commerce, "mother-like ladies" prepared the "best food we would ever have." Leon Rogers found the offerings much improved over the army's chipped beef on toast or "shit on a shingle." Rogers was "thrilled with the upgraded living conditions and excited about school again." After the bare facilities of the "Jap Trap," James McIlroy asserted that East Texas State Teachers College seemed "like paradise, with green grass, trees, girls, clean sheets and all the milk we wanted to drink."[33]

Although they followed a regimented program and marched off to class in columns, carrying books instead of rifles, no sergeants barked at their heels. In fact, leadership roles rotated among the men. Regular faculty taught the classes, though the quality of instruction was uneven. Joseph Thimm claimed the math professor at John Tarleton Agricultural College was "only one page ahead of us, and some of the guys were way ahead of her." They took heavy loads (double the usual number of classes) of the standard college fare: English, history, geography, mathematics, chemistry, and, depending upon educational background, engineering courses. But they helped each other with a real sense of solidarity. Risto Milosevich and his three roommates divided up the schoolwork, studying past "lights out" at 10 p.m. by using blankets to cover their flashlights. Rex Whitehead discovered "that in many cases the worst soldiers during training proved to be best students" and the best tutors.[34]

Unfortunately the army didn't solicit course and career choices from individual soldiers. Joseph Thimm and Louis Pedrotti would have preferred to put time and energy into foreign languages. Instead they were forced into engineering, a one-education-fits-all mold, which they disliked. Pedrotti scored high on a medical examination and was offered the opportunity to leave John Tarleton for dental school at Baylor University. He declined the offer: "I didn't want to be separated from my friends," particularly fellow classmates from Occidental College in Los Angeles.[35]

There was an added incentive to study hard and pass the courses; everyone feared that those who failed would be sent directly to the infantry. "We studied enough," James McIlroy stated, "so that dreaded assignment would not happen." Pedrotti, who lacked an aptitude for mathematics, broke his head "over logarithms, sines and cosines," so he would not be sent to a rifle company. Besides, if he could make it through the program and Officer Candidate School, he would "come out with bars on [his] shoulders, or so he was led to believe."[36]

The ASTPers knew they had a caught a break, and they were pleased that education and intelligence had saved them from the awful lot of other recruits. On marches to classes they proudly sang of their brainy ineptitude:

Take down your service flag mother, your son's in the ASTP
And ever a German I see,
I'll take out my trusty old slide rule
And square root the Sine of B.

In contrast to those less accomplished GIs dodging bullets and shells on dirty battlefields, ASTPers would happily spend their army

days pursuing lovely college women. Mel Richmond remembered
they sang:

> I'm in the ASTP
> Foxholes and trenches ain't for me.
> I will serve out World War Two
> Gazing into coeds' eyes of blue.[37]

Male students at colleges and universities had departed for the
service, so women were readily available. Never before or afterwards
would the ratio of women to men be so favorable for these young
guys in uniform. There were dances, dates, romances, engagements,
and even marriages in some cases.

• • •

While the ASTPers studied and prepared for engineering careers,
no one knew when and how they would put this training to use.
Many speculated that by the time they completed their degrees and
Officer Candidate School the war would be over, and they might be
utilized in rebuilding Europe or improving postwar America. A few
guys like Thor Ronningen thought, "I was not serving my country by
going to school." Eager to be a "real soldier," Ronningen deliberately
flunked a course in the vain hope of being sent overseas. But being
a soldier in uniform was proof enough of a young man's commitment to his country. While at John Tarleton Agricultural College in
Stephenville, Texas, Louis Pedrotti broke his little toe playing volley-
ball. Limping along with crutches on his way to eat a slice of pecan
pie at the Long Hotel, friendly local folks approached and praised
him as if he were a war hero.[38]

The arrival of more student-soldiers in the fall of 1943 appeared to
augur well for the program, so everyone enjoyed furlough visits home
that Christmas. Then in early February 1944, after a return to the classroom, disquieting rumors began to float about that the program might
be in trouble. In the army rumors flourished, a never-ending flow of
real and false facts conjured up and passed along to thousands of
enlisted men who were rarely given information. Those at the top of
the hierarchy deemed it unnecessary and unwise to inform underlings
of decisions and strategy. Consequently, soldiers constantly wondered

and worried about what might happen next, a source of uneasiness and anxiety. Finally in late February, official word came down; ASTP was canceled and thousands of bright young men would be immediately transferred to various divisions. Or as Richard King put it, "The army decided they needed more dirt soldiers than they needed engineers." Nearly three thousand men studying at colleges in Texas, Oklahoma, Louisiana, Arkansas and New Mexico were consigned to the 99th Infantry Division. Not only would these GIs not be allowed to finish their degrees, they would remain lowly privates in the next phase of their army career.[39]

CHAPTER 2

Training for War

The army activated the newly formed 99th Infantry Division on November 15, 1942, at Camp Van Dorn, near the hamlet of Centreville in the southwestern corner of Mississippi, a backwater area of abandoned cotton fields and decayed farmhouses. Hacked out of the wilderness, Van Dorn was not even completed when the first recruits arrived (from Pennsylvania, Ohio, and West Virginia) to see their living quarters—flimsy, tarpaper, one-story barracks erected on red clay. When the rains came and the ground turned into reddish muck, the cadre (training officers transferred from the 7th Infantry Division) set the men to work constructing duckboard walkways and digging ditches for water drainage. Cold and wet in winter, hot and humid in summer, weather added to the misery of basic infantry training, which involved forced marches, rifle range firing, close order drills, and trench digging as in the First World War while being tormented by chiggers, mosquitoes, and poisonous snakes. Physically isolated from any large towns, enlisted men (draftees and volunteers, privates and noncoms) had little chance to escape the camp's dismal confines in search of recreation.[1]

On August 2, 1943, Brooklyn-born Brig. Gen. Walter E. Lauer became division commander. Lauer spent several interwar years with occupation forces in Germany as a commissioned officer and then taught military science at two colleges. From December 1938 until January 1943 he served on the staff of the 3rd Division that participated in the occupation of French Morocco. Before the final Allied victory in North Africa, the army reassigned him to the United States.

Humorless, abrasive, and arrogant, senior officers found Lauer disagreeable. He told his men he wanted the division to "have a reputation of being outstanding," but Lt. Col. Matthew Legler reckoned Lauer was "more interested in his own reputation," a characteristic not uncommon among generals. Others agreed with this assessment; Maltie Anderson regarded Lauer as a "tooter of his own horn," and Furman Grimm remarked that with Lauer you got "windy speeches on hot days." His oft-repeated slogan, "Do it now, do it right, and do it with a smile," hardly roused men to action, though they wondered jokingly if "it" might refer to sex. Once while Lauer inspected an unheated supply room at Camp Van Dorn, Warrant Officer Willis Botz asked the general for a stove because typing requisitions in the cold proved difficult. Lauer replied, "When I was a lieutenant at Fort Benning we lived in tents without heat. I was a better officer for it." So no stove for Botz; apparently Lauer thought Botz would become a tougher typist by confronting the elements.[2]

• • •

In steamy mid-August 1943 the division engaged in "D" series maneuvers just outside the camp, mock battles to simulate actual combat conditions in which the men lived and "fought" against each other. General Lauer said these three weeks "were designed to accustom the men to [the] deprivation and hardships of field life." The only drinking water available came from area creeks; it was filtered, chlorinated, and distributed in large canvas (Lister) bags to the men, who then filled their canteens. Many thought the treated water tasted like rotting leaves and did little to quench their thirst. High humidity and temperatures over one hundred degrees took a toll on recruits, causing many to pass out from heat exhaustion. Private First Class John L. Kuhn, who landed in the hospital with hundreds of others, thought those days the "hardest and most strenuous" he faced during the entire war.[3]

In September the division loaded up and moved to the piney woods and swamps of Fort Polk in Louisiana for more maneuvers, again fighting venomous snakes, ticks, and chiggers as much as the fictional enemy. Mock warfare, this time against other divisions, involved hiking and hacking through heavy brush and sleeping on the hard ground with one blanket. Initially the troops enjoyed warm weather, but by November 1943 night temperatures dropped below freezing. First Lieutenant Charles Roland remembered a cross-country march of thirty-eight miles completed in twenty-three hours, the last stint in a torrential rain. The final exercise involved a simulated attack across the Sabine River (the state line between Texas and Louisiana); the division crossed in rubber boats, slogged through ankle-deep mud onto the opposite bank, and then boarded trucks that carried them more than two hundred miles to Camp Maxey, a new facility in northeast Texas.[4]

After the primitive shacks at Camp Van Dorn and pup tents in rainy Louisiana, Camp Maxey seemed comparatively plush with its white, two-storied, clapboard barracks, paved streets, service clubs, bowling alley, field house, hospital, dental clinic, mess halls, movie theaters, chapels, and a post exchange (PX). Yet the cold, rainy winter and brutally hot, humid Texas summer rivaled Mississippi and Louisiana for its capacity to inflict suffering. In July and August, according to Louis Pedrotti, it seemed as if "a hot, wet sponge was being squeezed dry all over us by a malevolent god." Jay Nelson wrote his mom that staying at Maxey for the duration of the war "would be worse than being a casualty" in combat.[5]

Camp Maxey came into existence in February 1942 when the U.S. government bought seventy thousand acres of flat land, much of it cotton fields gone to seed with scattered stands of mesquite and scrub oak trees. Construction on more than seventeen hundred buildings began that same month, and the base was activated in July 1942, nine miles from a small Texas town (population nineteen thousand) with the unlikely name of Paris. The base stimulated an economic boom for the town, which swelled overnight with construction workers, carpenters, roofers, plumbers, and prostitutes. Retail businesses, drug stores, movie theaters, dime stores, cafes, the Gibraltar Hotel, and residents with rented rooms benefited financially from the influx of civilian and military newcomers.[6]

• • •

In late 1943, three thousand of the original 99ers (mostly riflemen) transferred to the 85th and 88th Divisions; hence a need for the ASTPers, who filled the places of the departed, especially in the undermanned rifle platoons. According to Earle Slyder, the college boys arriving at the train station in Paris suffered a "cold awakening," for the town was nondescript, a mere "bus stop," completely "unremarkable," surrounded by "desolate" countryside. Those who had endured basic training in the "Jap Trap" knew they were bound for an infantry division. Others did not. As William McMurdie, who had taken basic training with an armored outfit in Arkansas, entered Maxey's main gate, his "heart fell" because he learned the 99th was an infantry division, and "none of us really wanted to be infantrymen." A first lieutenant addressed McMurdie and the new boys, "telling us a lot of baloney about the glories of being in the infantry. He treated us like a bunch of high school boys and failed miserably to improve our morale." Angelo Spinato made the mistake of arriving in a friend's convertible with tennis rackets and golf clubs visible in the back seat, ample evidence to the first sergeant that he was an uppity, "soft college boy . . . who needed to be seasoned and disciplined."

When Alfred Goldstein and other ASTPers arrived, a group of "uncouth" noncoms jeered at them. One sergeant yelled, "Hey school-boy! I hope y'all can walk, 'cause y'all will be doin' plenty of it here." George Neill and other newcomers marched to Love Company 395 headquarters not realizing what awaited them. When they learned they were assigned to a rifle company, Neill recalled, "I never saw so many dejected faces." After an officer told Lawrence Zonsius and his group they should forget about trying to leave the division, "some men cried."

It was an awful jolt for the ASTPers; they had been studying hard and enjoying the relative freedom of college, when suddenly their hopes for an engineering degree and officer status had been dashed for no apparent reason and with no explanation. ASTPers felt the army had misled them. They had done what the army had asked, and yet the army had consigned them to the infantry. Some accepted their new assignment with a sense of patriotism and a desire to do something physical. Mel Richmond was displeased but also excited at the prospect of becoming a "real soldier." Because of the overloaded class schedule and heavy amount of homework, everyone in Carter Strong's immediate group at Louisiana State University was "in the mood for change." But most ASTPers remained disappointed and upset although resigned to their fate.[7]

These "college boys" were destined to serve in the main as front-line riflemen, a dangerous assignment many believed squandered their abilities. They discovered all the noncommissioned slots were filled, so there appeared little opportunity for advancement in rank, pay, and privilege. Company commander Carl Byers told ASTP Tim Nugent: "I feel sorry for you; you're going to be a private first class throughout your army career." Nugent and others would not even receive a promotion from private to private first class until they arrived overseas.[8]

• • •

Most noncoms had a limited education, and some could not read or write. Consequently, ASTPers would be under the direct, daily control of men they considered less intelligent. "Some of us ASTPers were pretty arrogant," confessed William Meacham, and "we resented taking orders from poorly educated, even illiterate noncoms." Robert Mesler asserted, "Some of the Van Dorn guys weren't very bright. We were smarter, and they knew it." The cadre "resented us," Mel Richmond believed, "but they had the power of the army behind them; I was afraid of [noncoms], and we didn't rebel." Richard Weaver recounted, "The cadre let us know they were tougher and had more training, and a lot of them were big country boys." Harold Schaefer maintained a "chasm" existed between the ASTPers and Van Dorn 99ers: "Since they all knew we had scored in excess of 115 [on the Army General Classification Test] and mentally they were no match [for us], they had to prove how tough they were." The cadre assumed the college boys came from the privileged classes, so a degree of class hostility entered into the relationship; in reality, most ASTPers had ordinary backgrounds. Nevertheless, some training sergeants were determined to show these "whiz kids" what it meant to be a real man, namely, someone who knew how to drink, smoke, and swear, and who could endure rigorous training. (A sergeant told Leon Rogers, "If you don't drink, you're a sissy.") John McCoy recalled the cadre teased him about a lack of sexual experience and offered to take him to Hugo, Oklahoma, where he might "become a man instead of a math major."[9]

Some ASTPers talked in code about the cadre saying, "he's a sixty" or "that one is probably an eighty," a reference to army test scores.

Mel Richmond admitted they used to "joke that the cadre got their first pair of shoes when they went into the army." Cryptic discrediting of those with power offered a way of expressing frustration and scoring psychic victories over noncoms who controlled them. Calling the cadre and non-ASTPers "hillbillies" and "coal miners" labeled them as social and cultural inferiors. The ASTPers had demonstrated their superiority by being selected for the college program; they had studied and worked toward positions of authority and privilege, which they felt they deserved. Brains and education were often rewarded in civilian society, but the military ignored such qualifications and apparently bestowed rank based on length of service. To the ASTPers it seemed a rather stupid, ineffective way to run an army. Daily SNAFUs and the "hurry-up-and-wait" method of accomplishing a task confirmed for them the army excelled at inefficiency and waste.[10]

The ASTPers came in as a separate group and were placed in a provisional regiment for six weeks of training, which many ASTPers resented because it repeated basic training. It also permitted the Camp Van Dorn 99ers to identify and pigeonhole them as soft, untrained college boys who wouldn't be able to handle the physical challenges of infantry soldiering. According to Ronald Kraemer, the older (in their early and mid twenties) privates from Van Dorn were "not friendly; they wouldn't take you into the group and would challenge you to fights." One of the toughs socked Donald Wallace and knocked him down for no apparent reason. Wallace retreated to the latrine and cried, "not because I had been hurt, but because I couldn't understand why someone would do such a thing."[11]

General Lauer greeted the ASTPers with condescension, not approval: "Young men, you are the cream of the crop, but the cream is sour. We are going to train you and make you into soldiers." Lauer's speech angered James Bussen because it suggested he and the others did not measure up to army standards. From the beginning, the ASTPers met noncoms predisposed to dislike them. One sergeant remarked that college boys were "jerks who thought they were special and looked down on us." On the first morning in camp, a platoon sergeant handed Howard Bowers a Checkerboard shoulder patch and told him and his fellow ASTPers to "get those flaming piss pots off your shoulders"—a crude reference to the "lamp of learning" badge that identified a soldier as a member of the ASTP program. First Sergeant Jack Shaffer told Forbes Williams, "No smart-ass college bastard is going to tell me how to run the company."[12]

Some noncoms harbored a prejudice against these "college boys" or "GFUs [General Fuck Ups] with high IQs" even before they arrived. They believed these "quiz kids" (a reference to precocious youngsters who answered challenging questions on a popular radio show) had enjoyed a pampered college life, while the cadre and trainees had withstood brutal training in Mississippi and Louisiana. Staff Sergeant George Dudley thought these kids had "gotten a break, and they weren't tough." Homer Simons, a Van Dorn veteran, admitted they were "leery" of the ASTPers, "as they might be too well educated and might not want to do combat." Squad leader William Hofmann worried they "wouldn't blend in" because they "were well-spoken and didn't use slang." But Hofmann subsequently learned they "were my most dependable soldiers."[13]

The intelligence of the ASTPers threatened several members of the cadre, who feared these young men aimed to replace them. Company commander Joseph Shank warned Sgt. Hank Ankrom and other noncommissioned officers they could lose their stripes to the new guys "because they are smart." Insecurity in some cases fueled hostility towards the "whiz kids," who could read maps and use a compass with ease. ASTP arrogance and ability exacerbated the problem; Rex Whitehead bitterly observed, "For the first time in my life I was superior," but was being "lorded over by a nitwit."[14]

• • •

After completing provisional regiment training, the ASTPers joined regular platoons. For weeks they marched with a heavy field pack and rifle, learned patrolling and tactics, hiked along dusty roads, practiced shooting at the rifle range, attacked a mock German village with live ammunition, worked with tanks and artillery, crawled along an infiltration course with machine-gun bullets whistling three feet over their heads, and ran the obstacle course in timed competition. According to ASTP Byron Whitmarsh, training "was as hard as they could make it; they thought it was good for you. Every day they shit on you." The harsh treatment, exacting rules, lack of freedom, low pay, and bad food, "made you hate the whole world," said Whitmarsh.

Nevertheless, determined to disprove the cadre's assumption they were a bunch of "sissies," the "smart-ass college kids" held up well. Often they outperformed the older cadre on endurance marches where, at Maxey, according to Woodrow Hickey, you could "walk in the mud and have sand blowing in your face all the time." At training's end ASTPers felt proud to have overcome the obstacles thrown in their path, demonstrating, according to Louis Pedrotti, "We city slickers and sophisticates could outmarch and outdo our so-called superiors."[15]

• • •

This generation was accustomed to authority at home and in school, so obedience, not rebellion, was the norm. The army wanted soldiers who would follow orders instantly. As Leon Rogers put it, "Training destroyed your ability to ask questions. If you did or talked back, you would be given extra duties." Albert Davis tried to ask a question, but was rudely rebuffed and told, "You can't ask questions. You are a private. Just follow orders." Davis concluded, "They didn't want my brain."[16]

Privates obeyed orders and accepted punishment for misbehaving or violating rules, but petty, demeaning harassment undermined morale. Some ASTPers thought noncoms singled them out for more KP and latrine duties than the original trainees. Even though the army distributed power and privilege according to rank, those at the bottom wanted to be treated fairly. Petty tyranny seemed senseless and provoked suppressed anger, making military training more disagreeable and creating a rift between officers and privates that might not close even on the battlefield.

A few insecure (and in some cases alcoholic) noncoms imposed the tightest controls on the new arrivals, justifying their demands and insults with the military's premise that recruits needed to be shown the army was in total control. Humiliating and belittling a recruit was part of a regimen designed to break down his ego and individuality, then rebuild a sense of self with army values and pride in the group. But in a few cases the gratification of giving orders and punishing people satisfied personal needs, including the pleasure of exercising raw power over other men.

Captains, lieutenants, and especially noncommissioned officers supervised training in the field; noncoms also managed activities in the barracks on a daily basis. First sergeants (master sergeants), who administered the company, and technical sergeants, in charge of platoons, possessed higher rank and more power than squad leaders (staff sergeants). With their own sleeping quarters and dining tables, first sergeants and platoon sergeants were also somewhat physically removed from the recruits. This distancing enhanced their authority and impeded close relationships with privates, which the army discouraged anyway.

Noncoms and newly commissioned second lieutenants (the so-called ninety-day wonders from Officer Candidate School) as well as company commanders could create discomfort and even anxiety for recruits. Punishment included KP, scrubbing the barracks with toothbrushes, long marches, and denial of leave passes, which subjected recruits to additional irksome chores. Privates could not even relax in the barracks for fear of being assigned demeaning tasks; so they hid in the PX or the Service Club (where recreational activities took place).

According to David Reagler, the men feared and disliked 1st Sgt. James Cumstay, a short, florid-faced man, who ruled his company like a tyrant: "If you screwed up on some minor details, no passes for the weekend. If he found a single cigarette butt, he would make the platoon scrub the barracks with lye water and stiff brushes. If someone did something that displeased him, he would restrict the whole company." Harry Hagstad remembered when company commander Sidney Gooch came into a spotlessly clean barrack for Saturday inspection and proceeded to step on a footlocker and wipe his finger across a previously unseen smudge of dirt on a light bulb hanging from the ceiling. Gooch, whom the men hated, canceled all passes for the platoon that weekend. A few members of the cadre abused their power, such as when 1st Sergeant Vernon Selders sucker-punched Jack Prickett in the mouth. An ASTP friend wanted to retaliate, but Prickett, fearing the consequences, discouraged this urge for revenge.[17]

John Vasa recalled that 1st Sgt. John Shaffer would repeatedly swear and cuss the company when they stood at retreat, saying you "college fucks don't know sheep shit from Arbuckle coffee." Byron Whitmarsh watched a drunken Shaffer beat up a private and throw him into the barrack where his face was badly sliced on a footlocker. Disgusted by this behavior Whitmarsh requested and received

a transfer to Charlie Company, which had a "top-notch" first sergeant. But Whitmarsh's troubles with authority did not end. When
his platoon leader caught Whitmarsh smoking one night during an
exercise (a potentially dangerous practice on the battlefield), he
made him dig latrine trenches as punishment. On another occasion
the lieutenant decided Whitmarsh had done a sloppy job of shaving
and ordered him to do it over. Whitmarsh complied but deliberately omitted the mustache area. He was caught and sent back to
shave again. Deliberate disobedience of a direct order could result in
severe punishment, so passive-aggressive behavior provided the only
rebellious option.[18]

After Sgt. Shaffer became involved in a fight at the PX, he lost his
stripes and was transferred to another company. Forbes Williams
and the other men in his former company whistled and jeered at the
ex-sergeant whenever they saw him. But the harassment did not end
for Williams with Shaffer's departure, for his platoon leader worried
more about "spit and polish" than substance and punished the men
for minor offenses. Upon seeing Arthur Pellegrene discard a cigarette
butt without "field stripping" it, 1st Lt. John Vaughn ordered him to dig
a huge foxhole, throw the butt in, and then fill the hole. Once, Howard
Bowers entered his barrack without saluting Lt. Vaughn, standing some
distance from the entrance. Vaughn followed Bowers into the barrack
and confronted him: "Soldier, aren't you proud to be in the U.S.
Army?" Vaughn equated not saluting with being unpatriotic, thereby
inflating a simple misunderstanding into a sign of disrespect toward
the army. Of course, Vaughn really meant Bowers hadn't shown
proper deference toward him. Humiliated, Bowers quietly replied,
"Yes, sir." Bowers also made the mistake of sleeping in on a Sunday
morning. The platoon sergeant ordered Bowers to clean up after a
Saturday night party of commissioned officers, a humiliating assignment that reduced him to a virtual servant. In the process of hauling
out the garbage, Bowers discovered officers enjoyed another special
privilege—they had access to liquor whereas enlisted men could
only buy 3.2 percent Texas beer at the PX.[19]

• • •

Privates were not allowed to simply approach and address a commissioned officer of any rank. Regarded as a lofty elite, officers lived,

ate, and partied in special quarters far from the purview of common soldiers. "We considered," said Mel Richmond, high-ranking officers like Lt. Col. Matthew Legler, "who moved about with an entourage, to be like gods." But they were not benevolent deities, at least not to Robert Walter, who considered commissioned officers "an alien species to be avoided because no one ever had anything good come from contact with them."[20]

A few officers provoked genuine hatred. One company commander and a few sergeants were so despised that some men talked about shooting them on the battlefield. A replacement found himself repeatedly and unfairly punished by a platoon sergeant who assigned him "every shit job there was." The noncom "inflicted such indignities on me that I planned to kill him once we got overseas." A soldier could complain to superior officers but no one filed official charges of mistreatment; if he did, the private would suffer reprisals and likely be transferred away from his buddies. Nonetheless, everyone set about learning how to become a capable soldier to survive in combat, if it came to that.[21]

● ● ●

Many officers and noncoms did not abuse their power. As David Perlman put it: "Some were pains in the butt and others were very decent guys." Henri Atkins supported that assessment: "We learned that some were good and some were just plain mean and nasty; they had the power and many used it." Well-trained, natural leaders commanded respect, in part because they did not pull rank. Sergeant Harold Lange found the ASTPers to be cocky and even rebellious. He told them if they wanted to challenge him, he would meet them outside the barracks, but no one did. That seemed to settle the question of who was in command. After that initial episode, their playfulness did not appear defiant to him. Instead of counting off "one, two, three," they would say, "seventy, seventy-one, seventy-two," and when they reached seventy-six, they would yell out, "That's the spirit!" Lange, who was respected, found this behavior more amusing than threatening to his authority or to army discipline.[22]

Admired officers cared about their men and told them they were the best. Such officers, Byron Whitmarsh averred, "made you want to do what they asked." Sergeant Kenneth Juhl tried "to foster pride in his platoon, encourage the men on marches and make them fight for and with me." Wayne Cleveland found Plt. Sgt. Isador Rosen to be a leader who "treated us with respect," which made it easier to "buddy up with the regulars." ASTPer Joseph Thimm thought his 2nd Platoon "had a couple of outstanding training officers from the old 99th." George Lehr, John McCoy, Walter Malinowski, and Ernest McDaniel regarded Stanley Lowry, a "savvy," full-blooded Native American, as "the best platoon sergeant in the company." In August their platoon received a freshly minted, baby-faced second lieutenant, Joseph Kagan, who tucked his khaki pants inside his leggings and couldn't march correctly. Initially he did not inpire much confidence, but after the platoon went on several three-day field exercises, the men realized Kagan possessed good judgment and the ability to devise solutions to combat problems. These qualities, plus a concern for the welfare of his men, won over the platoon and produced "a close-knit team."[23]

The army however preferred an authoritarian managerial style; rough treatment was encouraged to toughen up the men; compliments and positive reinforcement were rarely employed. At Maxey and overseas, division, regiment, and battalion officers were too far removed to concern themselves with the plight of ordinary soldiers. Even company commanders and platoon leaders did not generally intervene to stop punishment; they did not want to undermine the cadre's authority. Lieutenant Harold Hill's company commander criticized him for "being close to the men." Captain Byers told Hill, "You must keep separation between officers and privates." This philosophy assumed that familiarity weakened authority, but some of the most effective leaders turned out to be those who bridged the distance between themselves and their men.[24]

During the retraining period, the ASTPers of the 1st Battalion 395 became involved in a dispute with one of the sergeants. It began as they were dismissed after a long day of marching. The recruits playfully yelled out, "hubba hubba," a practice they had adopted during basic training without repercussions. This was not however acceptable to the sergeant, who must have felt civilian expressions had no place in the military. The ASTPers believed he had no right to reprimand them, since after being dismissed they were on their own time. The next day the scene was repeated, but this time the sergeant told them to report back to the parade ground after dinner, whereupon he ordered them to stand at attention. After some time, he yelled: "Rest!" Whereupon a voice from the back row muttered "hubba hubba." This struggle of having the last word (literally) went on for several hours until both sides tired of the standoff. In a similar encounter with his group, S.Sgt. David Jones also heard "hubba hubba" from his recruits at the conclusion of drilling. Jones immediately ordered the men to perform more close-order drills. This group got the message and silence prevailed.[25]

One day Ernest McDaniel and his group marched to the rifle range where each soldier was given a wooden "sighting and aiming bar" designed to teach the most elementary steps in shooting a rifle. Since McDaniel had already qualified as a sharpshooter in basic training, he considered this a waste of time. Deciding to have some fun, he "entangled [himself] in the contraption in the most awkward way," which elicited laughter from his companions. Viewing this disruption as unacceptable, the lieutenant assigned the misbehaving private to kitchen duty on Easter Sunday. McDaniel did not venture to explain the reason for his lack of seriousness because in basic training a recruit learned what his response to an officer must be: "Yes, sir," "no, sir," and "no excuse, sir." [26]

As Harold Schaefer and his company returned to their barracks after a day of field exercises, they marched past the Service Club, and one of the recruits whistled at several women standing outside the main entrance. Punishment was not long in coming, nor was it restricted to the whistling soldier. At 2:00 A.M. the next morning the entire company was rousted out of their bunks, made to remove all beds and footlockers, and put to work scrubbing the barracks. Schaefer and his platoon mates learned an object lesson in army discipline: if one man misbehaved, all suffered the consequences. This rule placed enormous pressure on each soldier not to step out of line or express his individuality. Being punished for someone else's playfulness certainly did not seem right, but the recruit quickly learned fairness need not prevail in the army. Discipline dominated army training, and officers had the prerogative to mete out punishment.[27]

• • •

In July the ASTPers underwent "Expert Infantry" tests that consisted of shooting on the rifle range, performing nighttime compass work, running an obstacle course, and undergoing the much-hated gas mask drill—remaining in a room filled with mustard and tear gas. If the enlisted soldier passed, he received the Infantry Badge, (which became the much-esteemed Combat Infantry Badge, or CIB, awarded after engaging the enemy in a war zone) and a $10 pay raise. Acquiring the Infantry Badge provided tangible proof to the recruit that he had indeed become a soldier. Although Robert Walter resisted the transformation from peaceful civilian into combat soldier, he had to admit the army's training was successful. Before entering the army he would not have killed anyone, but later on the battlefield he viewed German soldiers simply as targets, not as humans. Most GIs did not give killing much consideration in training, as William Bray admitted: "I never thought it would happen or the war would be over before it came to that." Little did Bray or the others realize the death of a buddy and threats to their own lives would transform them into combat infantrymen willing and capable of killing strangers.[28]

One of the more disagreeable training exercises involved learning proper use of the bayonet, a stabbing weapon that required face-to-face killing. A throwback to an earlier era, the chief purpose of bayonet training was to implant a fierce martial attitude. Bryon Whitmarsh vividly remembered the training film, *The Battle is the Payoff,* which focused "on one guy who was in a bayonet fight. It was scary and guys around him were getting shot. You wished you weren't there." Harold Schaefer maintained, "Bayonet drills were the worst." Repeatedly charging and stabbing a burlap sack of straw seemed anachronistic and ludicrous. Schaefer also could not understand the logic of saving a round in the rifle chamber and firing it into the victim to extract an embedded bayonet. "Hell," he reasoned, "If I've got a round, I won't be sticking anybody. I will shoot him." The thought of going "toe-to-toe with some big German soldier or sticking someone else with a bayonet" repulsed Richard King: "I wanted to be patriotic but sometimes, even more, I wanted to go home." Louis Pedrotti found the idea of meeting an enemy soldier in

hand-to-hand combat "nauseating." According to his training sergeant, Pedrotti failed to show enough bloodthirsty rage when
plunging his blade into the ersatz enemy and had to repeat the
exercise several times, becoming more frustrated and angry all the
while. Pedrotti and his buddies took out their "anger on the drill
sergeant by yelling at the top of our lungs: 'and this is for you, you
damned son-of-a-bitch! Motherfucker!' The sergeant never realized
that we aimed all these juicy expletives at him" and not at the punctured dummy.[29]

Sometimes small victories offered some compensation. As Francis
Chesnick marched with the first battalion on a day so hot it felt as
though they were baking in an oven, a lieutenant went up and down
the line yelling exhortations to the men, spurring them on while
demonstrating his own fitness: "Keep going!" "Be tough!" "Learn to
take the heat!" After moving down the road some distance, Chesnick
spied the lieutenant sprawled in a jeep headed back to camp.[30]

B. O. Wilkins and other members of the platoon delighted in 1st.
Sgt. Donald Riddle's inability to pronounce his name correctly during
roll call. When Riddle came to the "Ws," he called out, "Wilcoxson."
Glenn Wilcoxson replied, "Here!" Next on the list was Wilkins, but
Riddle inexplicably shouted, "Werkerson!" No answer. Again, Riddle
yelled out, "Werkerson!" No reply. Finally B.O. responded, "Wilkins,
here!" Riddle angrily roared, "Hot damn it, Werkerson, when I call
your name, I want you to answer!"[31]

Sergeant Riddle exhibited another characteristic of some noncoms, namely hostility toward education and reading. One day while
addressing the company before tackling a field problem, Riddle
stopped speaking when he noticed a flap on Wilkins' fatigue unbuttoned. Riddle shouted, "Werkerson, button that pocket flap!" Wilkins
replied, "I can't, sergeant; it's going over my *Reader's Digest.*" Riddle
retorted, "Damn it, Werkerson, you tryin' to git intelligent on us?"
Radford Carroll, a loner, used reading as an escape from his unhappy
situation of being in the infantry and under the thumb of the cadre.
On one occasion a sergeant told him: "If you would stop reading
and exercise instead, you wouldn't be dropping out on marches."
Actually Carroll had always completed the marches. So he decided
to carry the Bible, a passive-aggressive act: "They couldn't very well
tell me not to read the Bible. I did it in part just to irritate the

sergeant." Reading smacked of effeteness and individuality, not toughness and conformity.[32]

• • •

Soldiers who accepted the army's indoctrination without reservations suffered fewer misgivings. Those who harbored doubts remained wary, lacking blind faith in what authority figures preached and ordered. Louis Pedrotti envied those "salt-of-the-earth" types who perceived "everything in simple black-and-white terms," for they believed what they were told. By contrast, Pedrotti and his ASTP friends "tended to think everything to death, intellectualizing everything in an endless analysis game with the army." Raising questions amongst themselves about military training made life more difficult; besides, the army did not want skeptical doubters but rather compliant automatons. Pedrotti and others went through the motions, pretending to accept everything directed at them because they saw no honorable way out of their situation. That they persevered despite so much physical and psychological discomfort testified also to their commitment to duty.[33]

At least they endured together. To express their individuality and rebelliousness Pedrotti and his fellow ASTPers recited poetry while on long marches. Howard Harris's company composed and sang ribald songs that poked fun at one another. When under the iron control of an imperious officer, the men sometimes bonded in silent, disgruntled opposition. John Thornburg and his platoon were tormented and belittled by Plt. Sgt. Warren Morgan, who told them, "So far as I am concerned I am king and you guys are shit." But they found an ally in squad leader Chester Gregor, who looked out for them.[34]

If the ASTPers constituted a majority in a squad or in a platoon, it was easier to build friendships. Moreover, the group could if necessary enforce its own rules of behavior. When a disgruntled draftee put a half bar of the army's reddish-brown soap in the food, members of Fielding Pope's platoon tracked him down and beat him up. William Blasdel lived with a platoon member who refused to bathe even after dirty, sweaty training exercises. Blasdel and his buddies solved the problem in peremptory fashion: "We took him to the shower, removed his fatigues, and brushed him clean with a bar of heavy duty GI soap. After that he took a bath every day." As Mel Richmond put it, "We would take care of the fuck-ups."[35]

Goldbrickers, those who shirked onerous assignments (scrubbing barracks, cleaning latrines, etc.) and who avoided marches by claiming injury, sickness, or a death in the family were disliked and shunned. Goldbricking might be viewed as a form of resistance to the army, but this selfish behavior only benefited the slacker, leaving distasteful tasks to others. Concocting a phony excuse to miss a long hike meant the goldbricker was not suffering with the group. Shared pain, and later shared danger, brought squad members together. The individual who refused to bear the same burdens had effectively opted out of the group and was not trusted as a result. William Blasdell recalled a gold-bricker in his platoon who would place empty buckets in his field pack, thereby carrying much less weight than the others. One day before a march, a member of the group lured the goldbricker to the PX. In his absence, the others filled the buckets with sand. The goldbricker discovered what the others had done only as they were forming up—when it was too late to empty the buckets.[36]

Those who fell out on marches were held in low regard. This was especially the case for ASTPers because it confirmed what the cadre said about them. Robert Mitsch broke a bone in his foot while marching, but refused to go on sick call because he didn't want to be labeled a goldbricker. Louis Pedrotti was dismayed to discover one of the worst offenders was a fellow ASTPer. He expected better of the college guys, but came to appreciate some non-ASTPers, whom he found to be decent and generous, unlike some of "us smug, educated, and spoiled college brats." One squad member shared pecan pastries from home with him, and another volunteered to tackle KP duties when Pedrotti went to Dallas for the weekend. Pedrotti realized it "takes more than ivy-covered walls to make a gentleman." The acknowledgment that men of limited education were worthy compatriots brought the men together—that and the fact they would need each other to survive. On the battlefield formal education mattered less than steadiness, perseverance, toughness, and an ability to deal with stress and physical hardship. Frontline soldiering placed everyone on the same level: in a combat zone country boys and college boys were equals.[37]

• • •

For those who had eaten at Camp Van Dorn, the food at Maxey represented a marked improvement, though a wide variety of opinions existed about the quality of the meals. Each company had its own mess, and the quality of the food often depended on the skill and ingenuity of the company cook. For Depression kids who had not enjoyed an abundance of anything, the food was at least plentiful, if not tasty. Having grown up in an Oklahoma oil patch without much to eat, Leon Rogers "was happy to have lots of food." Mel Richmond, who had only eaten kosher ("I thought non-kosher was poison"), tasted and liked pork sausages and pork chops. The meals loaded up on carbohydrates (pancakes, potatoes, bread), greasy pork chops or lamb, canned peas and peaches; fresh vegetables, salads, and fresh fruit remained in short supply. There was fresh and powdered milk and the same for eggs, though Louis Pedrotti thought powdered eggs had the taste and consistency of "yellow glue." Having enjoyed his mother's excellent Italian cooking, Pedrotti found army chow dreadful—steaming black-eyed peas "tasted like boiled hay," cooked okra "wallowed in its own goo," and grits consisted of "a tasteless pile of corn discards that even a sow would reject."[38]

Civilized dining gave way to chowhounds fighting for every item of food plumped down in big bowls on long cafeteria-style tables. When Alfred Goldstein entered his company's mess for the first time, he was shocked at what he witnessed; it reminded him of a James Cagney prison movie. Everyone stood at attention around the tables. Then the first sergeant blew a whistle, and each man plopped down and grabbed whatever food was set in front of him. Because Goldstein was slower than the others in helping himself, his evening meal consisted of candy purchased at the PX. And, he recalled, the scramble for food "was the same at every meal." Jay Nelson thought the meals resembled a rugby scrum. He wrote to his mom that there was plenty to eat but "it's always a case of eating fast and a long reach." Later, on the front, when provisions consisted of unheated, bland prepackaged food, even these meals would be missed.[39]

• • •

For most recruits Camp Maxey constituted a new living experience, although all had gained an introduction during basic training. They existed in a society of men who wore uniforms or fatigues and acted in concert with others. No longer autonomous, they could not operate independently. All decisions (when to arise in the morning, when to go to bed at night, when and what to eat, what activities to perform, and when they could come and go) originated with army authorities who issued orders to be obeyed immediately and without question. The squad and the platoon became a recruit's family and social circle, replacing parents, siblings, sweethearts, and friends. Enlisted men were not hermetically sealed off from the rest of the world, for they could write family members and occasionally visit civilian society; however, they were undergoing a relentless process of being pulled away from a previous life and forced into a new one. Their outlook, values, and behavior were being altered as they were transformed into combat soldiers.

After completing the six-week retraining program, ASTPers became eligible for passes to leave the base on Saturday afternoons and Sundays, provided there had been no infractions and the platoon had passed inspection. Getting off the base and away from the army as often as possible became a high priority. The men would take a bus to Paris (but there were always long lines for the few buses), pay a civilian to drive them to Dallas ($5.00 per soldier), or hitchhike to Hugo, Oklahoma, where liquor was legally available. They sought out food not available on base: fresh fruit, salads, steaks, pecan pies, and the watermelons Paris residents grew and sold in their yards.

Men also wanted female companionship, not only for romance and sex, but also for a connection with the domestic world they missed. Paul Jillson was riding in a bus crowded with GIs headed to town when suddenly a lovely young woman got on. Everyone stopped talking and just stared at her. She looked "angelic," remembered Jillson, for "I hadn't seen a girl for months. I just wanted to meet and talk to her." Likewise Ernest McDaniel delighted in going to a local dime store for the opportunity to speak with a salesgirl. Others went to USO dances on the base, in Paris, and in Dallas. Radford Carroll frequently escaped from Camp Maxey on the pretense of attending a religious service in Paris. Actually he wanted to meet women at the church to date. On one trip to Dallas, Robert Davis rented a hotel room with two buddies and invited some women they had met to an ad hoc party. Unfortunately the gathering ended abruptly when two MPs knocked on the door of their hotel room. ("They seemed to know where every serviceman was.") They were ordered back to Maxey; it was D-Day (June 6, 1944) and all soldiers were restricted to quarters.[40]

• • •

On July 24, 1944, the division marched out of the camp with full field packs beneath a broiling sun on the way to another mock battle in southeast Oklahoma on the Choctaw Indian reservation. Relay convoys of trucks helped move the troops along narrow roads through scrub woods. It was supposed to be a two-week exercise but the thick brush, steep hills, poison ivy, snakes, and unrelenting heat produced conditions that shortened the operation to five days. It is not clear what the division staff hoped to accomplish, unless they thought the 99th was destined for the island jungles of the Pacific. The heat was so intense that men could not sleep in the daytime, and since much of the "fighting" occurred at night, no one could rest; in addition, mosquitoes, flies, and chiggers gorged on the men, sending scores back to the base infirmary. In short, the operation became a complete debacle.[41]

In August 1944 orders arrived that instructed the division to break camp and head overseas. Without knowing the destination, the men set about constructing boxes in which to ship their equipment. Having trained in the scorching Texas heat, many feared they might be sent to the steamy, insect-infested islands of the Pacific. Marches and drills stopped, the cadre eased up, and the men worked at night when it was cooler. The atmosphere became more relaxed, even as everyone became excited but nervous about the prospect of ending arduous training and maybe becoming more directly involved in the war. Hershell Kennedy was "chomping at the bit to get over there and shoot some Krauts." But not everyone yearned to see action. Harold Kist remembered sitting around chatting with other members of his squad who thought they would not be coming back.[42]

After weeks of marching, drilling, cleaning, and performing various training procedures, the units had come together. The ASTPers proved to the "old guys" they could measure up physically to infantry training, and the college boys recognized the enlisted men from Van Dorn could perform ably. Joseph Thimm admired two men in his platoon, both illiterate, who could nonetheless "strip the BAR and put it back together again, which I could never do." The ASTP guys "were smart enough to know these old soldiers had something to teach, and we paid attention." When it came to field problems and day-to-day training they melded as a unit. Socially the groups remained apart but their ties as soldiers strengthened.[43]

In late August, Col. Don Riley assembled the three thousand men of the 394th regiment for a pep talk. Because of the relaxed atmosphere—the men were allowed to sit on the grass instead of standing at attention—everyone expected a congratulatory speech for having made it through. But they were mistaken, for Riley shouted into his microphone, "From now on this regiment will be called 'Riley's Regiment!'" The colonel apparently anticipated loud, resounding shouts of "Riley's Regiment!" But the troops remained silent. So Riley yelled once more, "Riley's Regiment!" Again, silence. Worried that the colonel might not appreciate the men's lack of enthusiasm, the officers jumped up and began exhorting the men to answer excitedly. Finally, on Riley's third attempt, the men reluctantly responded, "Riley's Regiment!" On that occasion Riley displayed his vainglory; later, during the battle of the Battle of the Bulge, he would reveal his incompetence.[44]

On September 5, a final division parade was held with generals, colonels, and soldiers' wives in attendance. Waiting for three hours in the heat before the ceremony began caused some 99ers to pass out. Jay Nelson reckoned it took thirty minutes for the 14,208 troops, fifteen abreast, to march past the reviewing stand where the brass stood. After the whole division reassembled, Gen. Lauer gave a farewell speech, announcing three men had failed to achieve "Expert Infantry" status and had left the division. A collective groan arose from the assemblage as the 99ers realized some misdirected shots on the rifle range and failed training tests could have resulted in their dismissal. Lauer then boldly proclaimed the 99th "ready for combat as the greatest fighting outfit in the world." Many of the older guys didn't think so; Joe Herdina and other ASTPers snickered at Lauer's inflated rhetoric. Jay Nelson, however, wrote to his mom: "We are all proud of our outfit and its achievements and confident that we can take care of anything they give us to do." Nelson looked forward to a "chance to show our stuff." Having successfully completed their rigorous training, the men felt a sense of accomplishment. They did not realize they would never again be together as a group.[45]

• • •

Because of his father's death in July, James Crafton was offered an opportunity to remain in the States, but he opted not to stay behind, unwilling to leave his buddies. When Walter Kellogg went home on leave late that summer, he became lonely: "All my friends were in the service as were the men I was training with. I was in a hurry to get back to camp to be with them." Jack Prickett had a chance to leave the division but decided to remain. He and his good friend, Leslie Miller, "Felt like we had too many friends to go to some other army unit." Al Boeger begged company commander Aaron Nathan to quash orders that would have transferred him to regimental headquarters as a clerk-typist. Nathan told him he was a "damned fool" for not accepting the transfer. Even though "I would have landed in a safe place with a typewriter in my hand instead of a rifle, I wanted to stay with my friends."

When Allan Nelson stood at the train station before heading back to Camp Maxey, his father, a Swedish immigrant who had driven an ambulance in World War I, said to him: "Son, stay low. Whatever you do, stay low." Charles Roland recalled a painful parting with his father, "a person of remarkable self-control," who never hugged or kissed him. However, on this occasion he shook his son's hand and said, "Goodbye, son," his voice breaking. Charles remained mute, but "was stricken to the center" as if an arrow had pierced his heart. Those moments of separation between parents and sons or husbands and wives, reenacted millions of times during the war, produced anguish and sadness, especially for parents and wives, for all they could do was wait and worry. Tony Aiello "dreaded the thought of how my loved ones would take it when and if they received notice I was dead."[46]

A few days before departure life became more serious; the base was sealed, phone calls ended, leaves canceled, and no unauthorized personnel could enter the camp. Officers began censoring the mail of enlisted men, a practice that would continue throughout the duration of the war. All GIs were ordered to remove division insignia so no civilian or spy could identify the troops. Yet, when Harold Kist and his buddies ventured into Boston, it seemed that cab drivers and bartenders all knew they belonged to the 99th Division.[47]

The movement of the 99th Division from Camp Maxey to Camp Myles Standish in Taunton, Massachusetts, began September 10, 1944. The division boarded trains day and night for a week—eight trains per regiment—that followed three different routes. A few days before departure, Rex Whitehead said "the hardest" goodbye to his parents, who visited him at the camp: "I kept trying to keep the thought out of my mind that I may be talking to them for the last time." As William McMurdie waved goodbye to his parents at the railway station in Pasadena, California, a soldier sitting across from him said, "Take a good look. It might be the last time you see them." John Baxter said the saddest moment came when his mother and father accompanied him to the train station: "I watched as they tried to smile and hold back their tears as they waved at the departing train." Sergeant David Jones remembered seeing his wife Virginia as he marched out of Camp Maxey. Jones had declined an opportunity to serve as a clerk because he "wanted to fight and feel more important." While wondering what the future might bring, he and most other men remained optimistic about a successful return. Married soldiers had to part from wives who had followed them to Texas and lived in town. These women returned alone to their parents' homes (some with infants or babies yet to be born) and waited out the war afraid they might become young widows. The most feared individual in America was the Western Union Telegraph man or boy who arrived by car or bicycle, bringing devastating news of death, wounding, or missing in action.[48]

Regardless of the route, the three-day trip was long, boring, and uncomfortable, made more so by the lingering summer heat that baked the travelers and made sleep difficult. In some trains men shed their khaki shirts and pushed open the windows, allowing dirty smoke and soot from the coal-powered locomotives to sweep into the cars and blacken everything. Others kept the windows shut and sweated it out inside the passenger cars. Day and night the troops played poker and shot craps in the aisles. Since no one told them where they were going, they speculated about their destination. If they traveled eastward, it would be Europe, which they preferred. Haskell Wolff's train left at night, so it was difficult for him to ascertain their direction until the train passed through Fayetteville, where he had completed his freshman year at the University of Arkansas. When he looked out the coach window and saw "George's Place," his beer-drinking hangout, he knew they were headed east.[49]

As his train pulled into Hugo, Oklahoma, Milton May looked out and spotted a Bond Bread truck driver he knew. May leaned out a window and asked the driver, "in defiance of the strictest orders," if he would mind telling his dad, J. M. May, that his son had left Camp Maxey and was on his way to the port of embarkation. The driver promised he would speak to May's father the next day when he made a delivery to the tiny village of Fort Towson, where every resident would soon know the 99th had left Texas. William Bray's train also headed north through Oklahoma and Missouri. Somehow Bray managed to contact his parents in King City, Missouri, and told them to drive down and meet him at the St. Joseph depot. They were waiting when the train pulled in, and Bray hopped off briefly for one final goodbye. As Bray started back for his coach, he saw his dad walk away and stand behind a post without looking at the train. Bray learned after the war that his father had moved out of sight because he didn't want his son to see his tears.[50]

The prospect of going to Europe energized the troops. Walter Gregonis, a second-generation Lithuanian and All-American football player at the University of Pennsylvania, believed "the best thing we can do is get rid of the Germans." Frank Hoffman, "glad to be on the move," hoped "the war would be over by the time we got there." Like most everyone else, Howard Bowers became excited about the chance to "see some of the places I had read about and studied," but also "apprehensive about what combat would bring and whether I would be able to do what was expected of me." T. J. Cornett "worried how he would react under fire, whether he would stay and fight or be cowardly and run." Lieutenant Harold Hill pondered how he, "a country boy from Washington," would handle this adventure. A few like Jack Prickett "actually looked forward to combat, young idiots that we were. At our age we did not worry; it would always be the other guy who bought the farm." Most, however, were not eager "to knock the knockwurst out of Fritz." They were curious about what they would encounter, eager for adventure, and ignorant of the horrors that awaited them.[51]

When the train reached Camp Myles Standish, the men disembarked on a platform and heard from a loudspeaker: "You men are now at a port of mobilization. You will make no telephone calls and you will give no one your address." The message suggested that matters had become serious, but most everybody ignored the warning about phone calls; some officers, knowing their destination, sent word to their wives who traveled to Boston to be with their husbands for the last time. There began a fresh round of injections, physicals, haircuts, and perfunctory psychological evaluations. The troops endured more inspections and lectures, marched, enjoyed trips to Boston, played football, and relaxed.

The evening before departure, the 394th Regiment gathered in an outdoor stadium to hear a final pep talk by Lt. Col. Riley, who told them "war is fun!" This remark irked the audience. The GIs showed their irritation by blowing up condoms, punching them into the air, and batting them down the rows. Officers ran up and down the stairs yelling at them to stop, but these orders were ignored. It wasn't often enlisted men had the opportunity to express their displeasure with leadership and not suffer any consequences. (Later, after spending nearly a month in a cold, muddy foxhole on the front, Harry Hagstad had occasion to pull regimental guard duty for a week in Hünningen, three miles behind the main line of resistance. He noticed that regimental officers slept in houses, ate three hot meals a day, and lived out of danger. He concluded, "War might be fun for those people.")[52]

But all was not just trips into Boston and rebellious merriment. The night before departure Easy Company 395's chaplain held a special service and communion for the departing troops. Paul Weesner remembered, "It was the largest attendance that we had."[53]

• • •

On September 29, 1944, 99ers left Camp Myles Standish on trains bound for Boston Harbor where troopships awaited them. A band on the pier blared "Stars and Stripes Forever" and "Over There," while Red Cross women volunteers passed out cups of coffee, donuts, and ditty bags containing a small copy of the New Testament, a cigarette lighter, and cigarettes. Loaded down with rifles, steel helmets, backpacks, and barrack bags stuffed with clothing and personal items, the

99ers slowly boarded the ships. First Sergeant David Spencer wrote in his Day Notes: "I am a little shaky walking up the gangplank because it may be the last time I will ever see the land I love."[54]

Under cover of darkness the ships slipped silently out of the harbor and joined a huge convoy headed for Great Britain. Walter Kellogg stood on the fantail of the SS *Exchequer* watching the lights of Boston and the harbor slowly recede from view. Suddenly Lafayette ("Leroy") Wadsworth approached Kellogg with tears running down his cheeks and said, "God just told me I wouldn't be coming back." Sadly, he was right.[55]

CHAPTER 3

Going to War

In the early morning hours of September 30, 1944, the fourteen thousand men of the 99th Infantry Division departed in six troopships for the deadly battlefields of Europe. Accommodations for enlisted men rivaled steerage passage endured by poor, nineteenth-century immigrants. Deep below the waterline, men squeezed onto canvas bunks, five or six high on racks twenty-four inches apart, while officers shared cabins on the main decks—the class system remained in effect during the voyage. Sergeant Richard Byers of the 371st Field Artillery lucked out by being assigned to a converted stateroom with a private toilet and shower. He knew these pleasant quarters contrasted favorably with those below him; he wrote his wife Jean, "The other poor devils are down in the hold—dark, dirty and crowded."

In the ship's bowels space was so cramped that gear piled up everywhere, making a quick exit impossible in the event of a submarine attack. Two meals a day were served to an almost continuous feeding line of men standing, gulping, and trying to keep their balance in rough seas. Roger Stottlemyer remembers food flying off high counters whenever the ship took a violent dip, and how angry he became when he spied officers sitting down to meals served on nice white tablecloths. Milton May watched as British Indian cooks hacked frozen codfish into chunks, threw them into a twenty-gallon pot half filled with powdered eggs, and then dropped a steam hose into the whole mess, and cooked it for a few minutes. The food approached the inedible—green eggs or "scrambled eggs that tasted like burnt horsehair" for breakfast, and hot dogs, beans, boiled salt pork, boiled potatoes, and hash for the second meal; consequently, "an awful lot of food was thrown overboard." Men resorted to purchasing candy at the PX or buying food from the ship's crew, who, Joseph Thimm said, "were very willing to sell sandwiches for an inflated price."[1]

Tasteless chow wasn't the only problem; many of the men became and stayed seasick during the entire voyage. John McCoy recalled, "It was not uncommon for those who were seasick to lean over their bunks and puke down toward the floor. Of course, some of this would hit others in the lower bunks." The floors and stairwells were slippery and smelly. Ten-foot urinal troughs became clogged with vomit, and urine sloshed over the sides and poured onto the floor. "If you weren't sick already," Roy Putnam remembered vividly, "you would be after you visited the latrine." The mixture of vomit, sweat (only cold sea water showers were available, so everyone passed), diesel fuel fumes, spoiled milk, and tobacco smoke transformed the lower decks into a steerage cruise from hell.[2]

To escape cramped, stifling quarters below, men spent as much time as allowed on deck where, sitting on stairs and lifeboats, they wrote letters, played chess, "shot the bull," listened to the all–St. Louis World Series on the ship's radio, saw two movies, voted in the presidential election, and gambled. Some men, according to Thimm, wanted to read *A Tree Grows in Brooklyn*, because it had been banned in Boston and one of the characters used the word "fuck." Others studied a book of French phrases distributed by the army. Rumor had it the division might be headed to France, and fantasies about meeting lovely French women no doubt spurred a newly acquired interest in the Romance language.[3]

At one point, a German submarine scare near one troopship sent everyone scurrying topside to watch a destroyer drop a few depth charges. For the most part, however, days passed slowly and uncomfortably (the more so if you were seasick), providing ample time to ponder what might lie ahead. Innocence and an itch for new experiences prevented most from contemplating the possibility of a violent death. Some hoped the war would end before the division reached the Continent, and they would serve as occupation troops who wouldn't have "to actually shoot our rifles"; surely, they reasoned, the army wouldn't send so many talented enlisted men into harm's way. Others were cautiously eager to see combat. Jay Nelson wrote his mom that if the men in his platoon "all do what they say they are

going to do [in combat], the war will be over in a week." This bravado
masked uneasiness about what they might encounter and how they
would react to infantry warfare.[4]

In early October 1944, after eleven days, the ships mercifully arrived
at various ports in Scotland and England. When the SS *Argentina*
docked at Southampton, Harry Arnold was disappointed no crowds
or bands welcomed the troops. One bored soldier blew up a condom
and let it fly onto the dock. A worker retrieved the condom, let the
air out, and pocketed it. Other GIs followed suit, and more inflated
condoms floated down. "Soon the air was filled with the white latex
globes, and everybody in the vicinity seemed to have a considered use
for them, even the women." Apparently food was not the only scarce
item in Britain. Those soldiers who kept their condoms would use
them in a more practical way, namely, capping their rifle barrels to
keep out rain and snow.[5]

The troops boarded British Railway cars that seemed small compared to American coaches and watched the "pretty" countryside of
"brilliant green fields, set off with quaint old stone houses and hay-
ricks." On the way to their camps the men shouted out greetings
but local citizens ignored them, probably because the British had
already seen too many Yanks. Having learned that American soldiers
meant candy and gum, kids approached troop trains ("any gum,
chum?") wherever the opportunity presented itself. At one stop
Charles Roland remembered the kids swarmed around the "dinky"
railroad cars begging for sweets. One of the soldiers threw them a
packet of "inedible" K-ration crackers. A pretty girl about eight years
old looked down disdainfully at the ration and then up at the soldier
who tossed it. "Those fookin' biscuits are useless!" she shouted. Obviously
she not only knew about army prepackaged food but had learned
army vocabulary as well.[6]

Quartered for three weeks in camps near Dorchester in southern
England (thirty-five miles west of the port city, Southampton), the
division hiked in cold fog and rain through the "lovely countryside,"
cleaned weapons, and participated in close-order drills. Some men
received passes and visited English pubs in nearby towns where they
drank warm pints of stout and played darts. David Perlman watched
with amusement when an elderly Englishmen offered his well-trained
dog a bite of food, calling it "Hitler's grub." The dog growled and

turned away, refusing to eat the treat. But when the owner made a second attempt while saying, "Churchill's grub," the dog wolfed down the morsel.[7]

Those GIs granted three-day passes rode trains to London and took in historical sites, including Piccadilly Circus where droves of prostitutes approached them. These working class girls (dubbed "Piccadilly Commandos") from London's East End often performed their services in alleyways standing up. Not everyone welcomed the easy opportunity for quick sex. Richard Byers complained by letter to his wife that hundreds of commandos swarmed the sidewalks accosting GIs, and "innocents like me had to fight like hell to save myself from a fate worse than death." Others, freed of hometown behavioral constraints, did not share Byers's sentiment. John Thornburg and a buddy "semi-seriously" propositioned two prostitutes, who carried tiny flashlights to spot potential customers in the blackout. Shining their lights at Thornburg's army shoes and leggings, one prostitute said, "Sorry boys, only officers." Where better to suffer again from institutionalized inequality than in Britain, where social class determined privilege, power, and pleasure.

Since the army appeared in no hurry to transport the division to the front, rumors persisted the 99th would be used as "a constabulary force to take over and run the occupied areas attired in white helmets and leggings." Other speculation involved more dangerous assignments, including an invasion of Norway as winter approached. Shortly before final orders arrived, Harry Arnold received a visit from his older brother, a major in the medical corps. Wilbur Arnold said he could wrangle a transfer to the medical corps where Harry might serve the rest of the war in Britain. Harry declined the offer because he "wanted to go on with the boys." Emotional attachment to the group, a source of much-needed psychological support, could also lead to decisions that might prove hazardous.[9]

• • •

In the predawn hours of November 3, 1944, five months after D-Day, the division began departing for the Southampton docks. James Bishop, who drew maps for the 1st Battalion 394, knew their ultimate destination, hence at "evening chow my appetite was poor." The men wore the greenish-brown, woolen uniforms (also known as olive drabs,

or ODs), and long, heavy, wool overcoats, while lugging full field
packs, duffel bags, and individual weapons. Around 1:00 A.M. Bishop
and Headquarters Company marched through the darkened cobblestone streets of Bridport on the southern coast. Despite the lateness
of the hour, people stood in doorways or leaned out upstairs windows
and softly offered words of encouragement: "Good luck, boys," and
"God bless you all." From one of the upper windows a gruff voice
sang out, "Give 'em 'ell, yanks!'" Some of the men flashed the familiar
V-for-victory sign as "we moved quietly on our way." So began the
greatest and most dangerous adventure of their lives.[10]

• • •

Because of a steady rain and choppy English Channel seas, the departure from Southampton for the Continent was delayed thirty-six hours.
Some men waited patiently in dockside sheds listening to drops pelting
the metal roofs; others marked time sitting aboard troop carriers. In
poor lighting they played poker and shot craps; others wrote letters, an
important way of staying connected to home and family thousands of
lonesome miles away. Finally LSTs (Landing Ship, Tank) and British
coastal steamers began the 115-mile journey to the port of Le Havre,
France. Except for a few impetuous types, the men were nervous,
unsure of what they might encounter, and as Harry Arnold commented, "in no particular hurry to mix it up with the Krauts."[11]

After waiting all day on the Southampton dock, Milton May and
Cannon Company, whose departure from Beaminster the villagers
ignored, boarded an old, weather-beaten LST. Despite a howling wind
mixed with an icy ocean spray, the men were left on deck to fend for
themselves. After observing how the sailors ate "a fine meal," while
the company received canned beef and ration crackers, May "began
to see just how highly the enlisted infantryman rated in the American
army overseas."[12]

Probably most 99ers expected to sail into a spacious harbor and
walk down a gangplank onto a sturdy dock. Unfortunately an unwelcome
shock awaited them. Allied bombers had repeatedly attacked the
port of Le Havre, inflicting massive damage on the harbor and city;
hulls of sunken ships poked above the surface, and piers had become
piles of rubble, blown up by retreating Germans who departed the city
only three weeks earlier. Many 99ers therefore had to hoist themselves,

with full pack and weapon, over the side of the ships, climb down a rope landing net (a difficult and dangerous procedure), and use a shallow-draft Higgins boat to reach the shoreline.

Entire blocks of Le Havre had been leveled, and the sight of such massive destruction produced, according to Paul Weesner, a "rather serious note" among his group. Charles Eubanks wondered, "What have I gotten myself into?" Richard Render could not push out of his mind the realization that his father had landed at Le Havre twenty-six years earlier during the First World War and subsequently had been seriously wounded. Render also recalled his father's advice before he entered the service: "Son, don't go into the infantry; it is the dirtiest, most dangerous job in the army."

Walking along the streets Harry Arnold observed buildings "cleaved apart with sections still standing, interiors exposed, with furniture, plumbing, and the usual trappings of civilized existence suspended over an abyss as though defying gravity." This scene of destruction foreshadowed what these GIs would witness on a larger scale in Germany, for modern warfare technology permitted combatants to flatten and burn entire cities and their inhabitants in a way that had previously been unknown. In Le Havre, Allied bombers killed several thousand French civilians and left thirty-five thousand homeless.[13]

Consequently, as 99ers made their way through the rubble, French dockworkers cursed them. This was not the greeting they had expected, for weren't the Americans driving the Germans out of France? James Bishop didn't understand the reason for such unfriendliness, but "some of the guys shot them the finger." Hostile attitudes toward the French among many 99ers would persist during and after the war. Those GIs thought Frenchmen were lazy, unclean, ungrateful, and out to fleece the troops; by contrast French women were viewed more favorably.[14]

Proceeding several blocks through the city, 99ers met a long line of 2 1/2-ton 6 x 6 trucks (the army's six-wheel-drive prime mover of troops, supplies, and ammunition), weapons carriers, and jeeps (for commissioned officers) that would carry them from France to eastern Belgium. One black driver leaned out of his truck and yelled at David Reagler, "Whatch [sic] you all doin' here? We don't need you no mo'. There ain't no mo' Lootiewaffie [Luftwaffe]!" Reagler certainly would have preferred to be elsewhere, needed or not, but if the

German Air Force had departed, somewhere ahead German infantry and tanks might present a serious obstacle. The men climbed into trucks and began the long, miserable journey to Belgium, stopping the first night near Rouen, France. Pitching pup tents (two water-proof cotton duck shelter halves bound together) in an orchard while a chilly rain poured down, they discovered the protruding lumps under their thin, olive drab sleeping bags and blankets were not rotten apples but cow pies. Curses about the weather, cow manure, and the noxious odor could be heard throughout the encampment. "Cow shit! Goddamn cow shit! We're in the middle of a bunch of cow shit!" Then an anonymous voice rang out: "Welcome to France."[15]

Officers told the men not to trust anyone or accept any food from civilians, including the French and Belgians, because it might contain poison; or perhaps the army worried that local cuisine might spoil an appetite for its rations. Since they had received little information about the situation, some of the men believed Germans lurked in the area. Standing guard, a tense Jay Burke watched a figure riding a bicycle toward him. Pointing his rifle at the man, he yelled, "Halt!" and nearly scared the Frenchman to death. When William McMurdie's company returned to their tents after breakfast the next morning, they discovered French kids had stolen some equipment. For McMurdie and the others, this thievery seemed "a very thankless, low down deed after our armed forces had freed them from the Nazis."[16]

The huge convoy resumed (in a staggered schedule) its 285-mile trek bound for fields and barns near Aubel, Belgium, a few miles from the front lines. As the black drivers of the so-called Red Ball Express whipped along French highways and careened though narrow village streets, their human cargo had to brace themselves to prevent crashing into one another. In each truck, twelve to fourteen men, packed together on two wooden benches running lengthwise, sat upright for the long, uncomfortable trip. Rain came and then turned to sleet. The canvas cover protected the men somewhat from the elements, but several vehicles were open, and everyone suffered from the damp cold.

As they traveled eastward, traces of recent heavy fighting became more evident, for the 1st Infantry Division had liberated this area only a few weeks earlier. Milton May and his group came upon a smashed German 88mm anti-aircraft cannon and a dead German crew: "We stared at them in silence, not knowing we would get used to such sights." The troops passed buildings pockmarked with machine-gun bullets, houses with roofs blown open, doors missing, shutters hanging loosely, and walls caved in. The feeling of being on an exciting adventure gave way to a "sense of foreboding," Richard Byers recalled, "as we saw more signs of what war does." In one small village "every house and building had been set afire and all were completely gutted." Here and there stood wrecked, burned German army vehicles and tanks with "white Maltese crosses glistening in the rain," the wasted wreckage of war and "evidence of angry, deadly exchanges. As they approached a large American cemetery, Harry Arnold saw white crosses "as far as we could see— and more graves were being dug in readiness" for new arrivals. "We were acutely aware that most of them would be filled with infantrymen." Silently they wondered if they would end up there too—and many would.[17]

Dreary French villages appeared deserted, and the few people they saw displayed no interest in the passing convoys. As a King Company 393 truck crept through one town it happened upon an elderly Frenchman standing alone on an empty street corner. Travis Mathis leaned out the back of the truck and playfully asked in a Southern drawl, "Hey, Mister, how far are we from Okolona, Arkansas?" This humorous question produced laughter and a moment of levity on a trip that lacked both. Jay Burke and his buddies were appalled by the behavior of one Frenchman, who suddenly "took a leak" against the side of a house while holding a conversation with a woman who leaned out a window. Urinating in public in front of a woman, who apparently didn't mind, confirmed for them how uncivilized the French were.[18]

Once the convoy moved into Belgium, the reception by civilians changed. Belgians cheered, waved, yelled "kill *les Boches* [the Germans]," flashed the victory sign, and presented 99ers with bread, fruit, and wine. One elderly lady ran out with a pan and spoon, offering William Bray delicious, hot pea soup. The warmth and friendliness lifted everyone's spirits and showed at least the Belgians welcomed their coming.[19]

THE STATIC FRONT (NOVEMBER 10–DECEMBER 16, 1944)

When the 99th Division reached its staging area, men heard the distant but ominous rumble of artillery fire and observed at night intermittent flashes of light. They were told, however, theirs was a quiet, static sector and nothing would happen, if at all, until spring. Nevertheless John Midkiff considered it "the saddest day of my life. I thought of everywhere I would rather be, and I thought of my people back home and wondered if I would ever see them again." Just before they boarded trucks bound for the front, Francis Iglehart, standing in cold rain mixed with snow, received a jovial letter from a "Vassar girl" with whom he was corresponding. She described an "outing in Greenwich Village with 4-F type dates where everybody had a simply wonderful time smoking their first joints." Precisely at that moment the contrast between his miserable situation and the enjoyment of those sitting out the war came crashing down on him. This letter depressingly reminded Iglehart that some men, perhaps using contrived excuses, were not making similar sacrifices.[20]

The three regiments of the 99th deployed on the front line, which snaked its way more than twenty miles along the Belgian-German border in a hilly area interspersed with streams and covered by a dense growth of fir and deciduous trees. Although the distance was far too great for a single division to defend, army command assumed the difficult typography of the forested Ardennes and a weakened enemy would prevent a serious threat to this quiet sector. Richard Byers was told German forces opposite them comprised old men, young boys, ex-Luftwaffe, ex-navy, and convalescents from the Russian front. General Lauer thought the enemy could only mount a "limited attack of one or two battalions, and it was only a matter of time before the Germans folded up." Therefore, there was no reason to be concerned.[21]

The division took up positions opposite the Siegfried Line or West Wall, a strong defensive barrier along Germany's pre-war western border, composed of concrete anti-tank blocks (popularly known as Dragon's Teeth), steel-reinforced pillboxes, barbed wire, and mines. In addition, artillery, mortars, and machine guns were zeroed in on all likely avenues of approach, so breaching these defenses might prove difficult. By the same token, however, if the Germans decided to go on the attack, those superbly constructed defenses would offer no protection for their advancing forces.

The 99th's three regiments were assigned different sections on the main line of resistance (MLR). The 395th Regiment was to hold the north, with the 3rd Battalion occupying the German village of Höfen, whose eastern outskirts were part of the Siegfried Line. The 393rd Regiment was placed in the center, while the 394th occupied the southern segment near the Belgian village of Losheimergraben and the so-called Buchholz railroad station; the 394th's sector alone stretched sixty-five hundred yards or 3.6 miles of dense forest. As Raymond Perisin and others from Baker Company marched on a blacktop road up to the front, truckloads of 9th Infantry Division soldiers passed them headed in the opposite direction. Each group of veterans shouted out to the neophytes, "You'll be sorry!"—a refrain they had previously heard from enlisted men at induction centers when they entered the army.[22]

Undermanned in terms of the distance that needed to be protected, squads and platoons were spaced yards from each other, making them vulnerable to serious incursions. Upon arrival at the front, Lt. Samuel Lombardo, a replacement platoon leader, pointed out to the company commander that such large gaps would be "difficult to defend." Captain James Morris replied, "Forget what they taught you at Fort Benning. This is the way they told us to do it over here." Frontline riflemen also were aware of the potential danger that existed; Private David Reagler commented to his foxhole mate: "I hope the Germans don't come through here because our holes are spaced so far apart." What Reagler feared, the Germans already knew. If enemy forces breached the front, they could overwhelm and encircle the outnumbered 99th companies. But virtually no one at SHAEF (Supreme Headquarters Allied Expeditionary Force) thought this possible; rather, they believed German forces, reeling from a series of devastating defeats, would soon give up.[23]

• • •

It was gloomy and snowing when the 3rd Battalion 395, replacing the 5th Armored Division, arrived in Höfen after a long, frigid trip in half-tracks and uncovered trucks—uncovered because someone at the upper levels of command thought it would be easier for the occupants to escape if an enemy fighter suddenly dropped out of the sky to attack them. No sullen German villagers appeared to observe their arrival, for the inhabitants had fled eastward or had been relocated by American authorities. George Neill said the "area gave many of us a feeling of foreboding" as they arrived in Hitler's Germany. When Paul Putty approached a foxhole, four GIs "in a great hurry to be relieved" clambered out of their dugout enclosure and quickly disappeared into the darkness: "They neither said 'hello' nor 'good-bye'—or gave us any clue as to the direction or distance of the enemy." Joseph Thimm experienced a similar introduction upon his arrival; the 5th Armored GI pointed vaguely toward the east, warned him not to stray off the path as mines and booby traps might be planted in the area, and then left. Thimm stared at his future home, a muddy hole with a makeshift roof of shelter halves, a bleak, snow-covered field to the front and, to the rear, another field strewn with dead, bloated cattle, "a heck of an introduction to frontline combat."[24]

The other two regiments of the 99th replaced the battle-tested 9th Infantry Division, recuperating and reorganizing after the bloody, ill-conceived Hürtgen Forest campaign. Byron Reburn watched Love Company 394, "standing like harnessed draft horses, vapor rising from the irregular columns of young men, humbled by the penetrating cold, the impersonal discipline, and the gods of fate that put us there." Although happy to be relieved, the dirty, unkempt, and bearded 9th Division GIs expressed no gratitude to the clean-shaven 99ers; instead, John Mellin recalled, they taunted us by saying, "look at all those clean uniforms." Another group shouted derisively at Harry Arnold's platoon: "Is this what the War Department is using for soldiers?" Ridiculing the "green" newcomers gave them a sense of superiority and at the same time pressured 99ers to measure up to veteran outfits. Of course, this meant the newcomers would have to overcome their fear of the Germans and the possibility they couldn't perform. Radford Carroll confessed, "My biggest fear going into combat was that I would turn out to be a coward." Since each GI had to survive in a dangerous world of random violence, self-esteem would be measured in terms of self-control, carrying out orders, and being steadfast. The American ethos of masculinity, expressed in sports, movies, magazines, and in public discourse, held males to tough standards; it included the requirement that "real" men silently endure hardship, never show fear, and never back down from a challenge, especially one imposed by other males.[25]

Ninth Division soldiers had constructed fighting holes covered with branches, which offered protection from artillery shells that hit tall pines, shooting deadly wood splinters and metal fragments downward. The 99ers proceeded to expand dugouts and erect log huts behind the lines for sleeping, as they expected to remain there for the winter. A foot of snow lay on the ground when the 99th took up positions along the narrow International Highway that separated Belgium and Germany. The white fields and snow-topped pines created a picturesque winter setting. William McMurdie described to his parents the idyllic scene of "fir trees covered with snow from top to bottom like some Christmas card. It all seemed to be in a dream world and made the war sort of out of place." This contrast between beauty and destruction, peace and war, life and death, civilization and savagery would sometimes present itself in stark incongruity on the battlefields. But McMurdie could not allow himself to become enchanted by lovely surroundings, for deadly German patrols prowled in those dark forests.[26]

● ● ●

By the time the 99th arrived at the front, daylight lasted only eight hours—roughly 8:30 A.M. to 4:30 P.M. Long hours of darkness, morning fog, and overcast skies magnified the gloom and danger. Even though American forces had already experienced winter conditions in Italy, the army did not provide the 99th and other divisions in Northern Europe with proper winter clothing. Neither the wool dress uniform nor the combat field jacket proved heavy enough or sufficiently waterproof to keep soldiers warm and dry. GIs tried to overcome this serious deficiency by dressing in multiple layers that typically included several pairs of long johns and ODs. Nevertheless, the infantry soldier suffered greatly from the "bitter cold that penetrated the very marrow of every bone in our bodies and sapped our stamina and morale." They lived without heat in wet dugouts and shallow foxholes, so there was, according to Stewart Fischer, "very little

to do it except feel sorry for oneself." He soon learned "the contribution of the infantryman was not in heroic action but in existing
under miserable living conditions." William Bray echoed those sentiments. The "worst thing" about being a frontline soldier was not fear
of combat, but "living in mud pits in freezing weather with no way to
get warm."[27]

The Army's heavy wool overcoat proved burdensome, for it absorbed
water and would freeze, adding considerable weight to what a soldier
already had to carry; its length dragged in the snow, so some GIs
lopped off a foot of cloth from the bottom. Many soldiers abandoned
the coats altogether and discarded their bayonets to lighten the load.
The absence of white camouflage proved another dangerous deficiency,
hindering the GI's ability to blend with the snow. Infantrymen tried
to overcome this blunder by appropriating white tablecloths and
sheets from abandoned Belgian and German homes, but hardly
enough material existed for all riflemen; moreover, this material became
frozen and emitted cracking sounds easily heard in the woods.

The most grievous problem for the infantry was the lack of waterproof, insulated footwear. Initially many GIs wore World War I vintage
shoes with khaki canvas leggings. Not only did the shoes fail to keep
out the rain and snow, but soggy leggings also ensured that ankles
and calves stayed damp and cold. The newer World War II combat
boots included a leather cuff that replaced the leggings and gradually
most of the men received a pair. But the boots leaked, so soldiers
standing in or moving through snow developed "frozen feet," where
blood stops flowing to affected areas, or "trench foot," caused by constant immersion in cold water, which results in the loss of skin and
infection. Both conditions eventually immobilized the soldier, leading
to gangrene and the possible loss of toes and feet. From November 10
until December 15, four hundred fifty 99ers left the front because of
severe foot problems. Senior Army leaders did not adequately plan
for winter fighting and as a consequence frontline combat soldiers
suffered needlessly. One veteran commented, "I don't understand
why they treated the infantry so badly."

Men were instructed to put on dry socks daily, but this was difficult to do regularly, and, as John Mellin said, "your feet were soon wet
again anyway." General Lauer, who lived indoors and wore galoshes,
believed the men were not putting enough effort into keeping their

feet dry. He issued an order that trench foot was to be regarded "in the same category as a self-inflicted wound," which apparently would mean a court-martial offense. Although some men did not attend to their feet regularly, even the most conscientious soldiers could not protect themselves when they stood and walked in mud and snow. The Army also issued rubber galoshes but not in sufficient quantities or in large sizes to cover the leather boots; rear echelon troops and black market thieves helped themselves to those galoshes. GIs who obtained overshoes discarded their boots and wore multiple pairs of socks with straw and rags stuffed inside. It made for tough walking but feet stayed drier and warmer.[28]

• • •

Food is vital for combat soldiers, especially when fighting in winter. An inadequate diet diminishes a soldier's combat effectiveness: energy levels are reduced, susceptibility to illness increases, and demoralization sets in. Unlike divisional and regimental officer staffs who enjoyed sit-down, hot meals, frontline troops of the 99th Division often did not regularly receive adequate quantities of hot, nutritious food. The best meals were prepared by cooks and eaten behind the front line or carried to the troops in insulated marmite containers. But often the cooks could not reach those in forward positions, so hot meals, an important morale booster, could not be counted on. And when it rained or snowed, hot food, plopped into the metal mess kits, quickly turned cold and mushy. On occasion food became contaminated (e.g., the turkey served at Thanksgiving), producing dysentery that afflicted many frontline soldiers.

More commonly, the army quartermaster supplied infantry platoons with packaged and canned rations. K rations consisted of Cracker Jacks–size boxes that held a day's worth of meals—each box appropriately identified as "Breakfast," "Dinner," and "Supper." Entrees consisted of chopped ham and powdered eggs, cheese, and canned meat. A separate plastic bag contained four biscuits, hard candy, packets of instant coffee, a bouillon cube, four cigarettes, a pack of matches, and sheets of brown toilet paper. Light in weight, a soldier could carry a day's worth of "meals," and the waxed inner box was torn into two-inch squares and burned to heat a cup of bouillon or coffee. K rations represented one of many nasty shocks GIs faced overseas. David Reagler remembered his first K ration breakfast. He found "the odor so repulsive" he couldn't eat it. Eventually he ate K rations to survive but "never liked them" and found the food monotonous and awful.[29]

A meal of C rations included two medium-sized cans: one contained a greasy entree (ham and scrambled, concentrated eggs, meat and vegetable hash, or meat and beans). Stuart Kline thought the meat entrees "looked and smelled like dog food." Many preferred either spaghetti or beans with wieners, but James Langford (and others) suspected rear echelon soldiers seized these "before they got as far forward as we were." The second, olive drab C ration can held three biscuits, three pieces of candy, packs of instant coffee, sugar, salt and pepper, and brown toilet paper. C rations were heavy; if the troops moved into attack, the cans proved cumbersome, and in frigid weather the contents froze. If some heat could be generated, a soldier could warm a C ration entree. The food offered one advantage—fewer bowel movements, not insignificant when forced to straddle latrine trenches or use "cat holes" in rain, snow, and biting wind.[30]

Finally the army supplied an emergency D ration, a tart, semi-sweet chocolate bar, packed with calories and nutrients, but so hard that small slivers could best be chipped away with a knife; Cliff McDaniel thought eating one was "like a rat chewing and gnawing its way through a bridge plank." William Galegar (among others) considered the D bar "a life saver" against severe hunger when cooked food or other rations did not reach him. Fear about running out of food resulted in most soldiers constantly carrying several D bars; at war's end Galegar still had six D bars stored in his pockets.

Each man also carried a metal canteen (and cup) filled with water, a vital liquid purified with halazone tablets that added an unsavory taste. Water in canteens turned to ice in freezing temperatures, so men had to thaw them by using body heat. Finding potable water often proved a difficult and dangerous task even amidst the snow.[31]

Besides his nine-pound M-1 rifle, which a soldier must have at all times (one squad member toted the twenty-two pound Browning Automatic Rifle or BAR), an infantryman carried at least nineteen clips (eight .30-caliber bullets in each clip) of ammunition, two grenades, a 2.75-pound gray-green, steel helmet with plastic liner and knit cap (the helmet actually provided limited protection, but the infantryman "felt naked without it"), a first-aid kit, a web belt with ammo pouches, backpack, poncho, sleeping bag or blanket, a shelter half, pup tent pegs, a gas mask pouch filled with personal items (the gas masks were discarded), and a small entrenching tool that functioned as both a pick and a shovel. A human packhorse, the GI had to dig his own shelter, usually with the aid of a buddy. If First World War soldiers in Western Europe fought from trenches, Second World War GIs fired from foxholes. When the front line remained stationary, a hole functioned as a temporary home and could be reused, but once on the move (or ordered to relocate) the combat soldier had to repeatedly scoop out a new shelter, a tedious, enervating task, especially in frozen or root-filled ground.

These newly arrived combat soldiers had to contend with a series of shocks, both physical and psychological. Instead of barracks and indoor facilities, they found foxholes and latrine trenches; instead of mild temperatures, bitter cold and snow; in place of security and relaxation, danger and stress. While training at Camp Maxey had conditioned them physically, the Texas heat and humidity hardly prepared these GIs for a long, numbing winter in the Ardennes.

Although initially nervous and edgy, 99ers were surprised to find the heavily wooded front unexpectedly quiet, not what they had anticipated. When Howard Bowers arrived after dark near Losheimergraben (an important crossroads in the southeast corner of Belgium), 9th Division men "were running around shouting and yelling" beside a bonfire, no doubt celebrating their departure. The 9th Division GIs told William Bray: "Don't bother [the Germans] when you have to go on patrol, and they won't bother you. Don't tell the officers, as they know nothing of the agreement." To learn the opposing combatants observed an unauthorized truce completely amazed Bray: "This wasn't exactly war as I envisioned it." Since conditions remained mostly peaceful, Richard Byers felt as if he were on "an adventurous camping trip, which would be over as soon as the German army faced up to the inevitable and collapsed." That should have happened, but Byers and his superiors underestimated Adolf Hitler's madness.[32]

Since the officers stayed away, Bray and other squad members decided to preserve the informal arrangement with the enemy. When Bray occupied an outpost (a forward position manned by a few men to alert the MLR of any German encroachment), he and his mates built a fire to keep warm, and the Germans did not bother them. One night two German soldiers (a young boy and an older man) surrendered to them. The Germans showed the GIs a new carbine, and they all sat around a campfire and communicated as best they could: "We gave them some of our rations and after an hour or so," two men escorted the prisoners back to headquarters. "This seemed like a strange kind of war" to Bray, for it contradicted army films and combat instruction at Camp Maxey. Lathan Walker and his squad adopted a similar approach to the enemy, which any officer would have hotly censured. On patrol they spotted some Germans, but "since they didn't shoot at us, we decided not to shoot at them." The 99ers' behavior did not stem entirely from prudence; they carried civilian non-violent attitudes to the battlefield. But hostile enemy action, fear, and a desire to stay alive would in time provide the impetus to squeeze the trigger.[33]

• • •

Stewart Fischer pulled sentry duty one night in a Höfen farmhouse attic when someone came running toward him. He shouted for the man to stop and in turn received a burst of automatic weapon fire. Fischer retaliated by firing his M-1 rifle four times and soon thereafter heard moaning. When the Germans launched a flare, he spotted a German soldier lying on the ground. But Fischer stayed in the farmhouse, unwilling to venture outside lest he encounter other enemy soldiers. Over the next few hours the wounded German repeatedly groaned and cried out for his wife and children. Fischer, who had learned to speak German at home in New Braunfels, Texas, wished that he couldn't understand the soldier's words, but also believed he couldn't "do anything about helping him." Eventually the German became silent and died. At daylight Fischer examined the man he had killed and discovered two of his rounds had struck him. Rather than celebrating, Fischer felt guilty about not going to the wounded man's aid: "I was convinced that I had violated one of the Ten Commandments, and that I would be assigned to eternal damnation." At this initial stage of combat, Fischer could not ignore the enemy soldier's suffering; nor could other soldiers new to combat. In time, however, they would become inured to the sight of the dead and to the suffering of the wounded. While on patrol a few days later, Fischer stepped on a mine that badly wounded him. He concluded he had been deservedly punished for not helping the dying German.[34]

To Louis Pedrotti the "little German gingerbread town" of Höfen did not resemble the ersatz "Nazi village" they had fought for at Camp Maxey. Except for the noisy, scary V-1 rockets that loudly putt-putted overhead like a "one-cylinder Maytag washer, they could have been a crew on location from Universal Studios." Snowflakes were falling, so the scene seemed both picturesque and "surreal," not the murderous killing grounds of First World War newsreels and movies. Harry Arnold, whose company occupied ground a few miles south of Höfen, found the battlefield not what he had expected. Prior to his arrival at the front, Arnold imagined bravely crawling hundreds of yards while under "constant artillery fire" to relieve a comrade in a forward position. Although both sides regularly dispatched reconnaissance patrols and daily lobbed a few artillery shells at one another, the snow-covered forests remained relatively free of violent clashes. Arnold's fantasy about being subjected to murderous shelling would subsequently come to pass, but the outcome would prove to be a nightmare.[35]

In spite of the lack of fighting, those first nights on the front lines generated fear and uncertainty. One night near Kalterherberg, a little village over the German border, Easy Company 395 sent out a patrol to relieve another group. After someone mistakenly fired a round, the two American patrols launched a serious firefight against each other, killing three men and wounding several others. The army never acknowledged "friendly fire" losses, so such information never reached parents who would have been devastated to learn their son's life had ended in such a useless manner. The army wanted to make sure the public could not raise questions about the competence of leadership.

Standing guard duty alone in a foxhole "seemed like a lifetime," Jack Prickett remembered. Bill Lefevre "strained to tell if sounds in the dark were caused by animals or an enemy patrol," and on guard duty he held a "grenade in one hand, a rosary in the other." Peering into the dark forests at night, GIs imagined German soldiers (referred to as Krauts or Jerries) creeping forward stealthily behind the trees

John McCoy of Fox Co. 393 heads back to his foxhole after chow in early December before the Battle of the Bulge. Note that he is not wearing an overcoat or galoshes. Courtesy John McCoy.

with a stick grenade or a knife, eager to slit a throat. Snow dropping off pine branches or limbs cracking during breezy nights sounded like advancing hobnail boots. "Scared stiff," John McCoy had trouble sleeping because of a constant, "urgent" need to urinate. Yet when he tried to relieve himself, he could only produce a few drops. After several weeks his bladder returned to normal, and he could sleep again. Fear never left McCoy nor others at the front, but over time they learned to perform in spite of it.[36]

• • •

Division headquarters ordered all units to send out day and night patrols into no-man's-land to gather intelligence and to season green troops. Soldiers hated patrols because they had to leave the safety of foxholes and move into unfamiliar territory where the enemy operated. There were two types of patrols: reconnaissance and combat. Whereas the former consisted of a small (and, it was hoped, quiet) band of infantrymen whose mission was to gather intelligence concerning German strength and perhaps capture an enemy soldier for interrogation, the combat patrol involved a large group looking to engage the enemy in a deadly fight, a dangerous undertaking.

A few men initially thought patrols would be exciting, as William Bray admitted: "My buddy and I assumed it would be like playing cowboys and Indians." The boyish lure of mystery and adventure drew some GIs into the forests where adrenaline-pumping action might be found. On his first patrol Bray and others discovered a minefield and, upon returning to their lines, reported its presence; but "they [battalion staff officers] . . . didn't believe us. So they sent out a second patrol to make sure we weren't lying." On the second patrol, a sergeant tripped a mine and was castrated. Consequently Bray became disillusioned with patrols, as it seemed his group had risked their lives for information no one heeded. Shortly thereafter, on November 18, 1944, Love Company 394th suffered its first killed in action (KIA) when a lieutenant died on a reconnaissance patrol. Company commander Allen Ferguson personally led (an unusual occurrence) a daylight patrol to recover the lieutenant's body, but he and Pfc. Clarence Robinson Jr. were killed by German machine-gun fire. (Bray speculated they had moved too close to the German lines, thus revoking the non-shooting "arrangement" with the enemy.) These deaths jarred the men of Love Company. Bray recalled, "Ferguson's death was a shocker for me." He stopped volunteering for patrols.[37]

The death of Clarence Robinson, "a handsome youth of sweet disposition and innocent of world events, who accepted his station in life without bitterness or rancor," saddened Byron Reburn. He had last seen Robinson shouldering an air-cooled machine gun and walking off with his comrades into the woods. Later he watched as stretcher-bearers carried his body back to the platoon: "He had not changed. There were no signs of mortal wounds or suffering. It appeared as though he had merely fallen asleep. Still handsome. Still a picture of youthful innocence. I looked on impassively. Some cursed. One or two threatened revenge. No one prayed."[38]

The first death in a platoon stunned the survivors, for no amount of military training prepared soldiers for the suddenness of death and loss. It brought home the deadly consequences of infantry combat, serving notice to every frontline rifleman that he could no longer ignore the possibility or even probability that he might be wounded or killed. "When you are young," William Galegar explained, "you don't expect death," but when it happened, "it came as a shock not ever forgotten." While on a patrol, Stanley Hancock, a tough, aggressive rifleman, came upon a dead American lying alone in "the cold, snowy darkness of the Ardennes." To Hancock the "war was no longer a game, but terrifyingly real." Joseph O'Neill reacted similarly when he observed his first dead GI beside the road: "When you see another American soldier wearing ODs, helmet, and carrying an M-1 rifle, you see yourself."[39]

Before reaching the front, these young soldiers had repressed or discounted the possibility of their own death or that of friends. Most remained optimistic they would survive, a psychological defense that allowed them to function under difficult circumstances. Seeing dead comrades brought not only sorrow, but also the realization that a similar fate might befall them. At one point Jack Prickett depressingly concluded, "I am going to die in some unknown place in Belgium, and no one is going to know." Each soldier eventually realized, on some level of awareness, he could perish, and his death would have no meaning except to other squad members and his family, who would receive an impersonal telegram from the army. This "sobering" conclusion came to William McMurdie when, serving as first scout on a reconnaissance patrol, he came upon a dead German soldier, "the first dead person" he had ever seen: "He looked so small and insignificant, even though his body was bloated from lying there for some days. I could not help but ask myself if each one of us was so small and so insignificant as this." A soldier had to believe his life mattered and, yet, he could not shut out the realization that in an army of millions, he was a cipher, a regrettable but acceptable casualty in the drive for victory.[40]

The individual soldier needed to feel he counted and others cared about him. Given the impersonal conditions of the army and combat, a foxhole buddy and squad and platoon members became extremely important, helping a GI endure and survive the physical and psychological rigors of frontline service. In effect, a GI's buddies became a surrogate family, replacing loved ones back home who had no idea what he was going through and could not help him even if they did; only fellow soldiers experiencing the harsh, frightful conditions at the front could understand his plight. In becoming an infantryman, each soldier had left civilian life to join a special fraternity and, for a time, they were closer to one another than to parents, siblings, and perhaps even spouses.

• • •

Since most men preferred not to go on patrols, platoon sergeants picked "volunteers." There were exceptions to this unspoken coercion. The men of the 2nd Platoon, Item Company 394, volunteered willingly because they greatly respected their platoon leader, Lt. Samuel Lombardo. Like others, James Larkey trusted and admired Lombardo: "When Sam said he needed volunteers, I volunteered." Earle Slyder felt the same about 1st. Lt. Earl Bennett: "He would say come along and follow me, and we did." Most infantrymen, if selected, went on patrol; but a few would claim illness and head for the first aid station. On one occasion, just before a patrol, a BAR man "accidentally" dropped his weapon in the mud, an action which, William Bray thought, merited a court martial. Jack Prickett recalled an instance when the platoon sergeant designated a replacement to be a scout for a patrol. The replacement refused: "No," he said. "You want to get me killed. You can shoot me right now, but I am not going." The other infantrymen became angry at this response—refusing a direct order was unheard of. Prickett offered to lead but told the replacement, "I'll take the point this time, but next time you will, or I will shoot you myself."[41]

GIs felt anxious before going on patrol, especially if a long waiting period preceded the departure. Men would clean their weapons, sharpen knives, remove noise-producing equipment (including their second set of dog tags), and try to sleep. Ernest McDaniel, who developed a close relationship with John McCoy, would give him a "ring and other personal belongings with the unspoken understanding that these would be sent to the family" if he didn't return. Once underway in daylight the riflemen visually scoured the landscape, searching for likely ambush sites and, at the same time, picking out a tree or depression that might offer some protection if bullets suddenly cracked the silence. Nighttime generated even more fear because it was difficult to see and easy to become lost. The cold, quiet darkness seemed to amplify the sounds of footsteps crunching snow, coughs, and clanking equipment. Because the Germans made extensive use of mines and booby traps—vicious weapons difficult to detect— each step was fraught with the possibility of traumatic amputation and death. Returning to one's own line also brought considerable risk, for nervous comrades could and did shoot by mistake.[42]

Orders for patrols came from the regimental staff (situated some distance from the front) who did not know or chose to ignore the tactical difficulties patrols faced. Matthew Legler, commander of the 1st Battalion 393, was told to send out a patrol on a bright, moonlit night even though the dark-uniformed men would have to cross open, snow-covered fields. Legler attempted unsuccessfully to have the order rescinded; as he feared, the Germans attacked the patrol. Once, however, Frank Hoffman witnessed an exceptional scene in which company commander George Balach, took off his .45-caliber pistol, laid it on the battalion commander's desk and refused to dispatch a patrol. The battalion commander cancelled the order.[43]

Some patrol leaders (often noncoms), fearing the consequences of a dangerous excursion into no-man's-land, ventured only a short distance, hunkered down for an hour or so, and then returned. George Lehr went on such a patrol, moving out a few hundred yards and stopping; after staying put for awhile, "we slunk back to our lines. Needless to say I was not about to complain." John McCoy had mixed feelings about such patrols: "it was safer, but you felt like a heel." Joseph Thimm had a similar experience at Höfen when he and others headed eastward toward German positions. After they had walked some distance, the squad leader announced he had "lost" the map; they returned, much to the dismay of some patrol members. James Larkey went on a patrol led by an old cadre sergeant: "We moved out, lay down in the snow, waited a while and then went back; on the way to their lines he warned everyone to keep his mouth shut." Larkey was glad not to have confronted any Germans, "but I thought it was disgraceful."[44]

Although the United States and Germany fought in World War I and again were at war, no longstanding, nationalistic antagonism existed between the two countries. Except for Jewish soldiers, most 99ers harbored little animus toward Germans prior to combat and lacked a strong incentive to kill. Once the shooting and shelling started, they realized German soldiers were trying to kill them. Fear, frustration, anger, a sense of duty, and the desire to maintain self-respect provided the incentives for men to fight.

• • •

Other surprises occurred at the front. In Texas, friction had existed between the cadre (including the older, blue-collar privates) and the younger college boys from the army's Special Training Program. During the course of the long training period, much of the antipathy dissipated. Both groups came to recognize value in one another, though real unit cohesiveness did not form until they reached the front lines, where danger and mutual dependence eroded educational and cultural barriers at the lower levels of the military class system. When death threatened everyone's existence, steadiness and dependability counted, not rank or education. According to Francis Iglehart, "cultural differences melted away and innate merits as a soldier are what mattered." Combat had a democratizing effect on the lower ranks. Life became reduced to its simplest elements and, as David Reagler noted, "our interests were the same: try to keep warm and dry, try not to get killed or wounded, and try to have something to eat and drink."[45]

Officers and enlisted men alike lacked combat experience. Military training attempted to overcome this deficiency by preparing men for the rigors of combat, while culling out officers unsuited for leading and infantrymen who could not follow orders. No organization operates a foolproof system that selects only the qualified, and given the army's inexperience and desperation to fill the ranks, misjudgments happened. Only on the battlefield, where danger, stress, and unpredictability were ever-present, could true evaluations be made as to who had the ability to lead and who would carry out orders.

The army assumed that divisional, regimental, and battalion commanders were too valuable to operate at the front; they could better direct the troops if they remained behind the lines (the higher the rank, the greater the distance from enemy shells and bullets), sending orders and gathering information by phone, radio, or runner. Company commanders operated with their platoons, but how close depended on the situation and the character of the officer. Second lieutenants were expected to lead combat patrols and be with the men during attacks. Many enlisted men, however, complained they "never saw [commissioned] officers at the front," and the higher the rank, the less likely a visit to the troops where they might gain firsthand knowledge of conditions. To the GIs, it seemed that rear echelon staffs operated in safety without showing concern for the dangers and hardships the infantry faced.

Since company commanders and 2nd lieutenants came and left (wounded, killed, or relieved for incompetence), frontline troops were sometimes hard-pressed to feel connected to their commissioned officers. Consequently, platoon sergeants and squad leaders (staff sergeants) often functioned as the most important figures to the men; they stayed with frontline soldiers, sharing danger and deprivation. As squad leaders and platoon sergeants departed because of wounds, death, or frozen feet, replacements emerged from the ranks, and former ASTPers became the new noncoms. Combat infantrymen in some units felt they survived on their own, almost isolated, without lieutenants or captains to lead them. Because the army gave them few resources to deal with adversity and pressure, these soldiers relied on one another to fulfill their responsibilities and yet cope with the threat of violent death, the possibility of crippling wounds, physical suffering, and exposure to bloody horrors.

Some officers clearly lacked good judgment and did not understand that rules followed in training did not always apply on the battlefield. General Lauer issued orders for the men to shave every day and look sharp, while the men, short on hot water, preferred to concentrate on keeping warm and staying alive. Company commander Neil Brown gave Byron Reburn "hell" after he returned from an outpost with an unbuttoned field jacket. Howard Bowers was heating water in his helmet when Lt. Lawrence Moloney warned him the "heat would soften the steel, causing it to be less resistant to shell fragments and bullets." A few officers became excessively concerned about litter on the battlefield. When newly appointed Captain Stephen Plume came up to the front and saw discarded C ration cans, he ordered the men to police the area because "flies will be a menace by spring." Regimental commander Lt. Col. Jean Scott somehow mistook the dirty, debris-strewn battlefield for the well-ordered grounds of Camp Maxey. He yelled at Capt. Joseph Carnevale to have "the men pick up cigarette butts and C ration cans."[46]

When the 69th Infantry Division finally relieved the 99th (in February 1945), General Lauer insisted that every man be clean-shaven when arriving in the rest area, even though chilly wind and rain left faces raw and beards hard. Perhaps Lauer wished to present his troops in good form, although it was impossible to spruce up dirty, irregularly dressed infantrymen who displayed all the ill effects of winter ground warfare. Unreasonable attention to presentation, especially in these circumstances, demonstrated an insensitive appreciation of conditions at the front and only served to foster hostility toward command.[47]

Although military rank still counted, some leveling did occur. Saluting of officers was discontinued because it would alert snipers to the best targets. Lt. Herman Dickman told his 2nd Platoon, "Don't call me 'lieutenant' anymore; just call me 'Dick.'" Relationships became more informal, especially between sergeants and enlisted men. Regardless of rank, frontline soldiers felt their experiences and suffering earned them consideration. They respected those officers who shared their fate and demonstrated competence. Henri Atkins discovered "some you could look up to and some were despised by all." Rank counted less and natural leadership counted more; or, as John Thornburg put it, "We needed leaders and didn't want to be led by assholes." Oakley Honey said that if you had a "weak lieutenant, you were not going to be gung ho. You were not willing to put your life on the line for someone who didn't know what he was doing." At Camp Maxey, Francis Chesnick's platoon endured petty harassment by a sergeant, "but after we got to the front, we didn't pay much attention to him." According to James Larkey, a platoon sergeant in training had been "a condescending S.O.B who kept threatening us with disaster if we didn't toughen up." The sergeant could not, however, maintain this high standard for himself; at the front he "broke down completely and had to be assisted to the rear." At Camp Maxey 1st Sergeant Donald Riddle called James Crafton "a yard bird," a derogatory term meaning an inept enlisted man. But when Riddle could not handle the stress of combat, Crafton secured some measure of satisfaction in telling Riddle, "You get to go home; we yard birds are going to win the war."[48]

• • •

Strategic planning came from SHAEF and First Army staff. Orders descended through the chain of command and at each level (corps, division, regiment, battalion, company), strategy was transformed into tactical planning by the respective staff. The average soldier lacked information to evaluate strategic objectives and tactical plans. Generally this did not trouble the combat infantryman because he focused on the battlefield immediately around him, usually a hundred yards or so, and let others do the thinking for him. He could judge the competence of platoon leaders and company commanders. Did they seem to care about the men? Were they trustworthy or unsteady? Did they remain behind the lines in relative safety while the men were exposed to bullets and shells? Did they lead by example or simply pass orders on to others? Did they rely on rank rather than ability? Did they have common sense? These were the attributes that mattered most to the GI.

At the front combat soldiers could and did resist orders from second lieutenants, especially those of the "chicken shit" variety. One platoon leader told a member of Easy Company 394 to dig his foxhole, but the soldier replied, "You can dig your own damn foxhole." When Lt. Rolland Neudecker ordered Leslie Miller and Jack Prickett to dig his foxhole, Prickett replied: "Hell no. We are not going to dig you a fucking hole." Neudecker responded, "I am giving you a direct order!" Miller interjected sarcastically, "What are you going

to do, send us off the front lines?" As company commander Paul
Fogelman walked by, Miller told him, "This asshole wants us to dig a
foxhole for him." Whereupon Fogelman responded, "Everyone digs
his own foxhole." Prickett admired Fogelman because he had refused
to allow exploitation by rank.[49]

Receiving the Combat Infantry Badge (CIB) for fighting at the
front was highly esteemed by soldiers. It separated the recipients,
men who bore the greatest risk, from rear echelon troops serving in
relative safety. Although they occupied the bottom rank, soldiers took
pride in their ability to endure combat conditions. Some field grade
officers (majors and above) wanted to acquire the CIB as proof of
their veteran status and rugged masculinity. Upon returning from a
dangerous patrol, which earned Oakley Honey and others a Combat
Infantry Badge, he noticed three senior officers, who had not gone on
patrols, wearing the CIB. Oakley wondered, "Where did they earn
their badge? These officers probably hadn't been beyond the MLR, let
alone been fired upon."[50]

Jack Prickett and Leslie Miller witnessed how one officer attempted
to achieve this honored symbol. Armed with a rifle and sniper scope,
a major approached them and announced he wanted to fire a few
shots at a German pillbox from their foxhole. Prickett refused,
saying, "If you fire, in three minutes they'll mortar the hell out of
us." The major replied indignantly, "If I decide to, I'll fire." Prickett
brazenly retorted, "If you do, we're going to kick the shit out of
you." The major insisted hotly, "I'll have you court-martialed!" Then
he abruptly left without firing a shot. Prickett knew "he was out
there to shoot his rifle and testify he was in a gun battle" to earn a
Combat Infantry Badge.[51]

Bronze and Silver Stars, as well as the Distinguished Service Cross
and the Medal of Honor, were awarded for acts of bravery. Some
men earned them, others did not; having officer status certainly
enhanced a soldier's chances of winning a medal, even if his actions
did not merit the honor. General Lauer spent little time near the
front, not unusual for a senior officer, but in November he visited
Höfen, Germany, and requested that Lt. Col. McClernand Butler,
commander of the 3rd Battalion 395, take him to the tallest house
in the village so he could survey the defenses. When Lauer stepped
before a window on the top floor, Butler pointed to a bullet hole

and told him a sniper caused it. Lauer immediately spun away from the window and said, "Time to go." Butler never again saw him at the front; yet Lauer received two Silver Stars and later requested a Distinguished Service Cross, which was denied.[52]

• • •

The weather remained miserable with snow, fog, and frosty temperatures during November and early December, but the 99ers adapted to the static situation, quickly assuming the physical appearance of veteran soldiers though their combat experience was limited. As John Mellin noted, "During this period we were living and sleeping in the same clothes, and spillage of food and the nasal drippings on our field jackets built up day by day; we not only smelled bad but looked bad." They hoped Germany would soon surrender so they could go home. After capturing some old men and young boys they concluded the German Army was running out of manpower.

Although the 99th had not fought any battles, brief firefights, mines, and accidents had killed thirty-five from November 10 to December 12; moreover, wounds, frostbite, pneumonia, trench foot, and combat fatigue, had taken nine hundred soldiers from the division. The platoons that underwent training together in Texas were losing men, which had the potential to adversely affect unit cohesiveness over time.[53]

In early December Gen. Courtney Hodges, commander of the First Army, ordered Maj. Gen. Walter Robertson to lead his experienced 2nd Infantry Division northward through the 99th's lines, penetrate the West Wall, and capture the Roer River dams, an objective the Hürtgen Forest campaign failed to attain. Three battalions of the 99th (1st and 2nd Battalions 395 and 2nd Battalion 393) would assist the 2nd Division by attacking on its right flank, an area of deep ravines, icy streams, and steep, wooded hills. The troops shoved off on December 13 and advanced against the pillboxes of the Siegfried Line under heavy German mortar and artillery fire. Shells rained down, according to Radford Carroll, with "a shriek that has unbelievable power followed by the explosion that seems to drain the air from your body. The really scary part is there is nothing you can do to protect yourself." Jack Beckwith, among others, became a casualty. An exploding shell severed his left foot, smashed his leg, and propelled pieces of steel

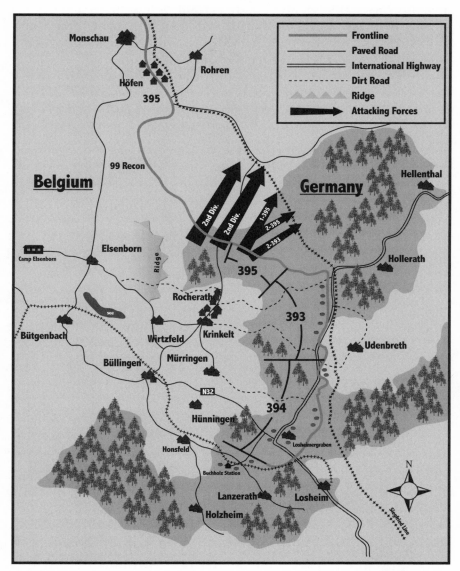

2nd Division and 99th attacks, December 13, 1944. Map by Paul Giacomotto and James Knight.

into his torso. His foxhole buddy Vernon Swanson, seeing "blood oozing from smoking holes in his abdomen and head," frantically yelled, "Medic! Medic!" But Beckwith was dead. Since the platoon had to move out, his mates buried him there; fifty-seven years later two Belgians (Jean Louis Seel and Jean Philippe Speder) found his remains, and Beckwith's family finally had closure.[54]

At 8:00 A.M., as Paul Jillson and Easy Company 395 began to move against a German pillbox, incoming artillery shells crashed into "the tall pine treetops, showering down razor-sharp steel fragments." Unfortunately, the 924th Field Artillery, situated miles behind American front lines, had unleashed a barrage of "friendly fire." After twenty minutes the firing stopped. The moaning of the wounded then broke the silence.[55]

Because no one had scooped out any foxholes, Paul Weesner and his squad "had to lie on top of the ground and take it." A shell fragment struck Paul Sage in the stomach. Weesner placed a compress over Sage's wound, but when he started "to vomit, [Sage's] intestines began to come through the wound. I couldn't hold them in no matter how hard I tried." Weesner and Double E Hill fashioned a litter out of a coat and tree branches and carried Sage through the woods, up and down hills and across exposed ground to safety. But their valiant effort came to naught. Sage died, and Weesner learned "we were gradually getting battle wise the hard way."[56]

Three days into the American offensive toward the Roer Dams, men of the three 99th battalions heard distant reverberations of heavy artillery to the south. The troops, SHAEF, and Omar Bradley, commander of the 12th Army Group, assumed the Germans were merely retaliating for the incursion toward the Roer, and the artillery barrage did not represent a serious threat. Unfortunately they were all dead wrong.

CHAPTER 4

The Battle of the Bulge

THE ATTACK

In the predawn hours of December 16, 1944, Pfc. Howard Bowers was sleeping in a log hut behind the front lines that zigzagged along the border of Belgium and Germany. Before turning in he had cleaned up in eager anticipation of going to Honsfeld, Belgium (a hamlet four miles to the west), the following day to see movie star Marlene Dietrich perform in a USO show. Neither Bowers nor Dietrich would make that performance. At 5:30 A.M. German artillery shells and rockets began crashing into the treetops near Dog Company 394. Jerked awake, Bowers immediately "crawled under a bunk and lay face down on the dirt floor." The shelling lasted for an hour: "All the time," Bowers recalled, "I was trying to bury myself deeper into the dirt floor, wishing I were in a foxhole and praying that it would come to an end." Unbeknownst to Bowers, those terrifying salvos marked the beginning of a gigantic German offensive that would become known as the Battle of the Bulge.[1]

William McMurdie was dozing in a primitive shack near Losheimergraben in the southeastern corner of Belgium when the shelling began: "I shook and got jumpy as everything. Then I got so cold I thought that I was slowly becoming a chunk of ice. My heart raced like a steam engine as I tried to decide what to do. Should I get out of this sleeping bag and get into a foxhole or just stay where I am?" He stayed, and the shelling finally stopped as suddenly and as it had begun. McMurdie did not know what to do next, but he now knew what it meant to feel gut-wrenching fear.[2]

When shells and rockets started exploding in the branches of pine trees near his foxhole, Harold Piovesan decided he needed extraordinary help. He feared one would strike the fir tree above him, and it "would be the end." Only one power could save him and that "was God." He pledged, "God, if you get me out of this, I'll serve you the rest of my life." Piovesan survived the barrage and, true to his word, became a minister after the war.

Caught in the open when the first shells struck the trees, Richard Byers dove into a slit trench and tried to become as small and flat as possible. The noise and concussive force of exploding shells made him feel as though he had put his head "inside an enormous bell while giants pounded it with sledgehammers." His youthful sense of invulnerability disappeared, and he was filled with terror.[3]

Maltie Anderson had just come off guard duty near the International Highway when the first shells exploded, showering his position with hot steel fragments and sizzling woodchips, filling the air with the pungent smell of burning pine. When the barrage ceased, Anderson and his squad waited nervously in their foxholes. After a while they spotted German soldiers trudging slowly toward them across the snow-covered field in front of their position. They opened fire at the approaching enemy soldiers, and Anderson heard a GI shouting, "I killed 'em! I killed 'em! I killed 'em!" not in celebration but in disbelief."

When the shelling stopped, BAR gunner John Mellin watched some forty gray-clad German infantrymen appear in a skirmish line on a hill. They advanced toward Mellin, who "wondered why they didn't turn around and go back. We didn't want to kill anyone." But he did not scream out a warning and the Germans did not know his thoughts. As they moved closer, Mellin and the squad began "picking them off one by one." Before long, bodies covered the snowy hillside.[4]

At 5:30 A.M. David Perlman was on guard duty, stomping his feet and shaking his arms to warm himself while the rest of his squad slumbered in their hut. In thirty minutes he and his foxhole buddy, Howard Stein, would be relieved. Suddenly, the shrill whistle of an incoming shell broke the silence. When a second shell exploded, Perlman and Stein ran and jumped into their foxhole. A third GI piled in on top of them and Perlman found himself hoping the soldier's body would protect him. More shells exploded, sending fragments humming in flight like a swarm of bees. When the barrage ended, Perlman climbed out of the foxhole and discovered an unexploded shell only a few feet away: "That was the kind of luck you needed to survive in the infantry."[5]

On Friday, December 15, rifleman Richard King and a few other fortunate souls left the front by truck for Honsfeld on a three-day pass. Like Howard Bowers, they also planned to catch the USO show featuring Marlene Dietrich. After spending four weeks in a frigid foxhole, King couldn't have been happier about a return to some minimal comforts of civilization. Once in the rest area he enjoyed a "lukewarm shower" (his first since mid-October), put on a clean uniform (actually two pairs of olive drab pants), ate a "big, hot meal," and then went to bed upstairs in a house situated on a side street off the main highway. Roused before dawn on December 16 by a "serious" artillery barrage, he lingered in his cot until explosions in nearby houses prompted a hasty descent to the cellar. After an hour everything grew quiet; concluding the worst had passed, he left in search of food, hoping to grab a meal before attending the USO show.[6]

At the *Eifelerhof Gasthaus,* King learned that Dietrich inexplicably had not arrived, but the USO show went on with entertainment provided by a four-piece band that ironically played, "There'll be a Hot Time in the Old Town Tonight." Afterwards King devoured another hot meal ("all you could eat") and went to bed "starting to feel safe." Unbeknownst to him, all leaves for combat soldiers had been canceled and trucks had been sent to fetch GIs in Honsfeld and rush them to the front. Somehow they missed King and two other GIs.

Early the next morning, King was awakened by "shouting and noise in the street." Looking out his second floor window, he detected German half-tracks moving down the main street less than a block away and heard the unmistakable scary sounds of squealing bogies and clanking tank treads in the near distance. Gripped by fear, King ran down and up the stairs several times, trying frantically to figure out what he should do. He decided to leave. Cautiously opening the front door, he spotted a small U.S. Army weapons carrier parked in front with its engine running. The driver informed King that he had orders to take stragglers back to the front. That unknown driver may have saved King's life; shortly after their hurried departure SS troops

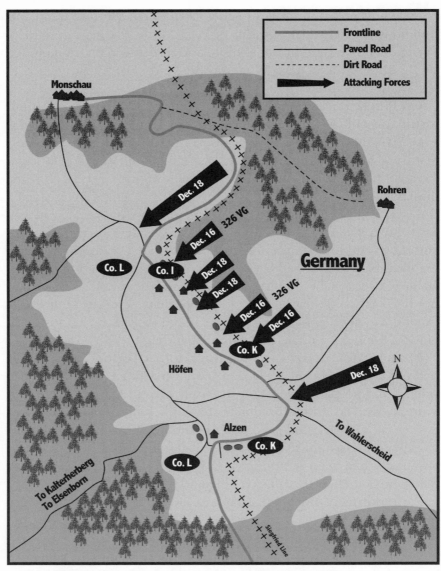

Defense of Höfen. Map by Paul Giacomotto and James Knight.

captured the town and murdered nineteen American soldiers who had surrendered. (During the course of the Ardennes offensive, SS forces would execute over one hundred captured Americans and an equal number of Belgian civilians.)[7]

King remembered his escape in the weapons carrier as "the wildest ride" of his life. Traveling toward the southeast without headlights in the predawn darkness, the four Americans in the weapons carrier nearly ran into half-tracks loaded with German troops heading toward them on the same road bound for Honsfeld. Upon encountering enemy vehicles, the driver steered the carrier into the roadside ditch, and the Germans moving in the opposite direction passed by without incident. At daybreak the Americans reached Fox Company's position, which appeared strangely unfamiliar: "The tall pines near our foxholes were all broken and the tops were pointing down at the ground. There had been tremendous shelling, and I could not recognize where we were for a while. It looked so different since we had left only two days ago."[8]

At the northern end of the 99th's line, the 3rd battalion 395 had constructed defensive positions in and around the German village of Höfen. Thor Ronningen was asleep in his deep foxhole on the morning of December 16. Since he and others felt the war "would be over soon, certainly by Christmas," the barrage that descended on their positions surprised and terrified them: "I woke up to a series of tremendous explosions" and the "ear-splitting scream" of rockets fired in salvos. "The ground . . . shook like a bowl of JELL-O." Ronningen "cowered" in his foxhole, reciting the 23rd Psalm: "Yea, though I walk through the valley of the shadow of death, I will fear no evil. . . ." The shelling lasted about thirty minutes, and then the eastern night sky became strangely illuminated by searchlight beams reflecting light off low-hanging clouds. The searchlights were intended to guide the poorly trained *Volksgrenadier* [people's soldiers or infantry] to their objectives, but they actually silhouetted the German troops as they advanced in a "slow, plodding march" toward positions held by Item and King Companies. Small-arms fire and mortar shells killed scores of German infantrymen with few American casualties. Two days later, on December 18, a German battalion-size force drove at the center of Item Company, managed to penetrate the line, and captured four large stone buildings. But two 57mm antitank guns fired point-blank into the buildings, killing many of those inside and inducing the rest to surrender. The Germans gave up trying to break through at Höfen, and the 3rd Battalion settled in and waited, not knowing that elsewhere the 99th Division faced vastly superior forces.[9]

• • •

In a desperate attempt to stave off defeat in the West, Hitler ordered two armies composed of some twenty-nine divisions with five hundred thousand men, one thousand tanks, and two thousand assault guns to attack American positions along a sixty-mile front extending from Belgium to Luxembourg. General Joseph "Sepp" Dietrich's Sixth SS Panzer Army, which included four panzer (armored) divisions and several hundred artillery pieces, was assigned the task of penetrating the 99th's lines.[10]

At the time of the attack the bulk of Allied forces were concentrated north and south of the breakthrough area in regions where the terrain suited mobile operations into Germany. George Patton's Third Army was preparing for a thrust into the Saar mining region, while the bulk of Gen. Courtney Hodges's First Army occupied a forty-mile area north of the Ardennes in preparation for an attack on the Ruhr industrial region. The First Army defended the Ardennes front with only four infantry divisions, two "green" or inexperienced ones, the 99th and 106th, and two veteran divisions, the 4th and the 28th, both recovering from bloody fighting with heavy losses.

The Germans knew the Ardennes region was weakly held, but the generals (unlike Hitler) reckoned that moving troops, artillery, tanks, and horse-drawn wagons along a limited number of narrow roads and across rivers with limited supplies of fuel would be a problem. They hoped to make up for fuel shortages by seizing American gasoline supply dumps in the path of their advance. Allied air power also constituted a threat, but Hitler counted on inclement weather to neutralize it.

The German plan called for three major assaults by the Sixth Panzer Army against the 99th: in the north at Höfen against the 3rd Battalion 395; in the center primarily against the 1st and 3rd Battalions 393, and in the south against the 1st and 3rd Battalions 394. The attacks were to begin with heavy artillery barrages, followed by advancing infantrymen with instructions to move quickly, bypassing

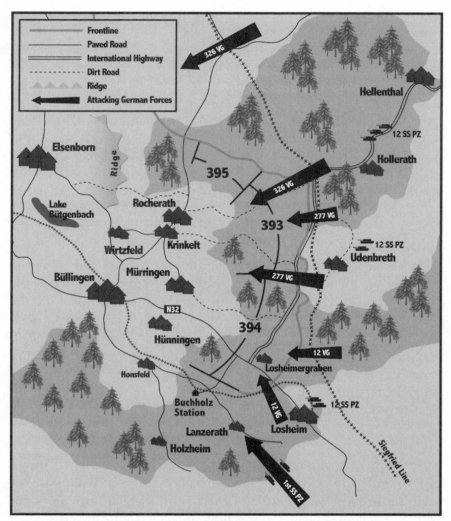

German attacks, December 16, 1944. Map by Paul Giacomotto and James Knight.

pockets of trapped American troops, and head northwest for the port of Antwerp, more than 120 miles away. To sow confusion, one thousand parachutists would be dropped some miles behind American lines, and teams of English-speaking soldiers, disguised in OD uniforms and riding in jeeps, were to infiltrate American positions, disrupt communications, and commit acts of sabotage. Although these two sideshow operations caused some confusion and paranoia

among the Americans, they had little effect on the course and outcome of the battle.[11]

After an initial infantry thrust through American lines, tanks,
assault guns, and artillery would follow four prescribed routes—three
(designated "A," "B," "C") for the 12th SS Panzer Division (*Hitlerju-
gend*) and route "D" for the 1st SS Panzer Division (*Leibstandarte* Adolf
Hitler)—all headed west-northwest to the Meuse River, more than fifty
miles from the border. Hitler expected this distance to be covered in
three days. Soft, slushy fields limited German traffic to a few highways,
secondary roads, and forest trails, which inhibited mobility and
striking power. Any delay in the timetable would give the Americans
an opportunity to regroup and bring additional force to bear.[12]

Route A followed the International Highway southward, then westward on forest trails to the twin villages of Krinkelt-Rocherath, 3.5 miles
from the border. From there German forces expected to use a logging
trail that connected to a narrow road from Wirtzfeld uphill to the
village of Elsenborn on top of a long ridge. Those units following the
second way or Route B faced the problem of moving through forested
terrain, but once the twin villages fell they would advance to Wirtzfeld
and then westward over secondary roads. The main effort would follow
Route C, making use of the major highway to Büllingen, then west to
Bütgenbach and north to Robertville. Capturing Krinkelt-Rocherath
quickly proved vital to the success of the German plan.[13]

• • •

After the predawn artillery and rocket barrage on December 16, troops
of the 277th Volksgrenadier Division walked and ran, yelling as they
went, across foggy, snow-covered fields toward the 393 Regiment's 3rd
and 1st Battalions (aligned, respectively, north to south) that defended
the main line of resistance along the International Highway. Weakened
by the absence of the 2nd Battalion, (attached to the 2nd Division) the
GIs had little chance of holding off the Germans who surged between
the two battalions, wounding and capturing many GIs, mostly from
Baker, Charlie, and King Companies. The 99ers, usually in small groups,
fought valiantly and inflicted heavy losses on the inexperienced
German infantrymen. In some instances the Americans were completely isolated and, not receiving orders to withdraw, stayed, only to
be killed, wounded, or captured.

The surviving GIs withdrew a short distance and, with the support of artillery barrages by Cannon Company and the 370th Field Artillery, halted the German advance. Not realizing the size and scope of the attack, Gen. Lauer and regimental commander Jean Scott envisioned a counterattack the following day to drive the Germans back. Shellfire severed many phone connections, leaving division, regiment, and battalion commands cut off from the front, so they did not fully comprehend what was happening. On that day hardly anyone at any level, from GIs on the ground to Supreme Allied Commander Dwight D. Eisenhower at the top, realized the magnitude of the German attack or the precariousness of the American position in the Ardennes.[14]

• • •

At the start of the German offensive, Gen. Walter Robertson's 2nd Infantry Division, plus 1st and 2nd Battalions 395 and 2nd Battalion 393, attempted to break through the Siegfried Line in the northern sector and capture the Roer River dams to prevent the Germans from flooding downstream lowlands. When reports reached Robertson of large-scale German attacks a few miles south of his force, he became concerned and drove from his headquarters in Wirtzfeld to Gen. Lauer's headquarters, located in Bütgenbach seven miles from the front. Robertson found the 99th's Division staff in disarray, with everyone talking at once and seemingly no one in charge. Lauer, who was playing a piano, assured Robertson everything was under control. Robertson didn't think so. Actually, Lauer was more concerned than he let on, for that afternoon he telephoned V Corps commander Gen. Leonard Gerow and asked whether he might have two reserve battalions of the 2nd Division's 23rd Infantry Regiment.

At midnight Lauer again telephoned Gerow to tell him "the situation was in hand and all quiet," but confessed to being "considerably worried" about his southern flank. Lauer may also have been concerned about his own safety, for at 7:30 A.M. on December 17 he departed precipitously for Camp Elsenborn, a military base four miles to the north, where he established his new headquarters. In doing so he effectively relinquished defense of the area to Gen. Robertson, who would use his 2nd Division to block the Germans from taking the twin villages and Wirtzfeld for three days.[15]

On Sunday, December 17, German tanks entered the fray. Breaking through the 393rd's line, they drove toward Krinkelt-Rocherath, cutting off the 1st and 3rd Battalions west of the International Highway. On that morning, Gen. Gerow finally received permission from Gen. Hodges to disengage the 2nd Division and send it south to establish a defensive line to protect the twin villages, a move that might allow the beleaguered 99ers to escape the onslaught. The 1st and 2nd Battalions 395 and 2nd Battalion 393 shielded the 2nd Division's southward trek along N 658, the road leading into the twin villages from the north.

• • •

Under cover of darkness and keeping to the forests to avoid detection, groups from the two battalions of trapped soldiers from the 393rd Regiment and the 324th Combat Engineer Battalion struggled to slip through the German encirclement and find a way back to their own lines, wherever they might be. Before they left, 1st Battalion commander Matt Legler and his staff urinated on a deer carcass hanging outside their headquarters, thereby spoiling it for the oncoming Germans. Cold, hungry, apprehensive, and sleep deprived, they hardly knew where or in what direction to go. Mark Beeman's platoon had captured seventeen Germans, but then wondered what to do with them as they desperately attempted to elude German patrols in the thick forests. One sergeant volunteered "to take care of them," which he and another GI did.

William Meacham "never hated anything more" in his life then having "to turn and run," but the "Jerries were coming . . . thick and fast." James Larkey asked himself: "How can this be happening?" They had been told the Germans were on the run, and the war would be over by Christmas. Angrily he concluded that Eisenhower and his staff had screwed up, a determination that other 99ers also reached.[16]

The men of Item Company 394, which held a reserve position near Buchholz, were directed to board trucks that would take them north to reinforce the threatened 393rd Regiment. The men could only take their lightly loaded combat packs; extra clothing and blankets were left behind (never to be seen again), and they spent a sleepless, anxious night in the cold woods not knowing what might lie ahead. On the 17th, Item Company moved into slit trenches not far from the International Highway. Soon after settling in, James Larkey recalled, a group of GIs came sprinting over the top of a hill toward them, their "faces contorted with horrified expressions of terror." Larkey watched in silence as they ran past Item's position, knowing that "whatever terrified them would soon be upon us." When the order came to withdraw, Item Company followed suit, scampering down the hill, hurried along by shells exploding nearby. They continued westward until they came upon defensive positions manned by 2nd Division GIs, who seemed "very calm." Larkey and the others threw them bandoleers of ammunition and kept going to a hill overlooking Krinkelt, where word was ominously passed along that the coming battle would be "a fight to the death." Looking down on Krinkelt ablaze with flames leaping high in the air, a "spectacular and horrifying" scene, they did not doubt the situation was desperate.[17]

• • •

The 2nd Battalion 394 manned defensive positions south of the two 393rd Battalions, one hundred yards east of the International Highway. Beginning on December 14, the machine-gun section of How Company fired intermittent bursts toward the German lines in support of the 2nd Division's incursion. Before dawn on the 16th, machine gunner Robert Corley heard "deep rumbling toward the Kraut lines." He turned to his buddy George and said, "listen to that, the air force must be up early pounding the Krauts." As the noise grew louder, Corley became happier. All at once, however, he realized it "was incoming mail" (shells). Corley commented, "I can't believe we caused all that by firing a few rounds at the crossroads." Later, he recalled, "We had every kind of Kraut artillery coming in on us." Luckily the 2nd Battalion's sector was spared the brunt of infantry attacks, though two Germans wandered into the area, where a machine gun killed them. Harold Schaefer and another GI ventured out to search the bodies and were "surprised and somewhat shaken by the fact that these soldiers were fifteen to sixteen years old." Apart from this incursion the Germans left them alone, but the Americans knew from the sounds of heavy fighting to the south that those units might be under considerable pressure.

The next day word reached the 2nd Battalion that they were surrounded and should attempt to break through the encirclement.

Using forest trails and firebreaks, they moved toward Mürringen, about three miles west of the International Highway, where the 394th Regimental Headquarters was supposedly located. George Company entered the town first and blundered straight into a large German contingent. In the ensuing clash thirty-three Americans were taken prisoner and and six were wounded or killed.

Under cover of a late afternoon fog, the remainder of the 2nd Battalion escaped, walking without food and water in a northwesterly direction, not knowing where friendly forces might be found. To add to their misery, American artillery mistook them for Germans and plastered their column with shellfire. Terrified, John Hendricks said a silent prayer, "Dear God, please let me live until Christmas, and I won't ask you for another thing." Maltie Anderson remembered wearily stumbling in the dark, holding on to the soldier in front of him, while stepping on dead GIs. After eight hours they finally reached Wirtzfeld, defended by the 2nd Division, and followed the muddy road up to Elsenborn, where they ate a hot meal and collapsed in a barn from physical and emotional exhaustion.[18]

When Rex Whitehead and others from the heavy weapons company 394 entered Krinkelt in the back of a truck at 3 A.M. on December 18, 1944, he experienced "fear, confusion, and hopelessness." Buildings were burning, German and American machine guns were firing, and "tracers the size of footballs were flying up and down the streets." He expected to be killed or taken prisoner. Then he spotted a 2nd Division GI standing guard and asked him what was going on. The GI calmly replied, "There is a Jerry tank group in town, but G Company [2nd Division] will chase them out." Whitehead could have "kissed the soldier, for with those words my confidence came back, and I felt there was a chance" of surviving.[19]

• • •

The Losheim Gap, situated in the southeastern corner of Belgium and named after the German border village, is a four-mile-wide corridor of open, rolling terrain bordered on either side by thickly wooded hills. With both the International Highway and a single-track railroad running through it, the gap provided an avenue of advance for large forces; invading German armies had twice used it—first in August 1914 and again in May 1940. Now it was the 1st SS

Panzer Division's turn to attempt its passage. An armored task force called *Kampfgruppe* [battle group] Peiper spearheaded the drive. Named after its aggressive and experienced commander, Lt. Col. Joachim Peiper, the strike force comprised seventy-two medium tanks, thirty massive King Tiger tanks, twenty-five self-propelled assault guns, a towed battalion of 105mm cannon, and four thousand panzer grenadiers.

A little more than two miles northwest of Losheim sits the Losheimergraben crossroads in Belgium, where the International Highway crosses N 32 (today N 632), the main highway running to Büllingen, Bütgenbach, and points west. The 1st Battalion 394 and the antitank company held this important road junction, which the 12th Volksgrenadier Division attempted to seize after a heavy bombardment on December 16. Despite repeated attempts, German forces could not take control of the crossroads that first day.[20]

On the 17th, flanking troops forced the bulk of the 1st Battalion to withdraw 2.6 miles to Mürringen where a battalion of the 2nd Division hastily established a temporary defense line; however, a large group of infantrymen, never notified of the pullout, were captured in the three customs houses in Losheimergraben. Fortunately, Col. Wilhelm Osterhold, commander of troops from the 48th Grenadier Regiment and a decent man, opted not to blow up the houses with the trapped GIs inside.[21]

• • •

Sixteen hundred yards southwest of Losheimergraben at Buchholz stood a railroad station defended by elements of the 3rd Battalion 394. On the morning of the 16th, German infantrymen sauntered down the railroad tracks toward the station, not expecting to encounter any opposition. But they did. Love and King Companies drove them off with rifle fire and employed an antitank gun to blast away at enemy soldiers who had taken refuge in several boxcars. After retreating, the Germans dropped an artillery and mortar barrage on and around the station. Regimental commander Don Riley, however, believed Buchholz was not seriously threatened and ordered his reserves to move towards Loheimergraben and assist the 1st Battalion. By the end of the day elements of the 3rd Battalion held on to Buchholz, but just barely, unaware a serious threat lurked to the south.[22]

The task of seizing Buchholz and opening the way for Kampf-gruppe Peiper was given to young, untried soldiers of the German 9th Parachute Regiment. All that stood between the paratroopers and Buchholz were fourteen men of the 99th's Intelligence and Reconnaissance (I&R) Platoon of the 394th Regiment and four men from the 371st Field Artillery Battalion, dug in on a hill above the Belgian village of Lanzerath. Using rifles and a jeep-mounted .50-cal. machine gun, the small group turned back two frontal assaults and held off the paratroopers until dusk, thereby disrupting the 1st SS Panzer Division's timetable.[23]

At midnight Peiper stormed into Cafe Scholzen in Lanzerath and angrily demanded to know why the paratroopers had stopped advancing to Buchholz, as his tanks had been sitting for hours on the road with engines running, consuming precious gasoline. The paratrooper commander told Peiper incorrectly that substantial numbers of American infantry blocked their way. Dismissing this flimsy excuse, Peiper pushed his long column of noisy tanks forward at 4:30 A.M., taking a battalion of paratroopers with him as he headed for Buchholz 1.5 miles away. The infantry and thirty of Peiper's tanks and assault guns led the way; behind them the entire panzer division stretched fifteen miles down the road.[24]

Private First Class Richard Render and four others had relocated to an outpost in the woods southeast of the railroad station in Buchholz. In the early, misty morning they heard the rumbling of tanks but weren't sure if they were German or American. Soon they saw columns of German soldiers marching along the road from Lanzerath. Previously Render had served on patrols that produced excitement without bloodshed; sometimes they had spotted Germans carrying little blue flashlights at night but never fired at them. Seeing large numbers of infantrymen accompanied by tanks and assault guns changed the dynamic. Render ran back to alert the platoon but discovered everyone had left. Render returned to the outpost and passed along the bad news to his buddies. The five GIs were quickly captured in a culvert where they had been hiding.[25]

During the night the 4th Platoon Love 394 led by Lt. Richard Ralston had moved up from reserve to the left of Buchholz. All at once GIs came pouring out of the forest. Ralston yelled, "What the hell is going on?" One frantic GI replied, "A thousand Jerries are right behind us! Get the hell out of here!" Another shouted excitedly, "Tanks are coming!" Ralston led his men north along with another platoon. Everyone was frightened and a couple of men began crying. The mortar squads discarded mortar plates to lighten their load but trudged on with the tubes; after a while, however, they ditched them too. For Frederick Feigenoff everything became a blur: "Somehow I felt this couldn't be reality; it must be a nightmare."

Captain Charles Roland reacted similarly to the unfolding catastrophe. Roland moved around in a daze, hoping he too would awaken from what he also regarded as a nightmare. His mind wanted to reject what was happening, but when he looked through his binoculars and saw the bodies of German crewman "hanging like rag dolls out of a smoking turret hatch," he knew that death and danger were real. A young lieutenant nearby began a strange rubber-legged dance, then twisted slowly to reveal a "blue bullet hole in the middle of his forehead." This was followed by the ghastly sight of Chaplain Hampton and his assistant lying headless beside their disabled jeep, "cleanly decapitated by an exploding enemy shell." Shocked by these events, Roland thought the "entire regiment seemed to be in peril of destruction."[26]

• • •

On December 17 remnants of 1st and 3rd Battalions 394 and a battalion from the 2nd Division established a defensive line at Mürringen. The 2nd Platoon of Love Company 394 was placed on the forward slope of a hill outside the village and assigned the task of guarding the road from the east. John Thornburg and others spent a few hours digging foxholes and then tried to sleep, their first opportunity in forty-eight hours, but the bitter cold kept them awake.[27]

In the morning they discovered the rest of Love Company had departed; for some reason their platoon never received word from the company commander they were pulling out. The thirty-four men of the platoon became engaged in a sharp firefight with advancing German infantrymen, and a few GIs were captured or killed. The survivors slipped away in the fog and headed north in search of the American lines. When their platoon leader proved useless, Sgt. Chester Gregor took command. Eventually they stumbled upon some well-constructed dugouts and decided to take refuge in them. That night Germans discovered and captured the GIs in one dugout, but never came to the second dugout even after Thornburg killed the German soldier who opened the door to their shelter.

Before dawn the group set out toward a faint glow on the horizon—Krinkelt burning. At one point American howitzers shelled the men as they crossed an open field. "Each shell," Thornburg recounted, "sounded like a powerful diesel locomotive rushing directly at us, and each blast stunned me for an instant, so I wasn't sure for the moment after if I was alive." As another shell came crashing through the air, he thought, "the last one missed, but this one can't. Will I die instantly or will I have time to feel the shrapnel knifing through me?"[28]

Thornburg survived but German troops subsequently captured his group. Five anxious days had been spent eluding the enemy in a perilous attempt to reconnect with their company. Tired, hungry, and emotionally drained, "It was," Thornburg confessed, "somewhat of a relief to be captured, for we would not have to risk anymore shoot-outs." He looked forward to food, drink, and a warm place to rest, never suspecting that hardships rivaling those of the battlefield awaited him. As the surviving POWs marched to the southeast, Thornburg saw "an endless number of Tiger tanks in double rows, stalled, but with motors running." "How," he thought, "could our side ever survive such massive power?"[29]

• • •

Charles Swann, a runner, arrived at Love Company headquarters in Buchholz to find his platoon missing. After wandering several hours trying to establish his bearings, he decided to follow a group of Germans advancing to the north. During the day, to elude detection, Swann dug a shallow depression beneath a stand of fir trees and covered himself with pine needles. After dark he walked a little over two miles to Wirtzfeld, where he met several 99ers but no one from Love Company. On the farm road to Elsenborn, his group of stragglers stumbled upon cocky 2nd Division troops who yelled at them, "When are you 99ers going to stop running?" Swann retorted angrily, "All right, you bastards, we'll be waiting for you after you get your asses kicked." Whereas "we were tired, depressed, and scared," the veteran 2nd Division troops seemed "unafraid and confident." Arriving in Elsenborn, Swann found Love Company commander Neil Brown and asked him where he could find the 2nd platoon.

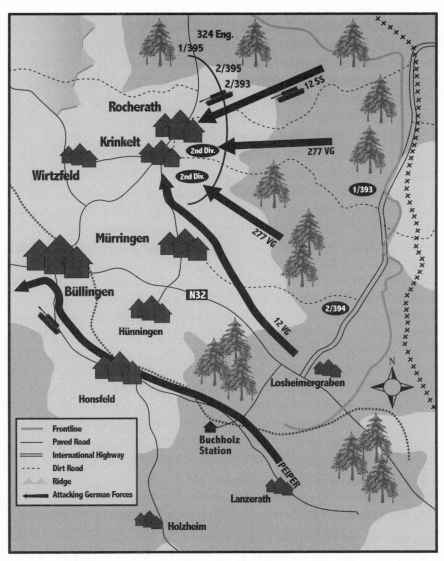

German attacks, December 17–19, 1944. Map by Paul Giacomotto and James Knight.

Brown replied, "It's right here. You are the platoon." No one else from his platoon had escaped.[30]

• • •

Peiper's tanks and troops left Buchholz in the predawn darkness and advanced three thousand yards to Honsfeld. James Bishop was also in Honsfeld for the USO performance when he and a small group of GIs were sent to a defensive perimeter at the edge of town. Sitting in a foxhole as night fell, he watched uneasily as a long line of 99th trucks, jeeps, and other vehicles, fleeing the German onslaught, streamed by their position, a disconcerting sight. Bishop was relieved from his post at midnight and went to bed. Well before dawn shouts in the street awakened him; the voices were German, as were the tanks rumbling down the street. His heart was pounding as he woke up two GIs and told them the Germans had occupied the town. He quickly tried to pull on overshoes but couldn't, so he gave up and headed for the back door of the building wearing his combat boots. After plodding through snow-covered fields for nearly two miles, he reached Hünningen and reported the enemy had captured Honsfeld. Other 99ers were less fortunate. Robert Gabriel and sixty 99ers were captured, but luckily led away by German paratroopers and not the SS. Gabriel was glad to be alive but embittered because "they had not been given a chance to escape or defend themselves."[31]

Peiper was supposed to continue west on Rollbahn D, but he opted to go north to Büllingen (a town of two thousand) because he wanted much-needed gasoline stored there. Once again his forward elements achieved complete surprise, capturing sixty-nine members of Service Battery 924. After ordering the prisoners to fuel his vehicles, Peiper hurried the tanks and half-tracks southwest and returned to his assigned line of march, Rollbahn D. Had Peiper chosen to violate the military plan and move north to Wirtzfeld in force, a distance of only twenty-five hundred yards, he would have trapped both the 99th and 2nd Divisions. That action would have achieved a substantial victory, but Hitler's grandiose plans envisioned splitting two Allied armies.[32]

Traveling on secondary roads, Peiper's tanks reached a crossroads at Baugnez, roughly two miles east of Malmedy, and captured more than one hundred GIs, including several medics. Peiper's troops massacred eighty-six prisoners in a field where their frozen bodies lay until the middle of January when American forces retook the area. Word of the mass execution (referred to as the "Malmedy Massacre") reached the 99th and other divisions, who resolved to exact revenge on surrendering Germans, especially fanatical SS troops.[33]

Peiper's armored column eventually penetrated twenty-six miles into Belgium, but on December 23, out of ammunition and fuel, he gave up the fight, destroyed his few remaining tanks, and began the long walk back to Germany with only eight hundred men. To the south panzer units of the Fifth Army advanced sixty miles into Belgium, but by Christmas Day the forward thrust had ground to a halt. The next day, elements of General Patton's Third Army broke the siege of Bastogne, an important road hub the Germans had encircled. In succeeding weeks, Allied forces slowly reduced the "Bulge" and pushed the Germans out of Belgium and Luxembourg.[34]

• • •

In the wee hours of December 18, remnants of the 394th Regiment left Mürringen on trucks headed north for Krinkelt on a road clogged with slow-moving trucks, jeeps, ambulances, and cannon, all trying to escape the German menace. Thinking that the Germans had already taken Krinkelt, regimental commander Col. Don Riley stopped the caravan and ordered the trucks abandoned, forcing the exhausted troops and the wounded to trudge cross-country over snow-covered fields to Wirtzfeld.[35]

Lieutenant Colonel Robert Douglas, commander of the 1st Battalion 394, led a long, disorganized column of survivors (only 260 out of the original 800) from the Losheimbergraben crossroads northward until they ran into the abandoned trucks. Douglas's group promptly appropriated them, drove to Krinkelt and then west to Wirtzfeld. From there they walked up the muddy wagon trail to Elsenborn, where they hoped to find food, sleep, and safety.

As Howard Bowers and a mixed assemblage of stragglers trudged along toward Elsenborn, they also happened upon 2nd Division soldiers moving in the opposite direction toward the fighting in Krinkelt. The 2nd Division GIs yelled "derogatory comments at us, asking why we were headed to the rear away from the battle, but I was too tired to care what they said." While Bowers sloughed off the derisive comments, he and others silently berated themselves for having withdrawn. Rex

Whitehead felt the "99th was the disgrace of the army, for we were [leaving] without a fight." Harry Arnold echoed that sentiment: "We pulled back . . . [with] sadness and anger for leaving the gained territory without a fight." To their credit the 99th had held back enemy forces for some thirty-six hours and upset the German timetable. Given the numerical and material superiority the Germans brought to bear against them, and the lack of intelligence concerning the enemy offensive, it is likely that even a large defending force comprising several divisions would have been hard-pressed to withstand such a massive, surprise attack.[36]

On the way up Elsenborn Ridge, Bowers spotted an overturned kitchen truck and some spilled goods. He picked up a can of tomatoes, opened it with a trench knife, and shared the contents with a buddy: "Those few cold tomatoes and a D ration on Sunday were my only food in almost three days." At noon Bowers reached the village of Elsenborn and made his way to a field kitchen, where he received a hot meal and enjoyed a sense of relief over having escaped the Germans. But this respite soon ended, for Bowers and others were ordered to dig and occupy foxholes in front of a 105mm artillery battery that fired all night, making sleep impossible. Returning to Elsenborn in the morning, Bowers found a cellar, where he immediately collapsed from exhaustion, even though German shells were hitting the village. Soon, however, he was rousted out of the cellar and loaded onto a jeep that joined a long line of bumper-to-bumper vehicles headed onto the ridge. Just then Bowers spied Gen. Lauer and his staff: "We were dirty, wet, cold, tired and headed back to the front, while the general looked like he was headed to the parade ground." Wearing an Eisenhower jacket, "pink riding breeches, polished cavalry boots and a clean helmet with two stars on the front," Lauer gestured at the troops with a riding crop.[37]

• • •

On December 18, Gen. Robertson (now officially in command of both the 2nd and 99th Divisions) ordered all remaining 99ers to leave Krinkelt via Wirtzfeld and proceed to Elsenborn. Meanwhile his 2nd Division, plus the three 99th battalions protecting his left flank northeast of Rocherath, held their ground in a desperate attempt to keep the twin villages (a mile long in length) from falling to the

Germans. In ferocious fighting east of Rocherath and in the twin villages German tanks and American tank destroyers blasted away, killing each other at close range. Whenever a German tank was hit, and the occupants scrambled out of their stricken panzer, American riflemen shot them dead, enraged that SS men benefited from the armor protection they lacked.[38]

From outside the village John McCoy and Fox Company 393 could see Krinkelt on fire, and "we could hear the frightening sounds of [German] tanks, the clank and squeak of the moving treads and the roar of powerful engines." First Sergeant David Spencer heard "cows bellowing as they burned to death; and the smell of death was everywhere." Harry Arnold and his platoon were "enveloped by the sights and sounds of contrived mayhem . . . a brawl peopled by madmen. Most eerie of all was the wail of a siren on a Tiger tank setting the tone and exemplifying the whole cataclysmic mess. A Dante's Inferno unglued."[39]

Frustrated by lack of progress in seizing Krinkelt-Rocherath and the loss of irreplaceable tanks, the German command pulled the 12th SS panzer and 12th Volksgrenadier Divisions from the fighting and sent the two formations around the twin villages, with orders to drive westward and seize Bütgenbach at the southern end of the plateau. Nonetheless, Robertson decided to abandon the villages during the night of the 19th, forced out by losses in men and equipment, lack of food and ammunition, and the accumulation of wounded. He led remaining 2nd Division troops to high ground south of Elsenborn where they established a new defense line tied into the 99th on its left.[40]

THE DEFENSE

The village of Elsenborn sits high (altitude: 1,968 feet) on a crescent-shaped plateau roughly four miles long and three miles wide. It consists of a series of long parallel ridges, or fingers; between the ridges, small valleys offered some concealment and limited protection against artillery bombardment. In the 99th's sector a dominant ridge sloped down to the valley floor and a creek, where it met a mixed forest of deciduous and evergreen trees. The Americans dubbed this long, sloping hill Elsenborn Ridge; it became a vital defensive position because the treeless terrain, covered by wild grasses in summer and (usually) snow in winter, offered 99ers (and other American divisions that occupied the ridge) good visibility and unobstructed fields of fire. If the Germans chose to attack the 99th, they would have to traverse six hundred to nine hundred yards of open ground on a slope up to the defenders. With the exception of some hedgerows and a small stand of trees, the Germans would have no cover; moreover, the snow, which blanketed the hill (especially after December 18), would hinder foot soldiers and tracked vehicles alike during the course of their ascent.

From concealed positions in the dense forest below the ridge the Germans could, with impunity, snipe at the 99ers and bombard them with mortars and artillery. For six weeks, any GI who ventured outside a foxhole in daylight risked becoming a target. The most terrifying German weapon was the high-velocity 88mm gun, the bane of American infantrymen and armor, rightly feared for its destructive, death-dealing capabilities. The 99ers tended to blame the 88 for all artillery shells that slammed into their positions.

Two miles west of the village stood Camp Elsenborn, a military facility built by the Prussians in 1896 after Germany annexed the eastern part of Belgium. Infantry and artillery forces trained on this open ground, hence the absence of trees and farms. After Germany's defeat in World War I, the annexed territory was returned to Belgium, and the Belgian Army took possession of the camp. From 1940 to 1944 it reverted to the Germans, but in September 1944 the camp became an American supply base where frontline troops might find a hot meal and a warm, dry place to sleep.[41]

• • •

The 99th Division took up positions (eventually three defensive lines) on the ridge, with the main line of resistance (three thousand yards from the village) stretching thirty-three hundred yards north of a dirt road that ran from Wirtzfeld to Elsenborn. The 99ers' foxholes followed a gentle arc that began in the southeast (overlooking Rocherath-Krinkelt) and looped around to the east. South and west of the road, the 2nd Division completed the defense line, followed in turn by the 1st Infantry Division in the vicinity of Bütgenbach. The 9th Infantry Division held the front to the north of the 99th, and behind the four divisions squatted a huge, murderous concentration of artillery (some four hundred howitzers) that could throw destructive power on attacking forces and German positions.[42]

During the night of December 19, the last 99th Division units (the 1st and 2nd Battalions 395 and 2nd Battalion 393) finally reached Elsenborn Ridge. In a short period of four days (December 16–19), the 99th had suffered significant losses: 14 officers and 119 men killed in action; 53 officers and 1,341 missing in action; 51 officers and 864 wounded in action, and 600 to battalion aid stations, half of those suffering from frozen feet. The survivors, including cooks and clerks, scraped out new foxholes or occupied existing ones on the front slope of the high plateau and awaited the enemy's next move. They were in bad shape—tired, weak, depressed, anxious, and cold. Henry Thomas thought the "world was going to end," and was so shook up that he couldn't light his cigarettes. Even before the German attack, the division had suffered substantial non-battle losses, primarily from trench foot and frozen feet. During the withdrawal, GIs had to walk through snow and mud for several days wearing porous boots; consequently, new victims had to be withdrawn from Elsenborn Ridge in succeeding days.[43]

• • •

It wasn't only the tanks and swarms of German soldiers that unnerved the men; unit cohesion had almost disintegrated in those companies hit hardest. In training, in transit, and during the first month on the battlefield, officers gave commands and men obeyed, even when the purpose seemed obscure or ill advised. Leaders maintained control. But intense fighting revealed several officers lacked the ability to lead (a few broke down completely, and one senior officer jumped in his jeep and drove away), units shattered under such great pressure; chaos and confusion replaced order and certainty. No one knew what was happening, and the division seemed on the verge of collapse. An enemy that had been hard to see, let alone find before the offensive, had come out into the open with massive force, ready to test the division's resolve and fighting capability.

The task for commanders was to rebuild their broken units, wait for replacements and new equipment, and assert their authority over the companies and platoons. Although tired and disoriented, the men would respond to directives and fight because they knew they had no other choice; the German onslaught had to be stopped. One thing was clear to them: the war would not end by Christmas.

• • •

Companies of the 393rd Infantry, the 324th Combat Engineer Battalion, and the 394th Infantry manned respectively (right to left) the 99th's forward lines southeast and east of Elsenborn, with foxholes located six hundred to nine hundred yards distant from the German lines. Two battalions of the 395th Infantry defended areas northeast of the village; the rest were held in reserve, though battalions were rotated, so the same men did not remain for extended periods on the dangerous forward slope. Many companies had suffered drastic losses in manpower. The 393rd had been reduced to 114 officers and 1,750 enlisted men, the 394th had only 119 officers and 1,904 enlisted men. The 1st Battalion 394, which originally totaled 825 soldiers, was down to 260 officers and enlisted men.[44]

The 99th Division would never be the same; many original members who had trained at Camp Van Dorn in Mississippi and at Camp Maxey in Texas, made the long, uncomfortable journey to Europe, and spent a month together at the front, were gone; some would return later after recovering from wounds. During succeeding weeks and months replacements would trickle in, but the companies would not regain full strength, and the rifle platoons, which suffered the most casualties, would never again achieve the same degree of cohesiveness.

Survivors of the 393rd and 394th Regiments barely had time to dig additional foxholes (some already existed) when the anticipated blow came. In the morning hours of December 20, the Germans began an attack they hoped would drive the 99th off the ridge and open up roads to Liège, Belgium, and beyond. Heavy German artillery and rocket barrages pounded the 99th for sixty-five minutes. Luke Brannon recalled hundreds of shells dropping on them, while he and his foxhole buddy recited the Lord's Prayer. At 9:00 A.M. a dozen self-propelled assault guns, armored troop carriers, and walking infantry of the 3rd Panzer Grenadier Division began the first of three attacks over open ground from the direction of Krinkelt. (At almost the same time, German tank and infantry units moved against the 1st Division at Bütgenbach and the 2nd Division west of Wirtzfeld.) Direct fire by

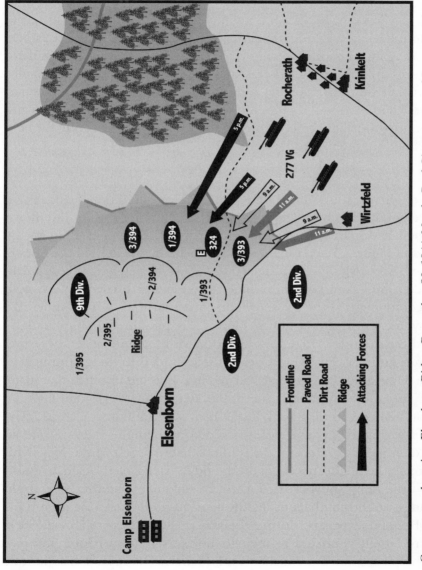

German attack against Elsenborn Ridge, December 20, 1944. Map by Paul Giacomotto and James Knight.

assault guns, according to James Larkey, "was the scariest experience because of the escalating scream of high velocity shells." The initial onslaught against the 99th, however, was stopped by heavy artillery that decimated German forces and drove them off. Two hours later the Germans made a second attempt with the same disastrous result. At dusk, using the hedgerows for concealment, the panzer grenadiers tried again, this time driving toward the 1st Battalion 394, while a second column assaulted the combat engineers. Machine-gun fire and time-on-target shelling inflicted severe losses on the Germans, who again retreated. Left behind were knocked-out assault guns and wounded Germans who lay on the snow moaning and crying for help throughout the night.[45]

• • •

Though no one knew it then (and despite additional attacks on December 21 and on December 28), the attempt to take Elsenborn Ridge had ended. From the latter part of December 1944 to the end of January 1945, the mission for the 99th was to hold the line on that barren, wind-swept plateau. Most 99ers lived in holes like animals, except they could not hibernate. The weather turned bitterly cold accompanied by heavy snowfall, particularly after December 27. Daytime temperatures hovered in the 20s, plummeted lower at night, and the denuded ridge was shrouded with fog and lashed by strong winds and blowing snow. Overcast skies added to the gloominess of the days. January snowstorms turned into howling blizzards that made life miserable and barely survivable. According to William Galegar, "you wished you were back in the heat and humidity of Texas." The subfreezing temperatures caused additional manpower losses and had a "demoralizing effect on the soldiers that were left." John McGilvray thought he might "never get off the ridge." The failed German attacks and the deep snow created a frozen stalemate. Neither side could budge, so the combatants mainly concentrated on staying alive.[46]

Because exposure during the day invited enemy shelling, 99ers were largely restricted to their foxholes. Nights were long and daylight passed all too quickly. Cliff McDaniel admitted his "morale would drop to zero, and I really felt low" as night approached. Heavy shelling during the month of December tapered off in January, but no one could relax because shells might be launched if German spotters detected movement. The snow did have benefits: it dampened the destructive impact of shells and camouflaged the defenders' foxholes. When Cliff Selwood, a replacement, arrived on the ridge in late December, he found the holes almost undetectable: "If you did not know where they were, you would never see [them], but think they were only mounds of dirt or irregularities in the land." Without the snow, the ridge would have appeared as an ugly moonscape of black holes. Each fresh snowfall created "a deceptively placid [white] blanket" that hid the shell craters. It was as though Mother Nature covered up man's transgressions against her. Mornings men shoveled out the entrances to their covered foxholes. Snow would fly into the air here and there, and finally figures, like groundhogs, would pop up for air and look around. A new day had begun.[47]

• • •

The biggest challenge was to keep from freezing to death while living in frozen ground. "This was our Valley Forge," Sam Lombardo commented. David Reagler believed the "worst part was the filth, the hunger, the cold, and the life of living like an animal." Shivering constantly in the bitter cold, William Bray concluded "there are worse things than death" and sometimes "you wished you would get shot so they would take you back to the hospital." It was difficult to sleep. According to Bray, "You would only doze, but you couldn't relax" because of the possibility of attack or a probe by an enemy patrol. Charles Swann and his foxhole buddy, who had no covering over their hole, would face each other and then lean on one another's shoulder to generate a little warmth.[48]

Men appropriated doors, wood, branches, and fence posts to cover their foxholes, which not only afforded protection from enemy shells, but also helped keep out wind and snow. If a heavy snow fell during the night, the men might be buried alive and suffocate. Limited by the length of their covering materials, foxholes tended to be narrow (about three feet for two men, five to six feet long, four to five feet deep) with an opening for exiting and firing. The small size offered certain benefits—easier to dig and better able to retain heat—but those subject to claustrophobia suffered. The men threw excavated dirt behind them, thereby creating a small mound to prevent German snipers from seeing their silhouette. Colonel Jean Scott, who had not been seen since mid-November, made a rare appearance at the front in mid-January wearing an air force fleece-lined jacket and polished leather jump boots. He demonstrated his ignorance about the disposition of the enemy and frontline conditions by bawling out Lt. Herring, telling him: "Those beards [of the men] have got to come off, and I want 360-degree, all-around fighting positions. Get those damn roofs off these foxholes. This position's a disgrace." After the colonel departed, Herring uttered "a rare burst of profanity" and told the men to forget about removing the protective coverings or the beards.[49]

Because of the dangers on the ridge, cooks set up their field kitchens some distance behind the lines. Before dawn or after dark, reserve companies would walk back to receive warm meals prepared by the cooks. Men in the first two lines of defense seldom ate hot meals except those they created by heating C rations. On occasion, cooked food would be brought forward in insulated marmite cans. Robert Waldrep recalled pancakes would be distributed with syrup but no butter: "They were cold by the time we got them, but we were glad to get them, because it sure beat K rations." William Bray's company mess sergeant would sometimes send up scrambled eggs and prunes mixed together, and "it tasted pretty good." Usually the men ate unheated food. Byron Reburn remembered wiping accumulated debris from his mess kit spoon, opening a can of frozen C-ration stew and munching on the ice crystals "woven into the lard and meat; it was like eating greased ice."[50]

The amount of food available varied from company to company. If squads were under strength, and many were, there might be extra rations, for allocations were based on the platoons being at full strength. William McMurdie consumed five or six K rations a day, while William Bray and his platoon stayed hungry, which couldn't help but provoke fantasies about favorite foods. J. R. McIlroy longed for a "good old American hamburger or my mother's home cooking." Francis Iglehart dreamed of Hershey bars, mustard, pickles, jam, anchovy paste, and Liederkranz cheese. Paul Jillson thought about fried chicken, corned beef and cabbage, mashed potatoes, spaghetti, and apple pie, eaten in a warm kitchen or at a dining room table.[51]

Packages from home, if they arrived, supplemented rations. The squad survivors also consumed food sent to the wounded, the dead, and the missing. Soldiers wanted cookies and cakes, even if they arrived as pulverized crumbs, not only for the pleasure such goodies provided, but because sweets interrupted the culinary monotony of army rations. George Miller, who received covered dates and other baked goods from home, consumed them right away because he "might not live long enough to enjoy them otherwise." Most importantly, packages and letters let the soldier know he was not forgotten, that somebody cared about him. Sharing treats also enhanced the bonding of fox-hole buddies and squad members.[52]

The desire to reconnect with civilization in the midst of war would assert itself, sometimes in odd ways. One morning Oakley Honey looked over at a soldier in the next foxhole. On the edge of his hole he had laid out a breakfast setting with white cloth, utensils, a plate, a coffee cup, and his little stove: "You would think he was at the Wal-dorf Astoria Hotel" instead of on a desolate hill in Belgium. All of sudden there was a "hell of an explosion" as a shell landed right on top of his breakfast, and a "black hole" replaced the setting. Honey concluded the soldier and his breakfast utensils had been blasted to bits, but then a head with a blackened face emerged from the foxhole. The GI had ducked in to retrieve salt and pepper and was spared, but the enemy had destroyed his modest attempt to bring fine dining to the battlefield.[53]

Haskell Wolff and Rex Whitehead had better luck. When the clerk dropped a mailbag into their foxhole, Wolff fished out packages from home: a three-month supply of the *Arkansas Gazette*, several five-pound packages of cheese, five pounds of anchovies, and tins of caviar. Shortly thereafter another GI came by to share a bottle of wine he had "liberated" from the village. The three of them sat in a "dank foxhole, sipping wine and nibbling on cheese, caviar, and anchovies," a surreal event in wintry Belgium.[54]

• • •

Like soldiers in all wars, American GIs learned to cope, improvise, and devise ad hoc solutions. Time and again combat infantrymen had to find clothing, shelter, heat, and food, and develop survival strategies to compensate for army deficiencies. Since the army failed to provide heaters, most men created a tiny stove by using two C ration cans and gasoline "taken" from five-gallon steel jerry cans that vehicles carried. By lighting a piece of cloth in gasoline-soaked dirt or a wick stuck in a wine bottle, the foxhole inhabitants produced a small, dirty flame that yielded a little heat to warm C rations. This primitive heater, however, presented a danger of asphyxiation if the hole was improperly vented; Plt. Sgt. Robert Walter found two of his men dead in their outpost, killed by toxic fumes in their tightly sealed shelter. The gasoline fire produced black smoke and soot that coated faces, hands, clothing, and lungs. Men complained of coughing up black particles for weeks after leaving the front. A German prisoner told battalion commander Robert Douglas he was surprised to have been taken by black troops. Douglas insisted he had no black soldiers. The prisoner retorted, "Black men captured me." When Douglas went to the forward line to discover what the German was talking about, he saw sooty-faced soldiers and sent them back to Verviers for showers. Yet even after rigorous scrubbing with the army's rough soap, it proved difficult to remove the greasy, black layers.[55]

In spite of primitive stoves and multiple layers of clothing, soldiers became sick or developed trench foot. One study estimated that 70 percent of World War II non-battle casualties during bad weather resulted from trench foot or frostbite. These maladies forced the evacuation of 539 men between December 16 and the end of the month and claimed another 587 men in February and March. Patrolling through deep snow or sitting day and night in cold, wet foxholes without exercise resulted in restricted circulation to the extremities, especially feet and hands. In some cases soldiers could not tell how damaged their feet were because they had lost all feeling in them. When they removed their boots, their feet swelled, and boots could not be pulled on again.[56]

Louis Pedrotti developed "frozen feet" and was transported to a field hospital in Liège, where he ended up on the floor of a huge warehouse along with fifty other men suffering from the same condition. Suddenly an officer appeared and said, loudly enough for everyone to hear: "Well, major, another set of amputees, eh?" That word provoked a chorus of groans from the patients. Happily for Pedrotti, however, doctors experimented with a new treatment of letting the feet thaw out gradually in unheated hospital wards. Though the outer skin turned black and dropped off, as did the dermis, leaving only red, raw flesh, his feet slowly healed.

Other victims of trench foot and frozen feet were less fortunate. When Edwin Stoch was wheeled into a hospital ward in Paris, he asked where he was. Someone replied, "The Butcher Shop," a place where afflicted soldiers were parked before being taken to operating rooms for the amputation of toes and feet. An athlete in high school, Stoch prayed that his blue, swollen feet would be saved. Luckily, the surgeon, who had participated in sports, was sympathetic. Consequently the doctor did not operate and, after months in an American hospital, Stoch eventually left with his feet intact.[57]

Jack Laisure, a typist in the engineer battalion, and other non-combatants had been rushed to the front on the afternoon of the 16th. After spending eight days in the snow, he hobbled his way to a battalion aid station where a doctor poked the bottom of his feet with a large pin, a method of separating serious cases from malingerers who wanted off the front. Since Laisure felt nothing, he was evacuated to a Paris hospital filled with hundreds of GIs suffering from frozen feet. Each ward had its own experimental method of treatment. In the first ward feet were rubbed with lanolin oil; in the second ward, where Laisure was placed, patients received sulfa tablets and penicillin shots to combat gangrene. In the third ward patients were given double shots of whiskey four times a day, and in the last ward nothing at all was done. After being transferred to Britain and then to a hospital in Colorado, Laisure eventually (after four months) regained the use of his feet, but like all other wartime victims he suffered during cold weather the rest of his life.

When James Bishop arrived at Elsenborn after narrowly escaping from Honsfeld, he reported to 1st Battalion headquarters. Lieutenant Colonel Robert Douglas told Bishop he had selected someone else to draw maps. Shocked and devastated, he couldn't speak to ask Douglas why he had been relieved of his position. He figured that Douglas mistakenly assumed he had run away when the Germans attacked Honsfeld. What made it so painful was that he respected Douglas and "felt personally responsible for his safety." Soon thereafter Bishop had to be taken off the line and sent to a hospital because his feet were in terrible shape. Embarrassed by his condition, he blamed himself for contracting "frozen feet." Knowing his friends were fighting on the ridge and seeing badly wounded and horribly burned GIs in his hospital ward, he felt even guiltier, for frozen feet didn't merit a Purple Heart. Although he recovered physically, Bishop suffered psychological wounds that never healed and never earned a medal.[58]

• • •

Christmas Eve 1944 in Belgium was cold and clear. For the thousands of men scattered about the frozen, barren ground of Elsenborn Ridge, nothing reminded them of the holiday season except the snow-covered landscape. William Galegar said, "If it had not been for the war, the countryside would have been considered beautiful." At Christmas and Hanukkah the men recalled a decorated Christmas tree or a lighted menorah, home-cooked food, and family. Rex Whitehead relived every Christmas and couldn't dismiss the thought that his "folks must be much more depressed than I was." The contrast between their civilian lives and the present situation could not have been more palpable. William Meacham sat in his foxhole heating a cup of instant coffee with a C ration can of gasoline: "All I could do was think about Christmas at home." Jay Nelson imagined his two little daughters opening presents under the Christmas tree and wrote to his mom and dad in Montana, "It would have meant plenty to me to have been there." Standing guard duty soon after dark, William McMurdie "felt so lonesome," he almost cried. "I could see my mom and dad, sister Jean, and brother Jack getting into our car and going to church for the usual Christmas Eve children's service." The kids would be reciting the different parts of the Christmas story and then singing "Silent Night." McMurdie expressed what many GIs were thinking: "Why should I have to be in this God-forsaken place in Germany [sic], perhaps to be killed?" Francis Chesnick wondered "if my family back home might be gazing at the moon at the same time." This emotionally charged thought expressed a deeply-felt longing to be connected in some small way with those left behind.[59]

Paul Weesner and others attended an "impressive service" conducted by Chaplain Stephens, who used the hood of a jeep for an altar. Robert Koch felt he "needed the strength of something, and it gave us a lift that we were alive." Wearing dirty, torn uniforms—their "Christmas best"—they prayed and sang hymns beneath tall, snow-laded pines: "There are some things a person will never forget as long as he lives—this is one of them," Weesner wrote. Afterwards they walked to new positions and only the crunching of the snow under their boots could be heard in that silent night. They were compelled to dig fresh foxholes that took until midnight to finish: "Everyone was feeling sort of blue and 'far away,' having to spend a Christmas Eve in such an undesirable way."[60]

R. H. "Luke" Brannon attended a Christmas Eve service conducted by a Catholic chaplain in a partially destroyed Elsenborn house. A table covered by a white cloth served as the altar, while a single candle provided the only light. Ten dirty, unshaven soldiers with heads bowed, rifles slung over their shoulders, helmets in their hands, solemnly listened for words of assurance. Although Brannon was a Methodist, it did not matter that a Catholic priest conducted the brief service, as "we were all Christians looking for the hand of God to guide us through this terrible ordeal." Four days later, during the attack on December 28, a German shell exploded near Brannon, knocking him unconscious and fracturing his spine.[61]

Despite the special significance attached to December 24, someone higher up the chain of command decided timeouts did not exist in war. That night Eldon Engel and other squad members had to go on a reconnaissance patrol under the command of Sgt. Paul Johnston. The sergeant led them out into a draw where the men lingered for an hour, making no attempt to reach German positions, and then returned to their foxholes. Johnston explained he didn't want anyone killed on Christmas Eve, a decision that greatly pleased Engel.[62]

Howard Bowers, "feeling melancholy and sad because it was my first Christmas away from home," heard the "sound of church bells coming from the German lines." This unexpected pealing, so out of place in the midst of war, conjured up thoughts of the family he missed. George Meloy drew guard duty at midnight on the forward slope. All remained quiet with nothing to see but endless snow. Looking up, Meloy observed, a "million stars that shone with a brilliance" he had never noticed before. Awestruck, the words flashed through his mind, "Glory to God in the highest, peace and good will to all men." In that moment Meloy expressed what everyone longed for: an end to the fighting and the chance to go home. On guard duty in Höfen, Joseph Thimm wondered if German soldiers across the field in Rohren were remembering past Christmases too.

He assumed they shared the same emotions. When the Germans fired off multi-colored flares, not artillery shells, he knew they were celebrating Christmas, perhaps for both sides.[63]

Ernest McDaniel, standing a two-hour watch in his foxhole, looked across the snowy fields before him. The little town of Krinkelt with its damaged church steeple and roof lines loomed in the distance: "In my mind, I could hear the words, 'Oh little town of Bethlehem, how still we see thee lie, beneath thy deep and dreamless sleep, the silent stars go by.'" A lonely sentinel, McDaniel felt kinship with those poor shepherds who tended their flocks nearly two thousand years earlier—a sacred scene and moment amidst the profanity of war.[64]

• • •

For Christmas Day the army promised everyone a traditional turkey dinner with all the trimmings. As in all matters, clothes, boots, sleeping bags, and food, there was no consistency or fairness—a few men received the best items available while others went without. Only rear-echelon troops had access to the most desirable equipment and hot food, usually to the detriment of the men at the front. Those in reserve positions fared slightly better than those manning the first line of defense. William Galegar enjoyed a hot turkey dinner with mashed potatoes, gravy, and cherry pie (with the food separated, not dumped together as usual), while Maltie Anderson's turkey dinner "froze before it hit the mess kit." Patrick Morrisey walked down the backside of the ridge to retrieve his turkey, but by the time he returned to his foxhole the food was frozen. Two men delivered a "not quite ice-cold drumstick" and white bread to Lionel Adda in his hole. Double E Hill thought it remarkable that the army provided him with a turkey leg, though he "would not have chosen dark meat." Jay Burke's dinner consisted of a piece of white turkey shoved between two slices of dry bread, but "it was the best Christmas dinner I ever had."[65]

The army's attempt to serve holiday fare, however meager, buoyed men's spirits but reminded them of a far-away home that William Galegar feared he might never see again. The enemy observed the special day by foregoing any shelling, and the snow sparkled in the sunshine, almost, Galegar observed, as if "angel dust had been sprinkled everywhere, covering up the marks of war." Time seemed suspended, and the war didn't exist. As the afternoon lengthened and nightfall approached, he meditated on home, family, a girlfriend, and "those who had not made it" to this Christmas.[66]

George Moon had looked forward to eating a turkey dinner on Christmas Day. But he, George Miller, and four others were ordered to leave their foxholes at 11:00 A.M. and proceed about half a mile down the slope and dig a listening post at the edge of the forest in which the enemy lay hidden. On this bright, clear day, Moon figured they would provide excellent target practice for the Germans. He tried to dissuade the assistant squad leader from undertaking this "suicidal" mission, but to no avail. When the patrol came within two hundred yards of their objective, the Germans opened fire. Unbeknownst to Moon, Robert Heinz and Beryl Mercer were killed immediately, while Moon was hit twice, in the left calf and back. Neither wound was life threatening, but Moon dared not move for fear of attracting more German fire. He lay in the snow all afternoon and through most of the night illuminated by a bright, full moon. Finally, when the sky darkened, Moon yelled "let's get out of here" several times to Heinz, his buddy. But there was no reply. He then crawled and stumbled up the slope toward the American lines where someone helped him to the battalion aid station. By then his hands and feet were frostbitten. In the early morning a medic handed him a cold drumstick, a remnant of the promised Christmas dinner.[67]

Richard King and his close friend Al Busse weren't sure whether it was Christmas Day or not. They argued about it and then yelled to the guys in the next foxhole, who confirmed the date. King and Busse gave each other a chocolate D bar and then laughed at themselves: "I usually had a couple in my pocket," King said, "but the one he gave me, of course, tasted much better than my own. It was my best Christmas present that year—my only one."[68]

• • •

For all soldiers, but especially those on the front line, mail was a form of sustenance, as important to their well-being as food. Jacob Hayes affirmed, "If you received a letter from home, you read and reread its contents till you memorized them." Letters connected the GI to the world left behind; as Ernest McDaniel put it, they represented "a slender thread that linked us to home." Soldiers hungered for news about family and community. Husbands looked forward to letters from their wives. James Langford, who married an Arkansas woman while in the ASTP, said the letters "made you feel good, but if there weren't any, you would get down in the dumps." Letters from his wife Alice gave Robert Mitsch assurance someone cared and a better life awaited him. Single men wrote to girlfriends, sometimes more than one. Al Boeger admitted expressions of "love entered more and more into these exchanges (in his case with more than one correspondent), and it helped to believe you were thought of, missed, and even loved by someone."[69]

Because GIs did not want to upset their families, and because enlisted men's letters were censored (on the unlikely premise that valuable intelligence could fall into the hands of the enemy), folks at home remained unaware of conditions at the front and thus could not comprehend what the men were going through. Some gifts sent to combat soldiers reflected this ignorance. John Vasa received a gallon can of popcorn (too heavy to carry and no way to pop the kernels), and a photo from his girlfriend set in a fragile glass frame. Robert Waldrep's mom sent him a camera but no film to take pictures of the lovely countryside. He wrote to her explaining no corner drug stores operated at the front. Whether for Germans or deer, Francis Iglehart's maiden aunt thought a leather-bound book on shooting game would come in handy; his girlfriend at Vassar mailed him a photo in a leather frame showing her in pearls and a formal gown. Fielding Pope's mom sent him a yo-yo, and George Miller received a wooden flute from his girlfriend. (Both gifts, however, did provide some amusement.) Don Gorsline opened a package from home hoping it would be full of cookies, but was disappointed to find a pair of wooden shower sandals. Sergeant Isadore Rosen wrote to his sister in Pittsburgh asking for soup. She, however, could not read his handwriting and began sending him bars of soap. Not every family was oblivious to the needs of the combat soldier on the front lines. James Larkey received a bottle labeled "cough medicine," but because he had no cough, he didn't sample the contents. When another soldier asked him if he had any cough medicine, Larkey gave him the bottle. Later the GI returned in an inebriated state to Larkey's foxhole and asked, "Hey, any more cough medicine?" After smelling his breath, Larkey realized "it wasn't cough medicine my folks sent me, and I missed out."[70]

On Elsenborn Ridge obtaining water often proved a serious and dangerous undertaking. Harry Arnold and his platoon had to walk almost four hundred yards through drifting snow to reach their water supply, a small stream. The trips could be hazardous as enemy gunners attempted to shoot anyone who could be seen. Once Arnold and his foxhole buddy were returning with a five-gallon jerry can when a shell crashed very close to them, sending a fragment into the can six inches from the top with a resultant loss of water. Other soldiers simply stuffed snow in their canteens and used body heat to melt the contents. Shell bursts could, however, saturate the water with the noxious taste of the chemicals used in the explosive charge.

The absence of streams and the difficulty in melting snow limited water's availability and forced soldiers to prioritize its use. Drinking it and making coffee took precedence. Then came cleaning mess gear, followed by washing hands and face. Shaving, brushing one's teeth, and maintaining personal hygiene came last. William Galegar and his two foxhole mates would heat a small amount of water in a helmet, and then each would dip a handkerchief into the warm water and scrub without soap.[71]

For reasons of safety, not modesty, soldiers relieved themselves in the dark, usually in the open or in shell holes. It was an activity a soldier needed to complete swiftly, otherwise the cold wind would freeze exposed private parts. The sudden whoosh sound of incoming artillery shells sometimes caused men to hop quickly to the nearest hole with their drawers dragging. The more cautious soldiers stayed in their holes, urinated and defecated in ration containers and threw the contents outside. Freezing temperatures neutralized the smells, and new snow thankfully covered bodily waste. Aware of a possible day of reckoning, Elden Hood told his foxhole buddy, David Reagler, "I sure hope we aren't around here when the snow melts."[72]

Long nights and short days in a foxhole made the hours drag. Ernest McDaniel commented, "We were locked in the prisons of our limited existence with low levels of emotional response to our daily experience and depressed by the bleak outlook for the future." Conditions in other combat sectors held minimal interest. Their world had shrunk to Elsenborn Ridge, an area encompassing about five hundred yards (more or less), and the situation on other battlefields scarcely entered their minds. They focused on the present and concerned themselves only with the men immediately around them. They stood guard, slept, ate, wrote letters, read, and talked to each other about family, food, and women, but J. R. McIlroy and his foxhole buddy "never mentioned what we were going to do in the future." Although Maltie Anderson and Cyrus Wells shared a foxhole and became friends, they did not discuss their plans after the war because it might "jinx" their chances for survival.[73]

Men concentrated on fighting the cold, finding something to eat, sleeping, and watching for the enemy. Life reverted to a primitive level, and except for manufactured equipment, mass-produced clothing, and canned rations, they could have been living in a premodern age. There were some compensations: no bills to pay, jobs to work, classes to attend, clocks to watch, no washing before meals and no shaving. But the losses were greater: no hot food, warm beds, toilets, baths, security, freedom, music, movies, female companionship or sex.

Usually each soldier had a partner or "foxhole buddy." The degree of compatibility and the amount of conversation varied. Living together and relying on one another for security and companionship under life-threatening circumstances created the possibility of a special bond. But incompatible personalities living in constant, close proximity could forestall friendships.

John McCoy relates that "tempers became short and arguments were the order of any day." Then too, a tremendous turnover in manpower limited the opportunity to build long-term relationships. The 99th had an 85 percent replacement rate, which meant ten thousand new men joined the division in the course of its overseas deployment. It was rare for a frontline soldier to share a foxhole with the same "buddy" for an extended period. The ASTPers had replaced the departed Camp Van Dorn men, and newcomers replaced the Bulge veterans. By war's end only a tiny percentage of the original group remained—an infantry division ravenously devoured its men.[74]

• • •

Replacements arrived at the front as individuals, not as members of a squad or a platoon. Peter Wolffe, a late arrival to the 99th, commented that going through the pipeline and joining a unit as an infantry replacement was "one of the most lonely experiences imaginable." Moving from a staging area in the States to a troopship loaded with other recruits, and then passing through a replacement depot in France, the newly trained GI, along with twenty-five other soldiers and their equipment, were loaded into a small, ancient railroad car for a long journey to the front. Eventually reaching a rifle company and platoon, the new man experienced the "trauma of combat for the first time, again among strangers."[75]

Because the army operated bureaucratically, it overlooked the importance of comradeship in enhancing morale and effectiveness. Replacements (in fact, all soldiers) were viewed as interchangeable parts that could be plugged into the war machine where needed. Some replacements had joined the division during the stateside training period, others during the first month at the front. After the severe losses of December, large numbers of new men arrived, many quite young or relatively old, and without much infantry training. Double E Hill remembered that camaraderie existed among the veterans, and the "replacements were almost considered outsiders." Veterans were "like brothers," Paul Jillson felt. "I was connected to some more closely than [to] a brother. But it wasn't quite the same with the replacements." Cliff McDaniel understood the replacements "had absolutely no opportunity to form comradely bonds with any old-timers." Ties formed during training and combat worked against the new men. Veteran soldiers felt connected to other platoon members and did not want to embarrass themselves by evading their responsibilities to one another. Newcomers did not feel that same connectedness or pressure.[76]

When a replacement came up, the new man was often placed with a veteran, which broke up an existing relationship and caused resentment. The veteran GIs complained, according to Robert Ortalda, about having "to baby-sit the new guys," who replaced men they had known in Texas. James Crafton felt a bond with those he had trained with, but "all of a sudden they were gone, and I spent the rest of the war with guys I didn't know as well." Because everyone had to stay in his fighting hole, it was difficult to meet or to spend any time with one another on the ridge. James Langford, whose squad defended some fifty yards on the MLR, said, "All we could do was holler back and forth to one another."[77]

The veterans were of two minds about the new men: they were pleased to receive additional help, but remained wary of them. Robert

Waldrep was "glad to have someone else in the hole, but there wasn't a lot of getting acquainted." Most replacements were frightened, nervous, and uncertain about what to expect, though a few initially viewed combat as "a big game," which also created problems. Francis Chesnick "felt sorry for them because it took a while to overcome fear, panic, and the unknown." "Imagine," said Robert Mitsch, "coming up to the front lines not knowing anyone and having to suffer the onslaughts of war." Unlike trained veterans, who had a month to adapt to combat and tough living conditions, many replacements had no adjustment time. Scores arrived directly from the States or came from the army air force, some with infantry training but others largely untrained; and there was no opportunity to instruct them. According to Byron Whitmarsh, a few had never fired an M-1 and didn't know how to dig a foxhole. Sergeant Charles Swann, complained the "new guys would get in their holes and not come out." David Reagler recalled leading some replacements up to the line, carrying all their equipment as they walked through snow: "Some of these men started throwing away their blankets or sleeping bags to lighten their loads. I told them they would regret doing so, but it did no good." Veteran soldiers would not have done that.[78]

Because of their inexperience, replacements would, according to Francis Chesnick, "do stupid things—walk around exposed or stick their heads out of the foxhole and look around." John Vasa said recruits would do "the damnedest things"—move around at night "when you could be shot by friendly fire" or light a cigarette in the dark. Some were "super cautious," others "macho and reckless." One night Plt. Sgt. Ken Juhl put two replacements in a fighting hole and told them to stay there: "The next morning they got out and both were killed." Lionel Adda was paired with a new guy who kept repeating, "I want out of here! I will do anything to get out of here." Adda found his behavior demoralizing; fortunately he was sent away. A few (including veterans) resorted to self-inflicted wounds, regarded by GIs as a form of desertion. One night (the time replacements could be safely brought onto the ridge) Charles Swann placed two new men in a hole together; early the next morning one of them shot himself in the foot: "We cursed him and then had to carry his heavy body all the way to the aid station." The next day the other replacement walked up to the aid station and shot himself too. Swann was furious. The newly wounded soldier asked, "Sarge, why are you mad at me? I saved you the trouble of carrying me up here."[79]

Veteran soldiers didn't know what to expect from the replacements and had to find out who could and could not be depended upon. The original 99ers believed replacements were killed and wounded at a faster rate than veteran soldiers, so it was thought best to avoid them. Platoon Sergeant T. J. Cornett fretted about the replacements: although he was glad to get them, it "bothered me when I lost [them]. You would be nice to them, but you didn't want to get too close to them." Jay Burke avoided knowing the replacements because they would "be here and then gone." Having already experienced the pain of losses, it was thought best not to become emotionally connected to the new men. Burke admitted he and other veterans "should have taught them how to survive." Certainly it took awhile to become combat savvy, to recognize where incoming artillery shells were going to hit, and when to take cover; but no amount of experience could protect any soldier, no matter how experienced, from a shell that landed in his foxhole.[80]

Francis Iglehart saw something of his former self in two eighteen-year-old replacements who arrived exuding a "boyish enthusiasm and an eagerness to help." The veteran soldiers thought the new guys were pretty youthful, but in reality they were only a year or two younger. Iglehart realized he and the other veterans, through "dumb, mule-like endurance and luck," had become the "old men" of George Company. Shared responsibility in difficult and dangerous circumstances caused them to have a possessive attitude toward their unit. Rank didn't matter, since few of the platoon and squad leaders had received stripes, but seniority and expertise earned them the respect of the newcomers.[81]

After a few patrols and a couple of weeks at the front, the replacements transitioned into veterans. As William Galegar said, "A rookie either learned fast or did not last very long." Cliff Selwood, a replacement, became squad leader after his sergeant stepped on a mine and lost a foot. Replacements who came in later thought Selwood was a seasoned combat soldier: "So you can see how quickly we had to learn and display what the real thing was, as opposed to mere training."[82]

Whether veteran or newcomer, the destructive power of artillery shelling terrified everyone because even the most experienced soldier could do nothing but burrow into the ground and wait for the barrage to end, never knowing when a shell might obliterate him. Of course, if caught in the open, chances of surviving greatly diminished. Artillery and mortar shelling occurred in two forms: the barrage that saturated an area with sustained fire, and the single shell that hit without warning, catching the combat soldier unaware. Both killed.

When the heaviest bombardment began on December 16, Al Boeger "could not believe you could survive, as the ground heaved and great gobs of earth, rock, and stuff came crashing down on you." The December 21st German attack, Cliff McDaniel reported, brought "a thunderous burst of shells" and the air was filled with "the whizzing and zinging" of shell fragments. Some men broke under the strain. In one case it was American artillery firing short that caused William Bray's foxhole buddy to break down. Suddenly in the middle of the barrage something landed right in Bray's foxhole: "I held my breath and waited for it to explode. Finally it moved; it was another GI who had gotten out of his hole and was running around and fell into ours." After the shelling stopped, the two men crouched for two days "whimpering and facing each other with their knees drawn up and blankets over their heads. They had gone to the toilet so many times in their pants" that the stench overpowered Bray, who asked they be sent back to the rear. Bray did not condemn the two men, for the "horror of that artillery would cause a breakdown in the best of us."[83]

John McCoy and Ernest McDaniel learned a lesson about how random shell violence could kill suddenly, without warning. One day they were asked to give up their foxhole to two newcomers. Although unhappy, they did as requested, and spent the rest of the day digging a new foxhole for themselves. That night the replacements moved into their old hole, which was hit by a shell, killing one and badly wounding the other. "Two replacements, one killed and one wounded, and we didn't even know their names," McDaniel lamented. Chance alone had dictated they should be spared and the new men hit.[84]

Death and mutilation could come at any moment in various guises: a single footstep could detonate an anti-personnel mine, a burst from the rapid-firing MG-42 machine gun could nearly slice a man in two, a fighter plane (Allied or German) could swoop down and strafe, or a sniper's bullet could strike an unsuspecting rifleman in an unguarded moment. While the experienced soldier tried to minimize his vulnerability, in truth, fate or luck (good and bad) often determined what happened. Byron Reburn likened the fate of a combat infantryman to the journey of the steel ball in a mechanical pinball machine. The trigger was pulled, the ball shot out and then rolled downward, pulled by gravity and directed by chance, bouncing off posts, momentarily landing in small holes, then falling into the reload magazine. The combat soldier was "propelled without volition or free will," not on a slanted board but "onto the killing fields." His chances of escaping harm, according to Reburn, was a "mathematical thing, a matter of permutations and combinations—not a good Las Vegas bet."[85]

Given the dangerous, unpredictable world in which they found themselves, most men prayed as a hedge against death and wounds. William McMurdie realized a combat soldier had to remain vigilant, but he also believed an infantryman needed divine assistance: "The Lord has to keep you in His protective care, or you will just not make it." Anxious, desperate men needed hope to maintain their sanity. Five or six days after saying his prayers, Joe Waskiewicz felt he had an angel on his shoulder: "I knew nothing was going to happen to me even though shells were dropping all around me." Fred Verdecchio asked God "to get me out of this, and I promise I will be a better Christian." Robert Waldrep, whose faith grew stronger because of his experiences in the war, "put myself in His hands" and "whatever He had in store for me was okay by me." Even McMurdie's foxhole buddy Sgt. George Dudley began "praying like everything," though he confessed to McMurdie that he wondered if "it will do any good." Prayer indicated the combat soldier's acute sense of helplessness and a recognition he needed a higher power to protect him. Despite the support of buddies and the army's formidable weaponry, in the end the individual was on his own. He needed to believe that an omnipotent God cared personally about him. Hopefully this God would prevent serious injury, but if death occurred, the believer would pass into heaven. The soldier knew other GIs were also pleading for help, even those who were subsequently killed; nevertheless, praying offered an important psychological defense against war's random brutality.[86]

• • •

Normally the infantry soldier envied and disparaged the army air force men. "Flyboys" returned to the U.S. after twenty-five combat missions, while "dogfaces" had to fight until war's end. After a mission, flight crews enjoyed clean, warm beds, hot meals, and, possibly, the company of women; whereas the combat soldier lived in cold, muddy foxholes without cooked meals or female companionship. Yet, when the weather cleared finally on December 23, the men on Elsenborn Ridge were elated, not only by the sun's appearance, but also by the sight of American bombers headed for German targets. To William McMurdie "it sure was a beautiful sight to see thousands of planes flying over with the vapor trails marking where they had gone." John McCoy knew "someone was in for a bad time when they reached their target; we actually cheered them on as we looked." That morning Cliff McDaniel "became aware of an all-pervading, ominous, low-pitched rumbling noise that enveloped the whole world about us." When McDaniel and the others looked up, they saw "the skies full from horizon to horizon with masses of bombers . . . and fighter planes everywhere. . . . It made us rejoice at being alive and proud to be Americans." The streams of bombers convinced Lathan Walker "we were going to win." Feelings of isolation moderated, and combat troops could rejoice in air power's ability to inflict massive revenge on the enemy. On one occasion a few GIs personally doled out punishment to a German pilot who parachuted from his plane; he was shot as he floated earthward. After another German fighter plane was hit, the pilot bailed out and landed a hundred yards from Jim Bussen's squad. They ran over, "took his leather jacket, boots, and pants and left him standing there for two hours in the snow before they finally sent him back" to headquarters.[87]

Bill Goss watched a British Spitfire pounce on and shoot down a German fighter. "Then the Spitfire went straight up, did some barrel rolls, came back, waved his wings and took off. It was great." Thor Ronningen cheered when P-51s "swooped down over enemy lines to strafe or bomb them." Among the few pleasures of being a combat soldier was the opportunity to observe battles in the skies overhead, exciting spectacles that no civilian would ever see. As Donald Wallace

Chaplain Herman Benner holds a Protestant service for GIs of the 394th Rgt. near Sourbrodt on December 31, 1944. Courtesy National Archives and Records Administration.

recalled, "watching dogfights" and seeing "planes go down leaving smoke trails . . . was like the movies" except these vivid scenes were real.[88]

• • •

Some fortunate enlisted men and officers were allowed to depart for Elsenborn or Belgian cities (even Paris and London) for a week to enjoy a shower, hot food, a warm bed, and relief from the tension of the front. Most hadn't changed clothes or bathed since they had departed from England in early November, so even the minimal benefits of civilized living seemed unreal. But going back could also lead to disappointments. David Reagler, who always envied those "who got to ride places instead of walking as I did," finally rode in a jeep back to regimental headquarters near Elsenborn, where he found a barber. His hair had last been clipped in England, so he asked for a haircut, but the barber refused because his hair was filthy. Without the slightest sensitivity to conditions at the front or Reagler's feelings, the barber told Reagler, "You're so dirty that you will ruin my instruments." After Lionel Adda arrived in Verviers, a city twenty miles northwest of Elsenborn, he showered and then visited a barbershop. Adda, who understood French, listened as one barber complained to another: "This soldier must have been working in a coal mine because his hair is full of soot particles." In Verviers, Maltie Anderson approached two attractive Red Cross women who were handing out coffee and donuts to servicemen. Looking at his dirty uniform one of them asked Anderson, "What do you do? Work in the coal mines?" So much for respecting the combat soldier and his plight; their haughty attitude let him know they "were too high status for an enlisted man."[89]

Harry Arnold and a few men from Easy Company rotated back for a twenty-four-hour respite. They began walking but subsequently hitched a ride into Elsenborn aboard a weapons carrier. Arnold's spirits rose as the distance from the front increased: "I can't express how new, fresh, and wonderful it was to feel relatively danger-free." He was amazed to see GIs walking about freely, "devoid of that gaunt, strained look common to the front." It seemed as if he had entered an "alien country, a land beyond imagination." After a shower and shave, new oversized clothing, and hot food, he lay down to sleep but decided "it was foolish to sleep through such civilized pleasure, comfort, and freedom from fear." In the morning Arnold and his comrades hopped a jeep and returned to the snow, cold, and tension of life at the front.[90]

In mid-January, Rex Whitehead left the ridge with a group bound for showers that had supposedly been set up at an evacuation hospital in the rear. As soon as they traveled beyond the reach of German artillery, everyone started talking and laughing at once. For the first time in a month, Whitehead later wrote, "We felt safe . . . and we were above ground." Whitehead noticed the GIs behind the lines looked "more like stateside [soldiers]—clean, pressed clothes, and even haircuts," in contrast to the dirty, soot-covered dogfaces from the front.

After wandering around lost for two hours, while the occupants froze in the back of the 6 x 6 truck, the driver finally found the evacuation hospital, a group of tents in a field. But the showers had not yet been erected, so a thorough cleaning was impossible. The food was typical hospital chow, but served with dishes, cups, and silverware, accoutrements of civilization not seen for months. Whitehead and the others stayed in a tent wired with electric lights, providing them a rare opportunity to write letters at night. A medic explained the hospital treated "mental cases," and admitted it bothered him "to see some big, husky guy sit and cry like a baby all day. Some of them would snap out of it all at once and go back, while some never got better."

The next morning Whitehead and his comrades climbed back into a truck that returned them to the village of Elsenborn. He noticed their happy mood evaporating because every man knew exactly what awaited him. As he walked past the shattered Elsenborn church en route to his foxhole in the snow, his stomach muscles tightened and his ears strained for the sound of enemy shells. He almost regretted having gone to the rear: "The worst feeling I had during the war was when our truck took us back the next day. I wished I had never left, for I had learned what it meant to be warm and safe."[91]

Ernest McDaniel received permission to go back to Elsenborn and clean up. But when a jeep came by, he and another GI impulsively flagged it down and found themselves happily riding to Verviers. They did not ask the driver to stop, even though it meant they were absent without leave. In Verviers they were amazed to find civilian life was "going on as usual." Men, women, and children were "scurrying about their business" as if no war existed. But McDaniel noticed people staring at them. He learned the reason when he looked into a store-front mirror and saw their appearance: "Faces totally black from the soot of our gasoline can lamps, clothes soiled and rumpled from two months of field living, and camouflage nets on our steel helmets caked with mud."

The presence of color—"women with red coats and children with plaid scarves and blue hats"—caught McDaniel's attention, for he had been subsisting in a drab chiaroscuro world of gray, black, white and olive-brown. Now he experienced a rainbow world of "brightness and light." Color and the absence of color separated peace from war, life from death, and civilization from savagery.

Women, the embodiment of life, companionship, and domesticity, also defined what was different about civilian society. When McDaniel entered a Verviers bakery, he first focused his eyes on the wares. The pastries were quickly forgotten, however, when the "young [counter] girl took my hand and examined my high school ring closely. We said things to each other that neither of us understood, but my heart swelled at her touch." Women meant softness, peace, romance, love, sex, and the end of loneliness. Soon, however, McDaniel returned to the front and the war.[92]

• • •

January storms dumped heavy amounts of snow on the region, hindering movement in the battle zone and vehicular traffic to and from the front lines, but German shelling lessened. No one was eager to go on the attack, for pushing through deep snow toward hidden enemy positions entailed a difficult and risky proposition. Nevertheless, reconnaissance patrols continued to be sent out to assess enemy strength and capture prisoners.

On January 15, 1945, Regimental Headquarters 394 ordered two combat patrols (one from Baker Company and the second from Love Company) to move off the ridge and engage the enemy in two separate sections of the forest. An incursion by a large number of GIs would naturally attract the attention of Germans troops who held advantageous defensive positions, so it was probable that American casualties would be high. No one told the men, but these two questionable patrols were merely demonstrations or feints designed to draw attention away from attacks farther to the west by the 1st Infantry and 82nd Airborne Divisions.

Charles Roland, S-3 for the 3rd Battalion 394, passed the order on personally to Lt. John Comfort, a first-rate officer, who was chosen to lead thirty-seven men drawn from the depleted platoons of Item and Love Companies: "We both knew," Roland recounted, "it was a patrol fraught with danger, but Comfort raised no objections." James Larkey recalled his friend Allen "Scotty" Maclean walking past his foxhole "with a terrible expression on his face, as if he knew he was never coming back from that patrol."[93]

The men started off toward the German lines in the morning. James Langford, who had no knowledge of the patrol, was standing in an outpost some two hundred yards in front of the company's foxholes when the moving figures caught his attention. He yelled out: "Halt, who goes there?" A prophetic voice came back to him. "It's only L Company going to get ourselves killed." Comfort walked over and spoke to Langford, who warned the lieutenant: "The Germans will know you are coming." Comfort said nothing, rejoined the patrol, and led the men down the slope, across the frozen stream, and then up an incline into the woods. They had edged forward several hundred yards when a German machine gun fired at them. They knocked out the gun and captured three German prisoners. The patrol began to retreat when it came "under intense enemy fire from three directions." They tried to call for smoke from the artillery but the radio, as often happened, wouldn't work. Except for William Bray and three others, who were taking the captives back to the American lines, the rest were captured, wounded, or killed, including Lt. John Comfort, who had predicted his company commander would "get him killed one day."[94]

Bray began the ascent to the ridge when a German bullet hit him in the forearm and shattered the stock on his M-1. As blood poured from his wound he thought, "I hope the bullet didn't hit my watch." He struggled on with the German prisoners when one of them began to laugh at him. Bray became so angry he took out his trench knife and slashed at the prisoner. Then he shouted to the men above him, "Shoot every one if they don't cooperate." When word of the terrible losses reached the rest of Item Company, James Larkey recalled, "We were furious, and talked about how stupid it was, wasteful of good men, and nothing was accomplished."[95]

Two days earlier, Cliff McDaniel and his buddy Arnold "Akie" Owens had gone on a patrol before dawn. The Germans heard them, popped a flare and opened fire with a machine gun, wounding the platoon leader. The rest of the patrol took off, leaving McDaniel and Owens with the difficult task of dragging the lieutenant, a big man, back to the American lines. Eventually they made it to a point where a litter team could carry him out. As they walked back to give a report to the company commander, Owens said, "Well, Mac, we made it again, but it can't go on forever." His words were prescient, for the January 15th patrol brought an end to their combat days. When the Germans opened up with machine guns and rifles, McDaniel was hit in the hand, the left shoulder, and the left knee. He yelled out to Owens, "Take charge, I'm hit." But then Owens called back, "Mac, I'm hit bad." Those were Owens's last words. McDaniel was captured and lost his left leg. Later he wrote, "I've grieved over Akie more than anything in all of life. We were practically residents of each other's bodies."[96]

The Baker Company combat patrol (thirty men and an officer) was also ordered to seek out and engage the enemy. B. C. Henderson, newly arrived, became tense when he heard the plan. The patrol jumped off at 4 A.M. and trudged a half-mile through knee-deep snow. They had gone only a short distance into the trees when the Germans opened up on them. The patrol responded in kind until they ran out of ammunition; then someone shouted for them to retreat. Henderson, who was wounded in the arm, ran back toward the American lines with the Germans firing at him. He ran as far as he could with German bullets kicking up snow around him: "I would fall face down in the snow from exhaustion and the firing would stop, but as soon as I'd catch my breath, I would get up and run some more and the bullets would start kicking up the snow again." He made it, but only thirteen members of the thirty-one-man patrol returned, and nine of them were wounded.[97]

• • •

On January 15, the 1st Infantry Division and the 82nd Airborne Division pushed eastward, capturing territory lost on the northern shoulder of the Bulge. On January 29, the 2nd Infantry Division began its offensive, capturing Wirtzfeld and then swinging north through the twin villages. At 3:00 A.M. on January 30, with no artillery preparation because regimental commander Jean Scott wanted a surprise attack, the 2nd Battalion 393 began its assault (Harry Arnold called it a "death march"), moving down the slope and then swinging to the north. Although they departed at 3 A.M., the deep snow hindered movement, and the battalion only reached a hedgerow some distance from the woods just before daylight. The Germans employed withering rifle and machine-gun fire, and Easy Company, according to Arnold, "was beginning to die, bleeding and freezing to death in two feet of snow in a remote field in an inconsequential action that would not rate mention on page three of a weekly newspaper." The men were pinned down, unable to move forward or determine where the bullets were coming from, a constant problem in combat. One newly arrived replacement, a "short, fat boy" had been shot; he was alive but trapped in the open where no one could reach him without being killed or wounded in the attempt. The boy raised himself weakly on an elbow and uttered a faint, anguished cry for the survivors to come to his aid. Finally a tall, gangling medic "stalked upright onto the field with a deliberate pace and stride, giving the Germans

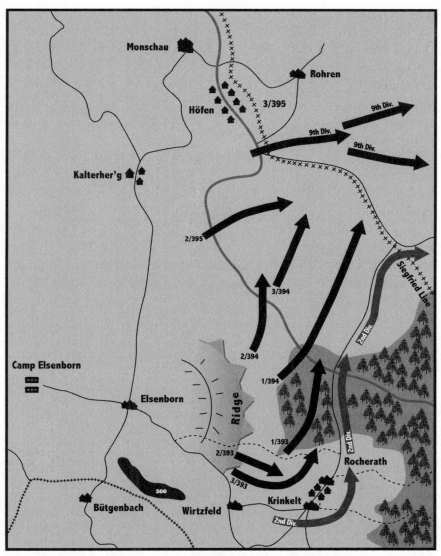

American counterattacks, January 30–February 1, 1945. Map by Paul Giacomotto and James Knight.

ample chance" to see the red crosses on his helmet and armband. But fifty feet out a bullet narrowly missed the medic's head, and he turned and jogged back. The Germans had established they would not allow anyone to rescue the wounded replacement, and his fate was sealed. He remained alive until mid afternoon when his movements became less frequent. Long after the war, Harry Arnold was haunted by "the tragedy of that boy who died so senselessly and so alone within sight of our eyes."[98]

Though the first attack had failed, a second was ordered. It fared no better, and the men spent the day crouched behind a hedgerow. Even after it grew dark, Easy Company was not allowed to retreat and spent the night in a howling blizzard. Three Germans attempted to surrender but after the day's events, according to Radford Carroll, the men of Easy Company "were not in a civilized mood, and the Germans were killed where they stood." Before dawn, the regimental commander finally approved artillery support and hundreds of shells rained down on German positions. At daylight the company walked into the woods and discovered the Germans had fled, leaving their dead, mostly young boys and older men, scattered among the trees. The 2nd Battalion 393 pushed northward for several days and then returned to the ridge.[99]

George Company 393 was also scheduled to participate in the attack. Francis Iglehart, BAR gunner and assistant squad leader, knowing they would "stand out like black bullseyes on a white background," raised objections with his squad leader to this movement down the Elsenborn slope under a full moon. Sergeant Mike Kelly lost his temper, called Iglehart a "smart-ass college kid" (the old conflict between the cadre and the ASTP resurfaced), and threatened to transfer him to another platoon where he would "become a rifleman among relative strangers, an internal exile shunned as a pariah." So Iglehart and the others had no choice but to follow orders. At 3:00 A.M. they filed across the moonlit plain and entered the woods, where they were hit by German machine-gun fire and mortar rounds. A number of men were wounded, including Iglehart; a mortar shell fragment hit his leg with tremendous force, as though "a giant had kicked [him] in the left thigh with football cleats." Iglehart survived but several of his squad members did not. Thirty-four men of the 393rd Regiment lost their lives during the last two days of January.[100]

On January 31, the 2nd Battalion 394 launched an attack to the north of 393rd's engagement. They left in a swirling snowstorm and succeeded in crossing the open ground without incident. Once in the forest, however, forward progress was halted by enemy fire that pinned down Easy and Fox Companies. This commercial forest had been planted like an Iowa cornfield with rows of pine trees separated at intervals by thirty-foot firebreaks. Richard King's squad was leading the way, and as they approached a firebreak, machine-gun bullets "sounding like mad hornets" buzzed over their heads. King buried himself in the snow. His buddy Al Busse ran by him into the firebreak shouting, "Come on King, let's go." In the next instant Busse stopped and sat down in the snow, which was above his knees. King yelled at him to get up and run into the trees but Busse couldn't hear him. Later, after a platoon from George Company, led by Sergeant Harold Schaefer, flanked the Germans and eliminated several machine-gun nests, King went back to Busse: "He was still sitting there, and he still couldn't hear me. There was one small hole just under his right eye where the bullet had entered his brain. I had seen other dead and badly wounded men before, but that sight burned into my mind. I should have stayed to say a prayer, but I didn't because I was too concerned for my own survival. But over the years I have said many prayers for my best friend." Al Busse and eight other men of the 394th died on that bleak winter day.[101]

• • •

The attack ended a couple of days later, and the sleep deprived GIs dragged themselves back to Elsenborn Ridge. A thaw had begun and melting snow filled the foxholes with icy water. Consequently, the men slept on the ground, but with fires burning. For the first time in eighty-four days the 99th was not in direct contact with the enemy. It seemed strange not to hear loud blasts of American howitzers and shattering explosions of incoming German shells. For six weeks this barren plateau had been occupied by thousands of men who endured bitter cold, shell fragment wounds, trench foot, and "an underlying dread that in due time death would find them." As they left the ridge George Miller was filled with emotion, a mixture of relief and joy, for he "had made it." Ernest McDaniel, one of the last to depart, scanned the empty rolling fields suddenly "devoid of movement or human activity." It was strangely peaceful, seemingly not the site of a cold, deadly struggle where young men died. Except for those who fought there, it remains unknown, holding no special significance. Only the survivors remember what happened on that wind-swept, isolated ridge in Belgium during the winter of 1944-1945.[102]

CHAPTER 5

Going on the Offensive

At the beginning of February 1945 the long Battle of the Bulge finally concluded for the 99th Division. After enduring weeks freezing in foxholes, the troops anticipated a break from combat. That didn't happen, at least not right away, for mopping up operations awaited them. The three regiments assembled in Elsenborn and were trucked eastward to the border between Belgium and Germany, the front line held two months earlier. Roaring through the Belgian villages of Büllingen, Krinkelt, and Rocherath, they witnessed the destructive aftermath of sustained artillery barrages and furious fighting—houses without roofs and walls, rubble-filled streets, demolished tanks and vehicles, dead GIs, discarded equipment, horse carcasses, and helmet-less German corpses lying along the roadways. Ken Stanger passed a blackened American tank where the stench indicated bodies remained inside. There is, he commented, "nothing worse" than the smell of burnt, decomposing bodies, almost like finding "a can of worms that had been left in the trunk of a car for a few days." Unforgettable, nauseating odors would, according to Peter Womack, "stay in your clothes for days" and in the mind long after war's end.[1]

Oakley Honey observed dead German soldiers scattered about, one lying beside the road without a head, a few propped up against walls and buildings, a figure in the middle of the street flattened by a tank, and all "covered with a thick layer of mud, almost as if they had been bronzed." Frozen, bloated Germans, with arms and legs sticking straight up, reminded B. C. Henderson of dead cows back home in Texas, and it bothered him "to see human beings, even Germans, lying there unattended, like some dead animals." William Bartow

135

saw a frozen American, stripped of his clothes with his arms up in the air, "his mouth was open," and he seemed to be "screaming." Twisted bodies and grimacing faces testified to the violent, horrific way lives ended.[2]

Preston LeBreton and his squad were detailed to remove American and German bodies: "Some were on the surface, while others were partly buried in deep snow with arms and legs protruding." The officer in charge warned them to be careful, because Germans booby-trapped the dead. As a precaution they made rope lassos that were placed around an arm, leg, or head of each body. Then from a safe distance corpses were pulled out of the snow and stacked in truck beds, Germans and Americans kept separate; in death as in life, combatants remained apart. On "several occasions," as a body was dragged, the helmet and head fell off. To LeBreton this was the "most unforgettable and depressing" experience of the war.[3]

Francis Haskins returned to Anna's farm in Büllingen, where he and a few other members of the Service Battery of the 371st Field Artillery Battalion had stayed before the Bulge. They discovered all her cows and two sheep had been killed in the barn. Only her hog was alive, but in "bad shape because it obviously hadn't eaten for some time." Anna wasn't there, so they decided to shoot the hog and end its misery. As they were about to leave, Anna returned to her farm and asked about the hog. They realized that killing her hog had been a terrible mistake, but nothing could be done. As they left, Haskins saw the middle-aged widow standing "alone in the world, [and] it was a pitiful sight." Another innocent victim of the war.[4]

Once beautiful forests had been slashed into jagged stumps and splintered branches. Emmett Jackson recalled the tops of pine trees had been cut uniformly by proximity fuses, almost as "if a giant lawn mower had been run over the forest." In his fictionalized memoir, Grady Arrington described seeing severed appendages "splattered with human blood and mud" and "battered heads with exposed brains," and he wondered, "how long such a life could be endured by men who had once considered themselves human beings?" Many soldiers witnessed one or more gruesome scenes of horror, and though they moved on, literally and figuratively, following orders and trying not to dwell on what they had witnessed, their minds photographed those moments and imprinted them in their memory banks where they

Büllingen in early February 1945, after the Battle of the Bulge. Courtesy National Archives and Records Administration.

remained. No one had the inclination to ponder its effects at the time, but these experiences, including terrifying episodes, would separate them forever from non-combatants and civilians back home.[5]

• • •

The Checkerboarders relieved the 82th Airborne and 1st Infantry Divisions, which captured territory that had been an objective in December. Leaving the 6 x 6 trucks, the 99ers hoofed their way along muddy paths through a countryside leveled by violent clashes. As Lt. Sam Lombardo walked onto the battleground he saw some two hundred or more American paratroopers, "all young, some intact, some in parts," lying in the "killing field." James Larkey remembered his platoon marching in the dark across a snow-covered field where moonlight eerily illuminated scores of silent, dead German soldiers. When the undermanned company reached battalion headquarters of the 508th Regiment, the lieutenant colonel flew into a rage because only a tiny replacement force had arrived to relieve the remnants of his battalion; he feared the ground they had captured with such heavy casualties could be lost. But the paratroopers departed, and Lt. Lombardo and his men spent the "longest night" alone hoping the Germans would not counterattack. In the morning they saw "the whole German Army" cooking breakfast, ignoring the Americans only a 150 yards away. Not a shot was fired and eventually both groups moved away.[6]

On February 4th and 5th the weather warmed a little, producing muddy conditions, in many ways worse than the frozen ground they had known. The 99th moved a few miles inside the German border and entered Hellenthal, Udenbreth, Hollerath, and Losheim, towns protected by pillboxes and dragon's teeth. Harry Arnold and the 2nd platoon Easy Company 393 marched under a cold, drenching rain into the tiny village of Udenbreth. Although assigned a roofless house without a rear wall, they considered it "better than a wet hole in the ground." After spending weeks on a barren ridge and before that in dark, damp forests, any structure represented an improvement. Despite the presence of two dead Americans in the yard, a lifeless German soldier caught in the middle of nature's call with his pants down to his knees, a knocked-out Sherman tank with its dead crew inside, and a "generous sprinkling" of slaughtered horses, cattle, chickens, and goats, Harry and his buddies acted "like kids in a candy shop, poking into and investigating the whole area." They collected German helmets, daggers, and rifles to be mailed home. In Arnold's case not a single war trophy arrived in North Carolina; "all were swallowed up by the heroic minions to our rear," he bitterly acknowledged.[7]

Arnold's squad patrolled the area while mortars and artillery sporadically harassed them, as did a gigantic shell hurled from a railroad gun (out of "Krautland") that sounded like a "railway boxcar hurled through the air end over end." Landing not far from Arnold, it spewed a plume of earth high into the air, leaving an enormous cavity in the ground. As frightening as that explosion was, Arnold and his buddies considered the mortar a more sinister weapon because its deadly projectiles arrived silently. If a soldier heard the "cough" of a shell leaving the tube, he could drop to the ground or jump in a hole. But if he failed to detect that muffled sound, the mortar shell could descend from a high arc without warning, spraying sharp, deadly metal pieces outward.[8]

• • •

The combat soldier constantly received orders from a remote authority that operated some distance behind the front lines. These orders limited the infantryman's freedom of action while placing him in danger. The frontline soldier advanced without knowing where he was or what the plan entailed. Subconsciously, he concluded his opinion, perhaps even his existence, had minimal value to those in charge. At the most basic level, he survived on his own, forced to make instant, possibly lifesaving choices. He had to decide where to plant his foot, what concealment to use, when to hit the ground, and whether to burrow or not. Should he expend energy digging a hole, maybe a shallow slit trench, or should he take a chance and simply spread out on the ground? Fatigue often tipped the balance, though veteran soldiers tended to be more cautious. Oakley Honey contended that guys with a background in hard, physical work were more inclined to dig, while "city slickers sometimes took the easier route." Frozen and rocky ground made it difficult even for the energetic or wary.[9]

Although Harry Arnold escaped firefights with the enemy, other companies met resistance. After some stiff fighting, they captured pillboxes and prisoners, but not without casualties—sixteen 99ers died during that week in February. Jay Burke's platoon used a flame-thrower and rifle fire to roust the sleeping occupants of one pillbox, hustling the barefooted, underwear-clad prisoners back to American lines. One young German was shot in the process, and he lay there, Burke recalled, "screaming and calling for his mother" for hours until he died.[10]

• • •

During the second week in February, after more than ninety days of contact with enemy forces, the reconstituted 106th Division (two regiments having surrendered during the first days of the Bulge) relieved the 394th Regiment; the newly created 69th Infantry Division replaced the 393rd and the 395th. No one could miss the contrast in appearance of the two divisions. The 69th's uniforms, Thor Ronningen remembered, were "clean and pressed, the noncoms wore their stripes, and all were clean shaven. We were filthy, our uniforms wrinkled and dirty, no one wore any rank or insignia, and nobody was clean-shaven." The 69th Division seemed to Oakley Honey as if they were headed for a dress parade, while "we were a motley, ratty-looking group with no one wearing the same uniform." Three months earlier the 99th had looked just as spotless and innocent when they arrived at the front, but combat, they proudly concluded, had transformed them into veteran soldiers.[11]

The 99ers walked westward from the Siegfried Line, enduring a miserably cold, sleepless night with men sprawled on the ground wrapped in raincoats, blankets, shelter halves, and ponchos. In spite of these conditions, Ken Reed, totally exhausted, lay down on the ground and went straight to sleep. He awoke at daylight, numb from the waist down because of the cold. The next day trucks carried the troops twelve miles to villages in the vicinity of Waimes, Belgium, where they stayed for a week in damaged homes and barns. The men were put to work cutting trees, building corduroy roads, and carrying stone debris from demolished buildings to fill large holes in the roads. Promised hot showers, comfortable quarters in local homes, clean clothes, picture shows, and rest, Jay Nelson wrote to his mom in Montana about the reality of his situation: "We have lots of water," but it "is running down the middle of the road." Instead of "nice houses, we sleep in barns," and instead of rest "we are put to work rebuilding roads with shovels and picks. "Boy," Nelson added, "will I ever be glad to get back up to the front lines where I can get a little rest. Nobody with . . . authority ever comes close enuf [sic] to bother you up there." Ironically, the place of greatest danger proved to be the place with the most freedom, especially from manual labor.[12]

After finishing the roadwork, the 99ers were granted a period of real rest. With roads too muddy for trucks, the GIs had to slog fifteen miles to Malmedy, a city mistakenly bombed three times by the U.S. Army Air Force. In late January, waterproof shoepacs (boots with rubber bottoms and leather tops) had been issued, long after their usefulness in snowy fields had passed. Shoepacs were not designed for marching. Byron Whitmarsh thought, "They were the sorriest things I ever saw. They were all right if you just wanted to sit around, but you couldn't walk in them." Loose-fitting (no half sizes), these shoes produced blisters, and the lack of arch support tired marching troops. "By the time we reached Malmedy," Carter Strong recalled, "our feet were killing us."[13]

When trucks finally arrived in Malmedy, GIs climbed aboard with standing room only during the cold, fifteen-mile trip northward to the city of Verviers. As the trucks rumbled through the city's streets, Belgian civilians cheered. Carter Strong found it "a thrill to see all the civilians and the attention they paid to us," for it seemed some people appreciated their efforts. But Harry Arnold spotted garrison soldiers, "resplendent of uniform," who "stonily" regarded "[our] rude looks— frayed uniforms, unkempt, holed helmets and hollow eyes." Arnold concluded combat soldiers "may have more in common with enemy infantry across the way than with the army in his rear." Awareness of the differences between those at the front and those out of danger became apparent when combat soldiers visited the comfortable world of the rear echelon, where, Y. B. Johnson wrote to his parents, they "stare at you as if you were some wild animal." When Lt. Sam Lombardo heard sarcastic remarks from regimental officers "who lived high on the hog," he soon realized he had nothing in common with them. Frontline GIs were viewed as outlanders deserving neither admiration nor gratitude for their sacrifices. Such attitudes provided incentive, Lombardo said, "to stay with your own group."[14]

The troops were distributed to villages in the vicinity of Aubel, the original jumping-off spot the previous November. Thor Ronningen and his squad finally enjoyed a hot shower in tents erected by the engineers. Afterwards, Thor commented, "I hardly recognized many of my friends; it had been so long since I had seen them clean." When platoon sergeant Charles Swann shed his layers of clothing, he overheard one of his men comment: "Jesus, I thought he was big, but he's skinny." In stripping down, Swann literally and figuratively lost "weight" in their eyes.[15]

The Checkerboarders rested, showered, drank beer and cider, ate hot meals, watched Hollywood movies, read, wrote letters, visited the old city of Liege, and enjoyed a respite from the tension of combat. Jay Nelson happily informed his mom he was "finally back in civilization," for it had been months since "I even saw a house in one piece." Besides electricity, which they hadn't enjoyed since England, there was an added treat, namely, "two genuine American girls" serving coffee and donuts from a Red Cross "clubmobile." Nelson thought it "the best coffee I ever drank." The female volunteers also served chow one night, and the troops kept returning to the line for seconds, apparently not only for food. Nelson added, "It's hard to explain just how good it is to hear and see the girls." American women represented home and nurturing, which they had not experienced in months. Knowing their break would not last, this fleeting exposure to civilization made returning to the fields of battle even more difficult.[16]

No one looked forward to misery and danger. The break from combat gave Maltie Anderson time to think about his family in Georgia, and he grew homesick and sad. Understanding what combat entailed, Anderson and the others had every reason not to defy the odds. When told they would move out on February 27, Oakley Honey became depressed as he imagined what was to come: "I had the feeling if I go back into combat, I'm not coming back." For several days he pondered how he might avoid further action. On the front men shot themselves, several deliberately froze their feet in snow, and a few broke down emotionally, unable to continue. The shame (which in some cases haunted them the rest of their lives) of thinking they had "behaved badly," even those afflicted with "combat fatigue," seemed a better choice than facing lethal shells and bullets. Honey did not want to be labeled a coward, for that would "smudge the family name," and a self-inflicted wound "could get you court-martialed." Eventually he overcame his apprehension by adopting a fatalistic approach. He told himself, "If I am going to get it, I am going to get it, but I am not going to run off." Being resigned to fate provided soldiers with a coping mechanism for dealing with life-threatening circumstances over which they had so little control.[37]

More replacements arrived to fill the depleted ranks, an ongoing process that persisted throughout the war and after Germany's surrender. Recognizable by their clean uniforms and youthful appearance, these newcomers had even less training than earlier replacements, and veterans remained leery of them, for rookie mistakes could put a platoon in jeopardy. Experiencing the long, difficult Battle of the Bulge became a defining event, and those who arrived afterwards lacked combat credentials, which some veterans impressed on the newcomers. Besides, Robert Hawn explained, "After three months in combat, those of us who survived found that we were reluctant to accept anyone as more than an acquaintance. It lessened the pain of seeing or hearing of their death if they were almost a stranger."

A replacement's probationary period could be difficult. When Ralph Oldroyd joined Easy Company 394 he "felt like a leper" because everyone ignored him. The veterans made him carry the orange-and-yellow aircraft identification panels—"load the new kid with the extra stuff." Upon Fred Kampmier's arrival at the 3rd platoon, Item 394, a veteran told him to empty his duffle bag and hand over his extra set of new clothing. According to Edgar Hensen, John Crampton went up to a replacement and removed a new jacket from the man's bag. When the replacement asked Crampton what he was doing, Crampton replied. "You won't be needing it. I will be wearing it in a day or two." Whether Crampton acted out of jest or not, his behavior doubtless unsettled the newcomer.

The new men eventually gained combat skills (sometimes quickly if serious clashes occurred) and became integrated into the group after demonstrating they could be counted on. Yet, according to Peter Wolffe, replacements felt estranged from the regulars. Max Norris, who joined the division during battles in the Rhine bridge-head, expressed a feeling shared by other newcomers: "I was never accepted as an equal either during or after the war."[18]

• • •

Before departure Gen. Lauer ordered a review and inspection. The troops spent a day cleaning equipment, clothes, backpacks, and weapons, an annoying return to pre-combat training. Lauer arrived (an hour late) for one group and moved along the ranks scrutinizing the soldiers. John McCoy remembered the general was displeased with "our raccoon faces," but he didn't understand that soap would not remove the layers of soot accumulated from gasoline smoke. Lauer stopped before a man with a bullet hole in his helmet. "Soldier," he asked, "did you put that hole in your helmet?" "No sir!" the GI replied. "Get a new helmet," the general ordered. Lauer failed to comprehend that a soldier who miraculously survived a bullet through his helmet had acquired a talisman, a good luck charm he believed would save him from future harm.[19]

Lauer then climbed onto the hood of his jeep and delivered several speeches to various contingents, like a college football coach giving a halftime pep talk. Oakley Honey remembers Lauer saying, "We fought the Krauts in the woods and the mountains and beat them. Now we are going to get a chance to fight them in the open. We are in for a lot of new experiences, and we are happy, happy because we are at long last to go on the offensive." Carter Strong recalled the general saying, "We will soon be meeting the enemy in a different way. We will be routing him out of his defenses with our bayonets as we attack, and attack, and attack!" Standing near the jeep, Emmett Jackson heard, "I have given you the opportunity of fighting in the woods, and you fought well. I shall now give you the opportunity of fighting on the plains. I know that you can fight because I can make you fight." A 99er near Jackson muttered cynically, "I know you can die because I can make you die."[20]

Despite Lauer's fervor for combat, the men remained unenthusiastic about more fighting, especially the kind entailing close, bloody killing. James Larkey was horrified "that such a jerk held my fate in his hands." The men also hated to leave Belgium, for its citizens, according to Jay Nelson, "didn't seem to be able to do enuf [sic] for us. When we left they were all lined up on the street and most of them were crying like they had lost their last friend." And they would lose some friends in the coming weeks.[21]

• • •

On February 28, 1945, the 3rd Battalion 395, attached to the 3rd Armored Division, shoved off under overcast skies toward the Cologne Plain, flat farmland of turnip and cabbage fields extending forty miles to the Rhine River; the rest of the 395th departed on March 1, while the 394th left a day later. Going into combat for the first time, newcomer Fred Kampmier found the war energizing: "You could see for miles across the countryside," hear the "swish of spinning shells constantly going over," watch the flash of explosions, and "see dead Germans along the side of the road." Previously, in the forested, hilly Ardennes, the division had fought from defensive positions, hunkered down in foxholes with artillery fending off the attackers. Now they were taking the fight to the enemy, coming out in the open, often supported by tanks, cannon, and fighter-bombers, so that

American superiority in firepower could be applied to the enemy. For those who endured the withdrawal from the Belgian border and the long, frozen stalemate during the Bulge, there was a sense of accomplishment in moving forward, perhaps to achieve victory and end the war. It was "a great sight," according to Robert Mitsch, to watch the coordinated effort of "a big powerful machine." Surveying the awesome display of force, William McMurdie "felt like we were all-powerful." Not everyone, however, viewed the fighter planes with enthusiasm. When the Germans pinned down a heavy weapons platoon, someone suggested they contact the air force. Platoon Sergeant Henry Thomas quickly rejected that idea: "We aren't that damn desperate yet. Air Force guys [would see us as] too good a target to pass up, and they'd probably kill all of us instead of the Krauts." Veterans who had survived strafing by Allied planes on Elsenborn Ridge knew something about friendly fire from the skies.[22]

The trucks traveled eastward through the ancient German city of Aachen, reduced to rubble the previous October when American forces captured it. The devastation was so complete that army engineers could only plow a single lane through the debris. Radford Carroll recalled in amazement that "the most intact building I saw consisted of two walls meeting to form a corner about two stories high." The Allies adopted a bulldozer approach to warfare. Using air and artillery bombardment, they smashed German cities and towns without regard for historic significance, architectural heritage, or civilian casualties. Much of this destruction proved unproductive, but it did not offend GI sensibilities; on the contrary, it lifted their spirits, providing tangible evidence the Allies were winning, while punishing the Germans for their transgressions.[23]

The Germans, in full retreat, wanted to pull back across the Rhine River and use it as a barrier against the Allies. Along the way lay hastily discarded equipment and gray uniformed corpses, including a dead German on his back with an empty wine bottle in his hand, placed there by a "GI joker" who assumed others would enjoy his macabre humor. Reducing the enemy to a harmless object of derision made it easier to perform the grim business of killing.[24]

In a few villages and towns, the 99th bumped into determined resistance, and suffered accordingly. After crossing the thirty-foot-wide Erft canal near Bergheim, about eleven miles from Cologne

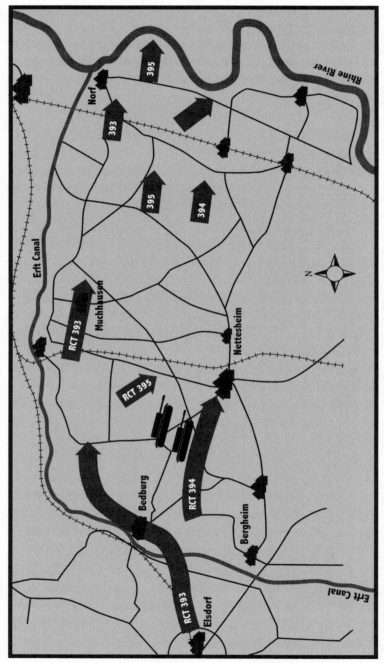

Across the Cologne Plain, March 1–5, 1945. Map by Paul Giacomotto and James Knight.

and seventeen miles from the Rhine River at Düsseldorf, Easy Company, 2nd Battalion 395 was moving over open ground when a single shot, fired by a sniper, struck Sgt. Frank Tezak in the left temple, killing him instantly. The rest of the company sprinted for a nearby erosion ditch and threw themselves into it. But this didn't stop the sniper, who fired at anyone who poked his head above the rim of the ditch, killing four more GIs in this fashion. Easy Company lay there most of the day until Baker Company arrived to drive the Germans out.[25]

The firefight left two Germans wounded. Easy Company commander George Balach walked over to where they lay and finished them off with his carbine. When his radioman, Sgt. Frank Hoffman, upbraided Balach, pointing out that the wounded Germans could have offered useful information, the officer turned to Hoffman and, with tears running down his face, announced, "I am relieving myself." He then left his company, never to return. Although he had committed two actionable offenses—killing prisoners and leaving his unit in the field—he was never court-martialed for either offense.[26]

The 99th advanced rapidly across the Cologne Plain, resisted by rear-guard German troops, mostly infantry composed of young boys and old men, but also tanks, rocket launchers, and artillery. At chosen spots, the Germans would suddenly spring into action and surprise the Americans with deadly results.

William McMurdie and other riflemen appreciated the added firepower of tanks and the chance to ride instead of walk. But McMurdie and the others soon learned tanks provided attractive targets for German gunners. When Able Company 394 approached a town thought to be "no problem," German tanks suddenly appeared and blasted two Shermans. Then another tank near McMurdie was hit. The vehicle's commander, standing in the open hatch of his turret, had his head blown off—but his body remained upright, blood gushing from the stump of the neck. The rest of the crew immediately bailed out and no amount of urging by McMurdie and others could persuade them to return to their tank.[27]

The German tanks broke off the action and withdrew, allowing Able Company to enter the village, whereupon German soldiers emerged from the houses with their hands up and helmets off. Evidently unwilling to sacrifice themselves so that others might escape, these inexperienced troops chose surrender over death, but there were no guarantees they would be spared. After a group of enemy soldiers gave up, a replacement, heady with a sense of power, borrowed James Tolmasov's BAR and fired at a POW's feet to make him dance. Unfortunately he lost control of the weapon and shattered the prisoner's arm. Another soldier recounted that Germans were killed "unnecessarily after they had surrendered or were trying to surrender." It bothered him, but "not enough to say anything."[28]

• • •

Through much of the winter the 99th had fought mainly in fields and forests devoid of German civilians, but now the Checkerboarders entered towns and villages where the enemy could hide behind doors or in cellars, sometimes among civilians, complicating tactics and increasing the possibility of killing innocent people. If white flags or sheets hung outside, troops moved in peacefully. If German soldiers in a town resisted, the infantry would radio for devastating artillery and tank shelling, resulting in massive damage and deaths. Squads would then go house to house searching for the enemy. It was potentially dangerous fighting, and, if civilians lingered or were trapped, they could become victims too. Bolted doors proved an inviting target. Y. B. Johnson took pleasure in "doing one thing I've always wanted to do," namely "cut a nice circle around the lock and door [knob]" with a Tommy gun. On occasion German civilians were forced to open doors just in case an enemy soldier might be hiding in a room or cellar. Typically Steve Kallas would kick open the front door and race through the house. When he reached the basement door, he would call out in German for everyone to surrender: "If we received no response, we would lob two to four hand grenades into the basement and then run out the door." It was hoped no civilians were hiding there, but no one knew for certain or cared. Once, right before Byron Whitmarsh was set to toss a grenade into the basement of a monastery, a priest came up the stairs. Whitmarsh stopped. He discovered the basement was full of old men, women, and children.[29]

James Larkey recalled that a member of another squad spoke Yiddish and scared the civilians with his tone of voice and accent, which the Germans must have recognized. To them, Larkey surmised, it must have seemed "like the vengeful Jew returning to haunt them."

Although Jewish Americans knew about the Nazi persecution of European Jews, none of the 99ers were aware of the death camps. Later, Larkey and others did come upon small slave labor camps filled with victims of the Nazi occupation. Had they known about this inhumanity earlier, perhaps more German prisoners might have met a quick end.[30]

In one village Angelo Spinato assisted in rounding up civilians and herding them into a community hall. One young woman frantically moved from soldier to soldier, crying and trying to tell the GIs something, but no one understood German. Finally an elderly woman told Spinato the soldiers had forced her out of her house while her baby remained behind. After Spinato heard the story, he agreed to escort the mother back to retrieve the baby. Another Frau then asked if she and her three children might return and collect loaves of bread she had baked. The group started out even though the Germans continued to shell the village. When he motioned them out of the street and against a house, the two women fell to their knees with the children hanging on and crying. Mistakenly assuming that Spinato was going to execute them, they begged for their lives. After assuring them he wouldn't shoot, they proceeded on. The lady and her three children turned down a side street, while he walked with the young mother. They came to an intersection covered by tank fire. Spinato tried to stop the young mother, but she dashed across the street with "complete disregard for her safety." Miraculously she made it, running at full speed to fetch her baby. He returned to the community center. Soon the Frau and children arrived carrying loaves of bread, and then the happy mother reappeared with her baby. The young woman came up to him, put the baby in Spinato's arms and kissed him on the cheek, all the while saying words to others he could not understand, but knew expressed her gratitude.

• • •

Towns offered the chance to sleep indoors away from the cold and rain (climbing into clean, feather-tick beds with muddy boots) and the opportunity to appropriate food, souvenirs, and alcoholic beverages. Steve Kallas said the army made sure "we had ammunition and grenades but not rations, so we behaved like Sherman's army." In Carsdorf, Fred Kampmier and his squad moved into a house and found canned fruit, dried meat, and live chickens that quickly hit the frying pan. George Meloy and his buddy grabbed one chicken in a hen house. As they were leaving with the dead fowl in hand, there, on the back steps of the house, stood the farmer, his wife, and two children who stared at the killer thieves with "blank faces"—a scene that could have been labeled "German Gothic." Meloy walked away speechless and later ate the chicken. Yet he could not forget that "scene of the enemy's loss and our theft of what was not ours."[31]

Army supplies frequently failed to keep pace with the advancing troops, so the men always felt famished. Like armies of old, infantry troops in the middle of the twentieth century frequently lived off the land, which meant confiscating civilian food. After entering the town of Bedburg (the troops called it Bedbug) and flushing out the civilian population, Fred Kampmier ate "a little breakfast at every house" where he found food cooking on the stove. Officers instructed enlisted men not to eat German food because it might be poisoned, but Virdin Royce said, "We ignored the warnings and ate anything we could get our hands on." Eating rock-hard, German black bread, which tasted like sawdust, transformed Royce into a lifetime devotee of white bread. When Leroy Wagner entered a house and found a table set with food ready to eat, he and the others sat down and gorged themselves. Soldiers raided German pantries, attics, cellars, and even haystacks looking for fruit, jam, potatoes, vegetables, and alcohol. Except for sauerkraut (one Jewish soldier urinated into sauerkraut-filled jars and placed them back on the shelf), anything was preferable to the unappetizing, monotonous regimen of K and C rations. Eggs, plentiful and easy to prepare, became a favorite. Since the men longed for fresh meat, no German chicken, pig, rabbit, or cow was safe from ravenous GIs, and no one gave any thought to consequences for civilians. Joseph Thimm remembered, "We thought about survival and creature comforts. If we saw something we wanted or needed, we took it without any pangs of conscience." GIs broke up furniture for firewood and took food to appease hunger; but they also smashed bookcases and picture frames—especially if the photos displayed a loved one in uniform—purely out of anger and frustration.[32]

In normal times taking from others would be considered a crime that should be punished. But this was war with no police around. Even before American troops encountered Germans, stealing or "acquiring" had become a fact of life for 99ers. Soldiers "appropriated" food, clothing, weapons, gasoline, and liquor wherever they could find it. Unlike rear-echelon thieves who stole supplies destined for the front and sold them on the black market for money, frontline troops often took what they needed to stay alive. When the army failed them, the combat soldier relied on individual initiative.

"Liberating" property from the Germans seemed morally justified because they had caused the war and had plundered others. According to Jay Nelson, the Germans "had been living in class off of other countries," so American troops felt warranted in grabbing anything they desired. Souvenirs included watches, silverware, jewelry, cameras, and weapons. Once a town was taken, citizens were ordered to turn in rifles, pistols (much-prized Lugers and Walther P-38s), swords, and daggers. The townspeople of Norf turned over an amazing collection, including rifles and revolvers dating from the middle of the nineteenth century. Souvenirs served not only as mementoes of combat service but also as valuable acquisitions, almost like bonus pay.

Cooks and service personnel with trucks, officers with jeeps, and military government detachments could and did accumulate great quantities of treasure. According to Willis Botz, Lt. Col. Frederick Maxwell hitched a wagon to his jeep, which he loaded with plunder. His well-known reputation prompted the men to sing a ditty to the tune of the "Blue Danube"—one line went: "Stop your shooting, Maxwell is looting." Bill Meyer recounted how the battery captain would send him and others inside houses to look for German soldiers and booby traps. When it was determined a house was safe, the captain would enter and search for valuables. In one house Meyer found a full-dress German officer's uniform, whereupon he cut off the epaulettes and stuck them in his pocket. Afterwards the captain inspected the house. He soon came out shouting indignantly, "Someone ruined this officer's uniform, and it would have fit me perfectly."[33]

Unlike an officer who had use of a jeep, the ordinary GI faced a serious handicap, for everything collected had to be carried, and weight became the infantryman's enemy. Robert Hawn "liberated" a 1928-model Thompson .45-caliber submachine gun, but then traded it to a tank crewman for a case of Ten-in-One rations. The appeal of the army's best prepackaged food took precedence over a valuable souvenir that had to be toted.[34]

Troops found and happily consumed wine, cognac, schnapps, champagne, and beer, which German families squirreled away in their cellars. Fred Kampmier and his group dragged several cases of liquor out of a cellar and downed the contents. The army granted a monthly allotment of hard liquor to commissioned officers, while abstinence was considered appropriate for noncoms and enlisted men, a policy no other army imposed upon its combat soldiers. Alcohol consumption (sometimes by stealing officers' liquor rations) became a way to rebel against such discrimination and momentarily obtain release from combat stress.[35]

Imbibing provided only one source of fun. Soldiers also availed themselves of bikes, motorbikes, and "half-pint" cars for joy-riding through the streets whenever the opportunity presented itself in captured villages. One group cut the top off a sedan and drove around in the open car with a large bust of Hitler in the rear seat. In the village of Anstel, Emmett Jackson and Headquarters Company 395 remembered "we ran all over town on bicycles and motorcycles having the time of our lives." Jay Nelson wrote his mom about "these crazy guys who are going around with high-top silk hats or derbies on and nearly everybody has some kind of fancy scarf or belt." Wearing fancy civilian accessories offered the opportunity to disparage upscale sophistication. These moments of levity interrupted long periods of boredom, discomfort, and stress, as GIs joyfully acted out youthful rebellion against army regimentation.[36]

• • •

Attitudes toward German civilians varied, though generally American soldiers distrusted and disliked them; however, the 99th did not mistreat the German people, even though Grady Arrington considered Germans "misinformed, desperate, and treacherous." Robert Ortalda conceded, "we weren't friendly to the civilians; we hated them." Most believed the German people had put Hitler in power and were responsible for the war. American soldiers blamed them for their misery and time away from home. Replacements were instructed to lump all Germans together. When Fred Kampmier arrived at a replacement depot (popularly referred to as a "repple depple"), the staff ranted about the "terrible Germans" and encouraged the new recruits to destroy German house furnishings and "throw radios

through windows." Robert Mitsch witnessed the "stupid" effectiveness of such harangues when his squad broke into a German post
office. To demonstrate their toughness, replacement soldiers went
on a "rampage," destroying numerous parcels of toys that had failed
to reach German kids. Maj. Thomas Sams Bishop wrote in his diary
on March 6, 1945: "We are not the liberators we thought we were.
We loot, burn, and pillage like the rest."[37]

Lieutenant Y. B. Johnson wrote his wife Olene that sometimes he
felt sorry for "some of the old people and kids, but when I stop to
think I could be home now if it wasn't for them, I don't care what
happens to them." In Bergheim, Grady Arrington described how
they rounded up the "aged and decrepit," along with the young, "a
despondent and anguished mass of humanity," and herded them like
cattle out into an open field. But he felt no mercy because Germans
were "responsible for the loss of our closest buddies." After finishing
their chow, Richard Weaver's weapons platoon Baker Company 395
emptied their mess kits into waste bins. Hungry civilians appeared
and tried to scrape out the remnants but were "unnecessarily and
inhumanely" chased away. Carter Strong witnessed a similar scene as
his unit ate breakfast. Germans kids, carrying little pails and buckets,
"silently begged" for scraps of food without much luck. Strong
admitted GIs had "no use for the German people, since we're headed
back toward the front again to fight with their menfolk and maybe
not come back." Because cigarettes became the universal currency
during the war, civilians followed GIs, ever watchful to pounce on a discarded butt. But some soldiers denied Germans this pleasure, deliberately "tearing up cigarettes butts and scattering them in the streets,
so no German could pick them up."[38]

• • •

GIs had been trained to fight and kill. They had been shelled and shot
at; in many cases they had seen fellow soldiers wounded and killed, sometimes in appalling ways. It was difficult, perhaps counterproductive, not
to hate the enemy, which included civilians, especially if the other
side did not fight fairly. General Walter Lauer reminded them of the
"ruthless sadism practiced by the Nazi beasts" and cautioned them to
be "on guard against booby traps and the treachery which they could
expect to encounter more and more, for the *Boche* was full of such

dirty tricks." According to Lauer, the "children were dangerous," and the women "were the most fanatical of the Nazi[s]." Rumors circulated among the troops that some civilians, including women, performed as snipers and artillery spotters. Village residents hung white sheets out of windows to indicate the town had surrendered. But sometimes German soldiers ignored the villagers' wishes and opened fire on the approaching Americans, who assumed the civilians participated in the deception, breaking one of the rules of war. One such incident occurred at Fortuna when a few German troops began waving white flags. Charlie Company commander Capt. Joe Budinsky stood up to tell his men to stop firing when a German rifleman shot him through the head, distressing his men, who believed the white flags had been a ruse.[39]

German soldiers made use of booby traps, nefarious devices that seemingly gave the victim little chance to avoid injury or death. American officers told their men to be particularly vigilant in German houses. Leroy Wagner had been warned not to even straighten a picture or painting hanging on the wall because it might be wired to an explosive charge. In one village the retreating Germans had stacked a large pile of mines against the outside wall of a brick building. Several curious 99ers were investigating the mines when they detonated, resulting in a terrific explosion, killing three men and wounding others. Immediately afterward, Robert Mitsch saw vapor rising from a nearby haystack. A closer examination revealed that the vapor was steam from hot body fragments scattered by the explosion, a sickening discovery that "made an indelible impression on my mind." Survivors believed the stack of mines had been booby-trapped. Francis Haskins and his buddy Don Royer had the "gruesome job" of hauling two badly mangled victims back to a graves collection point. They placed one body on a stretcher and gathered the second in a large clothes basket; the third victim vanished—not even his dog tags could be found.[40]

• • •

Often the soldier was conflicted, caught between compassion and anger, between the person he had once been and the person transformed by combat. When William McMurdie came to the door of a house with the intention of throwing everyone out, an old man met him and started wringing his hands and weeping. Inside he showed McMurdie a "flock of kids not old enough to walk, and all crying hysterically." McMurdie decided to let them remain in the house. John Scaglione offered testimony to the dilemma the combat soldier faced. As his platoon moved into a town, German civilians hurried down the road trying to pass through the American lines and out of harm's way. Scaglione spotted "two little boys not yet school age, running with their hands high in the air and tears streaming down their faces. "I felt bad when I saw them." Shortly thereafter he came upon a GI glove on the ground with a hand in it; "it looked like a piece of meat you'd see in a butcher shop. I didn't feel sorry for Germans [any more]."[41]

When Fred Kampmier and his platoon entered a farmhouse, they discovered a young girl and her mother. After chasing the occupants out, the GIs proceeded to "turn everything upside down," overturning drawers, looking for valuables, and depositing eggshells and discards on the floor. When the *Hausfrau* and her daughter unexpectedly returned for some clothing and personal items, they saw what a mess "we had made out of their house." As the two were leaving, the girl, with tears in her eyes, plunked two notes on the piano—a tiny, civilized rebuke to the soldiers who had vandalized her home. (Years later Kampmier could still hear those notes ringing in his ears, a shameful reminder of their behavior.) One of the GIs became angry, wanting to know who had let the mother and daughter back into the house. He told the others not to feel sorry for those Germans, as they were "the enemy." Then the squad descended into the basement and broke open trunks and suitcases. One soldier took his knife and cut off the leather side of one case. When several cans of American Red Cross food parcels tumbled onto the basement floor, they felt much better about ransacking the home because the occupants had acquired food intended for POWs.[42]

Robert Hawn found himself emotionally and morally conflicted after George Company 393 captured the village of Norf. His platoon was billeted in a chateau occupied by the wife of a German officer and her servants. Hawn and his buddies "were not allowed to fraternize with the enemy." Consequently the GIs moved into the upper stories of the house, while the mistress and her staff were banished to the basement during daylight hours. When evening came, all Norf's citizens, including the officer's wife, were escorted to several air raid shelters and kept there under guard throughout the night. A young German mother with a small infant approached Hawn and asked if she might return home to collect some necessities for her child. Hawn agreed and accompanied her to the house. Yet he felt "embarrassed and uncomfortable in doing this small thing for an enemy," especially after she softly uttered "*danke*" [thanks] to him as they returned to the shelter. The army expected him to be stern toward the Germans, but he could not ignore the plight of a mother and her baby.[43]

Sometimes it proved difficult to snuff out empathetic feelings toward enemy civilians. Francis Chesnik softened his attitude after one German lady kindly fixed potato pancakes for him and his buddies. Generally GIs found the German people (women, old men, and children) to be frightened, docile, hungry, and eager for the war to end. After American artillery bombarded a field, killing several cows and horses, the villagers emerged en masse armed with sharp knives to butcher the animals. They offered medic John "Smokey" Marcisin (so nicknamed because he was always the first guy in his unit to build a fire) a large piece of hindquarter horse steak, which he promptly cooked with garlic and scallions—a feast he rated a "ten compared to one-rated K rations." Perhaps they shared to curry favor; nonetheless, Marcisin appreciated the gesture.[44]

Carter Strong admitted it was "hard to be rough on little children, but that was the only case where our sympathy slackened." Some GIs commiserated with ordinary people. Under gray, cold skies, Strong watched dispirited people walking along a Stolberg street lined with destroyed houses, a scene emblematic of "hopelessness and of war." B. C. Henderson "felt sorry" for civilians coming out of towns, carrying all their belongings. Upon entering a house, James Larkey encountered a "little old couple." When he asked for some firewood, the man went to his oven and pulled out a single piece of wood. "I looked at the man, and he reminded me of my father. I thought, would I want this done to my father? I couldn't take the wood."[45]

As Charles Roland, S-3 3rd Battalion 394, entered Dormagen, he witnessed the "most unsettling sight" of the war. The town had been shelled from both sides. Countless dead and wounded civilians had been deposited on the grounds around a small hospital: men in business suits, women in dresses, and children in street clothes. The victims displayed "every imaginable kind of wound, some lay with brains or intestines spilling out on the neatly mowed grass." His eyes fell upon a "golden-haired little girl who bore a striking resemblance to one I had kissed while in the first grade." While steeled against seeing the dead in uniform, he turned away from "this ghastly tableau with a feeling of revulsion, horror, and remorse."[46]

• • •

After Bergheim, the division cut a six-mile swath as it advanced in a northeasterly direction toward Düsseldorf and away from Cologne, burning brightly in the dark sky. The infantry moved rapidly, attacking at night, which offered the advantage of surprise but the disadvantage of uncertainty and confusion. Such movement interrupted regular sleep patterns, and men grabbed moments of rest whenever possible. Swift advances and frequent changes of direction proved disorienting to William Galegar, who felt like a "bug skating on top of the water." B. C. Henderson agreed, complaining, "We hardly slept and ate our rations on the move because the push was fast and furious."[47]

After marching along at five-yard intervals, columns on either side of the road, hour after hour, the first units reached the Rhine. When the second scout of King Company 395 spotted the river, he turned and yelled to his squad, "I see it!" whereupon the group gave a "soft cheer of triumph and release." Some men expressed their feelings toward the enemy by urinating into Germany's most famous river. Francis Chesnick approached the Rhine opposite the city of Düsseldorf, heard train whistles blowing, and saw civilians hurrying to their destinations. The scene was surreal; on the far side of the river life appeared normal, while war raged on the other.[48]

Once the situation seemed secure, Harold Hill, the esteemed commander of George Company 395, ordered up the kitchen and had the cooks serve a hot meal in the courtyard of a large house. But tragedy struck after he left for battalion headquarters. A single mortar shell, fired from the eastern side of the Rhine, landed in the courtyard, killing five and wounding another ten soldiers. When Hill returned, he came upon a bloody scene where survivors were weeping openly over the losses. Hill blamed himself, reasoning that if he had remained, he would not have allowed so many men to congregate in that narrow space. The deaths hit him hard, and he retreated, "like a wounded rat," deep into the cellar of the house. His sorrow and despair were interrupted, however, by orders to have the company prepare for an immediate move.[49]

The Germans hoped and the Americans feared that crossing the wide, swift-moving Rhine River would prove difficult. Small, unprotected boats would present inviting targets for enemy machine guns and mortars. No GI wanted to think about the inevitable dangers of such an operation, which would certainly add to the total of 104 dead and many wounded suffered by the 99th in its drive across the plain to the Rhine. Then, on March 7, word came that somewhere upriver the 9th Armored Division had seized a railroad bridge. Early the next morning, the 99th Division piled on trucks and traveled south. No one knew what might lie ahead, but a bridge might be a better option than a boat ride.

CHAPTER 6

Crossing the Rhine

During World War I the German high command decided to build a double-track steel railroad bridge with two pedestrian walkways over the Rhine River to move troops and supplies from the industrial Ruhr area to the Western Front. The spot chosen was due east of Remagen, a small resort town of four thousand inhabitants. Construction began in 1916 on the Ludendorff Bridge (named after the quartermaster general of the German Army) but was not completed until 1918. The bridge stretched nearly eleven hundred feet from Remagen on the west bank to Erpel, a hamlet on the east side, where a huge tunnel 420 yards long was carved into a steep, black slate cliff (called Erpeler Ley), rising four hundred vertical feet to a barren, flat top. (Because of the bend in the river, geographically the bridge actually pointed north and south.) At each end of the span stood two neo-medieval stone towers with gun ports to defend the bridge in case of attack.[1]

In early March 1945 disorganized German forces began retreating toward the standing Rhine River bridges. Once troops and equipment had safely reached the east side, the bridges were to be demolished by explosives, thereby preventing the Allies from exploiting a passage into the heart of Germany; more troops and equipment could have been saved, but Hitler demanded they stay and fight to the last man. During the previous winter U.S. aircraft had repeatedly bombed bridges up and down the Rhine to prevent the movement of German troops and supplies to the front. By early spring only a few bridges stood intact. After disorganized and war-weary German troops

Ludendorff Railroad Bridge as seen from a quarried tunnel in the side of Erpeler Lay. Note the two earthen ramps leading up to the embankment. The 99ers first spotted the bridge from a forested ridge in the distance. Courtesy Friedensmuseum Brücke von Remagen.

evacuated over the river, the remaining bridges were destroyed, save one, the Ludendorff.

American bombers had attacked the bridge on October 9, December 26, December 29, 1944, and January 2, 1945, the last raid killing twenty-eight civilians and eight soldiers. These raids inflicted considerable damage on the town and the span, but German workers made repairs and kept the bridge in service. During the first days in March, however, train travel was suspended. German engineers laid wooden planks between the railroad rails and used two long dirt ramps up to the embankment so vehicles and troops could escape across the river.[2]

German soldiers fastened explosives around the support structures with the intention of blowing up the bridge at the last moment. On March 7, as troops and tanks of the U.S. 9th Armored Division approached the span's southern end, an explosive charge was detonated that shattered some beams and destroyed the upstream walkway, but the sturdy bridge remained upright on its stone piers. The Germans also exploded a huge charge at the approach to the bridge, slicing away part of the railroad embankment to prevent all vehicular and tank traffic from using it. Seeing the bridge still standing, troops of the 27th Armored Infantry Battalion cautiously advanced across the span, overcame light resistance, and moved into the Erpeler tunnel, capturing terrified civilians and *Volkssturm* [home guard] troops who sought shelter there. News of the bridge's seizure moved up the U.S. chain of command, and General Omar Bradley, Commander of the 12th Army Group, ordered all available divisions to assemble and move rapidly to Remagen. In the first twenty-four hours after its seizure, the 27th Armored, elements of the 9th Infantry Division, and two regiments of the 78th Infantry Division proceeded across the Ludendorff to secure the bridgehead.[3]

Initial resistance by the Germans proved spotty because Field Marshal Walter Model, thinking the Americans would attempt a forced crossing downriver, amassed his depleted forces near Bonn, fifteen miles to the north. He finally ordered a counterattack to push the Americans into the Rhine, but German troops, arriving piecemeal on the eastern side, could not prevent an American buildup.

The Germans employed fighter-bombers, howitzers, mortars, V-1 rockets, jet planes, and even a huge railroad gun in a desperate but unsuccessful attempt to destroy the bridge. Located behind the steep hills, the artillery could not hit the northern half of the span; consequently, German gunners aimed for the other side and its approaches. Although many shells splashed harmlessly into the river, intermittent fire scored hits on the bridge, its approaches, and the southern part of the city. Nevertheless, the damaged bridge stood until March 17 when it finally collapsed, killing twenty-three and injuring ninety-three engineers trying to repair it.

• • •

Ninety-Ninth Division troops assumed they would be granted a rest after overrunning the Cologne Plain. If the railroad bridge at Remagen hadn't fortuitously fallen into American hands, that wish might have been fulfilled. Instead, on March 9, 1945, they were ordered into trucks for a bumpy sixty-mile ride south to assembly areas west of Remagen. The 2nd platoon George Company 394 had a confiscated duck boiling in a pot at 10:00 A.M. when they were ordered to jump in the back of a 6 x 6 truck. Medic John Slubowski grabbed the half-cooked duck, climbed aboard, and the men consumed the slightly cooked fowl en route.[4]

Many GIs had no idea where they were headed or the urgency of the mission, but Maltie Anderson was happy to be riding instead of walking. John Hendricks remembered being crammed into a troop carrier with some men forced to stand. Only when a soldier going the opposite way handed Hendricks's group a copy of the *Stars and Stripes* did they learn about a captured bridge. No emergency was considered important enough to halt the southward movement of Hendricks's truck, not even nature's call, so a couple of men defecated out the back as it was rolling along. B. C. Henderson recalled their "Negro driver" drove so recklessly that "we bounced all over that truck." As William McMurdie's truck moved along, Sherwood Henry told the group he had a recurring dream they "would soon be coming to a hilly part of Germany and make an attack down a valley into a city and all [would] get shot up and all killed." McMurdie tried to convince Henry it was only natural for a combat soldier to harbor such scary forebodings, and it didn't mean anything. Henry's premonitions, however, would prove sadly prophetic.[5]

Carter Strong remembered his unit traveled more than eight hours in 2½-ton troop carriers. To fight the miserably damp weather, they put up the bench seats and crouched on the steel floor to avoid the wind. Movement alternated between swift dashes and long pauses along roads jammed with hundreds of trucks, tanks, ambulances, and jeeps. Charlie Swann recalled passing knocked-out American tanks and trucks with bloated bodies lying everywhere. While it bothered him to see dead GIs, the rest of his squad appeared "unmoved by these horrors," and his lieutenant thought "it was wonderful that the men had become hardened to this." Using only night beams (narrow slits called "cat's eyes") to light the way after dark, the convoys crawled along both sides of the highway as they moved south. On their way, those who looked off to the east could see a "big wall of flame" in the distance; it was Cologne burning.[6]

• • •

The 99th offloaded in villages near Remagen and were told they would soon cross the Rhine. After spending the night in barns, houses, and foxholes while 155mm "Long Tom" guns boomed away, a snake-line column of 394th Regiment troops began a five-mile hike into Remagen. As James Langford and a scouting party emerged from the evergreen forest and reached the ridgeline above the town near dusk, he observed a railroad bridge being struck by artillery shells: "Most of the time in combat you don't see what's ahead, but in this instance we could see where we were going." And the objective looked grim. During the two days of the crossing on March 10th and 11th, thirty-two 99ers would die.[7]

The third and second battalions 394 (the order of their crossing) approached the ridge after dark, which intensified the apprehension. The men could sometimes hear the scream of incoming shells followed by loud cracks or crashes, but usually, because of the noise, the deadly missiles exploded without warning. For Plt. Sgt. Harold Schaefer it was the most "harrowing combat ordeal" he would endure; "we had come to it and had to go through it." The gauntlet they had to walk presented a terrifying prospect, both for veterans and replacement GIs experiencing their first serious artillery shelling.[8]

Upon reaching Remagen the men of the 394th Regiment advanced in a southeasterly direction along narrow cobblestone streets lit by the flames of burning vehicles and buildings. Forming lines on either side of the streets, they clung to walls for protection and nervously trod along. With so many troops and vehicles vying for a single spot, movement was slow and irregular, adding to the terror and turmoil. As Guy Duren rolled through Remagen in a jeep, he spotted a sign that warned, "This street subject to enemy shell fire." Dead Americans along the way offered proof of the warning.[9]

When his platoon stopped, William McMurdie squatted on his helmet, pulled a poncho over his helmet-liner, and tried to sleep sitting up. Some platoons were shepherded into cellars until they received orders to move forward. Richard Jacksha and Cliff Selwood ducked into a basement just before a shell collapsed the building next door—one they had unsuccessfully tried to enter. After Byron Reburn stepped behind a large pillar to answer nature's call, a huge blast knocked him momentarily unconscious and killed the man who had taken his position in line. B. C. Henderson hunkered down beside a jeep hitched to a trailer when a shell detonated, sending a fist-sized fragment "completely through the trailer above my back." John Scaglione watched a large chunk of hot metal skidding along the street, clanging and throwing off sparks. He thought to himself, if that shell fragment "didn't immediately cut you in half, they'd have to use a mattress as a wound dressing." But nothing stopped the movement. Trucks hit by artillery shells were pushed aside, and columns of men and vehicles kept going. They advanced along *Alte Strasse* and then *Goethe Strasse* with orders not to stop for anyone, not even the wounded, which seemed "cold and inhumane" to Henderson. Although artillery shelling was intermittent (salvos roughly every thirty seconds), it was, according to executive officer Boyd McCune, who directed bridge traffic through most of the night, "the most intense" he had seen.[10]

394TH REGIMENT

A little more than two hundred yards from the west bank, infantrymen and jeeps approached a long, earthen ramp leading to the steep railroad embankment. As the troops came to the ramp, they turned left and headed up a rutted pathway to the bridge. Movement was spasmodic for each shell blast stopped everyone temporarily. Largely devoid of buildings (except for the Becher furniture factory) and protection, the area became known as "dead man's corner" for the many MPs, engineers, and combat soldiers cut down on this exposed stretch. B. C. Henderson saw dead and wounded GIs; some called out, "Help, I'm dying, please help me!" Harold Schaefer heard similar, desperate cries from those who had been blown off the embankment and lay on the ground below. As Charles Katlic and Fox Company reached the embankment, "three shells produced a number of casualties and sent the rest hurrying away in different directions."[11]

Guided by imperiled MPs of the 9th Infantry Division, who yelled at them to keep moving but maintain their spacing, foot soldiers and jeeps dashed for the bridge between salvos while dodging helmets, packs, weapons and other equipment that had been discarded. It was, according to Katlic, "hard to walk without tripping over the wounded and dead." Medic Saul Brechner sought shelter in a small building

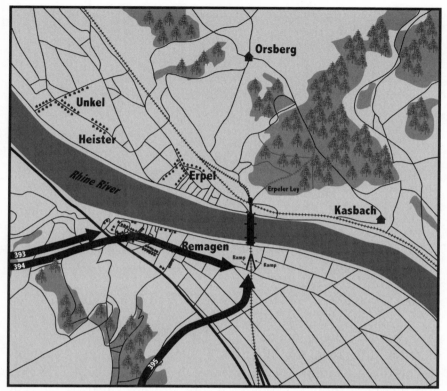

Crossing the Rhine at Remagen, March 10–11, 1945. Map by Paul Giacomotto and James Knight.

near the furniture factory where the wounded were placed. He offered his help, but when he attempted to use a rifle as a splint on a badly wounded GI, the soldier's leg came off.[12]

Shell bursts on the bridge's superstructure punched large holes in the steel crossbeams and temporary wood flooring, prompting both vehicles and men to move cautiously out of fear they might tumble into the rushing water below. Engineers and soldiers carried wood planks and steel plates out onto the bridge to cover the gaps. "Not only did you have to watch for the holes," James Larkey recalled, "but we didn't know what awaited us on the other side. We were scared." As Capt. Charles Roland stepped onto the bridge at midnight, he recalled that two thousand years earlier, Julius Caesar had crossed the Rhine at almost the same spot to fight the same enemy.[13]

When attacking, a combat soldier would seek some form of cover. But walking along the embankment or riding in a jeep out onto the bridge offered the GI no opportunity to protect himself. He felt vulnerable and could only hope fate was on his side, and the shells would land elsewhere. Robert Mitsch reached the middle of the bridge when the column came to a halt. He looked at the dark river and thought "that's a long way down." Feeling "terribly vulnerable" standing there, he quickly made a "plea to God that we'd make it across." Whether through divine intervention or not, Mitsch arrived on the other side safely and his "breathing became easier." But deadly harm could come even within the shadow of Erpeler Ley. Stanley Lambert saw an American jeep with a captain seemingly sitting at attention in the passenger seat while his dead driver lay on the ground. The captain didn't have a mark on him, but he was dead too. Lambert admitted, "I had a little feeling of happiness that it wasn't me lying there."[14]

Men became separated from their units, and disorganization added to the confusion. Uncertainty loomed over this dangerous enterprise. Rumors spread among the troops that German reinforcements aimed to drive them into the river, a point brought home by enemy leaflets dropped from a plane, warning the 99th they lacked reserves and therefore should surrender before all were killed. While only three GIs of the regiment died that night, the 394th would suffer another ninety-three fatalities the following week.

On the far bank Fred Kampmier slipped on shell casings and other debris, for modern battlefields produce instant junkyards. Ninety-niners waited for stragglers to arrive, reorganized, and then marched two miles south to the river city of Linz, which had been liberated by the 9th Armored Division. The late-arriving 1st Battalion was consigned to defensive foxholes, while the 2nd and 3rd Battalions billeted in houses and other buildings. J. C. Jones and his men found shelter in a tavern where liquid spirits flowed freely. David Reagler's platoon bedded down in a jewelry store full of broken glass. Everyone looked forward to seizing what he could when daylight arrived, but "as usual, we weren't the ones who would get to look for the goodies, as we moved out before light."[15]

Leroy Wagner and his platoon went into a home and discovered an older gentleman and his cache of wine. Fearful the wine might be poisoned, they made the owner take a drink from each bottle. Wagner recalled, "We got a chance to have what the officers got regularly with their liquor rations, but by the time we left, the old German was pretty tipsy." James Larkey entered a deserted house and found a nice bed with "fine quality bedding." Looking at his dirty uniform and muddy boots, he asked himself, "How can I do this?" He hesitated only for a moment, and then climbed into the bed, putting his filthy boots between the "rich, clean sheets." He felt guilty but enjoyed "a good night's sleep."[16]

The next morning they moved out on the attack. Robert Mitsch saw a dead American soldier "whose skull seemed to be crushed on both sides and his complexion was an ashen-green," a sight that would haunt him for the rest of his life. As Harold Schaefer came to a bend in the road, he saw the torso of a GI crushed by a tank track. His legs and left hip had been ground into the blacktop but there were no visible wounds on the rest of him. A frightening question entered Schaefer's mind: "Was that poor bastard alive when that tank ate him?" He did not know, but he would always remember the dead man's "blue eyes staring up at me."[17]

Cliff McDaniel, captured during an ill-fated patrol off Elsenborn Ridge on January 15, had spent six weeks in a German hospital west of the Rhine. On February 28, as U.S. forces moved closer, their captors hurriedly transported McDaniel and other patients across the Rhine to Linz. McDaniel was lying in his bed when a GI lieutenant entered the room, came over to him and asked, "How are you doing?" McDaniel replied, "Better now." Then McDaniel turned his head toward the wall and "cried like a baby." When McDaniel departed several days later he was overjoyed to see the streets of Linz "lined with fellows wearing the Checkerboard." (McDaniel may have seen rear echelon personnel wearing insignia, for veteran combat soldiers removed their badges.) He would be going home, but without his left leg and without his best friend, Arnold "Akie" Owens, who had been killed on that winter patrol.[18]

393RD REGIMENT

The 393rd Regiment arrived at the village of Werthofen before dawn on March 10, but had to wait until the following day before entering

Remagen. Robert Hawn was amazed at the sight of antiaircraft guns, tanks, tank destroyers, and artillery units assembled along the ridge-line giving supporting fire to the bridgehead. When Harry Arnold topped the high ground overlooking the Rhine River, he saw the bridge and for a moment "all seemed deceptively calm and peaceful below. Even in war the view was breathtaking." They proceeded down the hillside into the town, as the sound of "enemy incoming" grew ever louder, and, according to Hawn, "we became more tense." Gathering "strength and comfort from being one with my platoon, I was resigned to the job ahead and to my fate, whatever it was."[19]

On the road through the city, veteran squad leader Robert Waldrep snatched up K rations from dead soldiers, knowing from experience his men would need them in the coming hours. Lieutenant Frank Peck noticed one of his men down on his knees pointing a bazooka. Peck couldn't understand why the fellow didn't move along. He went over to the soldier and discovered he was dead: "I left him as he was in perfect balance—unbelievable." Upon reaching the embank-ment, the men saw the effects of earlier shelling: dead Americans beside the road. Ken Juhl caught sight of a GI who "had nothing below his belly button, as his legs had been blown away." Radford Carroll glanced at a corpse on top of the embankment. "The top of his head was gone, so I could see through his open mouth and empty skull into the river." As Daulton Swanner approached the bridge he saw bodies stacked head high between two posts and thought, "it could have been me." Normally medics quickly removed bodies so as not to upset the living, but in this instance there was no time to gather up the dead because they had to tend to the wounded.[20]

As George Company neared the bridge under shellfire, Robert Hawn looked at the twin, black towers guarding the approach and wondered, "What the hell are we doing here?" Hurrying along the bridge deck as fast as traffic would allow, "a considerable pucker factor occurred and our hearts came up in our throats." James Revell ran up the stone tower steps crowded with men too hesitant to budge and proceeded past them at a measured but tiring pace over the river. Guy Duren rode across in a jeep but "felt unsafe sitting so high up in the air with no protection." One GI, "spooked by all the shelling," dropped down, grabbed a beam and refused to move. Steve Kallas threatened to kick him off the bridge if he didn't get up and go.

The terrified GI released his grip and moved on. Halfway across they spotted the tunnel entrance on the other side, a safe haven that seemed to beckon to them. As Hawn's platoon members entered the dark tunnel and collected themselves, no one said anything but all quietly experienced a feeling of exhilaration, for they had arrived safely. They then headed south until they reached a huge winery. Robert Hawn grabbed five bottles of champagne and tasted it for the first time, a bubbly reward he certainly deserved.[21]

After reassembling, the 393rd walked southward two miles upstream along the eastern shore toward Linz, which possessed huge commercial wine cellars. Guy Duren and his buddy loaded their jeep with all the wine and brandy it could hold. John McCoy ventured into one cellar where he watched 99ers shoot holes in casks and fill canteens, bottles, gasoline cans, and even buckets with white Rhine wine. The intoxicating liquid quickly flooded the floor, producing a sweet aroma that filled the air and attracted every passing GI. After occupying a fancy apartment with thick carpeting on the floor, McCoy fired up a portable gas stove and put a quart-size can of bacon on the burner. Soon great quantities of bacon fat boiled over the edge of the can and down onto the beautiful carpet. His action generated "no regretful feelings at all."[22]

After Harry Arnold's squad occupied a large house, they found a basement stocked with alcoholic beverages, which they happily consumed, while encouraging the homeowner, an elderly man and an accomplished pianist, to play some music. But his repertoire turned out to be classical pieces, not popular American tunes the GIs wanted to hear. Either out of a macabre sense of humor or a deep-seated foreboding, Harry Arnold asked the German to play Chopin's mournful "Funeral March."[23]

395TH REGIMENT

Stuart Kline, a military policeman, was riding in a jeep, part of a long, bumper-to-bumper procession headed for the bridge, when German fighter planes appeared and began strafing the road. Kline and others jumped out and ran for the woods. Thinking the danger had passed, Booker Brown, another MP, stood up and instantly caught a bullet. Kline and the driver rushed Brown to an aid station but he died en route. Informed they would have to take the body away, Kline and Lt. Bowers laid Brown's body on the hood of the jeep, drove across the Rhine, found their unit, and bedded down for the night with the dead soldier still on the jeep. When Kline awoke in the morning, the body was gone.[24]

The 395th was the last regiment to arrive. Two soldiers from Able Company bedded down in a field with large draft horses. Agitated by incessant artillery, the horses bolted excitedly around, tearing themselves on barbed wire fences. John Scaglione became leery of them, fearing one might fall into his foxhole, which "would be a hell of a way to become a casualty—being trampled on by a crazy German horse." So Scaglione and his foxhole buddy left the field and spent the rest of the night in a barn.[25]

The next morning on March 11, the 395th Regiment began marching along roads and through muddy, plowed fields toward Remagen. (The 3rd Battalion left Heimersheim, south and west of Remagen, at 10:30 A.M. but did not reach their final destination on the east side until 4:30 P.M., six hours later.) A mile before the city, several trucks heading to the rear, each nearly full with dead Americans, passed Woodrow Hickey as he walked along—"a sight you never get used to" or forget. When George Company departed from Bölingen, eight miles from the bridge, the men were ordered to carry only the bare essentials, namely, rifle, ammo, K rations, D bars, and grenades. A replacement was to remain behind with instructions to bring up the packs later. William Galegar left his pack, including war booty (gold rings, watches, and an antique necklace set with rubies) on the ground. When the replacement subsequently caught up with the company empty-handed, "it almost cost him his life." The long trek into Remagen produced a general weariness, but as the 395th entered the town, Carter Strong recalled, anticipation over seeing the Rhine "kept us in a state of excitement."[26]

When William Galegar (nicknamed "Chief" because of partial Cherokee ancestry) reached the top of the hill, he noticed a single line of trucks stopped on the road west of the bridge and concluded they were simply waiting to cross. Descending the hill, he approached the trucks and discovered why they hadn't moved; the occupants were dead. To keep the approaches clear, two Sherman tanks equipped with bulldozer blades were at the ready. As 1st Lt. Harold Hill ascended the dirt ramp, he came upon a 6 x 6 truck that had taken a direct hit. The driver was slumped over the steering wheel, but Hill could not ascertain whether he was alive or dead. Nonetheless, one of the bulldozer tanks simply pushed the truck off the ramp.[27]

Joseph Thimm watched the chaos of trucks, tanks, and vehicles crawling toward the bridge while troops poured out of the hills above Remagen. U.S. Army vehicles jammed the main road from the west and headed toward the river, while helmetless German prisoners on foot or packed into trucks went the other way to holding pens. As he approached the "cold and battered steel structure," Thimm recalled voices screaming, medics carrying the wounded, and engineers repairing shell hits. Thimm's great grandparents had emigrated from Remagen to Detroit in the middle of the nineteenth century; after the war, when Joe returned home and mentioned being in Remagen, his grandmother asked if he had taken time to visit any of their relatives.[28]

William Galegar and two squads briefly ducked into a house before a sprint to the bridge, when another squad leader began talking incoherently about being killed, declaring "he wasn't going any farther even if they put him in jail forever." Seeing the men adversely affected by this fearful talk, Galegar threatened "to shoot his ass off" if he didn't shut up. The sergeant quieted down, and when the order came they departed for the tower, even though, Galegar confessed, "no one wanted to make that run across the bridge."[29]

After Bernard Brody discovered dead GIs piled up behind a building he began wetting his pants. Not understanding why he couldn't stop, he walked over to an ambulance and asked a doctor about his problem. The doctor replied, "I am scared too." Before they reached the river, Richard Gorby spotted an abandoned truck sitting by a curb with its tarpaulin tied down. Thinking it might contain "something good to eat," he untied the ropes. But inside "there was a load of American dead," and he quickly retied the ropes. John Scaglione arrived at the top of the ramp, only to watch a truck being manhandled back down. The hood and cab were riddled with shell fragments, and he noticed a large pool of blood sloshing on the driver's seat.[30]

As Francis Chesnik approached the bridge on foot, he looked up at a sign that read, "Cross the Rhine with Dry Feet—Courtesy of the

Ludendorff Bridge after it collapsed. Note the wooden planking placed on the bridge for motorized traffic. Courtesy National Archives and Records Administration.

9th Armored Division." Although Chesnick and others in Able Company 395 preferred walking over the river rather than fighting its swift current in a boat (especially because Chesnick didn't know how to swim), the danger from artillery shells remained. Driven by fright (according to Byron Whitmarsh "the worst place I ever was at"), they moved on, passing a smashed American truck where a dead driver, or what was left of him, remained inside. Along the route Carter Strong couldn't avoid seeing men "slumped over and lying in all position[s], some of them unrecognizable and others looking as though they were only asleep. It was not good for our morale." They entered the north tower, climbed the winding cement stairway that led to the bridge, then bolted out the door onto the pedestrian walkway for the nerve-wracking scramble to the far bank. Halfway across Forbes Williams accidentally dropped his .30-caliber machine gun into the Rhine; he not only worried whether he would arrive on the other side, but also whether he would have to pay the army $783 for losing the weapon. Lambert Shultz walked port high toward the other side (he was told not to run, though others did), but all he could think about was the bridge collapsing under him and the possibility that German soldiers waited for them in the tunnel and above on the imposing cliff.[31]

The engineers quickly completed the first pontoon bridge some 650 yards downstream (to the north) from the Ludendorff Bridge; a second pontoon was finished at midnight two miles upstream opposite Linz. Parallel to the river the army assembled a huge concentration of antiaircraft guns and trucks with four .50-caliber machine guns on a single mount to blast incoming German fighters and jet planes. As German aircraft approached from the north, antiaircraft fire escalated to a thunderous crescendo. GIs avidly observed the exciting spectacle unfolding above them. "Watching tracers making their paths through the sky," Galegar wondered "how any plane could get through such a dense firestorm of steel and smoke." Many did not. Of the 367 German aircraft that attacked the bridge, 109 were shot down either by antiaircraft guns or American fighters, and no bombs hit the railroad or pontoon bridges.[32]

Scores of tanks, tank destroyers, and howitzers fired steadily at targets in the hills, producing a deafening roar. Countless black telephone wires hung over trees, strung on hastily set posts, or lay in ditches connecting artillery batteries to forward observers and fire-control centers. On the Ludendorff Bridge mobile cranes, generators, truck-mounted welding machines, air compressors, and bulldozers operated at full tilt. All was racket and congestion. Homer Kissinger and Jim Crewdson drove to the pontoon bridge in a jeep pulling a trailer. The bridge could only support three vehicles at a time, and when it was their turn an MP signaled them forward with instructions not to exceed ten miles per hour. They rolled onto the first pontoons and inched toward the other side just above the water. Jim Crewdson confessed, "morning's nervous tension steadily progressed through apprehension, ordinary fear, outright fright, and well into tight-gut resignation." As they reached the middle of the river, the jeep ahead of them on the pontoon bridge took a near hit, killing two of the occupants and badly wounding a third. Arriving safely on the east bank they observed Graves Registration men collecting bodies of 78th Division GIs and loading them into jeep trailers. It offended Kissinger's sensibilities to see the dead treated with so little reverence—"it didn't seem right to stack them in a trailer that way!"[33]

• • •

For a few days the 395th was in reserve, bivouacked in the steep, wooded hills above Erpel or quartered in Rheinbreitbach, another village three miles north of the bridge. On Sunday Paul Weesner attended a Protestant service in a heavily damaged church in Erpel. During the service Chaplain Stephens paused several times until German planes made their fast runs at the bridge and the noise of antiaircraft guns stopped. Outside GIs hunkered down in their foxholes to keep from being hit by the spent antiaircraft shells falling among them. Shells struck Cannon Company's position, and, according to Ken Stanger, "one man lost an arm." Despite the danger, however, many watched the exciting air war unfold above the bridge. GIs contributed to the earsplitting barrage by firing rifles at passing planes, including speedy jets seen for the first time. Oakley Honey watched a two-man German fighter-bomber come in low when it was hit by ground fire. The pilot and co-pilot bailed out, but not in time to pull their parachute ripcords, and their bodies slammed into the hill with such force that Honey heard the deadly thud.[34]

394TH REGIMENT

On March 11, the 394th pushed south of Linz, capturing small villages situated on the narrow strip of flat land along the east bank of the Rhine; a day later the 393rd began its eastward attack in the hills above the river. The troops faced a series of steep, forested ridges running parallel to the river, where small groups of German infantry would fight largely unseen, hidden by brush and trees, and then retreat to the next hill. This defensive tactic fatigued and frustrated the advancing Americans. Progress was measured in yards not miles. Lack of roads and rugged terrain prevented tanks from taking part in the fight to enlarge the bridgehead. So it fell to the infantry to eliminate German resistance.

On March 13 and 14, the Germans launched three separate counterattacks to stop the American advance. All were repulsed with substantial losses on both sides. Machine gunner Robert Fickett remembered being surprised that German soldiers running toward him kept going for a few steps even after bullets and tracers slammed

81mm mortar team M394 prepares to fire at German positions in Ariendorf on the east bank of the Rhine. Courtesy National Archives and Records Administration.

through their bodies. The battles resulted in one of the worst weeks for the 99th Division—185 GIs fell. Warren Thomas recalled, "We went through fields that were carpeted with dead Germans and GIs. I saw more dead [than] anytime during the war."[35]

On the morning of March 12, the 2nd Battalion 394 moved east and southeast into the hills. The rifle companies faced only sporadic firing but progress was slow on the steep terrain. Around noon on March 15, Maltie Anderson and his squad were struggling up a hill when a German machine gun began firing. Then, without warning, an artillery shell crashed near them. Several GIs were hit, including a replacement who was decapitated, while hot metal tore into Anderson's legs—one shell fragment completely severed the two bones above his right ankle and a second steel shard tore into his left thigh cutting the sciatic nerve. Anderson lay there unable to move or apply a tourniquet to stop the bleeding. He heard moans from other wounded GIs throughout the night, and then only silence; he

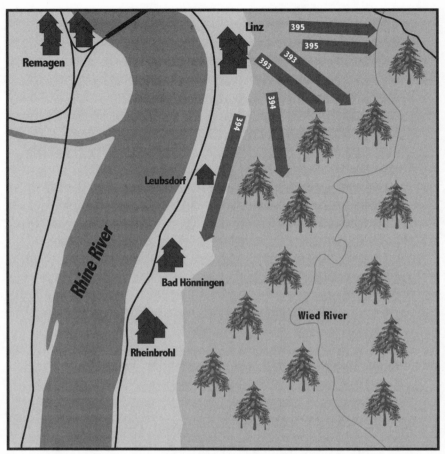

Rhine bridgehead, March 12–15, 1945. Map by Paul Giacomotto and James Knight.

assumed the others had died. In the morning medics called out from below, asking if anyone was still alive. Anderson yelled back and the medics finally came to his rescue. He was carted across the Rhine on a jeep, flown to Paris, and then on to England for several operations. Anderson was amazed the army actually took the trouble to transport him by plane: "up to that point I thought I didn't have any significance."[36]

• • •

At 6:00 A.M. on March 11, Item Company 394 left Linz headed south toward Leubsdorf and the hills above Bad Hönningen, a small industrial city six miles south of Erpel on the Rhine. Fred Kampmier's pulse raced when he almost stepped on an object in the middle of the road; it was a human, though barely recognizable because it had been flattened "like a pancake." The company then came to a steep valley surrounded by hills covered with grapevines. Tension mounted as they climbed up and then down a hill. All the while Kampmier expected a burp gun or machine gun to cut loose at any moment: "We were a perfect target. It would have been just like knocking down ten pins." But the Germans were not there to bowl them over.[37]

The platoon entered a tiny village and the inhabitants rushed out into the street waving white flags shouting, "*nicht* [not] Nazis," a cry American soldiers would hear repeatedly in Germany—few civilians wanted to be linked to the collapsing dictatorship, fearing repercussions if they admitted support for the Führer. The GIs left the village and climbed a steep hill, knowing that sooner or later they would bump into "some Krauts," but "where and when was what was worrying us." They ascended another hill and then another while taking a couple of casualties from American artillery firing from the west bank of the Rhine. After reaching the top of a pine-covered ridge they asked the squad leader if they could take a break and eat their dinner K rations. That delay saved them: another platoon entered the draw and was hit by automatic rifle fire resulting in casualties. Kampmier was "really out to get a shot at a Kraut" that day, but no potential targets presented themselves. Pinned down until dark, the platoon slipped away holding on to one another so no one would become separated from the group and lose his way.[38]

At 5:00 A.M. the next morning Kampmier's platoon groped its way back to the top of the ridge, where they ran into German fire from unknown locations. After a bullet struck one GI in the arm, they were told to retreat in an orderly manner, but the squad "all ran like hell" back some distance and dug foxholes—one soldier digging while the other stood guard. Kampmier was paired with an eighteen-year-old replacement from Missouri who "was nervous and scared of the least little thing." He did not enjoy the kid's company: "I had a hard enough job keeping myself brave, and when someone else is with you who is scared, it only makes you all the worse." They took turns catnapping and standing guard. Around midnight, Kampmier walked to the command post, where Lt. Norman Michelson explained their objective was the hill above Bad Hönningen, where the Germans had an artillery observation tower directing fire on the Ludendorff Bridge. As Mickelson briefed the men, Kampmier recalled, "I don't think I've ever smoked so many cigarettes in such a short time."[39]

At 3:00 A.M. on March 13, the platoon started out, noisily stumbling over dead branches as they clung to one another. At one point a German soldier fired two shots at them, whereupon they retreated back down the trail and waited until daybreak. When they moved out again they came upon a stand of large trees on top of a hill. Suddenly a burp gun opened up off to their left, and everyone ran to find a tree for protection. As Kampmier looked around, he noticed each man lighting a cigarette and puffs of smoke rising behind each tree. "It was a bad thing to do, but we hadn't been able to smoke for quite awhile and everyone's nerves needed a cigarette." Then a few German snipers tried to find some victims. Because of thick cover, the enemy couldn't be spotted. One sniper took a shot at Kampmier, which caused "me to cuss up and down because I couldn't see him."

When the Germans began to launch shells into their area, everyone started digging while prone on the ground, which proved a difficult task. After an hour Kampmier had scooped out a hole big enough only for his head and chest with his feet and legs dangling outside. When he heard a shell coming his way he was positive it was going to land right on top of him: "I'd bury my head in the hole with my hands on my head and every muscle in my body would tighten and I'd pray that it wouldn't hit me in any vital spot of my body." But a shell of unknown origin hit near where he had previously sprawled, and the nervous replacement from Missouri was killed.[40]

• • •

Two months earlier an eighteen-year-old orphan, Richard Curtis, had joined James Larkey's squad in the second platoon as a replacement, and Larkey "adopted" him, treating Curtis like a younger brother. Noticing that Curtis never received packages from home, Larkey wrote his father in New Jersey, asking him to send the young guy some treats, which he did. Curtis was quite pleased. On this day, the two of them were lying flat on a forested plateau when a shell crashed into tree branches hurtling deadly steel pieces downward. Larkey was unharmed but a chunk of metal punctured Curtis's helmet and skull. Larkey hurried over to him while yelling frantically, "Medic, medic!" John Marcisin, the medic, came running, looked at Curtis, and asked with irritation: "Why in the hell did you call me? He's dead. Doesn't he look dead to you?" Larkey admitted that Curtis did look dead. Upset, he began to gather up Curtis's personal effects, when he suddenly stopped, realizing he had nowhere to send them. Curtis's death saddened Larkey; he felt personally responsible for this orphan soldier who had endured such a tough life: "I couldn't function and went off to platoon leader Lt. Samuel Lombardo's covered foxhole to be safe and get away for awhile."[41]

Shells kept exploding, causing more casualties. After another tree burst, the cry of "medic" rang out, and Marcisin once again went to check on the new casualty. He found a shell fragment had practically sliced off one GI's shoulder and arm; the soldier was alive but in shock. Marcisin gave him a shot of morphine to ease the pain but "knew he would never make it."[42]

Kampmier was now alone in a hole; "it didn't help the matter any because having someone alongside puts a lot more confidence in you." After each shell burst, he would stick his head up and look around for another GI; "it just made me feel a lot better to see someone else around me." He didn't have any more rations, so he chewed gum and smoked cigarette butts. This situation lasted through the day until his "nerves were surely getting to an end." When it turned dark, tracers from German automatic weapons "were flying thick and fast over my head while I crouched in my two-by-two hole. I wouldn't stick my head out of that hole for anything." Finally an American artillery barrage began; "swish, swish they came over" landing among the Germans, and after the shells stopped falling, the GIs advanced. It was pitch black and Kampmier kept falling down and getting tangled in thick brush, but hearing the platoon yelling and shooting made him "feel good."[43]

The Germans withdrew down a long hill, and the GIs settled in on the top. Kampmier and another GI began digging a new foxhole, but were so tired they only carved out a hole large enough to sit in. They alternated between sleeping and standing guard. By 3:00 A.M. they both fell asleep despite the cold, damp air.

In the morning the sun came out and rations arrived, including a chicken sandwich ("since then I haven't tasted any chicken that tasted

GIs of I Co. 394 in foxhole above Bad Hönningen March 1945 during battle for Rhine bridgehead. Courtesy National Archives and Records Administration.

that good"), and Kampmier was "feeling a lot better considering" the previous day's events. The Germans fired up the hill at them but to little effect. Kampmier decided to crawl to the bank's edge and peer over the side to locate the shooters. Immediately an automatic weapon opened up on him. He recalled, "To this day I can still remember what those bullets felt like as they just skimmed my head. I backed up in a hell of a hurry." Night came and he joined his buddy George Maier in a foxhole. While on guard duty that night he watched American artillery shells exploding below in Bad Hönningen and heard shell fragments ping off the tile roofs. When no guns were firing Kampmier could hear the city clock sound the hours, and it didn't seem to him as though a war was going on.[44]

● ● ●

In Bad Hönningen several hundred German soldiers decided to resist the American incursion. Although undermanned and short of commissioned officers, the 1st Battalion 394 was assigned the task of seizing the city. The battle plan called for two companies to simultaneously attack from the east and north, but as often happened, the operation did not proceed as devised. Able Company became bogged down in an open field until nightfall, and Charlie Company confronted serious resistance as it tried to enter the city from the north. Urban warfare, especially in the dark, heightens danger, tension, and confusion, which happened in Hönningen. Hidden German automatic weapons poured out a steady fire of bullets and red tracers that struck acting company commander Charles Gullette and Sherwood Henry who sobbed, "I don't want to die!" His nightmare unfortunately came to pass. The company pulled back, leaving the mortally wounded behind. The next day, March 17, aided by tanks, King Company, including a newly formed black platoon, captured the city after bitter house-to-house fighting.[45]

• • •

Because of heavy losses during the Battle of the Bulge, Gen. Eisenhower decided to change army policy and ask blacks to volunteer for combat. Black soldiers served primarily as noncombatant service troops, in effect second-class soldiers, replicating their status in civilian life, especially in segregated Southern states. Despite the obvious dangers of choosing to be at the front, several thousand men (including some misfits and troublemakers shipped out by their unit commanders) offered to serve as infantrymen under white officers. Eventually black volunteers formed fifty-three infantry platoons—the 99th Division received one (extra or fifth) platoon in each regiment (King 394, Easy 393, and Easy 395).

Eager to dispel the widely held belief that black soldiers would disappear at the first sign of trouble, these infantrymen, according to Arthur Betts, wanted to show "they could fight as well as white soldiers." Betts, a supply sergeant, and others gave up their sergeant stripes because the army mandated that black soldiers could not outrank their white squad and platoon leaders. Empowered and resentful of past mistreatment, black soldiers proved fierce, "cunning," and brave warriors. Richard Ralston (the white lieutenant who commanded the 5th platoon King Company 394) said, "They had a lust to kill Germans and unlike other troops they did not hunker down in combat." As the 5th platoon was moving toward Hönningen, Stanley

Lambert watched one black soldier shoot a lone German who walked toward the Americans with his hands up. The platoon leader ran up to the GI and reprimanded him for killing the German who might have offered some useful intelligence. The black soldier replied, "It's past 6:00 P.M., past my capturin' time." His attitude was representative of many black soldiers who came to the battlefield filled with hostility. James Strawder confessed: "I had anger in me then, plenty of it, because of the way we was [*sic*] treated [in America and in the army], and I was just fit for killing—anybody, I was just right for it."[46]

Initially greeted with skepticism and insulting remarks ("Hey Sambo" and "night fighter") as they marched south toward Hönningen, their willingness to fight earned black soldiers a respect they encountered nowhere else in white society. Black soldiers also learned that combat forged a unique bond among fellow GIs. When told to drag the corpses of white GIs out of the rain into a shelter, Strawder couldn't understand the logic of the order, since the dead didn't know the difference. But soon he came to understand; "it didn't take me long to see the love they held for one another." In a few days he "was feeling the same way" toward fellow black GIs. Ironically, respect and love flourished where least expected, namely on deadly battlefields.[47]

• • •

On the hill above Hönningen, Fred Kampmier had a bird's eye view of the fighting below, watching GIs overrun the city. Jack Lamb saw tanks roll right up to windows and blast away; "it was like watching a movie." Despite the destruction to the city, Lamb "didn't feel bad for the German people, for they had caused all the trouble."[48]

The next day, March 18, as the sun brightened the hillside near the damaged, thirteenth-century *Schloss* [castle] Arenfels, Fred Kampmier and George Maier crawled out of their foxhole, brushed off the dirt, and sat down to eat K rations. It seemed strange "without shells bursting"; instead, the birds were innocently chirping away as if the whole world slumbered in peace. The battle for Hönningen and the hill had ended, and everyone would have preferred to sit out the rest of the war watching the Rhine River flow by. But it was not to be.

Toward evening Item Company packed up, moved off the hill, and headed south, skirting the city and then going up into the hills once more. The next day, as the Americans ascended a crest, the scouts came under fire and the company immediately attacked, with everyone running on the double some two hundred yards, firing as fast as they could. When the charge came to a halt, one German emerged from the woods with his hands high above his head hollering "*Kamerad.*" But this German never had a chance to surrender; the lieutenant raised his carbine and dropped him with the first shot. As the dying German was giving his last few kicks, a sergeant, spying a wrist watch, ran over and began to pry it off the German even as the mortally wounded soldier's arm kept jerking around, making removal more difficult.[49]

Afterwards a ten-man patrol from Item Company was dispatched to make contact with King Company. The men followed a muddy, winding wagon trail covered with fresh prints of hobnailed boots left by German infantry. Within a mile they came upon six German artillery wagons with horses attached but no enemy soldiers in sight. The patrol moved on until they spotted several enemy artillery pieces, which promptly fired at them. The patrol hustled back to the 3rd platoon, dug foxholes, and went to sleep without any food. The next day the patrol resumed the search for the missing company. They set off along the same trail and came upon the same German wagons, but the horses had been slaughtered by American artillery. The patrol advanced to the village of Hammerstein on the Rhine but failed to connect with King Company. After the futile search, they returned once more to the platoon. Rations finally arrived and at a farmhouse they uncovered a cellar full of cognac which, Kampmier recalled, the boys "really began to enjoy." The next day, relieved by the 2nd Division's 38th Infantry Regiment, the entire regiment walked downstream to the rear, where they rested for three days before resuming what Kampmier called "the rat race across *Deutschland.*"[50]

393RD REGIMENT

The 393rd Regiment departed from Linz on March 12, heading east into rugged, hilly countryside only foot soldiers could conquer. As they marched out of town, Easy Company paused, and Harry Arnold took the opportunity to sit on the stone steps of a house with his back against the front door. Suddenly a kind-faced, middle-aged woman opened the door, smiled, and silently thrust a handful of sardine cans into his hands. Whether this friendly gesture was prompted by a desire to prevent her house from being invaded or was a genuine act of goodwill, Harry appreciated the food, which he distributed to his squad. The columns marched on, trying to shake off the aftereffects of too much wine, cognac, and champagne. Robert Hawn recalled, "You could follow us up the mountain by a trail of empty champagne bottles we left behind."[51]

By afternoon on March 13, the 2nd Battalion reached Ginsterhahn, a drab farm community nestled on the side of a steep ridge some five miles from Linz and nine miles from the Reich Autobahn, the magnificent, four-lane superhighway that ran from Limburg north to the Ruhr cities. As Easy Company left the woods, they approached a pasture sectioned off by barbed wire fences. Upon spotting German soldiers in the village, a nervous scout fired his M-1 at them, and the element of surprise was lost. Alerted, the Germans immediately retaliated with their infamous, deadly MG-42s, sending bullets cracking through tree branches. Hugh Underwood crawled forward to snip the first barbed wire fence, but was caught in the open and killed, as were four others. The platoon leader ordered everyone to charge the village, which they did, rolling under the bottom strand of wire and then running forward with guns blazing. The Germans, no longer eager to die for the Führer, quickly surrendered. The surviving American foot soldiers gathered in a house and enjoyed "a sort of high at having come through unscathed."[52]

This initial encounter lasted less than thirty minutes but incredibly the *New York Times* reported that the First Army had overrun several villages including Ginsterhahn. To *Times* readers this news merited little attention or significance. Certainly it was not a momentous encounter with dramatic consequences, but rather a short-lived firefight, another in a seemingly endless series of clashes, some lasting several hours and still others only minutes, stretching from Belgium to the Danube River and beyond. The men on the ground had to take a stand, sometimes fall back, and then move forward until all German soldiers were dead, wounded, or captured, and Germany surrendered. Day and night the men on the ground performed the dirty business of infantry fighting, enduring weeks of fatigue, physical discomfort, and psychological stress. While this seemingly brief fight in Ginsterhahn had no overarching significance, certainly not to *Times* readers, it mattered to Easy Company. They had suffered casualties and yet achieved their assigned objective, which buoyed a sense of unit pride. It demonstrated to Sgt. Jim Bowers that even though his platoon was filled with replacements, they held together and proved their worth.[53]

Easy Company occupied the village, set up a perimeter defense, and awaited an anticipated German counterattack. That day the platoon of black infantryman joined the group. None of the 2nd Battalion company commanders wanted the blacks, but they joined Easy Company, much to the displeasure of Capt. Daniel Sutherland, who hailed from Mississippi. Sutherland was wounded the next day and left the front, so he never had the opportunity to reevaluate or confirm his views about the fighting ability of black soldiers. Radford Carroll, another southerner, shared similar sentiments about the "negroes," and even considered asking for a transfer, but discovered they were "effective fighters who we were glad to have with us." The black troops were told to dig in, but James Strawder decided to use a foxhole that contained two dead white GIs. He "pulled the bodies out, cleaned out the blood and gore," and jumped in. When the platoon lieutenant came down the line he saw the "two dead white men" pushed off to the side. The lieutenant yelled, "Strawder, I told you to dig a hole, not take one from the dead. I'm going to have trouble with you." Strawder angrily scooped out a new foxhole.[54]

At the crossroads south of the village, Item Company received fire from all directions, including short rounds from Cannon Company. Several GIs were killed or wounded and the cries for medics were heard throughout the day. At one point Al Nelson watched from his foxhole as a "big dumb hillbilly" crawled out with shells dropping all around to snatch the gold watch from a dead GI who lay in the sun. About mid-afternoon, Nelson and his foxhole buddy, John Makridis, decided to leave their foxhole and head for a nearby puddle to scoop up a bit of drinking water. But they never made it; a mortar shell exploded just as they were crawling out. Makridis suffered a nasty wound to his left hip, while Nelson absorbed two pieces of shrapnel in his leg, though he did not know it because he felt no pain. Nelson left to find some help and ran right past company commander William Coke, who was wounded; beside him lay his runner, screaming in great pain, "for in the middle of his forehead was a huge hole" gouged by by a shell fragment. Nelson and Makridis were finally loaded into an ambulance, which soon thereafter crashed into a 6 x 6 truck approaching the front with its lights off. The impact knocked their driver unconscious, and the ambulance sank into the muddy roadside so the back doors would no longer open. After crawling out the front door, the wounded were transferred to another 6 x 6 truck and transported to a crowded evacuation hospital where patients sat on top of filing cabinets, waiting to be treated by two doctors and one nurse.[55]

• • •

In the morning the Germans counterattacked Ginsterhahn with infantry, mortars, and tanks. Robert Waldrep and his squad, who had spent the night in a potato-filled cellar, watched from a house as one of the tanks hit an American machine-gun nest with its main gun, splattering two GIs and throwing a third man out of his foxhole onto the ground "still alive." Upon seeing the machine gunners blown apart, one of Waldrep's men went berserk. When a German Mark IV tank pointed its 75mm gun right at their house, Waldrep ordered his men out the front door while he shot at two German soldiers in a nearby foxhole. The tank fired at the house but its shell could not penetrate the structure's thick stone wall. After Waldrep retreated into the kitchen a German soldier tossed a grenade that sprayed his legs with metal fragments. Waldrep burst out the front door to join his men, who had sought shelter in another farmhouse. An hour later, after the battle died down, he discovered his legs were bleeding; he was evacuated, so "very, very glad" to leave Ginsterhahn and the war.[56]

Guy Duren, a radio operator for the 370th Field Artillery Battalion, crouched in another house with forward observer Lt. Erskine Hightower, who called for a barrage on the German tanks. His request was refused, however, because American troops were too close to the enemy vehicles. Duren peeked out of a window and saw the air filled with tracer bullets and every house in the town on fire with their slate shingles dropping off the roofs. Thinking they would soon be driven from the town or overrun, Duren prepared his own escape; but just as he was about to put a bullet into his radio and take off, the Germans withdrew.[57]

• • •

Experiencing his first action in Ginsterhahn, James Strawder discovered combat was "a whole lot different than I expected it to be, and I was 100 percent scared." In the battle's aftermath another black soldier, Arthur Betts, looked at the German and American dead strewn about the town and found himself wondering, "What have I gotten myself into?" Emerging from a cellar, Radford Carroll came upon the bodies of an old man and two little girls, apparently killed as they tried to run to safety.[58]

Having survived the battle, Carroll and his buddies scoured the town for food, appropriating chickens, home-canned beef, fruit, and "other goodies" from village homes. They brought out a nice tablecloth, china, crystal, candlesticks, and silverware, enjoying a brief return to civilization with a wonderful meal. Afterward the units involved in the fighting moved to the rear and were placed in reserve. Ernest McDaniel of Fox Company remembered lying on his back in a quiet meadow enjoying the warmth of the early spring sun: "For the first time since the long winter, I felt actually alive."[59]

• • •

On March 14, after spending three days in reserve north of Erpel, most of the 395th Regiment boarded trucks that took them to the southern edge of Linz, entering the town at midnight. That morning, the regiment moved east up into the mountains where the 1st and 3rd Battalions ran into heavy German fire from machine guns, mortars, and tanks. Oakley Honey dove into a foxhole to wait out the shelling. Suddenly he heard what sounded like a chicken squawking. He peered out to see Sgt. Dick Richards on his hands and knees making unusual sounds because his lower jaw had almost been sliced off. When Byron Whitmarsh moved forward, he asked the BAR man to shoot out the windows of a house they wanted to enter. As Whitmarsh rose on his knees to locate the target, a German soldier shot him in the upper arm. Since the arm fell limply in his shirt, he assumed it had been taken off; it wasn't, but Whitmarsh would eventually lose nearly two inches of his arm, endure several operations, and spend a year in various hospitals.[60]

One of the regiment's objectives was Stumperich quarry, where a company of infantry and a few tanks from the 11th SS Panzer Division decided to make a stand. The Germans put up stiff resistance and the 395th's attack stalled out for the rest of the day and into the evening. In preparation for a night attack, Item Company and Love Company were told to pull back so the artillery could blast the enemy. But the artillery fire was misdirected and shells fell among the two companies, inflicting casualties and effectively halting the operation.

The next day the 2nd Battalion, including George Company, was given the job of capturing the quarry. Losing their way in morning fog, company commander Harold Hill admitted, they missed the quarry and stumbled upon a German regimental command post located in the hamlet of Hähner. "Everyone thinks you are a hero," Hill commented, "but bad decisions sometimes turn out good."[61]

The fighting was intense, for the Germans defended with their usual assortment of weapons, including tanks. William Galegar heard one "armored monster" clanking down the road to the edge of the village: "If you have never faced one of these armed with rifle and hand grenades, then you don't know what fear is like." When a rocket from a bazooka penetrated the tank's turret, its crew scrambled out and were immediately shot. Galegar and his squad then sprinted one hundred yards to a building in the village. Arriving safely but out of breath and his heart pounding, Galegar looked across the street and there stood two GIs butchering a calf and cooking pieces of meat over a small fire. He understood their behavior, for combat infantrymen sometimes took great chances because fresh food, such as milk, eggs, meat, and bread, became "almost an obsession" when soldiers were "denied them for a long period." Shortly thereafter Galegar and his squad found the hindquarters of a large but unidentifiable animal in the basement of a house they occupied. Galegar thought it might have been a horse, but no one could say for sure. Nor did they care. Soon they, too, were eating cooked meat.[62]

After finishing his meal Galegar was resting outside the house when three German officers, oblivious to his presence, emerged from a building no more than two hundred feet from where he sat and began walking away from him in single file. He grabbed a BAR, rolled over into a shooting position, and lined up the targets as the platoon sergeant yelled, "Shoot, Chief, shoot the sons-of-bitches." Just as he was about to pull the trigger, the lieutenant, for some inexplicable reason, yelled, "Don't shoot!" Galegar held his fire and the Germans escaped without realizing how close they had come to being killed. Galegar was relieved the order had been rescinded because he felt shooting someone in the back, even the enemy, was unjustified and would have haunted him the rest of his life.[63]

Supported by tanks and tank destroyers, the Americans finally overcame enemy resistance in the quarry. Some two dozen Germans were killed in the two-day fight and another ninety surrendered. But the 395th also suffered heavy losses of thirty-four dead. A Luftwaffe medic, who had hidden in a quarry tunnel, surrendered when the firing stopped. As the GIs discussed what to do with him, one soldier began to whet his knife while starring and making threatening gestures at the German, who became visibly upset, but no harm came to him. Other prisoners were not so fortunate. The company commander sent a few captured Germans back with three 5th platoon GIs. The soldiers soon returned, saying an artillery shell had killed their prisoners. The captain knew they were lying, "but I didn't worry about them [the Germans]. You get real hardened."[64]

• • •

The Wied River, which meanders through the picturesque hills and valleys of the Dattenberger Forest, presented the next barrier to overcome. Though neither wide nor deep, the river was swift and icy cold. On March 22, at 11:30 P.M., artillery pounded enemy positions across the river, preparing the way for a midnight assault by the 395th. Al Eckert found the advancing Americans "beautiful to watch in the moonlight," but not everyone shared this sentiment: Virdin Royce was frightened by what he knew lay ahead and thought he "couldn't make it much longer."[65]

As Lambert Shultz and his platoon moved down a ridge toward the river, a mortar shell fell in front of Elbert Cain: "He flew up in the air and plopped down like a sack of potatoes, dead of course." At Camp Maxey, Cain, who was illiterate, had asked Shultz to read and write letters for him. Now, seeing Cain dead, Shultz suppressed an impulse to cry, knowing they "just had to keep going" and make it across the river. In combat, soldiers were not supposed to stop and minister to the wounded or grieve for the dead. Every soldier was expected to continue on with the mission without knowing the fate of the wounded, whom the medics would treat, while Graves Registration would retrieve the dead.[66]

With dawn approaching, Shultz and his unit waded across the river and scrambled up the riverbank on the other side to open ground. An American tank passing in front of the GIs was hit by an antitank gun; it lurched to a halt and began to burn. Shultz watched the action, wondering if the crew would escape. When three of them squeezed out of the vehicle's bottom hatch, "they came running towards us, and we were cheering like we were at a ball game." As he advanced across the battlefield behind another tank Shultz felt an urge to defecate ("can't go around with a load in my pants"), not uncommon among soldiers in combat. Even with shells falling all around, he put down his rifle, took off his combat pack, removed bandoleers of ammunition clips, then his cartridge belt, finally his fatigue jacket, and "dropped his pants just in time." Finished, with no time to cover up his waste, he put on his cartridge belt, jacket, and field pack, picked up his rifle and ran off to rejoin his squad.[67]

An artillery barrage pounded the village of Rossbach, situated on the east side of the Wied River. For Max Norris, a newly arrived replacement, watching artillery crashing into the houses was thrilling. He savored the "textbook perfection of the artillery's box barrage" as it "softened the town up for us." Forty years later Norris returned to a rebuilt Rossbach and found nothing familiar except the town's nineteenth-century church, severely damaged but not destroyed in the war. Walking inside the renovated church he came upon a plaque listing the names of eight civilians, mostly women, who were killed in March 1945. Like all young soldiers Norris had understandably focused on doing his job, fulfilling the expectations of others, winning the war, and going home. There was no time to dwell on destruction and death; in fact, that would have been counterproductive. If a combat soldier had paused to think about the horrible consequences of war, he might have stopped fighting, which the army could not allow. Long afterwards Norris faced a reality he had missed earlier, namely, "wars kill, destroy promise as well as property, rip permanent holes in families, and break hearts."[68]

German soldiers, captured by 395th Regiment, march through heavily damaged Rossbach near Wied River during battle for Rhine bridgehead. Courtesy National Archives and Records Administration.

• • •

That same night the 393rd also crossed the Wied River a few miles south and captured Waldbreitbach by surprise. The 2nd Battalion pushed on over forested hills to Kurtscheid, with the German troops withdrawing as the Americans entered the town. On one street, the GIs found a second-floor shoe store and began to throw shoes down to a crowd of women who scooped up the free footwear, ironically looting for the benefit of enemy civilians.

Fox Company advanced to a small cluster of farm buildings and, drawing rifle fire, put a bazooka round into a barn, which began to burn. Ernest McDaniel saw a squad advance and "felt something of the exuberance of a conquering army, powerful, strong and controlling events rather than being victims." But such an army also caused considerable damage. McDaniel and others were watching the barn burn when several farm women became visibly upset because one burning wall was on the verge of collapsing into their house. The GIs found a long pole and managed to shove the wall away from the house. McDaniel was struck by this paradox of war. One minute they destroyed the women's barn and a few minutes later they struggled to save their home. He recalled how, a few days earlier, his unit came upon a handsome, blonde-haired, young German soldier lying dead in the road. Moving on a short distance, his squad entered a house where a *Hausfrau* served them soup, saying she did not fear American soldiers because she had known several during the American occupation following World War I. McDaniel wondered how she could be so friendly with GIs while a German soldier—a veritable poster boy for the Third Reich—lay dead in the road nearby. Americans, he reflected, were killing Germany's young while being treated like favored houseguests.[69]

• • •

John Hendricks's machine-gun squad hiked up and down forested hills for two weeks without seeing many Germans. They were tired, frustrated, dirty, and sick of existing on K-rations. One night two deserting German soldiers came toward them in the dark, and a sentry shot and killed one instantly. The other soldier ran over to Hendricks, knelt down, grabbed his ankles, and begged for his life. For a moment Hendricks entertained the thought of killing him, "for you become pretty hardened living like an animal. Feelings of mercy disappear pretty fast because the other guy is responsible for your misery." But he did not kill the German, and the prisoner was sent to the rear.

Pushing on, his squad finally emerged from the forest on high ground overlooking the Autobahn: it was like "coming out of nature and reentering civilization." They stood and watched as American trucks and tanks zoomed by, and Hendricks wondered with amazement where they had come from. The next day Hendricks and other members of the 2nd battalion 394 headed east, hopeful that the tide of war had definitely turned.[70]

When Francis Chesnick climbed up the bank to the Autobahn he found himself impressed by the highway he had read about in high school. Soon he and Don Wolfe from Able Company were ordered to scout the village of Willroth some one thousand feet on the other side of the road. The ground leading to the hamlet was flat, treeless, and open, and Chesnick thought, "this could be the end of me." As they approached the village Chesnick told himself, "If I am going to die I want it to happen on a dreary, cloudy day, not a bright, sunny day like this." When they reached the village, the two scouts ran down the single street spraying bullets into the windows of houses. At the end of the village they nervously approached a big barn and were about to fire into it when suddenly a door opened and out walked Easy Company. It was a good day after all.[71]

• • •

The 99th Division had helped secure the bridgehead on the eastern bank of the Rhine at a cost of 271 dead. On March 27, tank destroyers arrived, and the 395th Regiment climbed aboard and motored onto Hitler's Reich Autobahn. It had taken two weeks to move from the west bank of the Rhine to this vital roadway. Not only could some troops ride instead of walk, every rifleman's dream, but also with this added power and mobility, they could bring the war to a speedy conclusion. At least, that's what they hoped.

CHAPTER 7

The Soldier's World

"War that touches our person . . . death that touches our heart. We look for purpose in their happenings. We find no purpose. Instead, we find camaraderie and thought too deep for tears. And, in the long corridors of one life, we hear doors closing forever. Warriors are killed and the sadness is cloaked, in God's own time, by fragile acceptance."

Pfc. Byron Reburn, Love Company/394th
Regiment/99th Infantry Division

• • •

None of the young men who arrived in Europe held a realistic conception of what combat entailed. George Dudley assumed the fighting would resemble the Tom Mix movies he watched as a boy, with exciting gun battles in which his fearless cowboy hero gunned down evildoers with deadly accuracy. Instead Dudley learned the enemy proved difficult to hit, a single gun battle did not determine the outcome, and killing happened at a distance. B. C. Henderson remembered how the bad guys killed off in one Western would reappear in the next. But reality replaced filmic fiction on the battlefield for him: "I realized this time, if you were killed, you weren't coming back."[1]

These new, government-issued soldiers were not eager warriors, but young guys who believed it their duty to serve the country; they would have thought badly of themselves if they had shirked this responsibility. Displeased at being assigned to the infantry, they made the best of the situation. Joseph Thimm's attitude was typical: "I was going to do my job, but I was not looking for trouble." Enlisted men did not view aggressive officers favorably because they feared bold or reckless behavior might have dire consequences. Killing and capturing the enemy was the goal, and soldiers took pride in eliminating combatants, but not by making the ultimate sacrifice. Each soldier became aware of his impotence and realized that his infinitesimal contribution could hardly affect the outcome. So the individual GI tried to perform honorably and yet remain alive.[2]

Their knowledge of the world conflict was limited, though everyone considered Hitler and the Germans to be a dangerous, evil threat. A desire to serve the country informed their thinking but did not motivate them to perform. The army exploited their youth, innocence, and energy. Virdin Royce admitted, "We were just kids. We didn't know any better than to do what we were told." Trained to follow orders, they also persevered because others in the platoon expected them to do so. Henri Atkins confessed, "We wanted to show up well, to appear fearless while inside we were scared to death. As a soldier you do not wish to let your buddies down." Terrified like everyone else by artillery barrages, Francis Chesnick held his ground because the "guy next to you was doing his duty, so you had to do yours. If you stayed down or stayed behind, the guys would think less of you." Al Eckert confessed, "I was scared shitless but I was worried what people would say." Combat required masculine skills and behavior, which placed extreme demands on each soldier to prove his virility. Self-respect and the respect of peers weighed heavily on conscientious soldiers, who were forced to stay until dead, wounded, or the war ended.[3]

Combat proved to be a dirty, difficult, deadly enterprise, especially for those who manned the front lines. The most dangerous and arduous duty befell a minority of all men in the Army. The possibility of being violently killed or seriously wounded created stress, apprehension, fear, and at times heart-pounding terror, which no one anticipated before arriving in a combat zone. Rex Whitehead learned, "War is not thrilling or exciting but consists of misery and being scared to death." Even men with considerable infantry training were not ready for the physical hardships and psychological demands of ground warfare. Seeing fellow soldiers and close friends killed, sometimes in the most horrific manner, challenged mental stability and moral integrity. Joseph Herdina admitted he was "emotionally unprepared for the brutality of war." Living in primitive conditions, while facing an enemy who wanted to kill them, placed extreme demands on individuals who arrived from a safe, "civilized" environment. Survival required combat soldiers to become hardened, even benumbed, to death and destruction, or else they could not function.[4]

Staying alive and intact meant learning in a hurry under pressure even as the army kept enlisted men uninformed about where they were, what enemy forces they faced, and what the division's military plans entailed. Each platoon often operated in isolation from other units, and combat for the average soldier often consisted of a series of isolated encounters between relatively small groups of combatants. As Patrick Morrisey commented, "You have no sense of the grander scale. A soldier is only aware of what is happening in his little area." Living each hour as it came, the combat infantryman usually did not know the day or the date and didn't care. He only focused on the demands each day brought. Few planned for the future, but most individuals remained optimistic they would pull through amidst the omnipresence of death.[5]

Although artillery, tanks, and fighter-bombers could and did provide effective support, an infantryman needed to fend for himself, in concert with others, to survive. There was an adjustment period in which the GI became adept at learning enemy artillery firing patterns, spotting enemy positions, and determining the origin of small-arms fire by sound. Combat accelerated the learning process and taught the soldier to react automatically and adapt quickly to new situations. Over time, according to William Galegar, "our perceptions and reactions became quicker. Your senses became more attentive to signals or conditions of danger." Unusual sounds or the complete absence of noise raised the alert level for the veteran soldier. T. J. Cornett developed a sixth sense: "I would suddenly feel I needed to move, and I would move. Sometimes nothing would happen but still I obeyed that sense of danger." While no one was safe from unexpected, random violence, the veteran acquired experience and hunches that increased the odds of surviving, or so he had to believe. "It was in the back of your mind that you might get hit," Joseph Hineman recounted, "but you thought your skills would get you through." (In Hineman's case a shell exploded near him, severely damaging his right leg, which he lost.) If the enemy refused to abide by the Geneva Convention, a GI's odds of escaping injury and death declined appreciably. Tilden Head was struck when Germans opened fire with machine guns from the basement windows of a hospital: "It had never entered my mind that I would be shot. But here I was, covered in blood, paralyzed from the waist down, feeling no pain." Head's real struggle took place in four hospitals where he underwent six operations, in which he lost one kidney and half his stomach.[6]

Combat did not involve continual firefights and artillery exchanges. Short periods of adrenaline-pumping action, when artillery and mortar shells exploded and bullets punctured the air, interrupted long periods of inactivity, digging, waiting, and walking. The range of emotional responses varied by individual and situation. Paul Jillson maintained, "We were observant and scared, but it was not high pressure all the time; otherwise you would go nuts." Veteran soldiers learned to function during times of stress and dread, but not always. "Some days you behaved with little fear," Walter Kellogg confessed, but on other occasions "it was barely possible to demonstrate responsibility toward others, and you behaved shamefully." No one could be heroic every day, and given the right circumstances, fear could invade the psyche of the steadiest soldier. The frontline soldier repeatedly balanced two opposing demands; he wanted to preserve his life and yet carry out an assignment that put his life in jeopardy.[7]

GIs who trained at Camp Maxey and endured the long trip to the front developed close relationships, especially within the platoon. Rex Whitehead perceived a big difference after they reached the front. At Maxey soldiers acted "indifferent, cocky and rude," but on the front lines men "were more kind and thoughtful; perhaps we thought in combat we had to take care of each other." Harold Schaefer noticed the squabbles of training days became muted in Europe: "You overlooked personality conflicts out of a great desire to remain alive." Each man needed the others, fostering interdependence more crucial in combat than in daily affairs back home. Eugene Eldridge avowed, "I never lost that sense of connection to the squad I started with. You can't survive alone in a combat situation." Enduring physical deprivation and psychological stress together strengthened relationships among soldiers in the squad and platoon that rear echelon soldiers could not develop. Paul Jillson said the squad was like a family: "You were connected to some of them more closely than to your own brothers." If a soldier found a buddy or two, and they stayed together on the front for a considerable length of time, the personal ties could

become extremely strong. Frontline combat could produce cooperation and brotherhood, the antithesis of the competition and individualism of civil society. After the war, men returned to hometowns and
resumed their individual lives, competing with others for a foothold.
The war created an unusual emotional bonding experience that could
not be recreated.[8]

Because the military and the war were impersonal, connecting with
others was advisable, even necessary. Removed from family, wives, and
close friends, the infantryman found his psychic and physical support
in the twelve-man squad. The group soldiered far from normal society
and the safe world of the rear. The front was frontier territory, like
the Wild West, with its own official and unofficial norms and rules.
Frontline soldiers almost became a different species, looking, talking,
and behaving in ways foreign to those who supported them behind
the lines. Tough, independent, gritty, and potentially dangerous, they
operated much like outsiders as the army's vanguard. These infantrymen took pride in their ability to survive in the harsh, spartan conditions of the front, despite the leadership's apparent lack of concern
for their suffering. The squad and platoon became the combat soldier's family, shielding him from uncertainties and fears that might
otherwise have overwhelmed him.

And yet combat conditions constantly assaulted the stability of
the group. Men left because of sickness, combat fatigue, wounds
(occasionally self-inflicted), and sometimes for disciplinary action. It
was unsettling. One day a member of the squad or platoon, including
officers, would be gone or missing in action. Ignorance and uncertainty permeated the unit's existence. As the war dragged on, unit
cohesion weakened. Luckily enemy forces disintegrated faster.

Combat riflemen not only suffered the most casualties, held the
lowest ranks, earned the smallest salaries, they also endured great
physical hardships, for rifle companies walked miles over rugged
ground carrying combat packs, ammunition, and weapons, including
mortars and machine guns. These soldiers mostly lived outdoors,
frequently enduring rain, mud, snow, and bitterly cold temperatures
without showers, haircuts, sanitary drinking water, and toilets; consequently, they smelled awful and frequently became sick. Unheated,
prepackaged rations never satiated a desire for fresh, hot food. Battalion

commanders launched night or predawn attacks, robbing GIs of needed sleep. In addition, all enlisted men had to dig foxholes and spend hours on guard duty, an onerous, boring task that reduced rest time. Most importantly infantry soldiers had minimal control over their lives; they were at risk from enemy attacks and subject to orders from army commanders.

Divisional, regimental, and battalion officers, who planned strategy and assigned objectives, rarely visited the front lines (with some notable exceptions) and therefore lacked direct connection with combat troops and the battlefield conditions they faced. For frontline soldiers, company grade officers (captains and lieutenants) mattered, not only in making decisions that saved lives (of course there were limits to what could be done) but also in maintaining morale. Platoon sergeants and squad leaders counted because they lived and fought in the muck and snow alongside the men.

William Galegar offered high praise for platoon leader Charles McNish and company commander Lt. Harold Hill because they "used their positions to improve the quality of life for the enlisted man." If combat soldiers trusted an officer's ability, and he seemed to have their welfare in mind, they would follow his commands more readily. The men in the 2nd Platoon Fox 393 had great confidence in and affection for Lt. Joseph Kagan (referred to as "Little Joe"): he treated the men with respect, led patrols, and made good decisions. Lieutenant Samuel Lombardo, a patriotic Italian immigrant who successfully navigated his platoon through a snow-covered minefield, exuded self-confidence and inspired trust. Although only a platoon leader, he actually ran Item Company 394. One of Lombardo's men, James Larkey, said, "We believed that Sam would keep us alive" through his judgment and leadership. If Sam made a request, his men would do it without hesitation or grumbling, a frequent response by enlisted men denied other means to express their unhappiness. Larkey confessed, "I knocked myself out to carry out Sam's orders, and I believed everyone else did the same." Once Lombardo told Larkey, acting as first scout, to reconnoiter the other side of an open field. Larkey perceived this might be a hazardous assignment but did not express his misgivings. As he slowly plowed alone though deep snow, he thought to himself, "If there are any Germans hiding amongst those trees, they can cut me down easily." But Lombardo had asked, and therefore Larkey would carry out the assignment regardless of the consequences. Fortunately for him, the enemy had departed.[9]

Any organization, especially one with a gigantic bureaucratic structure, always has its share of incompetent managers unable to perform the tasks and fulfill the responsibilities thrust upon them. In extreme situations, where lives hung in the balance, the fitness of officers proved crucial. Some GIs, whether justified or not, rendered negative assessments of their officers. Duane Shipman met "thankfully some good officers, but too many were not, and they treated the enlisted men as some lower life-form." Robert Walter considered officers "an alien species and the enemy responsible for everything bad." As the war continued, and 2nd lieutenants increasingly became casualties, the replacement officers, unless they came from the ranks and received a battlefield commission, lacked the necessary experience to reach good decisions. In many instances platoon sergeants and squad leaders carried the burden of leadership at the tactical level.[10]

• • •

Officers faced their own challenges, including ordering men to carry out perilous, sometimes ill-advised assignments passed down from higher authorities. Lieutenant Joseph Kagan observed that the men developed close relationships with each other, whereas a platoon leader or a company commander didn't have a foxhole buddy. Some officers wondered if the men respected them. Platoon sergeant Isadore Rosen thought the men didn't like him; only after the war did he learn otherwise.

Platoon leaders faced the unenviable task of writing letters to the deceased's parents. Lieutenant Richard Martin found it "hard to do," for he wanted to "say something that made them feel good," even though nothing could assuage the pain of their loss. The best company grade officers spent time among the men, sharing privation and stress but with the added pressure of demonstrating steadiness. Joe Kagan confessed, "You couldn't show you were scared" or appear unnerved. Lieutenant Art Clark was surprised and embarrassed that "I would get as scared as I did. I wanted to set an example, but sometimes I was shaking so badly during an artillery bombardment that I couldn't hide it." Exhibiting a calm, brave demeanor required an officer to be in control or appear so. Battalion commander McClernand Butler admitted he couldn't talk to anyone and reveal his "feelings and fears." The price of rank could be isolation and loneliness.[11]

• • •

Many of these young men had never seen a corpse before reaching the battlefield. Those who had attended funerals of grandparents or elderly relatives witnessed a dignified setting that honored the dead in a solemn ceremony in which the deceased resembled the living person. At the front GIs saw bodies (American and German) ripped to shreds with innards spewed on the ground, a revolting travesty committed against human dignity. It was felt that, in death, the human body ought to remain whole, not chopped up into pieces. The dead often lay scattered in muddy ditches and snowy fields, like discarded animal carcasses; and when the bodies were collected, stacked like cordwood in the back of 6 x 6 trucks, and hauled away to military graveyards, few combat soldiers could ignore the realization that death on the battlefield would result in a lonely, undignified ending.

During training soldiers learned how to kill from afar and up close. In combat, however, the enemy frequently remained distant and difficult to spot. The army emphasized marksmanship ("don't shoot until you have a target") over firepower (spraying an area), and the eight-shot, semi-automatic M-1 rifle limited the deadliness of the individual soldier, though most soldiers liked their rifle and considered it superior to the German bolt-action Mauser. (The Germans also possessed rapid-fire machine pistols or submachine guns that a few Americans coveted, especially when attacking towns.) The lack of firepower, dangers of exposure, and difficulty in spotting enemy soldiers caused GIs to use their weapons sparingly. Shooting stationary targets in training did not replicate chaotic conditions on the battlefield; moreover, three days on the firing range could hardly produce expert marksmen. George Meloy described one incident that illustrated the difficulty of hitting a moving target. Two Germans on a motorcycle with a sidecar headed unawares toward Item Company 393. Orders were passed along: "Hold your fire. Wait until they get closer and then fire!' The GIs waited patiently and then opened fire, producing a resounding blast that "let the enemy, two German soldiers strong, have a sample of our best marksmanship." The noise alone might well have frightened the two to death, but it didn't. The Germans jumped from the motorcycle and ran for their lives, disappearing over the crest of the hill to safety.[12]

• • •

Army training inculcated a kill-or-be-killed mentality, and government propaganda depicted the enemy as monstrously inhumane, which 99ers learned was true in certain instances. Initial indifference toward the Germans turned into hatred when shells exploded and GIs died. As James Langford said, "When someone is shooting at you and after someone is shot, you are ready to tear everybody apart." Byron Whitmarsh asserted, "The more you put up with crap, artillery coming in and they're shooting at you, the more you hated the Germans." Anger and fear made it easier to pull the trigger, fire the rocket, and drop a mortar shell in the tube. In combat situations soldiers reacted instinctively out of a desire to survive, and fighting could produce indifference to German deaths.[13]

What under normal conditions would be considered unthinkable and criminal became accepted in wartime; in fact, killing the enemy brought praise and medals. Joseph Herdina shot a German soldier riding a motorcycle. He walked over and took his wristwatch even as the German was dying: "I found no pleasure in shooting him. I even felt sorry for him, but there was nothing to be done." Stealing in civilized society was not considered such in war, but rather collecting trophies. A soldier was expected to behave in an upright manner toward members of his group, while ethical rules of civilized society need not apply toward the enemy, civilian or military. Food sent from home or found in German homes should be shared, while "souvenirs" and war booty belonged to the individual who seized them, in short, a male society that sanctioned cooperation and competition. War changed the rules and the mindset of infantrymen.[14]

In Höfen, William Huffman caught sight of a German soldier peeking around the corner of a house. When the German's cheek became visible, Huffman squeezed off a round; the German screamed and pitched forward into the snow with wooden splinters in his face. Still alive, the German stretched forward, "perhaps searching for the grenade he had dropped as he fell." Huffman aimed his M-1 behind the man's armpit and fired his rifle once more. "The German jerked once and then lay still." Huffman felt no remorse. He calmly smoked a cigarette "while a human being lay dead in the snow a few yards away. That was war. This brief interchange had been purely impersonal."[15]

In the village of Gleidorf, Lt. Jackson Goss came face-to-face with an SS trooper. Goss emptied his M-1 into the German before the trooper could react. He rolled the dead German over on his back, crossed his arms on his chest and put a flower in one hand, transforming a traditional gesture of respect into one of disdain. Word of Goss's action spread, and other GIs amused themselves in Gleidorf by imitating this belittling practice. Reducing dead German soldiers to objects of derision depersonalized the enemy and made killing him easier.[16]

Not everyone reacted so coldly. In Gleidorf William Blasdel refrained from shooting two retreating German soldiers who were in his sights at a distance of 150 yards because one was helping his wounded buddy. Many GIs would not understand Blasdel's aversion to shooting enemy soldiers. And yet the decent, humane self could not be extirpated, at least in most individuals. Antitank gunner Stanley Lambert watched as two older German soldiers tried to escape in a horse-drawn wagon. He aimed his 57mm gun at the wagon, zeroed in, but decided not to blast them: "These two guys were not a threat and despite your training, you retained a sense of right and wrong. And killing them would have been wrong." Subconsciously the individual soldier struggled to reconcile two worlds and their divergent demands and pressures. Different situations produced different actions, but many men did not lose their moral compass.[17]

The ordinary enlisted man, who occupied the bottom of the military hierarchy and was subject to orders from those higher on the ladder, sometimes felt unappreciated and neglected, especially because they endured the greatest hardships and dangers. Unhappy about the situation, GIs directed their frustration at the enemy, who was ultimately viewed as causing their misery.

At times infantrymen could enjoy freedom from officer supervision. Armed and operating with few restraints, the GI was empowered to do pretty much what he wanted. James Langford commented, "We did feel a sense of power. We had guns, and we knew how to use them, and there were some who did use that power to benefit themselves and push people around." Radford Carroll admitted to "a feeling of power and also a feeling of being anonymous—we were away from our homes and looked like all other soldiers."[18]

Occupying German territory permitted GIs to behave in a fashion that would be considered illegal and morally unacceptable. On Thanksgiving Day 1944, soon after troops arrived in Höfen and even before serious fighting began, a group of GIs butchered several cows and sat down in an unoccupied German home to an elaborate feast complete with linen tablecloth, crystal glasses, and fine china. When the meal was over "four men picked up the four corners of the tablecloth and threw the entire thing out the window—glasses, linen, plates and all." Operating in a world in which the normal rules of correct behavior no longer applied, senseless acts of vandalism could be rationalized as payback against an enemy people, and no authority figure was around to raise objections, even if they cared. Lindell Sawyers recalled, "This was a time when the rules of back home were not observed; it was like recess time." Charles Swann confessed, "We stole from German civilians, ransacked their houses and took everything of value, especially booze. We ransacked out of anger and a chance to get even; we were lawless and we could get away with it." The lowly GI found some compensation at the front where he could steal, destroy, and even kill without fear of retribution or punishment.[19]

When Lt. Col. Butler, commander of 3rd Battalion 395, began a tour of the front lines at Höfen, he and an aide came upon a dead German who had been dumped in a wheelbarrow. The aide, noticing the dead soldier had gold in his teeth, told Butler he would extract the precious metal later. When they returned, however, they saw someone else had already performed the dental work. The aide complained to Butler, "Someone stole my gold."[20]

Most GIs considered Germans, including civilians, to be enemies. Leon Rogers confessed he didn't care about German civilians: "I threw grenades into houses, and it didn't bother me. I hated them all and had as much fear of an old couple as a German soldier." Frank Hoffman watched houses burn to the ground, and he disliked the destruction, "but they deserved it." Angry and consumed with hostility, Y. B. Johnson wanted payback for the "miserable days" spent in combat. He grabbed linens, china, and silverware that he intended to send home: "Since the Germans stole most of it, why not us?" After finding

Red Cross packages in the "best German houses," Johnson avowed, in an angry letter to home, "my muddy boots will walk on the best rugs in town." Emmett Jackson watched men go into houses looking for treasure and souvenirs and end up sailing a record collection through the air into walls: "It seemed if they couldn't use it, they would destroy it."[21]

Competition among GIs for valuables and souvenirs motivated men to seize goods from prisoners and ransack homes. Earl Slyder said, "We knew we could take anything we wanted, and no one [in authority] would object." Additional weight, however, limited an infantryman's ability to haul loot. Slyder devised a solution to solve that problem and increase his take. He gave it to the cooks to carry in their truck with the understanding they could keep his "booty" in the event he was killed or wounded. Later, while on a looting expedition, Slyder stopped a German command car, but one of the officers got out and shot him. Now wounded, Slyder became upset about leaving the front because "the fighting was easy and the looting was good."

Being sent to a battalion aid station and a hospital usually resulted in the loss of loot, for medics often confiscated valuables from the wounded and dead. Charles Swann complained, "the "medics stole all my money and the watch given to me by my brother, who had been killed." When Peter Wolffe landed in an evacuation hospital after being hit by a mortar shell, the medics took his watch, Luger pistol, and other souvenirs.[22]

A few officers would not tolerate looting. After members of George Company broke into a large wooden safe and removed a dozen women's watches as well as jewelry and German marks, the owners came back and asked for their possessions. Lieutenant Harold Hill made his men return the stolen property to the German couple. Captain Horace Phillips had a soldier court-martialed for shaking down a civilian: "I thought it was highway robbery." Company commander Erskine Wickersham, who "couldn't stand thievery," came up to a wounded German soldier and noticed his watch missing. He screamed at the medics, "One of you bastards took his watch. Put it back on his wrist!" While squad leader William Blasdel allowed his men to break mirrors and tip over china cupboards, he chewed out one replacement who cut off the ring finger of a German to secure a wedding band; this barbarous act of mutilating a body out of greed, even the enemy's, seemed a gross violation of civilized standards. Later when an artillery shell blew off four of the replacement's toes, Blasdel considered it just retribution.[23]

• • •

Frontline units in the army sometimes shot prisoners; the massacre at Malmedy in particular gave license to exact revenge. The occurrence of these incidents depended on a number of factors, including the behavior and reputation of the enemy and the emotions of individual GIs. After the loss of a buddy, combat soldiers were not so resistant to killing captured Germans, usually referred to as "fucking Krauts." One GI admitted he "killed German soldiers who were trying to give up. The meanest man in the world is a mad GI. I have remorse for what I have done, but that was my mindset at the time." Radford Carroll acknowledged, "We were animals, and we were dangerous. We could kill at any time. We were selfish and didn't consider the welfare of others, only our own comfort and safety." Carroll acknowledged there was no danger of being punished for transgressions, so an enemy soldier relied on the mercy of his captors.[24] James Langford commented, "You live like an animal and also at times act like an animal. I am sure all combat soldiers at one time or another did things that later they were ashamed of and were never mentioned again." The combat soldier, who killed enemy soldiers or witnessed executions, could put it out of his mind in the midst of battle. But afterwards, when action slowed down, or later after returning home and settling in, some GIs found it difficult to forget or repress memories of those killings.[25]

When a group of GIs trapped a German soldier in the loft of a barn in Höfen, they ordered him to drop his rifle and come down, which he did. Then someone in the group shot him. He was an older German conscript, and Joseph Herdina recalled, "We looked in his wallet and there was a photo of two young girls. I didn't expect this to happen. I believed in fair play. I thought it was murder, but no one said anything." Richard Weaver watched two German soldiers raise their hands and walk toward the American lines. But a couple of GIs opened fire and killed them. Weaver recounted, "It made me realize that we weren't always the noble liberators." Robert Justice saw a fellow GI go up to a German soldier who had been shot in the stomach and was writhing in pain. The GI simply ignored the

German's suffering and went through his pockets, "cleaned him out and he wasn't even dead. I never got to that stage."[26]

Even though the American army trained and used snipers, German snipers were despised and could not expect to survive if cornered or captured. According to B. C. Henderson, "a sniper is kind of like somebody slipping up behind your back and taking you out without a chance to defend yourself." Well-concealed, hard to locate, and a specialist in killing, according to William Galegar, the sniper represented a "much bigger factor" than just another enemy soldier with a rifle. Fred Gole recalled how everyone in his unit became upset when a sniper killed company commander Joseph Jameson. Subsequently a group of Germans were captured. The first sergeant told the GI escorts to take the prisoners back to regimental headquarters and return in five minutes. Since headquarters was located some distance behind the lines, the unspoken message was to eliminate the prisoners, which they did. On other occasions, prisoners were shot simply because the escorts didn't want to walk them back to a holding cage. This wasn't army policy and most soldiers would not partake in such killings, but they did happen, and no one was ever court-martialed for these offenses.[27]

An enlisted man, lacking rank and authority, could hardly file formal charges against a GI who committed murder or rape. To remonstrate against an unnecessary shooting might indicate to others the critic lacked the manly toughness necessary to be a real soldier. But even officers ignored executions. Captain Raymond Talbird, company commander of Able Company 395, came upon a scene where a number of Germans had been killed by artillery. When one wounded German soldier suddenly propped himself up on one elbow and lit a cigarette, a GI shot him dead. Talbird pretended not to see the killing: "If I would have brought charges against him, I would have lost a man at the front; besides, the German may have died anyway."[28]

Once, near the end of the war, squad leader Paul Jillson and his men spotted an unarmed German soldier running away from them. One man raised his rifle, but Jillson ordered him not to shoot; however, other squad members pumped bullets into the German. Jillson commented, "Killing that one guy wouldn't have made a difference, but that's what we were trained to do."[29]

When Radford Carroll took aim at a German scout, fired a round and saw the enemy soldier flop over backwards, he was exuberant: "I felt like I had won first prize, and I had done my duty." When the German suddenly jumped up and scooted safely away, Carroll became disgusted with himself and then bitterly disappointed. Nevertheless, Carroll was no cold-blooded killer. Later, accompanied by a prisoner, he came upon a German soldier who had been struck in the head, chest, stomach, and knee. The severely wounded man was not likely to survive, so Carroll asked the German prisoner if he would shoot his compatriot. The German refused, so the burden was placed on Carroll. Even though it would have been a mercy killing, "I could not bring myself to shoot."[30]

The majority of 99ers did not kill and those who did found little pleasure in it, particularly up-close killings that made it difficult to deny the humanity of the enemy. During the German assault at Höfen, Robert Smith shot a German soldier at the edge of his fox-hole, and the German fell over the parapet and began thrashing about. Smith then shot him three more times, screaming, "Die, you bastard!" When he discovered the next morning the dead soldier was a handsome youth, he would not touch the body. During the Bulge, after mortars bombarded enemy positions, Leroy Wagner saw "pieces of German soldiers hanging from the trees like Christ-mas ornaments"; one German officer remained alive, even though his forehead was split open and his brains were leaking out. "Angry, confused and keyed up," Wagner decided to smash the German's head in with a rifle, but the medic stopped him; he later learned gratefully the German had lived.[31]

In tense combat situations, soldiers reacted instinctively out of a strong desire to survive. But such actions, even those wholly justified, often burdened the combat soldier with troubling memories. When Charlie Swann killed several Germans in a machine-gun nest he was at first exhilarated; afterwards, however, he thought about the men he had killed, admitting "it bothered me." Leroy Wagner shot a young German soldier who turned "snow white in color" and then died. A couple of days later "I thought about that kid I had killed." After killing a German infantryman, Edgar Henson turned the body over and looked through the dead man's wallet. Upon finding a photo of his wife and children and a letter to his wife, Henson became upset. In the Ruhr pocket Jack Stevens ran across a street and jumped behind a three-foot wall near a church. All at once he saw someone running for the rectory: "I cut him down with my BAR; it turned out to be the parish priest running for cover." Decades later he sadly remembered that unfortunate killing.[32]

Robert Hawn shot a German who was about to throw a grenade at him: "I watched him die. He didn't die right away and later I had nightmares about it." In the Ruhr a machine gunner, spotting a group of Germans, ran forward, set up his gun and sprayed the soldiers. James Bussen saw a German boy catch a bullet in the eye: "He ran around in a circle screaming in pain until he fell over dead." The sight of this horrible death left him shaken and convinced him that war was senseless. Radioman Fred Verdecchio carried a .45-caliber M-3 submachine gun (or "grease gun") whenever he moved forward with the artillery observer. When Verdecchio and the observer came to a building, they kicked open the door, encountering five young members of the Hitler Youth with their backs to them. Suddenly one of the teenagers turned around, and in his anxiety, Verdecchio opened up with his grease gun: "It was terrible, bullets tearing through their bodies, and they screamed and blood was everywhere. I had forgotten the terrible damage the gun could cause. It shook me up, and I sat down feeling lousy."[33]

James Tolmasov and other squad members entered a house with plans to evict the occupants, an elderly couple, and spend the night. All at once they heard shots. Rushing outside, they discovered a BAR gunner from another squad had fired at someone moving behind some trees; it turned out to be the couple's young grandson. While Tolmasov and the others became upset over the boy's death, the shooter seemed proud of himself. When the grandfather carried the dead boy into the house, Tolmasov and the others decided they could not stay there.[34]

Robert Story and his squad happened upon four Germans soldiers whom they could have killed. Instead they shot around them, and the startled Germans dropped their weapons. He later wrote, "As I have reflected back over the years on this incident, I have been so glad that we let our consciences be our guide and did not take the lives of those men."[35]

It was much easier to accept the slaying of German soldiers—after all, they were killing Americans—but civilian deaths bothered most GIs. After entering a village that had been shelled, tough Cyrus Wells became unnerved when he saw a "seven-year old German girl in a blue dress carrying her two-year old dead sister." Alfred Schnitzer watched a bazooka rocket slam into a house and set it on fire. Trapped inside was a woman who began screaming in agony: "it was one of the most devastating experiences I remember. Just the dark night lit by the fire of the house and accented with the screaming—impossible to forget." William Galegar rushed into a house and came upon a dead grandmother sitting in a motionless rocking chair. She bore no visible wounds though a shell had crashed into her bedroom. Galegar surmised she had died of shock, alone in her own house. Seeing this innocent victim of war disturbed him as much as any death on the battlefield.[36]

Sometimes the most upsetting death scenes involved animals trapped by the destructive forces of war. As Rex Whitehead rode in a jeep on a road that twisted through a narrow canyon, he came upon a column of German horse-drawn supply wagons that had been destroyed by strafing U.S. aircraft. Evidently, Whitehead concluded, the fighters had caught the convoy with no place to hide and raked it with .50-caliber machine-gun bullets that blasted huge holes in the hapless animals. Whitehead found himself deeply disturbed by the cruelty and pain inflicted upon the animals. Byron Reburn became distressed when he entered a village square at night and saw two Sherman tanks "burning like giant candles" that illuminated a small, abandoned group of agitated sheep bleating in fear. For Reburn the scene dramatized the "biblical innocence of the sheep" trapped in the "violence of war." A few days later Reburn again happened upon a blameless animal casualty. Love Company was walking down a winding road on a spring day when suddenly a saddled but riderless horse with a polished harness came galloping toward them. The troops stopped the "sleek and innocent" horse with blood pumping from a single head wound. Although the fate of the rider and how this magnificent horse came to be so badly injured would remain a mystery to Reburn and his buddies, they understood all too well that the war would soon claim the life of yet another innocent creature.[37]

• • •

The slaying of American soldiers impacted the survivors, even when the dead were strangers and the circumstances of their demise remained clouded; but then ignorance often accompanied death in combat. Walking along one peaceful, sunny morning, Byron Reburn and his machine-gun section came to a turn in the road where several recently killed GIs "lay like discarded toys" along its edge. Reburn had not heard any shellfire, and he wondered what brief and violent drama had unfolded there a few hours earlier. The contrast was not lost on him: "the beauty of the day and the beast of death." No one in his group said anything, and they marched on, the silence disturbed only by the dull thud of rubber-soled combat boots as they trudged on toward the next hill.[38]

Grisly deaths proved particularly difficult to bear. Wayne Cleveland remembered painfully how a young, married GI with a one-year-old son accidentally blew himself up when a grenade hanging on his jacket snagged a barbed wire fence and exploded. Joseph Herdina could not forget how his best buddy Paul Kreider Jr., a "sensitive, sophisticated son of a college professor," was killed by a German machine gun. Richard Gorby watched a mortar shell fall under a scout, ripping off most of his head except for the face: "it looked like a body holding a false face about his shoulders. I kind of wish I had never looked at him because he wasn't a very good sight."[39]

One afternoon Steve Kallas led his squad into a village searching every house for enemy soldiers, kicking in doors and throwing grenades into the basements. As they turned the corner of a street, an enemy tank opened fire, wounding one man, a new replacement, whom someone dragged into a house. Everyone then beat a hasty retreat. Once the squads had reached safety, the mortar section lobbed white phosphorous shells into the town, setting many houses on fire. Later that night the platoon leader selected Kallas and two other men to return and find the wounded man. As Kallas and his companions edged quietly along the darkened street, they suddenly heard the metallic clank of a gun being cocked. Frightened and uncertain which house the wounded man was in, they decided to leave and return in daylight. The next morning they came to almost the same spot where they had been the previous night. Kallas went into a house and discovered the remains of the GI, his body badly burned with most of the flesh gone and a pickax stuck in his head. Kallas was haunted afterwards, not only by the recurring image of the dead GI, but also by the thought they might have saved the man's life if they hadn't waited until morning to retrieve him.[40]

Lambert Shultz and his buddy, James Jackson, the BAR gunner, were walking together uphill through tall timber when they received rifle fire. Jackson instantly dropped to the ground. All at once Shultz heard a loud explosion very close by, which he assumed a mortar shell had caused. Then, to his horror, he realized Jackson had been hit in the head just below his helmet, and the loud noise came from a bullet that had forcefully shattered the skull: "In a half minute Jackson gurgled and died. His death was the low point for me. I actually broke down and cried. Why did they not shoot me?" The death of a friend produced sadness, and yet there was no opportunity for prayer. In combat the survivor had to keep moving; grieving for a slain buddy had to be postponed. An unspoken feeling of relief passed through the survivor's mind because the bullet had missed him, but he often had to deal with a sense of guilt for having been spared the cruel randomness of death.[41]

• • •

Most everyone wanted to escape the front, but not, of course, in a body bag. The most honorable reason to leave was to be wounded, but hopefully not severely. Albert Eckert "preferred to die rather lose a leg or my eyes. What woman would want a disabled man?" Men wished for the "million-dollar wound—a slight wound that led to evacuation was worth that princely sum. It was considered acceptable but not heroic to leave if you became very sick or got frozen feet. Mel Richmond, whose feet froze, "was glad to get out of there, and I did not want to go back." Hershel Kennedy's feet turned black, and he left Elsenborn Ridge on Christmas Day: "I was happy to be out of there. I did the best I could." Transferred to England for a foot wound, Charles Swann would hang his foot over the edge of the bed before the doctor arrived so his toes would turn purple. It worked, and he was not sent back to the front. One day the doctor told him he could stop dangling his feet as he was going home.

After being wounded Stewart Fischer entertained "a small feeling of remorse at leaving the platoon, but this was far outweighed by the feeling of relief that I was getting out of the snow." Wounded early in the Bulge, Jack Prickett was sent to England. In March he had an opportunity to return to his unit, but an Irish doctor offered him the option of being placed on limited service in the air force: "I chickened out and decided to stay." In April Prickett learned his best friend Miller had been killed. Thereafter he was haunted by the thought that his return to combat could have prevented Miller's death.[42]

Most GIs welcomed the opportunity to escape combat; others, however, recovering from wounds in a hospital, missed their platoon and wanted to return to the front. Don Wallace, who had to leave Elsenborn with an infected hand, "felt like I was deserting my buddies. Boy, I missed them." When Joseph Herdina ended up in a ward, he became bored and lonely: "I wanted to get back; the company was my home." So he asked to rejoin his outfit early even though he hadn't completely healed. Walter Kellogg also left his hospital bed and returned to the second battalion but found it "sobering to go down the list of those killed and wounded while I was away." Byron Whitmarsh, who was seriously wounded in the Rhine bridgehead, wished he could return, as he was "homesick for the company."[43]

On January 17, while sitting in a foxhole on wintry Elsenborn Ridge, Plt. Sgt. Harold Schaefer learned he had won the "lottery prize," namely a seven-day pass to Paris. Rounding up a stash of cigarettes, chewing tobacco, and chocolate candy, he rode back to division headquarters at Camp Elsenborn and hopped aboard a 6 x 6 truck in a convoy headed away from the front. All the men aboard the trucks happily anticipated good food, alcoholic beverages, adult entertainment, sightseeing, and perhaps a short-lived romance. Schaefer had been sick with a bad cough, which grew worse on the long ride. By the time the trucks reached St. Quentin, he was coughing blood. Consequently, he entered an air force hospital while the others helped themselves to his barter goods and went on to fun in Paris. Five days later he was well enough to leave. The doctor asked Schaefer if he would still like to go to Paris as he could have him transferred to the general hospital there. Schaefer declined because "I had a platoon of replacements that needed me, and I had to get back to them." The next day the trucks from Paris picked him up. The returning

GIs were in terrible shape; having lost some of their clothes and boots while on leave; they looked more like displaced persons than American soldiers. Schaefer could only console himself with the thought he would be returning to the front in better shape than his compatriots.[44]

Those who left the front discovered rear-echelon GIs wearing the coats and boots desperately needed by combat soldiers. Riding to Paris in a hospital train, Jake Langston angrily noticed "all the personnel had insulated rubber boots and some wore fleece-lined tanker clothing." In England Jack Prickett and his paratrooper buddies physically assaulted soldiers wearing jump boots and winter clothes: "We took that stuff away from those bastards who came into the pub wearing them." Mel Richmond saw guys wearing galoshes when the infantrymen at the front had none: "They thought they were soldiers but they weren't. It was disgusting." Frontline troops suspected that support personnel were siphoning off the best rations, cigarettes, and apparel for trade on the thriving black market. Had they known for sure, their outrage would certainly have created even more divisiveness in the army.[45]

• • •

The lucky few to whom the army granted short furloughs learned firsthand the sharp differences separating the battlefield from the civilian world. To the returnees it seemed incredibly unreal to be trapped one moment in the grimy, destructive nightmare of the front lines and a few hours later to be deposited back into civilization, where even in lean times, a semblance of order and normalcy existed. When squad leader Frederick Feigenoff arrived in Brussels on a three-day pass, he was shocked that everyone was walking around and acting normal. It seemed so strange that it threw him into "a daze." He couldn't handle the transition and wanted to go back to his squad, as he "felt responsible for his men, who were all replacements." When Capt. Charles Roland arrived in Paris, teeming with people and "throngs of pretty women dressed in high fashion," it was like "passing from hell to heaven." After enjoying a hot bath and clean clothes, George Meloy and a few GIs mingled in the Place de la Opera and ogled French women, who emitted a lovely perfumed smell, adding to the "joy of being in Paris in the spring and away from the war of ugliness." Loaded with cartons of cigarettes, the currency of exchange, Donald Wiberg and Charles Eubanks savored the City of Lights, watching the Folies Bergère and other shows, their fun only diminished by guilty thoughts about abandoning their buddies, "some of whom might be dead when they got back." After luxuriating in clean, dry clothes and sleeping in a warm bed, Lt. Y. B. Johnson dreaded going back; in a letter to his parents he wrote, "Everything is so nice here, and we know where we are going there is nothing nice." Captain Horace Phillips took in the sights of Paris on a five-day pass but decided he didn't like the French, who "seemed as if they were trying to get all they could get"; nevertheless, Phillips did not want to return to the front "where you saw such gruesome sights." Vern Swanson spent time in a Paris hospital but became angry seeing the soft life of civilians while "guys were suffering and dying at the front."[46]

All combat veterans were acutely aware of what awaited them. Those who had recovered from wounds faced an additional burden. Robert Story, who had caught a mortar shell fragment on January 31, found it difficult to go back to his unit, having experienced combat and "all the emotions and fear that you undergo." Soldiers like Story wondered if they were pressing their luck; they had survived a first close brush with death, but what about the next time?[47]

While the indifference of the French and rear-echelon troops infuriated combat soldiers, Ernest McDaniel, who received a special, seven-day pass to London, did not think about such matters because he immediately fell in love with an attractive British woman who erased "all the loneliness of the past months." But when she asked for his Combat Infantry Badge, he would not part with the medal that marked him as a frontline soldier. Despite a powerful desire to remain in London, he boarded the train and began a long, sad journey back to his unit and the war.[48]

CHAPTER 8

Closing the Ruhr Pocket

Reaching the Autobahn signaled a major accomplishment for the 99th because the division was now in command of Hitler's prized highway. In the early morning hours of March 26, Guy Duren watched 7th Armored Division Sherman tanks rumble down the battered Autobahn, and he reckoned that nothing could stop the First Army. While happy that a potent armored force had joined them, Duren thought the infantry had accomplished the tough work of capturing the bridgehead. Tanks clanked down all four lanes for a few miles and then turned east, roaming at will, racing through villages, while leaving mop-up operations to the infantry.[1]

Over the next two days, elements of the division piled on trucks and tank destroyers (an open-turret, tracked vehicle with a powerful 90mm gun) and hurried to catch up to the rampaging tanks. On the Autobahn Emmett Jackson witnessed "such horrible carnage I had not seen before"; strafing American fighter-bombers left dead horses, overturned artillery, and equipment scattered everywhere. Max Norris was stunned to observe a German tank turret blown off completely and the tank's steel plates peeled back "like a sardine can." While captured German soldiers marched down the median headed in the opposite direction, American army vehicles of all types clogged the highway as they drove deeper into Germany. Trucks and tank destroyers dropped off infantry squads that fanned out over the countryside and captured demoralized German troops.[2]

Resistance melted away and the GIs spent nights in houses, which meant beds and more opportunities for plundering: rifles, pistols, wristwatches, cameras, eggs, ham, preserves, wine, and liquor. While many German villagers, fearing the worst, closed their shutters and hid from sight, other families seemed pleased the Americans had appeared. Paul Weesner wrote: "We arrived in these towns like conquering heroes just returning home. Everyone in town seemed to line the crooked streets and cheer and wave white handkerchiefs and cloths." The friendly reception by some Germans eased the tension. When Harry Arnold's platoon reached one house, a family received them warmly. He and his buddies shared rations with the family and in the morning, as the Sherman tank they were riding pulled away, the Germans "stood by the house waving farewell, tears rimming their eyes and streaking their cheeks." It was, Arnold thought, "a crazy war."[3]

Fred Kampmier and his squad occupied a nice home with two mothers, two kids, and an elderly grandfather. Shocked and scared by the GIs' entrance, the women began to cry and rush about excitedly. The squad assured them they only wanted a place to sleep and cook and that nothing would be taken. The next morning one of the GIs, concerned about the two young boys, brought back an armful of milk bottles he had taken from neighboring homes. The GIs enjoyed their stay and, although there was a rule against fraternizing with the enemy, Kampmier liked hanging around the kitchen with the women to soak up "a homey feeling that we all missed."[4]

The division headed eastward toward the cities of Wetzlar and Giessen, some thirty-eight miles and forty-seven miles respectively from the Autobahn. West of Wetzlar, Carter Strong's jeep came upon thousands of newly freed foreign laborers, including groups of Frenchmen who shouted and waved excitedly, which "made us feel that maybe all those winter months of hell were worth it." As the companies swept into Wetzlar, swarms of newly freed, hungry slave laborers, mostly Poles and Russians, cheered the 99th's arrival and began breaking into German houses taking food, clothes, shoes, and bicycles. Some also took revenge on their former captors: in one case the prisoners forced a particularly brutal guard to eat feces and then beat him to death. Witnessing the joy of these people and knowing the unbelievable cruelty they had suffered at the hands of the Nazis confirmed the righteousness of the American mission.[5]

Robert Hawn was assigned to keep the former slaves from escaping a Wetzlar labor camp, as the army feared a massacre of German civilians and the possible spread of diseases. The prisoners, including pregnant women, were sick, dirty, smelly, and lice-ridden. Overjoyed by their liberation, the victims attempted to hug and kiss Hawn and his fellow platoon members, much to the uneasiness of the GIs. Saving these people, Hawn admitted, "made you feel good about yourself," but he preferred receiving their gratitude from a distance. One night the freed workers staged a party with music furnished by concertinas and violins, and Hawn danced hesitantly with the DPs (Displaced Persons), despite their physical condition.[6]

The swastika flag was lowered at Nazi Party Gestapo headquarters and torture center, popularly referred to as the *Braunhaus* [Brown House] by German residents, who renamed it the *Weisshaus* [White House] after the American flag appeared in front. In an adjacent building GIs flung open steel doors and freed slaves from their dark, damp underground bunkers where they had lived and worked without fresh air or sunlight. In the city's center GIs pushed into the world-famous Leica factory and grabbed as many cameras as they could lay their hands on. Discipline among some American units deteriorated in the jubilant atmosphere. Radford Carroll and another soldier shattered front doors with a sledgehammer and ransacked apartments with DPs following after them, scooping up food and valuables. A few German women offered to share a bed with any GI who would keep the looters out of their houses. On a railway track outside the city, GIs discovered an abandoned string of boxcars packed with malnourished, lice-infected American POWs, including a number of 99ers captured during the Bulge. Since Hitler had ordered that no POWs should fall into the hands of the advancing American Army, guards had to march or transport their captives deeper into the German interior, causing incredible suffering to the internees. In this case the guards had moved their prisoners from Limburg, but fled with the appearance of American tanks and infantry.[7]

The 99th then moved a few miles north of Giessen and rested a few days in scattered villages. On Sunday April 1, 1945, soldiers attended Easter services in local churches. Richard Gorby and other men squeezed into the "dinkiest" church in a tiny hamlet. Because of heavy attendance, the chaplain conducted the service in the doorway, but to Gorby it was "one Easter I'll always remember." Lindell Sawyers attended a Lutheran service with fellow GIs who crowded into church pews with M-1s on their backs. Sawyers found it ironic they were sitting in a church of the conquered "whose goods we were systematically looting." Sawyers was "appalled" by the amount of plundering that took place—watches, cameras, "anything not nailed down." When he heard a mother with two small children wailing, he entered her house and discovered some men in his squad had taken the woman's traditional Easter cake. Sawyers found this theft so utterly offensive that he retrieved the cake.[8]

Ralph Shivone recalled that two GIs, one playing a violin and the other a church organ, began a duet of beautiful music: upon hearing the lovely sounds, various townspeople drifted into the church, creating "one of the most memorable happenings we had. It brought us all together for a day." In the village of Alzbach, Chaplain Brechenridge pumped a foot-powered church organ as the church bells rang, signaling the beginning of the service. As each GI entered the church, he was handed a lighted candle, which cast a soft glow across the twilight dimness. German villagers climbed into the balcony and "worshipped with us." It was, according to medic Richard Tobias, "a solemn, quiet, impressive moment."[9]

The silent reconciliation between enemies on this religious holy day was not limited to church events. Richard Switzer and his squad took over a German farmhouse occupied by a wife, her parents, and two children. Herman Weissman, a Jew who spoke Yiddish, inquired whether the family had any eggs. The frightened family said nothing. But upon lifting up a couple of loose floorboards, the usual hiding place, the GIs uncovered several water-filled crocks full of eggs. After satisfying their craving for fresh food, Switzer and his buddies colored the remaining eggs and hid them, much to the delight of the two little boys. Similarly Oakley Honey and several squad members let an old couple stay in their house while they bunked outside on a screened-in porch. As they left that Sunday morning, the elderly woman gave an Easter offering to each departing GI. "As I got to the woman, I could see tears in her eyes as she placed a hard-boiled egg in my hand."[10]

• • •

In late March 1945 Gen. Eisenhower decided British and American forces would relinquish the capture of Berlin to the Russians. Once that decision was reached, Gen. Omar Bradley, commanding the 12th

Army Group, set into motion a plan to encircle the Ruhr area with two powerful armies, thereby confining Field Marshal Model's Army Group B inside. General William Simpson's Ninth Army, which crossed the Rhine River on March 22, proceeded eastward through the devastated industrial cities of the Ruhr. At the same time, Gen. Courtney Hodges's First Army drove east and then circled to the north. On April 1, armored divisions from the two American armies met at Lippstadt, trapping more than three hundred thousand German troops.[11]

On April 4, the three divisions, (99th Infantry, 5th Infantry, and 7th Armored) from positions in the southeastern corner of the trap, began to move in a northwesterly direction in coordination with six other First Army divisions. Unlike the urban-industrial area north of the Ruhr River, this region, known as the Sauerland, featured steep, forested hills and narrow valleys through which small rivers ran, with villages scattered along valley floors. The topography hampered vehicular movement by confining it to the roads and valleys; it also aided the Germans, who could easily threaten American forces by seizing the high ground. Consequently, the ground troops had to capture the ridges, a task that entailed endless, enervating tramping up and down hillsides.

• • •

At 2:39 A.M. the soldiers of George Company 395 began a long trek in darkness toward the mining town of Meggen. To reach the village they had to wade two small streams and then climb a ridge, while carrying their combat gear and weapons, including mortars and machine guns. After reaching the top, they crept down the other side of the ridge toward the town with houses and buildings built into the slope. German defenders, expecting the Americans to attack from the valley entrance, were caught by surprise and surrendered without a fight. Afterwards, the whole company entered a huge cave at the end of the street, threw down their equipment, and collapsed from exhaustion. When Harold Hill, company commander, reported to battalion headquarters, he was told their job wasn't finished— they were expected to seize the next ridge too. Hill returned to the cave unsure how he could possibly tell or expect his tired men to continue. He gave the new order to his platoon leaders and sergeants, but they reacted with "blank, unresponsive faces," as if they had "not heard a single word." After passing on the information to the men, the platoon officers returned and reported to Hill the men were too fatigued to continue and were not responding. Hill entered the cave and told the men he was going to start up the ridge and, "if anyone wants to go with me, [he] had better get off [his] ass and join in." Hill left and began climbing the hill with a couple of sergeants, half expecting to encounter resistance without any support. Then he looked back and saw "those loyal, wonderful, worn-out soldiers filing out of the mine to join us."[12]

German resistance varied from weak to moderate; in some places fighting turned fierce and deadly when the Germans decided to make a stand, often with powerful antiaircraft cannon. On April 6, as the 3rd Platoon of King Company 395 approached the village of Gleidorf, a group of German soldiers on a hillcrest waved a white flag at the GIs indicating their desire to surrender. Platoon leader Jack Musser and others started walking toward them when all at once the Germans dropped to the ground and fired their weapons, killing Musser and several others. The rest of the platoon, consumed by rage, ran toward the Germans in a staggered skirmish line. Robert Ritchie fired several shots at a German soldier and saw dust flying off the gray uniform as each bullet struck. None of the Germans survived. Ritchie could not understand why the Germans didn't surrender: "We were killing them and they were killing us. It was mass insanity, almost as if the world had gone mad." Ritchie was not unaware of the mission's overarching goals, but these larger issues seemed secondary to men trapped in the "nightmare" of combat.[13]

When the 3rd Battalion 395 attempted to capture Gleidorf, tank and 40mm flak fire initially drove them back. As Joseph Thimm, the BAR gunner, and other squad members approached the first houses, German small arms commenced firing, and the GIs ran for cover behind fences and outbuildings on the edge of town. Thimm ducked into a house and fired two magazines from his BAR through a plate glass window at the German troops hunkered down across the street. Warren Thomas and his mates, finding themselves outgunned by the Germans, hurried into a house cellar. While the others exited through the cellar door, Thomas, being the last man, had no time to escape, so he jumped into a large bin and covered himself with potatoes. Intent on following the other GIs, the Germans failed to search the potato bin, and Thomas lived to fight another day.[14]

By late afternoon King Company had achieved considerable progress securing Gleidorf. Thimm's squad, including a bazooka team, moved down the main street into the center of the village looking for a tank that had been harassing them. Soon after Thimm crossed to the other side of the street, a shell exploded in their midst, sending a steel fragment into his ankle and another piece into the back of Harry Threlkeld Jr. Thimm crawled across the street and dragged Threlkeld onto a house porch. The medic arrived, slit open Threlkeld's combat jacket and poured sulfa powder into the terrible back wound. Threlkeld spoke haltingly, "I can't breathe." Then he stopped breathing and died. Thimm recounted sadly, "I saw him die. I admired him. He had so much talent and promise. His life was wasted. He would have moved ahead in life afterwards." Threlkeld wasn't the only loss, for eleven men of the 395th died during those two days of fighting.[15]

In the early afternoon of April 8, Love Company 394 approached another typical village of that region. After struggling up and down hills with German artillery following them, the company stopped at the top of a treeless hill. Ignoring a warning from Lieutenant Sam Lombardo that German troops occupied the village, company commander Neil Brown ordered his troops down the steep hill. As the company began its long descent, the enemy opened up with mortar and rifle fire, some bullets coming from a large haystack. Since the hill offered no cover, the men ran down the slope as "black explosions that bloomed like evil flowers" caught the troops in the open. Byron Reburn, the last to depart, thought to himself as he prepared to follow the others, "I will either be in heaven or in a hospital." But neither place was Reburn's destination, as he made it safely to the bottom. Off to his right he spotted Neil Brown lying wounded in a ditch. Although the Germans resisted vigorously, the company secured the village that evening at a cost of three dead and seven wounded.[16]

• • •

As Harry Arnold and Easy Company 393 approached the village of Oberhundem on April 7, all seemed well, for white sheets hung from

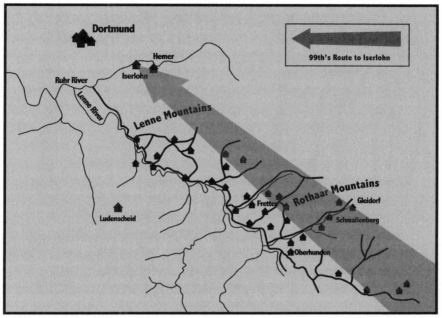

Ruhr Pocket drive, April 1945. Map by Paul Giacomotto and James Knight.

houses. Suddenly, however, a hail of bullets and shells erupted from across the valley. GIs hugged the ground or ran uphill seeking cover in the undergrowth. The Americans retaliated with a massive artillery barrage and white phosphorous mortar shells, while P-47 Thunderbolts bombed the village. Arnold wondered if this devastating battering wasn't mostly an act of vengeance, since the German onslaught had come from across the valley and not from the town. Easy Company, accompanied by Sherman tanks, filed into Oberhundem, but the Germans troops simply withdrew, leaving the town in ruins. As Radford Carroll walked through the village he could "not forget the look on the villagers' faces as they watched everything they owned burn." One grim-faced, older man with nine children expressed his anger to Harry Arnold over the loss of his home. While somewhat sympathetic to the German, Arnold deflected the criticism by telling him (in sparse German) that if Hitler had not waged war on his neighbors, the house would still be standing. When Lt. Col. Thomas Bishop, who had ordered the "immensely enjoyable" air strikes, entered Oberhundem,

Alert for snipers, infantrymen of 395th Regiment move cautiously into Saalhausen in Ruhr Pocket, April 9, 1945. Courtesy National Archives and Records
Administration.

all the people were sitting in the streets crying while their homes
burned. Like Arnold he blamed the villagers for what happened,
commenting in his diary: "Maybe the Germans will think twice before
starting the next war."[17]

• • •

GIs were usually distrustful of German civilians, and even when they
appeared friendly, many Americans assumed that fear drove them "to
do things for us." But these suspicious feelings softened when combat
soldiers encountered terrified women and children. When Fielding
Pope approached a woman and two young girls, a plane flew over and
the girls ran off terrified into the woods. Pope felt sorry for them
because of "the horror they had endured." Sammy Oliverio and other
GIs began to dig foxholes at the edge of one town, and the villagers
starting wailing because they assumed the holes would soon become
their graves. Oliverio had to explain the holes were for the his men.[18]

Encountering Germans who spoke English surprised GIs. Item
Company 394 was attacking in a forest when James Larkey heard a

Civilians from Saalhausen await screening and questioning after their village was captured by the 395th Rgt. on April 9, 1945. Courtesy National Archives and Records Administration.

voice shout, "Stop firing, we want to surrender." Larkey recognized an accent from New Jersey. The speaker was one of a dozen young soldiers, born and raised in New Jersey, who had graduated from Irvington, New Jersey high school, a rival school to Larkey's. The grey-clad soldiers had emigrated to Germany to serve in the Wehrmacht. Realizing the war was lost, as was their U. S. citizenship, the boys asked to join the American army. Their offer was declined; instead they were loaded up with all heavy, bulky equipment as the company moved forward.

Charles Eubanks and his squad rounded up a group of men, children, and women, including a buxom blonde. One GI commented aloud, "Boy, I'd give five bucks to chew on those tits." The blonde responded, "You son-of-a bitch. Why don't you give it a try?" It happened that the bosomy woman had been born and reared in Brooklyn.[19]

When Tim Nugent entered a house with three armed medics, two women with little children came up from the cellar. They were afraid and crying. Nugent tried to calm them by saying, *"Nicht scheissen,"*

Infantrymen of Dog Co. 394 pass through the burning ruins of Odingen, April 10, 1945. Courtesy National Archives and Records Administration.

(mispronouncing the word "*schiessen*" with a long "i" instead of an "e" sound) Nugent did not realize it but he actually said, "no shitting" instead of "no shooting." The women immediately burst into laughter, which so angered red-haired Nugent that he turned and fired several shots into the wall. The women and children resumed bawling louder than before, so he again had to try and calm them down. (Only after the war did Nugent learn of his pronunciation mistake.)[20]

• • •

On April 13, while the 99th pushed deep into the Ruhr pocket, word reached the troops that President Franklin Roosevelt had died the previous day. The news shocked and saddened most GIs. To David Williams it was like "losing a member of your own family," for he saw FDR as a "father figure." Charles Roland "seriously wondered how the nation could go on without him." Carter Strong was disquieted but thought nothing would change, and "we went right on with the war." Y. B. Johnson wrote his parents that he and the other infantrymen were sorry to hear about Roosevelt, but GIs "have seen too many of

Riflemen of Item Co. 393 ride on a tank in Deutmecke, thirty miles southeast of Iserlohn in Ruhr Pocket, April 1945. Courtesy National Archives and Records Administration.

their buddies fall to be unnerved by his death." For Fred Kampmier, a Republican Party supporter, it didn't leave much of an impression, for "we had our own problems." As Omar Paxson marched along with Mike Company 394, someone yelled out, "Who the fuck is president now?" Paxson responded proudly, "'Harry Truman!' I was the only one who knew the name of the vice president."[21]

On a warm day, Harry Arnold's column, dusty, sweaty, and tired, marched past a military convalescent hospital. On the hospital grounds, leaning against the building and looking out from windows and doors, were hundreds of wounded German soldiers, including a number of amputees. They stared at the American soldiers, and the GIs responded in kind. Neither group spoke or waved. Arnold felt the "bitterness of combatants hung in the air," for "we were healthy and they were hurt," and "we were the victors and they were not." And yet Arnold believed there existed a "mutual compassion for the other, an unspoken bond [for] we were all soldiers." Then Germans nurses with buckets, pans, and pitchers of water came to the roadside and stood offering each GI a refreshing drink. "We passed in minutes, but those minutes will forever be impressed on my mind."[22]

Enjoying letters from home before moving out in a 6 x 6 truck. Courtesy National Archives and Records Administration.

Each succeeding day more Germans surrendered and in numbers so large that it initially created unease, because in many instances the soldiers carried weapons. A long, grey procession of young and old infantrymen, arrogant SS troopers, paunchy reservists, female nurses, and teenage members of the Hitler Youth traipsed south. GIs generally reacted with aversion or indifference to German POWs, but every once in a while an incident would momentarily soften attitudes toward the enemy. Joseph Shimko accompanied a large group of prisoners back to a POW holding pen. As they passed through one village, a six-year-old boy standing by the side of the road, began yelling out, "*Vater! Vater!*" when he spotted his father in the group of internees. The boy ran to his father, who reached into a knapsack and handed his son a couple of bread slices, saying, "Mama, Mama." Shimko was quite moved by this demonstration of a father providing in a small way for his family at the expense of his own well-being.

When company commander George Maertens entered Altena, a town nine miles from the garrison city of Iserlohn (the final objective), he came upon an amazing sight of German tanks, mechanized vehicles, command cars, and units all lined up in formation. Maertens thought to himself: "That force could have liquidated us." Escorted to a nearby house, he confronted several high-ranking German officers prepared to surrender. The disparity in appearance of the two groups could not have been more noticeable or more ironic. The victorious Maertens appeared unkempt and shabby in his olive-drab field uniform, while the defeated Germans in their dress uniforms and polished boots looked the part of consummate professional soldiers, almost a reenactment of General Robert E. Lee's surrender to the disheveled Ulysses S. Grant at Appomattox Court House. In contrast to certain spit-and-polish American generals, the typical enlisted man took pride in his slovenly appearance, an image captured by cartoonist Bill Mauldin's two scruffy combat GIs, Willie and Joe, who expressed rebellion against army correctness and discipline. It also evoked the mythical tradition of the Revolutionary War Minutemen, yeoman farmers who ventured forth from their modest homes to fight for freedom against Old World aristocracy and uniformed Hessians.[23]

When a German commander learned that Maertens was only a lowly captain, he refused to accept him as worthy of receiving the surrender. So they awaited the arrival of the main force with high-ranking officers and staff. In the meantime, German unit commanders gave passionate farewell addresses to their troops, followed by "Heil Hitler" salutes, tears, and a singing of *Deutschland Über Alles*. After the formal surrender, the sound of hundreds of hob-nailed boots crunching on cobblestone streets could be heard as the Germans marched off to hastily constructed POW cages.[24]

German troops surrendered in record numbers, marching south, sometimes with only a few American infantrymen shepherding them. Paul Weesner watched a company go by in step, commanded by their officer who had perfect control over these men marching proudly in defeat. Weesner's admiration for the tightly disciplined German soldiers ran counter to the widely shared attitude that German infantrymen, fighting as mindless automatons, could not match the resourceful, individualistic GIs. According to the American view, the more self-reliant, independent GI could outperform the vaunted, disciplined German soldier. This belief offered combat GIs a sense of superiority, even though, like their German counterparts, they too had to obey orders that put their lives at risk.[25]

Thousands of prisoners, according to Carter Strong, headed to the rear in vehicles with their own military police organizing and directing their movement. At points along the road German MPs directed American traffic to the front. Strong came upon negotiations between company commander Harold Hill and a German general. Strong spotted a shiny new military flashlight hanging from the belt of the general's aide. He was about to reach for it, when the lieutenant stepped back, snapped to attention, unfastened the light, made a stiff bow and handed it to Strong, who found it delightful that a perfectly groomed German officer was "bowing and scraping to me, a lowly enlisted man in dirty combat garb."[26]

Riding on tanks, Harry Arnold and his squad ran into captured Germans marching in a double column. The mass of prisoners so clogged the highway that tanks moved to the roadside. At one point a convertible staff car crept along in the midst of marching men. Only the driver and an old, monocled officer seated in back occupied the car. Seeing this arrogant representative of German militarism and aristocracy riding comfortably, Arnold pointed his rifle at some POWs and motioned for them to step into the car so the "rigid line between master and servant [could] be breached." With great reluctance the soldiers climbed in, one even took a position next to the officer. But the old Junker steadfastly ignored the rabble riding with him. As Arnold put it: "You could have smeared dung between his lip and nose, and he would have ignored that as well." Arnold and other GIs hated the Prussian class system that symbolized the German Army: after all, Americans viewed the struggle as a fight between democracy and despotism. It gave Arnold and other enlisted men great pleasure to exercise power over high-ranking German officers, something they couldn't do in their own army.[27]

At 11:00 A.M. on the 16th of April all German units in the 99th's sector surrendered, with the exception of *Oberleutnant* Albert Ernst, who commanded a contingent of *Jagdtigers* (heavy tank destroyers) in Iserlohn. Lieutenant Colonel Robert Kriz, commander of the 2nd battalion 394, met Ernst under a white flag and asked him to surrender. At first Ernst did not believe Kriz was in charge because he had covered his helmet insignia with mud, the usual practice for officers to lessen the chance of being killed by a sniper. Kriz had to take off his field jacket to show his rank before Ernst would talk to him through an interpreter. Kriz convinced Ernst he should avoid needless bloodshed; besides, all other German ground forces in that region had already given up. Ernst agreed but requested a formal surrender ceremony. Lining up his depleted company beneath the long-barreled 128mm guns of his huge tank destroyers, Ernst shook hands with his men, called them to attention, had them count off, delivered a short speech, executed an about-face, saluted Colonel Kriz, and formally surrendered. The 99ers' military operations in the Ruhr pocket had ended, but 122 men would not return home.[28]

• • •

Seven kilometers to the east of Iserlohn, the 3rd Battalion 395 came upon a large POW prison on the outskirts of Hemer. Originally established by the German Army as a military camp, it was transformed into a prison (Stalag VI-A) for thousands of Poles and Russians—Slavs whom the Nazis considered an inferior race that need not be saved. The overcrowded, unsanitary prison had functioned as a distribution center, processing over two hundred thousand men, who were shipped off to work in Ruhr steel mills and coal mines, where thousands succumbed to mistreatment, malnourishment, and disease. If a POW became too sick to function, he was sent back to Hemer, where, without adequate food or medicine (only captured Russian doctors tended to their countrymen), he usually died. The dead (estimated to be twenty-four thousand from 1939 to 1945) were stripped of clothing, wrapped in paper or left naked, piled high in carts and unceremoniously dumped into mass graves on the edge of town.[29]

The 7th Armored Division arrived first at the Hemer prison, freeing more than twenty-three thousand emaciated prisoners. Of these some nine thousand suffered various maladies—TB, dysentery, and typhus—and none had received food for three days. The recently deceased were simply thrown into the basements of the four-story barracks. Weak and mad with hunger, the prisoners went searching for something to eat, breaking into German homes and grain cars on a railroad siding. William Bartow and his section were eating at the edge of town when a horde of these prisoners appeared, begging for food, holding out their hands to catch the uneaten remnants as the GIs dumped

Newly liberated Russian POWs in Hemer prison. Courtesy National Archives and Records Administration.

their mess kits. But giving these prisoners a D bar or K rations could have killed them because their intestines could not handle this sudden rush of food.[30]

A horse-drawn wagon loaded with flour and other supplies arrived in the camp, and a small group of French prisoners were told to bake bread in an enormous barn-like building chosen as a mess hall. Holes in the sacks allowed some flour to spill out. Upon spotting the leakage, the Russian POWs began pushing and shoving in a desperate attempt to reach the flour; the lucky few stuffed the flour, mixed with dirt, into their mouths. According to David Williams, when the baking began and the Russians smelled the food cooking, they went into "a frenzy"; Williams and another GI had to threaten the prisoners with (unloaded) rifles in an attempt to stop the meleé. The French prisoners added to the hysteria by cruelly throwing bread out a second story window to watch the Russians fight for the crumbs. Eventually the doors were opened and the hungry Russians surged inside.[31]

Meanwhile the horses were slain for a horsemeat stew. A German POW tried to pass through the crowd with a wheelbarrow full of intestines, but the starving prisoners grabbed the steaming innards and stuffed them into their mouths. William Bartow thought it "the awfullest thing I've ever seen in my life." Battalion surgeon Dr. Herbert Orr, sympathetic to their plight, set up an aid station in an attempt to save the POWS he saw on the street. Despite his efforts, however, many did not survive.[32]

• • •

With the liquidation of the Ruhr pocket, everyone assumed there would be a period of relaxation. Maybe, they thought, the war would end. But as in the past, the 99th would not be allowed to rest. On April 17 trucks arrived to transport the division to Bavaria to join General George Patton's Third Army and hunt down German units that refused to surrender. How much longer could the war go on, they wondered, and how many more would be killed and wounded before the fighting ceased?

CHAPTER 9

Prisoners of War

On Sunday morning December 17, 1944, Alfred Goldstein, a member of the service battery for the 924th Field Artillery Battalion, walked from his billet to the kitchen for breakfast in the Belgian village of Büllingen. After eating pancakes with syrup (later he wished he would have stuffed himself) he started back to his quarters, unaware of the onslaught taking place just four miles away. Upon hearing staccato machine-gun fire and seeing dotted lines of tracer bullets flying through the air, he decided to lie down in a ditch at the side of the road and wait with his carbine at the ready. Suddenly over a rise in the road there appeared an enormous German tank propelled by a pair of menacing steel treads that could easily chew him into ground meat. Goldstein crawled away and dashed back to their house where he watched a column of enemy tanks, half-tracks with troops, and vehicles passing through the village. The startling appearance of this armored German force behind American lines generated considerable anxiety and confusion for Goldstein and his mates. Radio operator Earl Peters called battery headquarters and excitedly reported a German tank in the village. Not believing what he heard, the major asked Peters, "Are you sure the tank is German?" Peters simply hung the receiver out the window so headquarters could hear the ripping sounds of a German machine gun. The major instructed Peters to leave Büllingen at once, but it was too late, and he was captured.[1]

Lacking experience in combat and lightly armed with a carbine, Goldstein decided nevertheless to attack the armored phalanx. A Jew, harboring an intense hatred for Nazis and wanting "to kill all those bastards," he began to fire at German soldiers riding in passing vehicles. The first sergeant, someone he did not respect, asked Goldstein to stop shooting as it would draw return fire, but he did not comply. Outside he spotted an assistant cook near the house trying to load a bazooka from the wrong end. Thinking this weapon might offer a better method of killing the enemy, Goldstein ran to the cook, took the bazooka, and jumped in a foxhole. Normally two men were needed to load and fire the bazooka, but Goldstein somehow managed to launch a rocket that missed the tanks and hit a house across the street.

Goldstein returned to his billet and descended into the cellar where others had gathered out of harm's way. Some time later he heard voices speaking in English, calling for everyone to surrender. Looking out a basement window, Goldstein saw two American officers standing in the road. He laid down the rifle and discarded his dog tags because the "H" stamped on the little metal plates would have identified him as Jewish, and he correctly feared the consequences of that discovery. Exiting the house with hands raised, Goldstein and the others were surrounded by young, tough, camouflaged SS troops. A huge SS soldier approached Goldstein, kicked him in the rear after Goldstein muttered something audible, and then relieved him of his D bars, saying he had devoured (*gefressen*, a verb describing how animals eat) enough chocolate.[2]

The service battery GIs and other captives marched two miles to Honsfeld where they caught sight of German and American dead, including a few flattened by tanks—the crushed skull of one American reminded Burnett Hartley "of a coconut that had been shattered." Frank Garrett and his buddy wanted to pull an American corpse off the road, but the German troops stopped them. After spending the night without food in a recreation center, the POWs resumed their trek toward Germany. Some regular German soldiers came marching by headed in the opposite direction; one approached Goldstein, demanding his field jacket, which he meekly surrendered. But when another German tried to take his gloves, he jerked his hands away, and the trooper relented. Soon thereafter he saw two Germans attempting to take overshoes from a GI. Goldstein inexplicably and boldly ran over and protested in broken German (he knew Yiddish), "*Nein, nein, Er ist krank*" [he's sick]. Surprisingly the enemy soldiers walked away, and he realized that resistance could work.[3]

• • •

When the Battle of the Bulge began on December 16, German troops sliced through gaps in the 99th's defensive positions and circled behind exposed units, including King Company 393. Tony Dodd felt angry and embarrassed they had surrendered, for he had joined the army "to fight, not to become a POW." After being captured, rifleman Robert Grant turned over his galoshes, overcoat, personal items, and chocolate D bars to the enemy. One German officer confiscated stuffed dates that Howard Harris's Jewish mother had sent and began eating them on the spot without knowing the "contaminated" source of the goodies. Grant and others in the company were ordered to carry wounded German soldiers back to an aid station inside a bunker. They made numerous, tiring trips through the snow to retrieve more wounded while dodging American artillery shells. From a POW assembly area, B. O. Wilkins and another GI were forced to lug a box of ammunition to the front, even though it violated the Geneva Convention protocols. Seeing his company commander Stephen Plume coming in as a prisoner, Wilkins asked him, "Captain, they can't make us do this, can they?" Plume replied, "It looks like they're doing it." When a German soldier told Wilkins, "Your war is over," he assumed combat had ended and his remaining days would be spent in a warm, dry barrack with regular food. Little did he know his struggle for survival had only begun.[4]

Teenage German soldiers captured Wendell Cathey and, after cutting off all the buttons on his pants but one (presumably to hinder his ability to run away), forced him to cart their wounded for the rest of the afternoon. (To retaliate, Cathey and his foxhole buddy twice deliberately dropped a wounded, helmet-less German on his head.) Robert Grant and three others were carrying a German soldier with a terrible stomach wound when he slipped from their grasp. In a moment of instant triage, the guard motioned them to pick up someone less severely wounded, leaving the German soldier to die alone in a field. When the number of wounded exceeded the space available inside, the rest were left outside the bunker in freezing temperatures, and the next morning Grant and others piled the frozen corpses into a cart and hauled them to the nearest town.[5]

After spending the night in crowded pillboxes with scores of crying, moaning Germans, this group of captured 99ers marched in subdued silence eastward through the West Wall. On the way they saw long columns of tanks, tank destroyers, troop carriers, horse-drawn artillery, and infantrymen all headed west toward the 99th Division; they suspected the Germans had launched a serious attack, though no one had any inkling of its massive size. Some German soldiers shouted insults and tried to hit the prisoners with their belts; one German in a troop carrier slammed his rifle down on David Thompson's left shoulder as he walked along. But not all enemy soldiers were unfriendly. As William Mudra and others stopped before a large house, a group of young Germans came by and chatted without enmity. Everyone laughed when one of the Germans piped up, "Hitler drafted me. Did Roosevelt draft you?" Both sides enjoyed the light-hearted moment, realizing they shared a common fate.[6]

The following day the prisoners gathered in a large dance hall where interrogations began. Before they arrived, a 2nd Division GI boasted to Harold Wagner, "You won't find any captured 2nd Division guys, just 99ers." But Wagner noticed 2nd Division prisoners there too. When other prisoners arrived, the GIs realized the American army had suffered significant losses. Sitting behind a desk with a huge swastika flag and photograph of Adolf Hitler on the wall, officers questioned them. When asked for information, everyone offered his name, rank, and serial number. Besides, the Germans knew more about the disposition of American troops than the GIs. The German officer who questioned Elton Kerbo found him carrying a humorous postcard showing Hitler being tossed into a toilet. Kerbo worried what might happen, but the German just grinned and said, "Oh, Roosevelt." Raymond Perisin's interrogator told him, "We will be in Paris by Christmas." When Perisin stepped outside the building the next day, he saw a line of tanks as "far as you could see." Maybe, he thought to himself, the German officer was right.[7]

• • •

Jack McElroy, part of the forward observation party for Cannon Company 394 (a battery of 105mm howitzers) occupied a house close to the German-Belgian border in the village of Losheimergraben. When the German artillery barrage of December 16 stopped, McElroy and his group withdrew in search of the company, which had moved from its original position. Unfortunately the howitzers mistakenly relocated to a bare hill in a highly vulnerable spot just north of Mürringen. Finding the company just as it turned dark, McElroy joined ten other men who decided to sleep in a shallow, covered shelter constructed by an antiaircraft unit that had wisely moved back to Elsenborn.

At 2:00 A.M. on December 17, McElroy awoke to sounds of gun-fire and the excited yell of the night guard: "There's some Krauts out here!" followed by, "They hit me!" German paratroopers then began throwing grenades that exploded on the shelter's roof. Since only one small exit existed, the men were trapped in their hole. To their surprise, a German-accented voice shouted in English, "Come out or you'll be killed." Seeing no alternative, they complied, despite their fears of what might follow. The Germans lined them up in the snow and began removing watches and other jewelry; the men assumed they were being prepared for execution, but no one was shot. McElroy quickly took off his 1940 Tekamah, Nebraska, high school ring and dropped it in the snow; neither the Germans nor anyone else ever found it.[8]

In the morning, soon after they started moving eastward, American artillery shelled the road, and the heavily armed paratroopers and their prisoners scrambled up a ridge top and lay flat. After the shelling ceased a small convoy approached, and the Germans set up machine guns, opening fire at the Cannon Company trucks. Some men were killed, others wounded, and the rest surrendered.

• • •

On Friday December 15, 1944, Robert Gabriel and a buddy had the chance to go to Honsfeld for a shower, a few beers, hot food, and a cot. On the morning of December 17, German troops shouting in the streets awakened Gabriel and two dozen others. The GIs surren-dered and came out of a building in various states of dress and undress. Troopers of the 1st SS Panzer Division shouted at them to move away from the house. One SS officer carrying an American .45-caliber submachine gun came up to Gabriel and told him in

Captured 99ers in Honsfeld being escorted toward Lanzerath, Belgium, December 17, 1944. Courtesy National Archives and Records Administration.

German, *"Mach dass es nicht schiesst"* [make it so it won't shoot]. Gabriel, who knew some German, closed the dust cover, which also served as the safety. The German placed the gun against Gabriel's stomach and pulled the trigger. When it did not fire, the German blithely commented, *"Gut."* Nonetheless Gabriel worried what might happen next, but no one in his group was executed.[9]

The SS troops departed when German paratroopers occupied the town, easing tensions considerably. Gabriel and other 99ers marched a few miles south to Lanzerath, Belgium, where they joined roughly two hundred POWs, including many from the 106th Division that had been overwhelmed south of the 99th's position. Gabriel and others were forced to collect frozen German corpses and wheelbarrow them into a barn where they stacked the bodies. Afterwards they walked to German defenses, where more POWs joined them in a large concrete bunker.[10]

• • •

German forces had raced behind the 2nd Battalion 394, essentially cutting off those troops. For two days the men tried to find their way back to American lines under overcast skies, which made it difficult to determine directions. Thinking that Mürringen (regimental headquarters) remained in American hands, the officers in charge carelessly ordered 2nd platoon, George Company, to enter the town without first reconnoitering it. But regimental headquarters had pulled out, and the Germans held the village in force. Upon receiving machine-gun fire, Sgt. William White led his squad into a stone barn, hoping they might hold the enemy off there. The Germans began firing through windows, and bullets bounced off the walls, hitting the cows, wounding several men, and killing three. To avoid a massacre, the remaining squad members put down their weapons, yelled "*Kamerad*," and surrendered. After a miserable night locked in a garage with no food, they were marched out of town with their hands over their heads. They passed enemy tanks and equipment headed in the opposite direction, while German soldiers stopped GIs and took what they wanted.[11]

Exhaustion replaced anxiety as columns of POWs trudged along to collection points where the captured GIs, numb and disbelieving, assembled. Having lost galoshes, helmets, overcoats, and gloves to their captors, they suffered from the bone-penetrating winter cold, especially when forced to stay outdoors or confined in poorly heated buildings. In addition to inadequate protection against chilling temperatures, the main challenge for survival would always be lack of food. Over time the men grew weak from malnutrition, became ill, and lost weight—fifty pounds on average over a period of more than four months. Privates were forced to perform manual labor, further sapping their energy, although sometimes presenting opportunities to pilfer food and stay alive.

After observing the military might of the German army, the battle's outcome remained uncertain in the minds of POWs, and they realized the war would probably not end any time soon. In many cases the men were shocked and ashamed to have been captured. William Mudra admitted, "The pain within was great: a hard fight against self-pity, bitterness, and absolute melancholy."[12]

The German Army imposed its class system on all prisoners and isolated the men from their leaders. The Germans segregated officers (commissioned officers from enlisted men), and sergeants, who did not have to work, from privates.The cohesiveness of the squads and platoons was destroyed, for prisoners were thrown together without regard for their company or regiment. A few members of the same squad and platoon managed to stay together, but often GIs were detached from their mates, ending up in separate barracks and even different prisons and work camps. Men were mixed with soldiers from other divisions, and many Americans were placed with British and Australian POWs. The individual POW had to create connections with a few familiar faces or with strangers in a sequestered world of extreme duress.

• • •

William Mudra's group marched seven miles and at noon rested in a children's school. There two young, friendly guards obtained half a loaf of dark bread per man, two cans of sardines among three men, six biscuit crackers apiece, and a real luxury, all the water they wanted. Mudra assumed conditions might not be so dire for the POWs, but he was wrong; this little "feast" would be the most food he and others would consume in one meal until their liberation.[13]

They moved on, walking for hours, even after dark. The long trek gave everyone time to think about the miserable situation. Mudra asked himself bitterly what other soldiers must have thought: "Why we had to suffer, while others safe in the snug comfort of home were probably oblivious to the smallest hardship." After receiving a telegram from the army that identified a son or husband as MIA (missing in action), families had to endure the pain of not knowing for a month or more if their GI was alive or dead, let alone having any idea of the deprivation he faced. Moreover, the POW could not console himself with the belief he was fighting the enemy—his combat career, such as it was, had ended. Henceforth, the battles he faced would be for survival.[14]

At last Mudra's group turned into the courtyard of a palatial building swarming with German Army officers, who ignored the prisoners standing in the cold. Finally, at 10:00 P.M. guards divided the POWs into two groups, sending one to a barn and the other bunch into a stockade. In the morning the Americans were permitted to enter the stockade's yard where they quenched their thirst with snow. Wandering about the area were a few emaciated Soviet prisoners, some on crutches, all clothed in tatters, all barely alive. American POWs tried to give these wretched men leftover bread, but the Germans wouldn't allow it.[15]

The guards produced a small mobile boiler and heated a thin pea soup for the Americans. Before ladling it into the helmets of the Americans, the Germans forced the Russians back into the building. It was a meager breakfast, but it could have been worse—and it was better than nothing, which is what the Russians received. At midmorning the guards hustled the Americans into old trucks that puffed and crawled along, finally reaching Flamersheim, a village three miles southeast of Euskirchen, where Mudra met others from King Company. After receiving a cup of "ersatz" [substitute] coffee and a bowl of barley soup, two hundred POWs were squeezed into two rooms where burlap mats filled with straw served as beds. Several times during the night they were awakened and marched downstairs to be counted.[16]

The next morning, after eating a slice of hard black bread and a piece of sausage, they walked to the city of Euskirchen and worked the next two days at the railroad station, a dairy, a warehouse, and a produce center. Mudra's group unloaded and sorted the vegetables farmers had carted in. Four Russian boys, captured three years earlier when they were ten and eleven years old and billeted with a German family, worked alongside them and at noon brought a large pot of rice soup cooked by their German *Hausfrau*.

On the night of December 21, several hundred more prisoners arrived in Flamersheim, and all were shoved into two rooms on the prison's second floor. With no space to lie down, everyone sat all night with knees drawn up. By now just about everyone suffered from dysentery caused by contaminated food and water. The only latrine was a barrel placed in one corner of the smaller room. Trying to step over bodies and find the barrel in the dark or wait one's turn proved impossible; many defecated in their pants.

The next day a large group of POWs walked twelve miles to the old university city of Bonn, situated on the banks of the Rhine River. Their departure relieved some overcrowding, but most of Mudra's buddies left with that group. He stayed two more days in Flamersheim and worked unloading boxcars. When U.S. planes passed overhead on bombing missions, Mudra fantasized about what he hoped would be their not-too-distant liberation, but he knew there wouldn't be any turkey dinners that Christmas, and no C rations or D bars either.[17]

December 24th dawned bright but cold as the four hundred remaining prisoners in Flamersheim departed on foot for Bonn; along the way some men found and ate raw potatoes and turnips. In one village an angry mob of citizens shook their fists and shouted curses at the GIs because Allied planes were making their lives hell. GIs speculated that the policy of marching prisoners through towns was designed to boost civilian morale by demonstrating Germany was indeed winning the war. At 2:00 P.M. the POWs reached a transit prison camp dominated by French inmates, who received more food— or so the Americans believed. Inside the concrete-block buildings, divided into spacious rooms, the Germans had placed small stoves but would not allow them to be used at night; consequently, the cold easily came in through broken windowpanes. As Milton May lay down on the concrete floor with an empty stomach, he imagined what his folks at home would be eating for Christmas dinner. William Mudra and the other shivering POWs wondered what the future held, other than movement farther away from American forces.[18]

Christmas Day turned out a little better than most expected. First, everyone received a bowl of hot cabbage soup, including a few potato chunks, and one-sixth of a loaf of black bread. Milton May thought, "No stateside turkey would have tasted better." Second, they enjoyed ringside seats to an exciting dogfight between a gray German Messerschmidt and a high-powered American P-51 fighter. When the pursuing American's machine guns struck the German plane in the midsection, it burst into flames, eliciting cheers from the POWs.[19]

Bonn served as a central distribution center for POWs, and the guards locked a large group of POWs in boxcars (known as "forty-and-eights" because they were designed to carry forty men or eight horses) headed for Limburg, a city sixty miles southeast of Bonn. A few German civilians came to gawk at the scruffy Americans, but one "courageous lady" brought a platter of cookies; Furman Grimm took one and told her, "God Bless you."[20]

The haunting "whoo—whoo" of the locomotive's whistle signaled an ominous warning to its human cargo. Shipped like livestock headed for a slaughterhouse, the men suffered deprivation and humiliation, underscored by close quarters and the lack of sanitary facilities. William White, who had no gloves or overcoat, remembered the freezing temperatures and the ice on the inside of the boxcar. Squeezed together on the floor, the men tried to lift their spirits by singing Christmas Carols, with little to celebrate except they were still alive. As White's first Christmas apart from his wife Rena, he, like so many others, could not dispel the pain of homesickness and melancholy.[21]

• • •

HAMMELBURG: STALAG XIII C

Although the distance to Limburg was not far, the trip lasted hours, mostly at night to avoid being strafed by American planes. Richard Render's group arrived early on Christmas Day and marched through the city's streets to the prison camp designated Stalag XII A. Their guards had told them upon arrival they would be given showers, food, and a warm place to stay; however, on the night of December 23, British aircraft mistakenly bombed the camp, killing American POWs and destroying several barracks. So when the new batch of prisoners reached the prison, they learned there was no room for them. For Richard Render Christmas Day 1944 "was the low point of my prison experience."[22]

The POWs did not know that seven 99ers from B Company 394 were locked inside the prison at Limburg. Two 99ers, Pendleton Woods and Clarence "Red" Deal, and five others were captured on December 10 while on a reconnaissance patrol near the Siegfried Line. Their captors marched them into a vacant, snow-covered field where Deal assumed they would be executed—rumor had it the Germans shot prisoners. Instead, two giant doors opened, and they descended into an underground bunker. Their interrogator, a German officer, knew they had trained at Camp Maxey, identified where they had been stationed in England, and correctly named their company and battalion. The officer, who had traveled extensively in the

United States, stunned Deal by asking whether Bishop's Restaurant remained a good place to eat in Oklahoma City, Deal's hometown.[23]

The seven 99ers were subsequently transported to Düren and placed in the city's unheated, windowless jail. For two days and three nights they lay in a circle with a single blanket covering their feet and legs. Then they were placed in a boxcar with other prisoners and transported eighty-five miles to Limburg, a trip that took several days to complete.

At Stalag XII A Woods and Deal were locked in a large building, so crowded that not all the POWs could recline simultaneously on the concrete floor. Woods, suffering from dysentery, began crawling over his recumbent fellow prisoners toward the latrine located at the end of the building, but couldn't move fast enough and soiled his boxer shorts and long underwear. All he could do was remove the underwear and try to wipe the mess off his body and then throw away the fetid clothing. From then on he lived and worked without underwear.[24]

• • •

Prisoners who had been turned away from the overcrowded camp were sent back under guard to the train station and waited outside on the platform for the train to return. As they moved about to keep from freezing, a German guard toyed with them by cutting a slice of bread into small pieces and throwing them onto the railroad tracks. Stanley Colby refused to humiliate himself, but other hungry GIs scrambled after the crumbs. Robert Grant and Howard Harris recalled German housewives handing out pastries to the guards, but not to the POWs. Robert Grant said bitterly, "All we could do was watch [the guards] and think about Christmas back home."[25]

One prisoner collapsed but the guards would not allow him to be taken into the station; he died a few days later. It was as if, Marvin Snyder concluded, "they didn't care what happened to us." A group of prisoners, including Sgt. Dwight Bishop, began to softly sing "White Christmas" but lost enthusiasm in the cold. Finally, in the evening, the train reappeared and the prisoners were herded into boxcars and transported without food or water to Stalag XIII C near Hammelburg, one hundred miles to the east in Bavaria, north of the Main River and Würzburg.[26]

Since the boxcars were enclosed, except for two small, wired-covered rectangular portholes located high up at both ends, the POWs could not even pass the time watching the scenery as they sat between their neighbor's legs. Some light penetrated holes and cracks during the day, but at night they shivered in total darkness not knowing where they were going, except farther into Germany's interior. Most of the men remained quiet but sullen; a few expressed anger, and others wept. Everyone endured a certain degree of fearfulness, for they had no idea what might happen to them. Some thought about Christmas and home, but they would have to focus on survival, then, and in the coming months.

The POWs relieved themselves in helmets which they passed to men nearest the two portholes, who threw the smelly contents through the small 12 x 18-inch wired openings. Others urinated in the crack of the door. Once the train stopped the men were allowed outside the boxcars for a few minutes. They used these short breaks to toss out the waste in their helmets (if they still had them), empty their bladders, and drink some water. Most of the men had become heavy smokers and suffered from nicotine withdrawal; the lack of food only increased a craving for cigarettes. William Heroman remembered how, when the train halted and the doors opened, the smokers jumped out and frantically gathered leaves, grass, and even rose stems, anything they could smoke in lieu of tobacco.[27]

During a stop at one railroad junction, British planes bombed the yards. Robert Gabriel recalled the darkness, the screams, the noise, the ground shaking, and their feelings of helplessness, as the guards would not release them from the boxcars. On December 26, after twenty-four hours in boxcars, the first 99th POWs reached Hammelburg. As they walked through the narrow cobblestone streets, German civilians poked their heads out to look at the American prisoners. Some residents handed baked goods to the guards but not to the prisoners, who walked south three miles to Hammelburg *Lager*, a former German Army training center converted into a large prison camp. Since the prison was located in a saucer-shaped hollow on top of a plateau, the walk uphill with snow on the ground proved especially difficult for men with frozen feet. Dwight Bishop was in such bad shape that two men had to carry him up a long hill from the railroad yards. The camp, which eventually held thirty thousand enlisted men and four thousand officers, was divided by nationality (Russian, Serb, French, British, and American) and by rank: commissioned officers at the north end, Oflag XIII B; noncommissioned officers and privates in the south, Stalag XIII C.[28]

According to Marvin Snyder, enlisted men of the 99th Division and the 106th Infantry Division became the first group of American POWs at Hammelburg. The privates were assigned to wooden barracks while noncommissioned officers stayed in a one-story, brick-and-plaster horse stable. Two rows of barbed wire fences with guard towers, lights, and machine guns surrounded the entire camp. Close to the inside fence, the Germans had placed a warning wire one foot off the ground. The prisoners were told that anyone who stepped over that wire or who ventured outside the locked barracks at night would be shot.[29]

The Germans were unprepared, in terms of shelter and food, for such a large influx of new prisoners accumulated during the Battle of the Bulge. This problem worsened as the Red Army advanced through Poland toward eastern Germany, forcing the Germans to march their prisoners westward. Hitler foolishly believed POWs could be used as a bargaining chip with the Allied powers. By the end of 1944 the Germans held 2 million POWs, including 95,000 Americans.[30]

Heating was minimal in the prison quarter, so everyone suffered from the bitter cold. German guards issued each man a thin, wool blanket, which the prisoners kept wrapped around themselves. At night most slept two to a narrow bunk, with two blankets on top, so that each benefited from the body heat of his bunkmate. Initially prisoners in Emil Wieleba's barrack stripped to their underwear for additional warmth, but the guard stopped this practice, fearing it would encourage homosexual behavior.[31]

Lice thrived in the mattresses, gunnysacks filled with wood chips. Day and night men scratched their bodies, especially about the stomach, ankles, and head. They spent considerable time and energy killing the lice and squeezing the eggs, which settled into the seams of their clothes. Some men were permitted a cold shower and deloused, but as soon as they returned to their bunks, the lice hungrily jumped on their prey.

Each morning began with roll call (*Appell*) or a count of prisoners, a practice repeated twice a day, often taking forty-five minutes or more in cold weather—a method of determining if any escapes (or deaths)

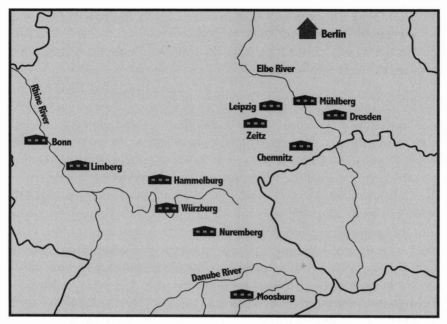

German POW camps. Map by Paul Giacomotto and James Knight.

had occurred during the night and a reflection of the German obsession with numbers. During the first roll call an officer asked all Jews to step forward, warning of terrible consequences if Jewish soldiers failed to follow this order. The German assured the group no harm would come to the Jews unless they failed to identify themselves to camp authorities. Sensing danger, Al Goldstein refused to move, but other GIs, either out of concern for Goldstein or for themselves, kept saying, "You'd better step out, Al." Finally, the murmuring grew so loud he felt he had no choice but to step forward. (In other barracks some Jews did so voluntarily.) The Jewish prisoners were collected and escorted to a separate barrack. Worried about what might happen, Goldstein slipped out that night and returned to his original barrack. No one said anything. That daring move may have saved his life, for Jewish POWs were sent to Berga, a satellite camp of Buchenwald, where some 20 percent died.[32]

Later, when registering and receiving German dog tags, Goldstein and other Jews identified themselves as Protestants. A short, mustached

German guard asked Raymond Wenzel, "What are you doing here with a German name like that?" Wenzel replied, "I was born in the U.S.A., thank goodness."[33]

In training and in transit GIs conversed about women; in prison they talked almost exclusively about food. A young male needs about 2,150 calories per day to remain active; in cold conditions even more; the POWs however received fewer than than 1,000 calories per day. Consequently prisoners suffered from severe malnutrition and, had the war lasted longer, would have faced the possibility of starvation. Several men died and were buried in a field away from the barracks. (The starving Russians, viewed by the Germans as an inferior race, were dumped in a separate plot.) Earl Peters, one of the gravediggers, remembered the German guards measured exact dimensions for each hole the POWs dug. Then the wooden box was lowered unceremoniously into the ground. No prayers were said, and no marker was erected.[34]

After rising at 6:00 A.M. and making their beds, each prisoner received a cup of ersatz coffee and a bowl of thin barley soup. When Burrell Hartley looked at his first serving of barley soup, he saw little white worms in it. He dumped it. Driven by hunger, the next day he shut his eyes and drank the soup, worms and all.[35]

In the late afternoon a pint of awful-tasting soup usually made from sugar beats or dehydrated vegetables was ladled into cups; five or six men also shared a loaf of black bread made of rye flour, sugar beets, and sawdust. Because it was impossible to divide a loaf equally, a certain amount of bickering ensued until a system was put in place that eliminated conflict. One group used a deck of cards to determine who would select first, second, etc. Frank Smollen, who sliced the loaf for his group, distributed the pieces in alphabetical order, and the man who chose first one day would be last the next day, so even the man with the knife could not favor himself. Everyone intently watched the cutting process, eyeballing the slightly larger pieces. Sometimes in the evening POWs received a few small potatoes and infrequently some kind of sausage.[36]

Red Cross parcels, weighing eleven pounds in compliance with German postal regulations, contained graham crackers, cheese, canned meat, dried fruit, a large can of powdered milk, a regular-size can of condensed milk, instant coffee, a chocolate bar, raisins, two bars of soap, and five packs of cigarettes, which served as the coin of the prison realm. Given the meager rations provided by the Germans, Red Cross parcels meant the difference between a tolerable existence and absolute misery for French, Serbian, and British prisoners captured early in the war.

International Red Cross parcels were distributed to all prisoners except the Russians (the Soviet Union refused to join the Red Cross) at the rate of one parcel per week per prisoner. For the first three years of the war the prisoners received regular supplies, but after D-Day (June 6, 1944) and subsequent transportation disruptions, the number of parcels reaching prisoners declined drastically. In August 1944, Berlin mandated that prisons could no longer stockpile reserves of parcels and instructed the Red Cross to limit its shipments to one-day food supplies only. During their stay in prison many Americans shared one or two Red Cross parcels among several men; some POWs never received even one until the final days of the war.[37]

• • •

Almost everyone suffered from dysentery, requiring frequent visits to a limited number of latrines. One type consisted of a long trench with a round pole the user could sit on; another was an outhouse with multiple holes. Despite a lack of food, the prisoners had to relieve themselves(especially if they suffered from dysentery), which resulted in long lines to use the primitive facilities. The Germans provided no toilet paper, so everyone, as Robert Grant said, "had a constant reminder in [his] shorts." Once Herb Netter was assigned the nauseating task of "honey dipping" or emptying a latrine. Using a six-foot pole with a helmet attached, he scooped up the reeking muck and dumped it into a two-sided garbage wagon while spattering himself with filth in the process. The contents were given to a farmer who, it was assumed, used it to fertilize his fields. Since prisoners were not allowed to leave the barracks at night, they had to plan their trips to the latrine before lockup or else use a five-gallon can placed in the center of the room.[38]

Confined to their barracks and the immediate surrounding area, there was little to do, so time dragged, as the prisoners dealt with cold, hunger, uncertainty, and lethargy. The guards, a collection of misfits unsuitable for combat, neither brutalized nor threatened the prisoners. Sensing their lack of enthusiasm for the job, the prisoners sometimes took rebellious pleasure on good weather days in throwing off the prisoner count during *Appell.* On Sundays chaplains held church services, and German movies were shown for a while until the guards discovered POWs were disassembling the wooden benches for firewood.

Prisoners could send a few cards and letters informing families of their plight, but the absence of incoming mail from loved ones severed that tenuous but important connection to home. In the mid-twentieth century most Americans had grown up with warm clothing, hot meals, baths, soap, toothbrushes, haircuts, and entertainment. In the camps these basic components of civilized living had disappeared, and prisoners' lives had been reduced to a primitive level that drained them physically and psychologically. Having seen the comfortable conditions German POWs enjoyed at Camp Maxey, the men were outraged by their circumstances. Burrell Hartley could not understand "how a people [who] were supposed to be civilized could treat their fellow man so terribly."[39]

Men read the Bible, played cards, and slept, but mostly they thought, talked, and dreamed about food. Pendleton Woods explained that the gnawing pain in the stomach disappears after a while as the stomach shrinks: "Hunger is in the blood, which means it is all over your body," so the entire body craves nourishment. POWs spent hours naming all the candy bars they knew, exchanged menus of favorite dishes, and discussed foods they longed to devour. Patrick Morris fantasized about stacks of pancakes with "oodles of butter running over the edges and covered with maple syrup." John Thornburg longed for ice cream covered with caramel and chocolate mints. Harry Hagstad had more pedestrian but nonetheless civilized dreams about elimination rather than consumption, namely, a bathroom with a flush toilet, real toilet paper, and a normal bowel movement after which he could wash his hands.[40]

Those men who couldn't adjust to such debilitating conditions became extremely depressed and lay in bed day and night. As Harry Peterson commented, "Starvation brings on general listlessness and apathy." Unlike British compounds, where senior noncommissioned officers established order, rules, and activities, American enlisted men did not create a hierarchy of authority. Consequently each man had to fend for himself, usually among strangers. To enhance one's chances for survival, the POW needed to establish a relationship with a buddy or a small group to maintain morale in the face of gradual starvation and an uncertain future.

Each barrack contained two small stoves but without sufficient fuel for heating. German guards asked the noncoms to go on work details and cut wood, with the promise they could keep most of what they gathered. But when the initial ten-man party returned with branches, the guards confiscated the wood for themselves. On the next detail into the forest, the sergeants organized a sit-down strike and refused to work, citing provisions of the Geneva Convention. The German guards became angry, put shells in their rifle chambers, and pointed them at the strikers. Burrell Hartley thought the guards might shoot them, but "we sat tight." Finally the guards gave up and escorted the POWs back to the camp. That ended wood-gathering details for noncoms, a small victory over their keepers, but one that resulted in the loss of additional firewood.[41]

WORK CAMP IN BERGSINN

After a few weeks, the Germans drafted thirty-five POWs for an extended work detail outside Stalag XIII C. Because the prisoners were ostensibly paid for their work (actually a pittance never received by the captives) the German military could claim it did not violate Geneva Convention protocols forbidding the use of forced labor. In reality, ordinary soldiers of all nationalities became part of the huge slave work force the Nazi regime exploited. Had Germany won the war, a permanent caste of slaves would have been forced to perform the manual labor the German people considered beneath them.

The POWs from Hammelburg rode in passenger cars to Bergsinn, an attractive village on the Sinn River twelve miles west of Hammelburg. Here they chopped down beech trees that were ground into wood chips and then burned in lieu of gasoline (increasingly in short supply) as fuel for steam-powered trucks. William Kirkbride reckoned Germany's desperate use of wood indicated it was losing the war. Felling medium-height trees with axes and then cutting the trunks into one-meter logs with a two-handled crosscut saw required considerable physical labor. However, the five guards, older men disabled in combat, did not demand extraordinary effort, though one German did remark that the "Americans were lazier than the Poles"; he failed to realize the POWs had no desire to work for the German war effort. Anticipating Germany's defeat, Herman, the head guard, who had lived in America and spoke English, reminded them to tell the American troops, "I was not mean to you." To endear himself to his charges, he once took the POWs to town for a haircut, but no bath unless they wanted to jump in the frigid Sinn River. At least prisoners could build small fires in the woods and bake the odd potato or carrot they somehow acquired. Working outdoors in winter could be harsh, but they were not cooped up all day.[42]

Housed on the second floor of a sturdy stone barn in Bergsinn, POWs could bring firewood back at night and burn it in a stove, another advantage over the Hammelburg barracks. Otherwise, living conditions were much the same in both. Breakfast, served at 7:00 A.M., consisted of 500 grams of black bread (sickly non-workers received just 250 grams), a slice of baloney, and a cup of ersatz coffee. Since no lunch was served, most men saved half their bread to eat in the forest. Supper included a bowl of beet or vegetable soup and a cup of tea. On Sunday, their day off, the soup might contain potatoes and a little meat, which they guessed came from either a horse or a dog. On one occasion the POWs unloaded potatoes from a damaged boxcar; naturally some of those spuds found their way into prisoners' pant legs.[43]

Living conditions improved somewhat compared to those in Stalag XIII C, but the captive GIs remained prisoners in a facility ringed by a chain-link fence topped by barbed wire. They had access to an indoor latrine with stools, but only until 8:00 P.M.; so, as Robert Gabriel put it, "We made our toilet plans based upon business hours." Finding any kind of paper to use in the latrine presented a real challenge, but given the limited amount of food, William Kirkbride recalled, "They only had a bowel movement every third day." Even though the guards behaved decently, the prisoners delighted in vexing them. The POWs picked lice off their skin and placed them in a Red Cross–supplied matchbox. On Sundays a small detail had the responsibility to clean up the guards' quarters on the first floor. Whoever was assigned that day would take the matchbox and spread lice in the beds of the guards. On Mondays the POWS enjoyed watching the guards scratch themselves as they stood by the fires in their heavy wool greatcoats.[44]

TASK FORCE BAUM

On March 25, the POWs watched in amazement as an American armored column rumbled through Bergsinn and crossed the Sinn River, firing at and wounding one of the guards in the process. Two POWs ran and jumped on a half-track as the convoy passed by, while the rest of the prisoners cheered, mistakenly believing forward elements of General George Patton's Third Army had arrived to liberate them. But this Armored Task Force, commanded by Capt. Abraham Baum, consisting of ten medium and six light tanks, twenty-seven half-tracks, three self-propelled 105mm assault guns, and 293 men, had been ordered to rescue Patton's son-in-law, Lt. Col. John Waters (a prisoner at Hammelburg, fifty miles behind enemy lines), not the POWs at Bergsinn.[45]

This suicidal mission had no chance of succeeding. Hit by *panzerfausts* (a recoilless antitank weapon) and tank destroyers along the route, Capt. Baum lost half-tracks, jeeps, tanks, and men as the column blasted its way to Hammelburg. The depleted force finally reached Oflag XIII B (the officers' camp) in the evening on March 26 and knocked a hole in the fence. In the ensuing melee, however, a German guard shot and severely wounded Lt. Col. Waters, defeating the purpose of the risky raid. Moreover, Capt. Baum was stunned to discover the camp contained fifteen hundred U.S. officers, but he could only take a small group, made even smaller by the loss of vehicles. Freeing enlisted men was not part of the operation, but when the guards scattered, those POWs assumed they would soon be liberated, and according to Richard Render, everyone unwisely consumed their stocks of hoarded food.[46]

Most officer POWs at Oflag XIII B concluded it would be too dangerous to walk out and stayed in the camp. The remaining tanks, half-tracks, and jeeps departed with some POWs, but German forces almost immediately surrounded them. Fifteen of Baum's men and two POWs escaped to the American lines; twenty-five men were killed and the rest captured, including the POWs who tried to leave the prison camp. On April 6, 1945, the 14th Armored Division liberated the camp, but found only seventy wounded American officers, including Baum and Waters, remained there. The Germans had already shipped the prisoners to Nuremberg.[47]

BERGSINN TO NUREMBERG

After Task Force Baum left, the prisoners in Bergsinn returned to their compound and found the guards missing. For several days the POWs lived as free men, but decided to wait in their farmhouse/prison until the rest of Patton's forces arrived. As William Kirkbride wryly commented, "We didn't have sense enough to leave." The guards returned, however, and the brief interlude of freedom ended. Alerted to the imminent arrival of American forces, Herman announced the POWs would be walking to Nuremberg more than ninety miles away. Not only wouldn't they be freed, as they had anticipated, but they would be walking away from American forces.

On Sunday April 1, 1945, the thirty-five POWs and the guards departed Bergsinn on foot. After proceeding a few miles, Robert Gabriel and two buddies decided to slip away into the dense forest along the route. Surprisingly, no guards came charging after them. Walking all day and most of the night, the escapees used the North Star to guide them westward toward Frankfurt, which they knew U.S. troops had seized. On the third day, upon hearing the engine roar of what they thought was an American tank, they carelessly rushed out into the open, only to encounter a German patrol led by an older man and three teenagers. Luckily the German soldiers were friendly, offering them cigarettes and sausage, because they wanted to surrender to American forces. The Germans escorted them to their company's area where a German MP sergeant (and two other MPs) assumed command of the group. Instead of trying to locate American forces, the MPs decided to follow orders and take the prisoners to Nuremberg. At one point an SS trooper rode up on a motorcycle and told the German MPs that Hitler had ordered all prisoners to be shot, and all soldiers should report to the nearest line of resistance. But the three MPs pointed their rifles at the SS trooper, who angrily barked at them but then drove off. The POWs and the German MPs proceeded to Nuremberg without further incident, but Gabriel's escape attempt had failed.[48]

• • •

Apparently unconcerned about the missing prisoners, Herman and his four guards escorted the group along back roads toward Nuremberg, because using the main highways would provide easy targets for prowling America fighters. Having survived nearly four months in captivity, nothing would be more tragic for the POWs than to be killed as the war drew to a close, especially by friendly fire. Besides, Herman was not eager to reach their final destination, fearing he would be sent to the front. Looking like a bunch of filthy tramps, they staggered along, sleeping in barns and taking food from fields and farms when they could find it. After ten days the group reached the outskirts of Nuremberg where they came upon a beautiful park with green grass and newly leafed trees. William Kirkbride, who had a badly infected foot that made walking difficult, and the other POWs relaxed on benches, taking in this peaceful scene as small gatherings of German soldiers and civilians stood talking and enjoying the spring day. The soldiers paid no attention to the POWs, though a few civilians told the Americans about the recent, destructive bombing of the city. Amidst destruction and death, the park briefly offered a time and place out of war, a glimpse of what existed before and hopefully what would return once again for everyone.[49]

The prisoners moved on to Stalag XIII D, located in Langwasser, just outside Nuremberg. Other American prisoners had departed, so their group was alone, except for twelve Italian captives "uniformed like doormen," and several thousand starving Russian POWs, incarcerated in a separate compound. After one day Herman and the guards herded the POWs south but stopped in the village of Wendelstein, three miles past the camp, where they settled in a sizable barn. After a few hours, Herman and the guards appeared dressed in civilian clothes, bade farewell, and abandoned their prisoners. The POWs left the barn and walked to a nearby schoolhouse where soldiers from the 45th Infantry Division liberated them. Their ordeal had ended.

• • •

Because Kirkbride could barely walk, he had stayed behind in the Nuremberg camp with another injured American prisoner to receive medical attention. Standing inside the barbed wire fence, Kirkbride heard the loud roar of what he excitedly assumed was a swarm of U.S. Sherman tanks. But over the hillcrest came a single, noisy tank from the 45th Infantry Division, the Oklahoma national guard division from his home state. Kirkbride joked to his friend, "They have come for me!" The lone tank pulled up outside the prison gate, and the tank commander, not recognizing the shabbily dressed prisoners, yelled from the turret, "What is going on here?" Kirkbride replied, "We are American POWs. How about knocking down the fence?" The tank driver revved up the engine and rammed the fence, laying it flat, whereupon the German guards immediately slammed their rifle barrels into the ground and hollered, "*Kamerad!*"

Because Kirkbride was incapacitated, the tankers gave him a confiscated Volkswagen automobile so he might move around more easily. He drove into Nuremberg and happened upon the gigantic stadium in which Hitler and the Nazis once held their mass rallies. Having seen photos of the stadium filled with hypnotized crowds in the *Weekly Reader* he read in high school, Kirkbride immediately recognized its significant history. Here thousands of Germans once hailed the Führer with Nazi salutes and chants, but the place was strangely silent and empty, like the promises Hitler had made to the German people.[50]

WÜRZBURG

In Hammelburg, on February 1, the Germans rounded up 160 enlisted men in Stalag XIII C, mostly 99ers, who were transported by passenger train to Würzburg, a lovely, old medieval city straddling the Main River, thirty miles south of Hammelburg. Quartered in a large gymnasium with double bunks and stoves but no fuel, the POWs had access to wash basins (without hot water or towels) and toilets without toilet paper. Their diet remained much the same, but they found opportunities to steal supplies and food. The men were farmed out to perform various jobs: sixty POWs transferred supplies from boxcars to trucks in Zell three miles downriver; others stacked goods in a warehouse, and one party baled hay until a prisoner deliberately broke the machine. The general attitude, a form of passive compliance, was to exert the least amount of effort, although Richard Knoblock maintained his group worked efficiently because they liked their civilian overseer.[51]

The POWs worried constantly about their survival. Al Goldstein imagined a mob of angry German civilians might seek revenge for Allied bombings or, alternately, war planes would unwittingly obliterate them. The most demoralized prisoners did not bother to wash or keep their quarters clean, and they relieved themselves wherever the urge came instead of using the latrines. The German sergeant in charge, a First World War veteran who resembled film actor Wallace Beery, dismayed by their appearance and behavior, organized Sunday inspections and close-order drills to instill discipline in his slovenly charges. The sergeant told Goldstein, "The Russians I had before you were bad enough, but you Americans are much worse." Goldstein himself was disgusted by the "shameful" behavior exhibited by some of his fellow POWs: groveling before the guards for cigarettes, showing no interest in personal hygiene, fighting, bullying the weak, and worst of all, stealing food from others, including the sick. While a prisoner might count on a small group of friends or a buddy for help and protection, no one took charge or had the rank to impose discipline or promote cohesiveness.[52]

Goldstein served as an interpreter, translating orders from the German guards to the American POWs. Feeling a responsibility to obtain medical care for the sick, Goldstein repeatedly requested that a doctor see the ill; but the German sergeant rejected his entreaties, arguing the men were not sick, just lazy. Then one morning the sergeant told Goldstein he could take the sick to an infirmary. Goldstein collected about twenty men whom the German doctor treated, including one POW he sent to the hospital. The physician, however, complained about having to examine so many filthy patients. Consequently, the sergeant told Goldstein that in the future he could only send a small number for medical treatment, and diarrhea did not qualify. This stricture placed Goldstein in the uncomfortable and unpopular position of having to decide who would receive care and who would not. Then, one day the sergeant abruptly and inexplicably fired Goldstein as triage nurse, saying he could "not have a Jew in a position of such authority." Apparently the German was not actually an anti-Semite, for he never alerted the Gestapo, and he appointed, perhaps unwittingly, another Yiddish-speaking Jew (Murray Fox) in Goldstein's place.[53]

• • •

During the night of March 16–17, 1945, British bombers dropped tons of incendiary bombs on Würzburg, creating a firestorm that burned the city to the ground, killing some five thousand inhabitants. The POWs, sitting in a bomb shelter escaped injury, but their living quarters, the bakery, and the warehouses were destroyed. The guards led the prisoners through the burning city and out into the country-side. Looking back on the inferno as they walked, Robert Grant thought the scene resembled General Sherman's torching of Atlanta in the movie, *Gone with the Wind*. Although it was March, the heat blowing from the city "made it feel like a balmy August evening."[54]

Since everything had been leveled in Würzburg, the prisoners were relocated to Zell and housed in a small, frame building near four large concrete warehouses and the railroad yards. Their new quarters contained no beds or blankets, so sleeping conditions dete-riorated. Ten days later, American fighter-bombers bombed and strafed the rail yards, damaging several boxcars in which the POWs discovered cigarettes, cheeses, blood sausages, chocolates, cigars, salamis, Red Cross parcels, and bottles of cognac. Some prisoners grabbed gunnysacks and filled them with food, while the guards insisted the prisoners carry cases of liquor to their quarters, where they proceeded to get drunk.

The inebriated German sergeant became rather talkative and revealed to Goldstein that soon he would march the prisoners to Nuremberg. Upon hearing that information, Goldstein realized he and his five companions needed to act fast. They had previously discussed their escape plans with one of the guards, a melancholy German whom they called Curly. He was to accompany them, and if any German troops stopped them, he would simply say the Americans were his captives. Goldstein dashed off to find Curly, but discovered he was too drunk to leave. So the men collected some food and they departed without him, heading west in the direction of the American lines. After walking several hours they climbed a hill and found a con-crete dugout, where they decided to hide. A few days later a group of German soldiers stumbled onto their hiding place but ignored the POWs out of a desire to flee the fast-approaching American forces.[55]

The next day the escapees spotted three U.S. Sherman tanks on the other side of the river valley. The POWs descended the hill, planning to threaten an old man with a knife and take his boat to cross the river. This proved unnecessary, for the German cooperated with them, instructing his two grandsons to row the Americans to safety. On the other side the POWs ascended a long slope and came upon a flat plain. Stretched out before their eyes were scores of tanks. They ran toward the nearest one, shouting, "Don't shoot! Don't shoot! We're GIs." The surprised tankers escorted them to an officer, who immediately offered them a swig of Old Crow whiskey. Freedom never tasted so good.[56]

ZELL TO MOOSBURG

On April 1, Easter Sunday, the guards in Zell told the remaining prisoners to go into a warehouse and fill a gunny sack with canned goods, cheese, and enough food to last several days, as they were going to walk to Nuremberg. From there they were to continue on to Stalag VII A at Moosburg in southern Bavaria.

Heretofore the POWs could have slipped away at any time, for they were not fenced in, and only a few elderly guards watched them. Not knowing where they were or if they might encounter German troops, no one thought, especially during the cold winter months, that escaping offered a viable option. But when the prisoners realized they would be heading away from nearby American forces, some decided to take action. The group marched several hours and then halted for a break in a forested area, whereupon seven 99ers ran into the woods and walked a mile back to a village they had passed earlier. When the sun poked through the clouds and created a rainbow, they took this as a favorable omen and decided to approach a farmhouse. Asked if they might stay in his barn, the owner declined but suggested they hide in a nearby stone quarry, which they did. Several days later a German infantry squad spotted them crouched at the bottom of the shallow quarry. The Germans could have easily killed them, but the war-weary lieutenant in command simply told the Americans to go back to sleep and led his squad away. When the seven escapees heard recognizable sounds of U.S. Army vehicles, they emerged from the quarry and saw Sherman tanks everywhere. The hungry POWs

returned to the farmhouse, but this time the German family prepared a breakfast of hot potato soup for them. They instructed the
owner to go into the village and tell the Americans that U.S. prisoners were staying in his house. After eating, the POWs looked out
the window and saw the farmer with hands raised, walking in front
of a single Sherman tank approaching the house. The seven were
free at last.[57]

• • •

The remaining Zell prisoners continued on the road by way of
Nuremberg toward Moosburg, 150 miles away. Other POWs joined
the column, which stretched out for a half-mile. Undernourished
and weak, the prisoners could not sustain a fast pace. Even those
who carried food, and many did not, soon depleted their supply
and had to scrounge for potatoes and frozen sugar beets they took
from farms. Emil Wieleba, who learned Polish at home in Detroit,
bartered with Russian and Polish slave laborers for food, but with
limited success: "hunger was a word we walked with every day." Three
weeks later they finally reached the outskirts of Mainburg, only twenty
miles from Moosburg, where Wieleba's group spent the night in a
barn. When they awoke the next morning, the guards were gone,
leaving their rifles behind. Several slave laborers on the farm told
them American forces were already ahead of them, so they walked
into Mainburg and found the city overflowing with U.S. 6 x 6 trucks,
weapons carriers, and jeeps. The next day they climbed aboard trucks
and rode to an airfield in Regensburg, boarding DC-4 transport
planes that flew them to France, where they impatiently awaited a
ship homeward bound.[60]

HAMMELBURG TO MOOSBURG

One day after the abortive Baum raid, the guards escorted all the
POWs in Stalag XIII C to Hammelburg's train station and put them
in boxcars for a trip to Nuremberg. When an American fighter strafed
the train, the guards ran off, leaving the POWs locked inside. But the
prisoners survived. After arriving at Stalag XIII D in Nuremberg, the
group was crammed into several circus-sized tents. The next day they
heard the thunderous roar of approaching American bombers and

fighters. The guards allowed the POWs to leave the tents and run for ditches along the road where they took cover, scared and hungry, hoping and praying the fighters would not attack the camp. They didn't.

The following day a long column of POWs clothed in dirty, ill-fitting outfits, crawled southward like drab insects being drawn by an unseen force toward Moosburg, ninety miles away. The guards warned the prisoners that anyone who attempted to escape would be shot, a threat most took seriously. The men walked for ten days, sleeping in barns, churches, hay mounds, and on bare ground. By the time they reached Stalag VII A in Moosburg, the prison camp, originally built to house fourteen thousand, had swelled to more than eighty thousand prisoners of all nationalities. Because the barracks were filled to capacity, the late-arriving Americans had to live in large, white tents with mud floors.[59]

On the morning of April 29, a tank from the 14th Armored Division and troops from the 394th Regiment of the 99th Division appeared at the front gate and received a tumultuous ovation from the prisoners. A Red Cross truck arrived and served coffee and donuts while playing, appropriately, the song, "It's Been a Long, Long Time." Although most of the original members of the 394th were gone, POW William White found two officers from his old company and enjoyed a happy reunion with them. General George Patton came two days later. Standing in a half-track, he told the men they were heroes, which made Robert Davis feel better about having surrendered to the enemy. After being deloused and given clean clothes, the ex-POWs were trucked to an airport in Landshut where they climbed aboard C-47 transport planes that took off for France. During the flight William White looked out his plane window and spotted the Rhine River, which he had not seen four months earlier when locked in a German boxcar.[60]

MÜHLBERG STALAG IV B

Late at night on December 26, German guards packed another group of prisoners into boxcars on a train headed for Mühlberg, a town in eastern Germany near the Elbe River, eighty miles from the Polish border. Besides the abominable, crowded physical conditions —lack of space forced the passengers to alternate between standing and sitting—the prisoners had to deal with the psychological stress of not knowing their destination or what awaited them at journey's end. Harold Wagner remembered receiving a bowl of steamed sauerkraut before departure from Bonn; any food was desperately welcomed, but this cabbage had the unfortunate result of producing a need for bodily elimination. William Mudra said the Germans also gave each prisoner a half loaf of bread and some cheese, but no one had any water.[61]

No direct railroad route existed, and the trip's duration lengthened because American fighters had knocked out sections of track. When the train stopped for long periods, "It made us feel," according to Mudra, "as though we were being abandoned to vultures in a strange desert." They wondered if the trip would ever end and whether they could survive the journey. Everyone was miserable, hungry, cold, and depressed, so conversation was limited. In John Thornburg's car the men argued and complained so much that he was ashamed of their behavior. Richard Folmar felt vulnerable, for they had not been registered with the Red Cross, so no record existed of their capture, and the German guards could, he feared, take them off the train and shoot them if they felt so inclined.[62]

On December 28, the Germans provided the POWs with barley soup and tea, but the welcomed and needed liquids contributed to more elimination problems. John Thornburg remembered in his boxcar men defecated in the so-called crap helmet, which was passed around until it was full, then dumped out the ventilator (difficult to accomplish, especially in the dark); others defecated and urinated in a corner. But since Thornburg and others had diarrhea, their underwear became the main receptacle. Once when the train stopped, the men relieved themselves in the railroad yards while the townspeople watched. Unsympathetic to their plight, the guards commented on the Americans' uncivilized behavior.[63]

During the third day an American fighter swooped down like a raptor with easy prey in sight. Hearing the engine noise, the prisoners boosted one fellow up to the ventilator who spotted the plane and yelled out, "Here he comes!" In Harold Wagner's car everyone "hit the floor in the muck and mire," and in John Thornburg's car someone overturned the "crap helmet," which added to the stench. German train crew and guards dashed for cover while the prisoners cried and shouted to be let out, but to no avail. The plane made a pass at the sitting target and raked the flimsy, wooden boxcars with .50-caliber bullets, killing one prisoner.[64]

On December 30 the weather turned cold, producing a coating of frost on the inside of the boxcars that the men licked in a desperate attempt to quench their thirst. Another weary night and day passed before the prisoners reached the camp three miles east of Mühlberg on New Year's Eve, 1945. Stumbling down from boxcars halted on a railway spur, the bleary-eyed POWs observed a bleak, snow-covered landscape, barren except for a few clumps of leafless trees. Barely able to walk after being confined so long, the men dragged themselves toward the prison where they spotted ominous guard towers, snow-covered wooden barracks, double barbed wire fences, and the main gate above which hung the sawed-out block letters: "M Stammlager IV B." The camp contained some fifteen thousand prisoners with French, Russian, Dutch, British, and other nationalities kept in separate compounds.[65]

Having lived there more than two years, the British made it plain they were in charge of the compound, and the "Yanks" had to obey their orders. There was a noticeable difference in appearance, as the clean-shaven British POWs in dress uniforms scrutinized the unshaven, bedraggled Yanks in their soiled ODs. The first day the senior British noncom, flanked by German guards, addressed the newcomers, saying: "Welcome to Stalag IV B, Yanks. This is going to be your home for some of you for quite awhile. It's going to be crowded, so everyone is going to have to cooperate. We are not interested in your story of how you had the misfortune to be captured, so stow it. Most of us here have had it a lot rougher."[66]

The newcomers were assigned to the British, who were, according to Richard Folmar, "extremely irritated" at having to take the Americans into their living quarters. In each barrack a British noncom explained the rules to be obeyed, which included a prohibition on planned escapes except with the approval of a compound escape committee. After toughing it out for so long, the Brits didn't have much sympathy for the new arrivals, whom they considered soft and pampered; the British complained they ate hardtack while the Americans enjoyed yummy chocolate D bars. The Brits acted, according to Jack McElroy, "very superior in manner and action, and they looked down at us as not qualified to be soldiers." Milton May also harbored bitter feelings towards the British, writing in his memoir: "They were unwilling to help us in any way, and we did not have a bit of love for them." Having first suffered the indignity of being captured, American boys had to endure perceived insults from British allies.[67]

Not all Brits were unfriendly, and in time relationships did develop. Most Americans received a shower, their first in over two months, but since no towels were provided, they had to dry themselves with their dirty uniforms and put on whatever assorted clothes they had acquired. (B.O. Wilkins and his buddies from King Company 393 got much-needed shaves from British "barbers" armed with straight razors.) The head of Harry Peterson's barrack ordered the newcomers to shave, telling them, "Just because you are a prisoner, you don't have to go around looking like a bum." Standing undressed, they could see the effects of days with minimal food, for everyone had grown thin. After being photographed in groups of four wearing German dog tags, an English-speaking German officer interrogated each prisoner, an experience that concerned Harold Wagner, who was unsure what would happen and whether he might inadvertently reveal military information. But it turned out to be a harmless exercise.[68]

The "Limeys," as the GIs called them, were organized and maintained group morale and discipline (during inspections the privates stood at attention), which gained the respect of the guards; in fact, the senior British noncom conducted *Appell* with the German officer. Although the Americans may not have admitted it, the British exuded confidence. Having endured and survived imprisonment for such a long time, they showed it was possible to make the best of a terrible situation. The British shared communally prepared food and tea with the new boys. Also a few gifted craftsmen handcrafted plates and cups from the large cans of Klim powdered milk, which they distributed to or bartered with the Americans. During the first two years the British POWs received regular shipments of Red Cross parcels, hence their health had not deteriorated drastically, and they felt fit enough to organize military drills and play soccer. But by late 1944 the number of shipments had declined, as had packages from home, so they too suffered from lack of food. They established a central market where personal belongings or items from Red Cross packages the Americans received could be traded at fluctuating exchange rates. (The Germans also bartered with the POWs.) In John Thornburg's barrack, an enterprising Brit operated a wheel of fortune in which one could win or lose cigarettes.[69]

The British provided an important psychological boost to the new arrivals, namely news of the war's progress. The Brits possessed one or two hidden radios, and every night a messenger arrived in each barrack to deliver BBC news. The Americans learned the German attack in the Ardennes had been stopped, and the Allies had mounted a counterattack. They also received reports of Soviet advances from the east but, like the Germans, were uncomfortable with the prospect of being liberated by the Red Army because the Soviet Union had been an enemy before the war.

The realization they were trapped so far from the American lines added to the burden of imprisonment. Most everyone became depressed and demoralized by the situation. George Aaron worried about his parents, wondering whether they knew of his whereabouts and, if they did know, how they dealt with "such unfavorable news." After witnessing the death of some prisoners, he wondered if he would "end up that way too."[70]

The morning began with an ersatz coffee, which tasted so bad some prisoners used it for shaving instead of drinking. At lunch each POW received a cup of cabbage soup and a slice of bread. Twice weekly two tablespoons of sugar and one cup of small potatoes were distributed. On two separate occasions a few long strands of horsemeat were added to the meal, but immediately afterwards everyone had diarrhea. Since there was only a two-holer inside the barracks, long lines of men with urgent needs could not be accommodated. Waiting in line became intolerable, and most everyone dumped in his pants. Since the men were not allowed to leave the barracks at night, everyone who failed to reach the latrine slept in a stinking mess of his own making. John Thornburg, who never experienced a solid bowel movement while in prison, had to wait until morning when he ventured outside, stripped down in the cold morning air, and washed his stained shorts, long underwear and pants. But then he put the wet clothes back on because they were all he had to wear.[71]

WORK CAMP IN ZEITZ

After two weeks in Stalag IV B, most Americans were farmed out to out-lying work camps. Richard Folmar, Harold Demone, and 170 privates were loaded into boxcars and shipped to Zeitz, a city of thirty-six thousand inhabitants, twenty miles southwest of Leipzig. The presence of a synthetic oil plant attracted American bombers and the city had suffered severe damage. The prisoners were detailed to remove rubble, save useable bricks for rebuilding, and dig mass graves for the civilian dead. The wife of a Nazi *Gauleiter* [district leader], whose house had been destroyed, came around screaming at the POWs, insisting they find her iron in the wreckage. Her demands and arrogance offended the prisoners, and they decided she would never have her iron again. When the prisoners found the iron, they sneaked it back to the barracks and, despite a search of their living quarters—a former dance hall—the iron was never discovered.

On April 13, Richard Folmar and the other POWs heard tank fire as the U.S. 6th Armored Division began attacking the city. The guards quickly led their contingent of prisoners out of Zeitz in the direction of Chemnitz. After walking a few miles, the POWs and guards stopped at a village community center to rest. Suddenly P-47s attacked the village, and everyone retreated to the basement just before two bombs struck the building. In the ensuing dust and confusion, several Americans ran off. Most were soon captured by the Gestapo, thanks to information supplied by German citizens. Folmar and two buddies, however, went up to a house and asked the *Hausfrau*, "a large woman," if they could hide in her basement. Surprisingly she agreed and escorted them downstairs where they discovered a roomful of silent civilians all sitting on benches.

Instead of putting the POWs in with the civilians, the *Hausfrau* took them to a laundry room piled high with clothes. Some time later the local Gestapo agent and two assistants came down into the cellar and asked the civilians if they had seen escaped prisoners, warning them they could be executed for withholding any information. Perhaps fearful of the consequences if they did reveal the presence of the POWs, the civilians did not give away the hiding place of the Americans.

Afterwards the three prisoners left the house and spent the night in a mausoleum with a corpse. But their luck did not hold, and they were recaptured by a German officer accompanied by a sergeant and a "young private with thick glasses." The group started out with the captain and sergeant riding bicycles while the private and the prisoners trailed behind. When the two bicyclists rode ahead some distance, the POWs easily disarmed the hapless private and walked to a farmhouse, where an elderly grandmother agreed to allow them to spend the night in her basement. The next morning they looked toward the road and spotted five 6 x 6 trucks sitting in a field in front of the house. One POW with a white cloth tied to a broom-stick greeted the GIs, who turned out to be a platoon of combat engineers who were lost. The liberated POWs were happy to offer their assistance.[73]

Work Camp in Chemnitz

On January 19, Harold Wagner was part of a hundred-man group sent to Chemnitz, forty-five miles south of Mühlberg. Housed on the second floor of a warehouse, the group worked in an Auto Union automobile repair shop. One overcast day, several weeks later, as they were returning to their living quarters, British Lancaster heavy bombers attacked the city. A bomb landed on the northeast quarter of the warehouse, and the building burned to the ground. Along with a group of French POWs, the Americans relocated to a huge three-story concrete structure housing a power plant. On March 5–6, another attack by RAF bombers devastated the city, flattening the Auto Union shop in the process. Wagner and the others were assigned the gruesome job of digging out basements and recovering the German dead.[74]

On Good Friday, March 30, 1945, the booming of artillery could be heard in the distance. That night the guards vanished. The POWs held discussions about what they should do. Some prisoners wanted to make their way out of the city and head for the American lines. Others preferred to stay put, fearing reprisals by German soldiers and armed civilians. A day later German troops appeared, rounded up the pris-oners, and began marching them south toward Czechoslovakia on roads clogged with civilians and German soldiers fleeing the advancing

Red Army. After walking for days, Wagner and others decided they too did not want to be liberated by the Russians and slipped away, returning to Chemnitz, which had become a pile of rubble. West of the city they reached a mansion occupied by American MPs. Inside a tennis court, which served as a temporary holding pen, the liberated POWs saw captured German officers and their "lady friends." Now, Wagner thought, the enemy would experience what they went through.[75]

WORK CAMP IN BAD SCHANDAU

William Mudra left Mühlberg in a group of one hundred bound for Stalag IV A, located six miles from the Czech border. Traveling south in regular passenger cars—a startling and pleasant contrast to their nightmarish journey in boxcars—they arrived in Dresden, a beautiful baroque city with stately buildings, half-timbered homes, and civilians hurrying through the streets completely unaware of the terrible fate that would befall them. After living in POW hell, this sudden return to civilization was a shock for the underfed prisoners. But Mudra's group did not remain in the city; a train carried them into fir-topped mountains near Bad Schandau where a newly built sub-camp, mostly populated by British POWs with smaller contingents of Russians and Italians (each in their own enclosure), became their new prison. For the first and only time Mudra received a Red Cross parcel he need not share with anyone else. The Germans, as was their practice, punctured every can or food tin in the parcels they could find, so the prisoners could not hoard food and consume it during an escape. The POW who received a parcel or a daily ration, distributed in the camp once every twenty-four hours, faced a difficult decision. Should he "bash," i.e., eat everything on the spot, or should he delay gratification and stretch out the food as long as possible?

Work, for which the prisoners were supposedly paid six cents a day, involved laying railroad tracks and building wooden bridges in a narrow valley surrounded by mountains. Mudra, who initially malingered and then developed a bad cough, was able, except for four days, to avoid manual labor by remaining on sick call in the camp. There he combated arctic temperatures, boredom, and the frustration of no longer receiving much information about the war. When he and others heard a rumor that British Prime Minister Winston

Churchill had broadcast an ultimatum to the German people that, if they didn't capitulate within ten days, their cities would be bombed off the map, Mudra and others thought the Germans would surely give up, and they would be freed. Ten days later, on the night of February 13, the prisoners were awakened by the thunderous rumble of hundreds of British and American bombers, followed by incessant pounding and immense fires that lit up the skies. Since Dresden was only twenty miles to the north, they could see the massive conflagration, which burned for four days, killing some thirty-five thousand civilians. Dresden's destruction, however, did not end the war, nor did it liberate the American POWs, whose numbers soon increased with the arrival of a new batch of captives.[77]

BACK TO MÜHLBERG

A few weeks later a contingent of American POWs left Stalag IV A and boarded a passenger train headed back to Mühlberg. En route they passed through what had been Dresden, but all they could see was rubble, for the once "mighty and magnificent city had been completely leveled." Dresden, Mudra thought, was dead, buried beneath its own granite. The train rumbled on to Coswig where German soldiers, civilians, and American POWs crowded into the train cars. Late that night the POWs and their guards disembarked at Stalag IV B. Despite cold and howling winds, the prisoners could not enter the camp until early morning and so were led to unheated barracks where Mudra lay on the floor, shivering uncontrollably and praying he would not freeze to death.

Because of overcrowding, Mudra and other American prisoners were housed in a *Vorlager* or pre-compound and were not allowed access to the main camp, except on special occasions. The Vorlager consisted of five barracks: one for officers, two for Italians, one for Americans, and one for the British. One hut housed 140 men and, since there weren't enough bunks for everyone, many had to sleep on the floor. The food situation kept deteriorating, but daily BBC reports, heard on clandestine radios, informed them of Allied advances. As the end of captivity drew near, it became harder to bear, especially for those prisoners who had been incarcerated for several years. On Good Friday, March 30, even though large POW signs had been painted on the roofs, an American fighter suddenly dove out of the sun and with machine guns blazing, made two passes over the camp barracks, killing five prisoners and three Germans.[77]

Daily reports indicated the Red Army would soon arrive, and excitement inside the camp grew when the guards disappeared. Russian and Polish prisoners left and crossed the Elbe River, while American and British POWs from Torgau, a few miles down river, streamed into Stalag IV B. Early in the morning on April 23, the POWs heard shouts and, looking out their windows, saw Russian soldiers racing across the fields outside the camp. Someone happily remarked, "No roll call today." But liberation produced no raucous celebration; the long anticipated release seemed strangely anticlimactic.

In the days that followed, ex-prisoners made their way to Mühlberg and confiscated everything edible from German homes and shops. Back in camp, groans of indigestion replaced the usual cries for food. May 1 was set aside as a day of celebration: decorations festooned the camp, photos were taken in front of the main gate, and officers of the Red Army were welcomed. The next day the Americans marched out of the camp and headed for the city of Riesa, where the Soviets would provide living quarters. Walking through the open main gate, the 99ers took one last look at the empty guard towers and now broken barbed wire fences that had represented the limits of their world. The agonizing ordeal had ended, and they had survived.[79]

CHAPTER 10

The War Comes to an End

With the closure of the Ruhr Pocket and the demise of the German 12th Army Group, most 99ers assumed their combat days would end, and they could savor a well earned, maybe permanent respite. As happened before, however, these infantrymen were in for another unpleasant surprise; namely, orders to hop on trucks for a 285-mile "motor march" to southern Bavaria, because the Allied High Command believed (incorrectly) the Nazis and SS troops planned to make a last, fanatical stand at a so-called national redoubt or stronghold in the German Alps. The weather warmed as the first 6 x 6 trucks departed at 10:00 A.M. on April 17, 1945. While officers and a few enlisted men knew the destination, most remained uninformed. One rumor had the division headed for Berlin, requiring more fighting but achieving the final victory; another foretold the opposite, namely, the 99th would settle into safe occupation duty. Despite the lack of downtime and the abrupt departure, Harold Adkins said morale remained "very high."[1]

The 395th Regiment left after dark, and the drivers turned on the truck headlights to illuminate the roads, which unsettled William Galegar, because it was the first time full headlights had been used since their arrival in Belgium months earlier. Having learned always to stay concealed, giving away "our presence with lights seemingly made us vulnerable to any type of sneak attack." But nothing untoward occurred, at least not to the 395th. Discipline was relaxed, and men commandeered German motorcycles, automobiles, (Patrick Morrisey jumped into an enemy ambulance), and new trucks from a Ford production plant, driving them until gas tanks emptied, whereupon they joined their mates aboard uncomfortable, drafty U.S. Army vehicles. Continuing on in a southeasterly direction, they passed through Schweinfurt where Allied bombers had reduced ball bearing factories into "nothing but twisted steel and shattered bricks."[2]

Slow-moving armor, blown bridges, crumbled cities, and disabled vehicles hindered the rate of progress. After two days the troops finally arrived at an assembly area north of Fürth and Nuremberg; they stumbled down from the trucks, tired, hungry, and unhappy. Morale flagged when it was confirmed they had joined the Third Army, ruled by General George S. Patton, a brilliant tactician albeit martinet with an insatiable need for publicity and glory. According to Dewey Amos, "we knew he had a terrible reputation"; "we were familiar," Jim Bowers asserted, with "General Patton's nickname, 'Old Blood and Guts,' which many translated as 'Our Blood and his Guts'." When Patton, standing in his polished boots, observed 99ers looking unkempt and wearing dirty, mismatched clothing, he delivered a speech on military etiquette and ordered the men to put on clean Class A uniforms. Dewey Amos noticed even the tanks had to be clean; he didn't realize Patton obsessed about image, his own and that of his troops. For veteran soldiers like Leon St. Pierre, insistence on proper dress regulations in combat was "so much chicken shit" and so unproductive in a war zone. Patton employed army regulations and the threat of punishment to rule by fear, which he thought best motivated men to place themselves in danger.[3]

Even as the weather turned cold and rainy, Patton demanded frontline troops remain outdoors in foxholes instead of sleeping in village houses, an order that was counterproductive, since it undermined troop morale. Moreover, German homes made of thick masonry offered protection against artillery shells and saved combat troops from expending time and effort digging foxholes. Guy Duren thought it was "the screwiest order of the war. We'd be next to a house and couldn't shack up in it." Company commander Harold Hill became incensed about this "idiotic order" when he observed regimental and division officers staying indoors. With access to homes denied, it was more difficult to prepare hot food, which always boosted spirits. Battalion surgeon Herbert Orr, who wanted to be close to the fighting and the wounded, was upset with Patton because he "would not allow us to infiltrate our medical vehicles among" his tanks, which commanded first priority.[4]

Patton's lack of empathy for enlisted men was not limited to the infantry. Byron Reburn witnessed Patton yell at a tank crew that had placed sand bags on the front and thick boards on the sides of their thinly plated Sherman tank for extra protection against enemy tank fire. Wearing a lacquered helmet liner and his ivory-handled pistols, Patton bellowed at the tankers, "You rotten sons-of-bitches! Get that fucking shit off! A tank is to fight in, not hide in!" After Patton departed, the tank commander asked the driver, "Do you think we should take this stuff off?" The driver replied, "By the time he sees us again, we'll be dead."[5]

Sergeant Charles Eubanks experienced Patton's wrath when he escorted a squad back for showers in pyramidal tents set up by engineers. The group was loitering on a highway when Patton's three-starred jeep came rolling along. No one paid much attention and no one came to attention, for as Eubanks said, "We weren't use to saluting officers on the front lines in the First Army." Noticing the lack of proper military courtesy, Patton barked at his driver to stop; he then angrily marched over to the group, choosing to dress down the shortest soldier, Pvt. Fortier of Brooklyn, leaning against a truck, legs crossed, smoking a cigarette with his helmet hanging over his back. Patton roared at him: "Soldier, who is in charge here?" Not wanting to get Eubanks in trouble, Fortier replied: "I don't know. This is my first day up here in this goddamn army." Patton flew into an expletive-saturated rage, ordered Fortier to put on his helmet, stand at attention, and perform a proper salute. Casting a withering look at the slovenly group, the general yelled in his high-pitched voice, "I am leaving, but I'll be back in thirty minutes, and you bastards better be lined up at attention on that highway when I return or else!" Sure enough, Patton's entourage drove by again, but this time the men stood on both sides of the highway, ramrod straight with right hands raised in salute. The general did not stop, and Eubanks did not lose his stripes.[6]

In the staging area GIs rested, cleaned weapons and themselves, received clean socks, and wrote letters. Some units practiced with twelve-foot wooden boats on small rivers and lakes in anticipation of crossing the Danube River, a worrisome prospect, according to Jim Bowers, if they had to paddle while under direct enemy fire.[7]

On April 22, it began to rain and the temperature dropped, which signaled, the men assumed, the resumption of combat; the 394th and the 395th Regiments would lead, while the 393rd would follow (initially) in reserve. On secondary roads and cross country the division moved rapidly to the southeast, walking and riding on tanks of the 14th Armored Division. At river and canal crossings the enemy would stop and fight, hoping to slow the rapid American advance, and then retreat. But the Germans knew the war was lost, and many soldiers (not the SS) surrendered if the opportunity presented itself.[8]

Energy for so much exertion was mainly fueled by K rations, so everyone yearned for hot food prepared by the cooks. According to Kenneth Haas, the 99th barreled through Bavarian villages whose fearful residents draped white surrender sheets out the windows. Sick of living on cold rations, the infantry jumped from tanks, rushed into houses of panic-stricken inhabitants and shouted, "*Eier, Eier!*" The fearful villagers ran to them with baskets and pails full of eggs. Then, at each brief stop, out would come "liberated" frying pans, down would come fence-rails, and soon fried eggs were devoured without toast or seasoning.[9]

• • •

On April 25, George Company 395 ran into stiff opposition as it attempted to cross the shallow, fifty-foot wide Altmühl River at Kinding, thirty-five miles south of Nuremberg. The Germans had destroyed all the bridges but one, left standing for approaching American troops, whom they planned to hit with mortar and machine-gun fire. Sensing a trap, the scouts looked for an alternative and found the submerged remains of a bridge. The company proceeded single file into the icy water just before daylight. Harold Hill recalled the misery, "You have never lived until you wade a cold stream fully clothed in army woolens, loaded down with weapons . . . and wet shoes and socks are not comfortable items to conduct a war in." Once aware of this flanking maneuver, the Germans pulled out, and George Company did not have to fight for the village.[10]

A few miles farther south, the first platoon of Easy Company 395 led the attack on Kipfenberg, a village situated on the east side of the

Lt. Col. Robert Douglas, CO of 1st Bn. 394, and his men heading toward Danube in late April 1945. Courtesy National Archives and Records Administration.

river. According to Frank Hoffman, the new company commander, who "wanted to make a name for himself" kept rushing his troops ahead; consequently, he failed to reconnoiter the village where SS troops waited. Heavy machine guns (water-cooled .30-caliber) set up and fired at two German cleaning girls when they began yelling, "*Die Amerikaner sind hier!* [The Americans are here!]" Shots eliminated the element of surprise and the chance for riflemen to slip into town unnoticed. The Germans responded by dropping mortar shells behind thin-walled wooden houses where Paul Weesner and other squad members sought shelter. Shell fragments wounded eight riflemen and six from the two machine-gun sections; the American attack went nowhere. The concussion from one mortar shell burst a blood vessel in Frank Hoffman's face while a steel fragment tore through his arm into his chest. The wounded were carried into a basement filled with several inches of water, where they remained, tended by a medic, until evacuated the next day. At 2:00 A.M. the uninjured infiltrated across a dynamited bridge into Kipfenberg, only to discover the enemy had vanished. After a few hours sleep, the average during this rapid trek, they headed for the Danube River, eighteen miles to the south.[11]

• • •

Following a strenuous twelve-mile hike against light resistance, the 2nd Battalion 394 approached the village of Dietfurt, where the Ludwig-Donau-Main canal joined the Altmühl River. On the hill overlooking Dietfurt, an anti-tank gun lobbed a couple of shells to determine if enemy troops were lying in wait. When they observed Germans slipping away, the GIs concluded there would be no resistance and proceeded down the hill into the village. At 2:00 P.M. they reached the other side of the village. Suddenly the Germans shelled the American arrivals, and the attacking units took cover. Platoon Sergeant Harold Schaefer rushed forward to see why the lead company had stopped. Standing in the market square, a mortar shell struck the building behind him, sending a steel fragment slicing through his left leg and shattering the tibia. Until that moment Schaefer was the last original member of the platoon not to have been killed, wounded, or taken sick. He did not make it to war's end, but he did survive.[12]

At 2:00 A.M., under a bright, moonlit sky, the 2nd Battalion advanced to the next village where they halted for a few hours' rest. At 8:00 A.M. they began a ten-mile hike and then were picked up by tanks and carried some distance. After stopping to rest, guards were ordered out on the surrounding hills to provide security. One sentry, Pfc. Michael Popinny, was shot dead by a sniper. Two squads immediately slipped around each side of the hill from which the shot was fired, but the shooter escaped their determined effort to kill him. Back on the tanks, they traveled fifteen miles stopping outside Kelheim, the assembly area for the 393rd's crossing of the Danube River.[13]

During the five days it took the division to move south through rolling terrain and scattered forests, over rivers and a canal, from the outskirts of Nuremberg to the Danube River (some sixty miles), eleven men were killed in action. Everyone hoped, given the spotty resistance, that no more would die, for an armistice might not be long in coming. In fact, fighting would stop a week later, with the Division's last combat death recorded on May 4, four days before the official end of the war in Europe.

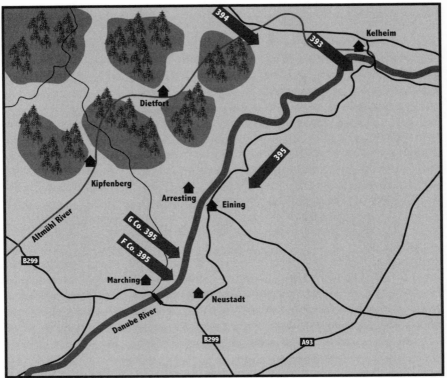

Crossing the Danube, April 27–28, 1945. Map by Paul Giacomotto and James Knight.

THE DANUBE RIVER

Crossing the famous Danube River, mucky brown in color (only blue perhaps in mid-nineteenth century or in Johann Strauss's imagination), and swollen by spring runoff to roughly eighty yards in width, might prove a dangerous, even deadly undertaking, if German units manned defensive positions on the opposite shore. On either side of the river, in varying distances (a few feet to one hundred yards) was a soggy flood plain that stopped at high earth-and-rock levees erected to protect the countryside from flooding. Between the levee and the sandy shoreline grew tall grass and small trees that might offer some cover to those who would need it. With the bridges gone, the first units would have to paddle the river in army-green plywood boats.

Fox Co. 395 rests before climbing levee and attempting to cross Danube, April 27, 1945. Note the wooden assault boats. Courtesy National Archives and Records Administration.

The operation called for companies from the 393rd and 395th to launch their attacks three miles apart at 11:00 A.M. on the 27th of April. On the afternoon of April 26, Lt. Earl Bennett, company commander of Fox Company 395, and Lt. Harold Hill, company commander of George Company 395, were called to 2nd Battalion headquarters and told they would lead the regiment's crossing of the Danube. After the briefing, the two officers walked to the levee to size up the launch site. Looking across the river they spotted German troops working on positions beyond the south levee. (Later they would learn teenage SS cadets and their instructors awaited them). Since the Americans would be crossing in daylight inexplicably without artillery preparation, the situation seemed fraught with danger and "totally against proven military strategy," thought Harold Hill. Bennett told Hill, "This isn't going to be good." Hill agreed, and they sent a message back to battalion headquarters arguing the plan was unworkable. They awaited a response, but when none came, they proceeded as commanded: "We received stupid orders all the time, and sometimes they turned out okay." Hill hoped the two of them were mistaken about this ill-conceived operation, and the crossing would not turn into a disaster. Unfortunately their assessment proved correct, while those in command didn't suffer the consequences.[14]

Army engineers transported boats to the levee in the early morning, but the 2nd Battalion's attack was delayed until 12:45 P.M. As Robert Piller crouched behind the levee, an American journalist from *Life* magazine came walking along on top and said, "Boys, this is going to be a cakewalk. There's nobody over there." Medic Alvin Cooper said, "We were laughing and kidding as we waited along the back of the levee." None of the enlisted men had an inkling of what awaited them.[15]

The first four boats of Fox Company were carried over the top and down into the high grass that ran to the river. When they reached the shoreline, intermittent rifle fire began. Nevertheless Lt. Bennett, the respected commander, shouted, "Let's go!" and four boats were launched. As they began to paddle, machine guns opened up, and Robert Piller heard the bullets exploding like fire crackers just above their heads. Lieutenant Bennett was riding in one of the two lead boats when a bullet struck him in the knee, producing a sound, according to Piller, like "a watermelon hitting concrete." Everyone stopped, momentarily stunned as to what they should do. But even in

GIs of F Co. carry assault boat toward Danube. Heavy brush and saplings provided cover after German troops on the south bank opened fire with machine guns and mortars. Courtesy National Archives and Records Administration.

pain, Bennett followed orders and shouted, "Keep paddling!"—a heroic decision with fatal consequences for himself. Bennett's boat and one other managed to reach the opposite bank, while two boats turned around and returned. Bennett lost blood, went into shock, and subsequently died because medics were unable to reach him with morphine. Later his driver, Woodrow Hickey, found an unfinished letter Bennett had written to his wife: "You know I suppose the people in the U.S. are reading fantastic headlines. They don't know how much blood it cost to make those headlines."[16]

Fielding Pope recalled the men were relaxed as they approached the levee because they thought the Germans, who had been withdrawing in great haste, wouldn't put up much of a fight. As they reached the top of the levee, however, a German sniper, sitting in a conveyor bucket hanging from a tower on the opposite bank, shot and killed his buddy, Arnold Zbornik. The squad climbed over the top and into the water. All at once bullets ripped into the boat and the GIs. Every man was hit except S.Sgt. Charles Neibert, who jumped

Trapped riflemen of F Co. take cover on sand bank in Danube, April 27, 1945. Note the dead GI, left foreground. Courtesy National Archives and Records Administration.

into the water and swam while holding onto the boat. At that spot a brush-covered sand bar sat in the river, and the sergeant managed to pull the damaged boat behind that marshy slip of land where they waited, completely soaked without food, until darkness, when the medics carried them to safety.[17]

The men in the two boats who somehow made it to the other side were trapped on the shoreline without food. Every time someone rose up, a German machine-gun nest would let loose with a volley; fortunately the levee prevented the Germans from depressing the gun. The Americans lay there all day and into the night when they finally made their break, even while German flares lit up the river. They paddled back, letting the current take them farther downstream, and landed in Easy Company's sector.

After carrying Lt. Bennett's body onto the shore, the two dozen survivors climbed over the levee and headed for a group of farm buildings where they bedded down wet, cold, hungry, tired, and emotionally drained. Upon awakening the next morning, they found themselves alone and ventured into a village where German families offered them potatoes and eggs. Not knowing what had happened to the others and not eager to resume the fight, they decided to sit tight and wait for the company to send someone to fetch them. Finally, after a week, another American unit discovered the men and radioed Fox Company to ascertain its location. When the missing two dozen caught up with their outfit, they learned everyone had assumed they were dead.[18]

• • •

John Oakes and his squad mates carried a boat upside down through yards of brush and dropped it into the river. But they had trouble climbing into the boat as the current pushed it downstream. When machine-gun bullets repeatedly struck the boat, the occupants simply let it drift away while they moved onto the sandbar, which supported some vegetation that concealed their presence. They lay there throughout the rest of the afternoon and into the night.[19]

Machine gunner Forbes Williams of George Company remembered they stayed the night of the 26th in foxholes three miles from the river. The next morning Capt. Carl Byers, S-3 of 2nd Battalion, drove up in a jeep and briefly spoke to the men. Williams asked, "Where are we going?" Byers simply replied, "You are in for a tough day" and drove off. He knew what awaited the men crossing the river on that spring day.

As Forbes Williams walked toward the levee, Oscar McLaughlin offered to carry the machine gun so Williams could better manage the boat. Soon after they hiked over the levee, a sniper, obviously looking to silence an automatic weapon, shot McLaughlin through the head. This death shocked Williams, for he realized that if he had been carrying the .30-caliber machine gun, he would have died instantly. As the machine-gun section carried their boat toward the river, bullets hit the plywood and sent wood splinters flying into Williams's face. He and others dumped the damaged boat, crawled back some distance, and hid in the high grass and saplings. As Williams lay there, he heard a boat drifting by with men screaming in pain.[20]

Squad leader Thomas Woznicki began moving toward the river, but the murderous rifle and machine-gun fire stopped him and the others. The platoon leader ordered Woznicki and his men to keep going, but they refused. Woznicki shouted, at him, "We are not getting into the boat!" The unlikable lieutenant repeated his command without results. Finally Woznicki said, "We'll go when you get into the boat first." The lieutenant made no move, and they stayed and lived.

When William Galegar's squad headed for the Danube, the combat engineer in charge of their boat said to him, "This is a death mission." The men hoisted the boat and carried it over the levee with no immediate objection from the Germans. But as Galegar's squad proceeded toward the sandy beach at the water's edge, "all hell broke loose"; machine guns and rifles poured out heavy fire, followed by mortar shells and even rockets. Had the inexperienced German cadets waited, they might have caught most of the boats unprotected in the water, and American losses would have been even greater. Galegar and the others in his squad discarded the boat and hurriedly took cover among the saplings. There they stayed, awaiting further orders, which they feared might entail a new attempt.[21]

As Harold Hill and eleven other men lugged a boat toward the Danube, "We met the most intense small-arms and mortar fire I had ever experienced"; it wounded five, killed one, and punched holes in the boat, rendering it non-buoyant. The survivors and the wounded hid behind the boat and in the brush. Trapped, unable to move, even as the adrenaline accelerated heart rates, they had to stay, hoping the erratic firing would miss them, all the while frustrated they couldn't defend themselves. Lying prone, each man scooped out a soggy, shallow hole with his entrenching tool and remained there while bullets sizzled a few feet overhead. Harold Hill radioed for smoke shells to be aimed at the opposite bank, but almost as if angered by this feeble attempt to blind the gunners, the Germans stepped up the mortar and artillery barrage. Trapped on the flood plain, Albert Eckert endured the day without food and urinated while laying flat. Others, suffering from diarrhea, perhaps exacerbated by fear, had to pull down their pants and empty their bowels from a horizontal position, a messy undertaking. As the afternoon wore on, it began to drizzle, adding to their misery.[22]

Ken Reed and Easy Company were in reserve with orders to follow after the two brother rifle companies had successfully navigated the river. As they moved toward the levee, mortar shells and rockets exploded in the area, and, Paul Weesner recalled, "Every so often we would pass a pool of blood with a cartridge belt or raincoat

Engineers build pontoon bridge across Danube at a peaceful site downstream from crossing by F and G Cos. 395. Courtesy National Archives and Records Administration.

nearby." Reed could hear German machine-gun fire on the other side; he figured Fox and George Companies were pinned down. Squad leader Paul Jillson kept thinking, "if someone offered me $10,000 to take another step, I would turn it down flat." One of the men in his squad, a recent replacement, fell down and became absolutely rigid, unable to move. (Jillson attributed his condition to "hysterical paralysis.") Reed saw Easy Company's assault boats leaning against the levee, waiting for occupants, and "my heart sank." It was "one of the worst periods mentally," for "to come this far and at this late date to have to try to cross the river was depressing."[23]

Reed sat down dejectedly waiting for the command that would be "tantamount to suicide." Some twenty yards away under a tree sat Morris Rosenberg, whom Lt. Hill had ordered to stay behind with the backpacks out of harm's way because he was a "talented musician and a tremendous morale booster." Suddenly a salvo of screaming rockets landed nearby, scoring a direct hit on Rosenberg, and Hill's effort to save a gifted artist failed. Upon impact the rockets shattered into razor-edged fragments, which, Paul Jillson recalled, splintered the upright bottoms of the assault boats lying inclined on the levee. When Reed moved back to his boat, he was delighted to discover several holes in it. When he mentioned the defects, an engineer told him, "We've got more boats." But Reed's anxiety vanished when word came that Easy Company's attack was canceled, so neither Reed nor the others had to force a crossing with the probability of heavy casualties.[24]

With nightfall, remaining members of Fox and George Companies finally left the flood plain, climbed the levee, walked back to the road, regrouped, and marched in a daze downstream. After the day's debacle, Hill recalled, they moved as "a group of defeated men in shock," for it had been a foreseeable disaster that should have been avoided. Tony Pellegrino and others vowed from then on they would take no more chances, even if it meant disobeying orders.[25]

Before dawn George and Easy Companies reached the spot where the 393rd Regiment had enjoyed a relatively safe crossing the previous day. When they learned the 393rd had used boats without opposition, their anger increased. The death of thirteen men from the two companies appeared inexcusable, the result of poor planning and an unnecessary rush to push ahead regardless of the consequences. Enraged at both their own commanders and the Germans, the troops were primed to punish those who had caused such havoc and killed their buddies.

In the early morning of April 28, they climbed aboard Dukws (amphibian trucks called "ducks") that ferried them to the south shore, an unremarkable crossing of a famous river that the dead should have made. Accompanied by tanks and tank destroyers, which had crossed on a pontoon bridge, George Company marched upriver to the outskirts of Neustadt (a cluster of some forty houses with barns and outbuildings), the town opposite their assigned launch site. Company commander Harold Hill ordered the tank destroyers to blast away, and they moved down the main street and "literally blew the town apart." Years later Hill felt remorseful for "leveling" the town: "I didn't need to. I didn't care. I was mad, tired, and disgusted."[26]

As Ken Reed and his platoon moved into the town behind the tank destroyers, a woman came running towards them, screaming that her husband had been killed. Inside they found a headless German, obviously a victim of a tank destroyer's 76mm shell that had struck their house. The men expressed regrets, but given the tragic circumstances and the language barrier, they could hardly appease her. The men proceeded to carry out the requisite house-to-house search, looking for the enemy. One GI entered a house and heard some noise in the basement. He called out, telling whoever was down there to come out. When no one responded, he tossed a grenade into the cellar. Afterward he and Robert Justice went downstairs and found a group of dead civilians. Similarly a soldier from the extra rifle platoon shot a fifteen-year-old girl who had taken shelter in a hole that served as an air raid shelter.[27]

Squad leader Paul Jillson came upon a house with a gaping hole that had been blasted in a wall. When he stepped through it into the kitchen, he observed four people, an elderly man and three women sitting at a table frozen in a state of shock, shrouded in dust, holding cups as if they were about to drink their morning coffee, except the cups were empty. Jillson could not understand why they hadn't all died. In halting German, Jillson assured them that no further harm would come to them, but they didn't acknowledge his words.

Out in the street again, Jillson saw a German soldier burst out of a building with his hands high in the air. Jillson waved him toward him, shouting *"schnell! schnell!"* and the soldier came running, but tumbled to the ground. Jillson turned him over and noticed a red stain spreading across his abdomen. A young man with blue eyes and blond hair, a "model of Hitler's concept of ideal German youth," lay there, his face very white, "eyes revealing pain and fear." Jillson wanted to offer some comfort to the boy, but all he could do was tell him, "I'll get a medic," even though none was available, and it was doubtful anyone could save him. Jillson returned later to check on the wounded soldier and discovered someone, "either more savage or more merciful than me," had put a fresh bullet hole in the boy's forehead.[28]

When Paul Weesner reached the town, "some of our company" (including the 5th Platoon) decided not to take prisoners, probably because of the previous day's losses, which were widely assumed to be high. In his history of the 99th, Gen. Walter Lauer delighted in their actions: "They routed out the well concealed enemy in cold fury and drove them away screaming for mercy." But Paul Weesner found this behavior reprehensible: "Scores of young prisoners were shot while crawling out of their holes or walking down the road with their hands up." The remaining prisoners, including one youth who had his left arm blown off, were beaten severely with rifle butts. Later when Weesner returned to the road, he saw that all the wounded had been shot. By his estimate, the battalion took forty-nine prisoners while eighty-five were killed (even Gen. Lauer admitted few prisoners were taken). Although the division lost twenty-six dead, Weesner thought the beating and killing of these "kid soldiers" was unjustified.[29]

AFTER THE DANUBE AND V-E DAY

The Danube River presented the last serious obstacle for the division as it hurried toward the Isar River, twenty-five miles to the southeast. While several units encountered pockets of resistance, the resulting exchanges were brief and haphazard; but the worrisome fear lurked in the back of each man's mind that he could die just as the war drew to a close. As Rex Whitehead and fellow mortar squad members were riding in a jeep, they saw the body of a GI on the side of the road: "No one said anything, but we all thought the same, for we had discussed getting killed on the last day of the war, after going through what we had."[30]

On a snowy May 1, foot soldiers of the 393rd reached Landshut where Love Company started across the Isar canal on a walkway above the gates of a power dam. In the middle of the dam a sniper killed Sgt. Merle Wright. The men rushed on, capturing six hundred troops as well as the city, whose inhabitants quickly bedecked their buildings with white flags of surrender. Afterwards Plt. Sgt. Ken Juhl and his men returned to retrieve Wright's body, but discovered it missing. They decided to inquire at a nearby Catholic church to see if anyone knew what had happened to their fallen buddy. Inside the church they spotted the dead GI lying in an old wooden box. The Catholic nuns had carried the body from the walkway and placed it near the altar, an act of respect that heartened Juhl and his men.[31]

Twelve miles upriver, the 395th and the 14th Armored Division reached Moosburg (Stalag VII A) where thousands of Allied prisoners, including many 99ers captured during the Bulge, joyously celebrated their liberation. Oakley Honey saw a ragtag mass of humanity shouting and yelling, and his group threw them candy, cigarettes, and K rations: "Boy, were they happy to see us." The liberators enjoyed the chance to free fellow GIs, and the freed POWs amused themselves by burning

Columns of infantrymen march triumphantly through Landshut, May 1, 1945.
The war is nearly over. Courtesy National Archives and Records Administration.

down the wooden barracks. The prison commandant, a hated colonel
who placed prisoners in solitary confinement for small infractions, was
dragged in front of the prisoners. GIs tore off his epaulettes, removed
his hat, and shouted to the American POWs, "What do you want us to
do with him?" They shouted, "Kick him in the ass!" When one soldier
delivered the blow, the prisoners cheered.[32]

A few days later, in the vicinity of Mühldorf, Cliff Selwood and members of Baker 394 went through a town and came upon a slave labor camp, where they encountered men and women who looked "hardly alive or human because they were nothing but skin and bones." These "poor creatures," wearing only skimpy, torn clothes with rags or newspapers wrapped around their feet, were pushing to get through the gate, some with tears streaming down their faces. Escaping from their confines, the hunger-driven foreign slaves poured into the city in a frenzied search for food and revenge. Battalion surgeon Herbert Orr watched several Russian women beat a German guard to death with sticks and farm tools.[33]

Skeletons with large, "dazed and desperate-looking eyes popping out of their heads," they glanced around not quite comprehending what would happen next. Seeing them shivering in the cold, Selwood and his squad raced upstairs in the house they occupied, stripped the closet of coats, sweaters, shoes and expensive fur coats, and threw them out the window where the slaves struggled with each other for a shirt or coat, all the while speaking in an unintelligible language. GIs in other houses followed suit.

Selwood watched one starving fellow scoop up lard and sauerkraut from two barrels under the side steps of the house and stuff his mouth. Selwood attempted to caution him by shaking his head while patting his stomach, but to no avail. Like a wild animal, the man kept on gorging "that horrible mess until he could eat no more." Selwood never saw the man again but assumed the sudden ingestion of large amounts of grease and pickled cabbage probably killed him. Others told Selwood they saw two slaves fighting over a dead cat.[34]

These shocking scenes, at once appalling and repugnant, angered the GIs who believed the "local people had to know about it." This experience brought home the cruel inhumanity of the Nazi regime and confirmed a sense that theirs had been a struggle for civilization.

As the troops advanced beyond the Isar River toward the Austrian border, they saw in the distance the beautiful but menacing, snow-covered Alps no one wanted to fight for. Luckily it did not happen; on May 2 the division was ordered to "halt in place" and await further instructions. Six days later, on May 8, 1945, the European war officially ended, exactly six months from the day the division had reached the war zone.

• • •

In villages throughout France and Belgium church bells rang out the happy news. In Paris, London, and other cities masses of people erupted in unrestrained dancing, singing, and drinking because the long, mad nightmare of death and destruction had stopped. Stewart Fischer watched Parisians pile into American jeeps and joyride through the city streets. When Donald Wallace heard the "Star Spangled Banner" being played in Paris through loud speakers he got the chills. Trapped on board a ship in the Solvent, only a quarter mile from Portsmouth, Great Britain, Richard Byers and other troops stood on the railing, "gnashing their teeth," as they watched bonfires burning, bands playing, people dancing in the streets, and delirious crowds going in and out of pubs. Recovering from wounds, Leon Rogers could only look out from the seventh floor of his Paris hospital room and watch the exuberant scene in the streets below. At least, he thought, "I am warm and comfortable and not lying in the muck with my rifle." Homer Simons had better luck sitting in a café, for French women came running in and kissed him. Peter Wolffe felt well enough to join the crowds when "it was great to be young and alive in a beautiful city in the springtime."[35]

• • •

By contrast, frontline troops, especially those who had served months with the division, reacted with subdued gratitude as the tension of combat slowly began to lessen. It was, Ken Reed recalled, as if a "tremendous weight had been lifted off me," particularly "the dread of going into the next action." They were grateful to have survived. Another GI told J. C. Jones: "Every day from now on is a bonus. You had no business living this long." In Landshut, George Lehr recalled, "We were too tired and drained to make any kind of demonstration." Ernest McDaniel felt "our entire capacity for outward emotions had been muted for a long time." William Galegar, a veteran of Camp Maxey, wandered around in a "daze for three days, not believing it was over, and I had survived." Even though the fighting had been winding down for several days, it seemed eerily strange that no bullets ripped the air. Platoon Sergeant T. J. Cornett found the quiet unnerving: "I couldn't stand it. I expected the shelling to break out again any

moment." After consuming a certain amount of wine, Tony Pellegrino decided to explode an artillery charge, which resulted in him
being sent to the hospital for severe facial burns. Some replacements
fired their weapons into the air, but the end seemed anticlimactic and
sad because they remembered those who had died. Then too, the war
in the Pacific, including an invasion of Japan, seemed likely to be in
their future.[36]

Joseph Herdina was riding a Sherman tank when the crew gave him
the news. He jumped off and went into a barn where he lay down in
the hay and fell asleep, not waking up until the next day. In Linz,
Austria, Bill Meyer and his buddies, staying in a cuckoo clock factory,
celebrated the war's end by unleashing a cacophony of "cuckoos."
When Guy Duren and others in the forward observer team sat down
at a table to play cards, he thought, "We should be up cheering or
downing some booze and acting overjoyed." After squad leaders Cliff
Selwood and B. C. Henderson saw liquor rations being distributed to
the officers, they figured the rumor about the war's end must be true
and decided to visit their lieutenant's quarters to confirm the news.
The lieutenant was not there, but a full bottle of scotch whiskey was.
While waiting for the officer's return, temptation overcame them:
after all, they felt entitled to a taste. Soon sip followed sip until the
entire contents disappeared. Standing the empty bottle upside down
on its neck, they departed seriously drunk and made it back to their
quarters where they fell sound asleep.[37]

OCCUPATION

Within forty-eight hours of Germany's unconditional surrender, troops
of the 99th climbed aboard trucks bound for their zone of occupation in northwest Bavaria, including the destroyed cities of Würzburg,
Schweinfurt, Aschaffensburg, and numerous agricultural villages.
According to Ken Reed, everyone was in high spirits (literally in some
cases after DPs handed them bottles of newly produced wine), for
they had defeated the enemy and were the victors. Initially wary, fearing
diehard fanatics might continue the war, they remained guarded and
somewhat negative because the German people had supported Hitler.
As the GIs assumed occupation duties—organizing DPs, controlling
civilians, and supervising POW work details—they realized the

cooperative German population, mainly older men, women, and young children, accepted their presence, preferring Americans to the hated Russians.[38]

Instead of climbing steep hills (with weapons and full packs), wading cold streams, trudging through sodden fields, and sleeping in muddy foxholes, the men settled into warm quarters with beds or cots. Instead of being awakened before dawn after a fitful sleep, they could slumber for hours, though enlisted men still had to perform irksome guard duties both day and night. They ate hot food, wore relatively clean underwear and uniforms, showered or took baths—sometimes in the clear water of the Main River—and drank alcoholic beverages, which were confiscated or bought cheaply (a bottle of champagne cost sixty-five cents). After months or weeks of hardship and stress, occupation duties, if nothing else, offered rest, relaxation, and a period of decompression before they returned home or left for the Pacific.

Even though the war had reduced many German cities to rubble, nearly obliterating vestiges of modern society, GIs began the physical and psychological journey from the dangerous world of combat to the saner life of civilization or what was left of it in Germany. This sudden change took getting used to; it seemed strange to Harold Hill to move around without seeking concealment and to have lights and fires at night. Steve Kallas had trouble dealing with the quiet; leaving the battlefield did not erase combat memories; vivid nightmares followed him "loud and clear, with all the screaming and yelling you can imagine."[39]

• • •

Much of Europe was on the move: Yugoslavs traveling to the southeast, German civilians returning to homes (if they existed) or fleeing the Russians, German POWs moving into hastily erected prisons, French laborers and POWs heading west, Italians crossing the Alps, and Poles and Russians forced into trucks and trains for the long journey to the east. West of the Elbe River, the Allies faced the enormous task of sorting, feeding, controlling, and moving this enormous mass of humanity stuck in the middle of a nation that had ceased to exist.

Peacetime occupation presented other drawbacks for American troops. Since the army hated and feared idleness, officers reinstituted stateside training—weapons inspections, close-order drill, guard duty, conditioning marches, reveille, retreat, and saluting of officers. To veteran combat soldiers the reintroduction of garrison regulations and practices seemed ludicrous and "chicken shit." In time these futile attempts were mostly abandoned; in fact, maintaining discipline became a problem. Charles Eubanks said that during combat the replacements looked up to him, but after the war "I couldn't get them to do anything."[40]

The army also maintained the non-fraternization policy that insisted GIs not have any contact with Germans except to issue orders and check identification cards. Soldiers who had lost buddies or who felt strongly about the concentration and slave labor camps agreed with this policy. Having been trained to hate and kill the enemy, it was not easy to simply discard hostile feelings towards Germans in general and soldiers in particular. When William McMurdie returned to Germany after recovering from his wounds, he saw uniformed German soldiers walking along the road; "it seemed funny not to shoot at them," he wrote his parents. Some soldiers never reconciled themselves to the Germans or their plight. When Fred Feigenoff entered the heavily bombed city of Nuremberg, he thought it looked "like the surface of the moon," but felt no sympathy for the inhabitants because of their eradication of European Jews.[41]

At first most 99th units observed non-fraternization, but this policy was disobeyed by soldiers affected by the plight of starving Germans. Following army orders, company commander Capt. George Maertens had leftovers from mess kits and serving pots emptied into a sump and covered with dirt. When Maertens learned Germans were digging for food in the garbage pits at night, he decided that his company "could not throw away food while hungry people, especially children, were nearby." Allan Nelson, who became a mess sergeant in a farming village near Passau, couldn't resist cute, blond-haired German kids who came to the kitchen door carrying little, empty pails. When William McMurdie walked out of the mess hall one day at Fürth, he encountered Germans lined up to accept any leftovers no one wanted: "It was such a pitiful sight. We could see they were thin, undernourished and in need, some horribly so"; after that, he and others supplied them with excess food. Over time, despite the fact that platoons were frequently shifted to different villages and towns, which made it more difficult to know one another, some GIs came to accept individual Germans. After other squads looted and wrecked an elderly woman's house in Lohr, Sgt. Edward Eimermann, embarrassed by this behavior, allowed the woman back into her house, which he visited regularly. Richard Tommey befriended a fifteen-year-old boy, Hans Frankenburger, who played classical piano for him; Tommey in turn supplied Hans and his mom with soap. At war's end Robert Ritchie "hated" all Germans, but with the passage of time, he came to realize "they were people just like us."[42]

In Ochsenfurt Omar Paxson and his platoon took over a physician's house, forcing the owner to find living arrangements elsewhere. The German doctor returned frequently to cultivate his beautiful flower garden. One day a sergeant tossed a large mattress out the second story window and flattened the entire pansy bed. Seeing the needless destruction, Paxson remarked to his buddies, "Whoever did that is no better than a dog." When the sergeant heard about this comment, he walked up to Paxson and punched him in the face. What bothered Paxson was not just the cowardly punch, but also the sergeant's vandalism, demonstrating an uncivilized disregard for the flowers and the doctor's property.[43]

While sympathy for hungry civilians caused GIs to violate official policy, the availability of German women played a significant factor in undermining non-fraternization. Given the absence of young German males, American GIs enjoyed an enviable position. This wasn't coercive power in which men took what they wanted, including sex (although rapes did occur); rather, Germans wanted cigarettes and needed food. If enlisted men occupied the bottom ranks of the army hierarchy, they stood in superior position to Germans. GIs could provide C rations, soap, sugar, chocolate, and cigarettes, especially attractive to a population that suffered from a food shortage and nicotine withdrawal. Guy Duren confessed, "It doesn't take long to realize as a member of the conquering army that you have immense power over people." While stationed at a town on the main railroad line running south, Duren's job (along with three men under him) was to check the identification papers of train passengers. One evening a "very attractive blonde" bound for the Alps ski resort of Garmisch stepped off the train to stretch her legs. Duren attempted to convince her she should delay her trip and "shack up" with him. He even suggested that he was "the local dictator" and could make her stay.

She declined, and to his credit he did not insist, but he became aware "how easily power can corrupt."[44]

Being in charge could place GIs in unusual situations for which they had no training. Robert Walter escorted a group of German prisoners to do roadwork filling in potholes. At lunchtime he and the prisoners retreated to a nearby *Gasthaus*. There was only one large table where the prisoners sat down to eat. Walter faced a dilemma: Should he join the POWs, thereby narrowing the gap between them, or not? "Here I was," Walter recounted, "a nineteen-year-old conqueror who had no clue how a conqueror was supposed to act." He decided to eat outside alone under a tree, while the POWs remained comfortably inside.[45]

Even with the threat of venereal diseases, sexual relationships with German women were not uncommon, especially for sexually experienced soldiers. A few enlisted men were shocked that GIs would take up with German women; one disgusted GI saw soldiers "lined up like dogs" to have sex with an "accommodating German woman." Anthony Aiello saw sweet, well-dressed, lovely German women who "sold their bodies for a bar of candy and most of our boys in the ETO [would] take advantage." It shocked and dismayed another GI that married soldiers committed adultery. An enlisted man had a sixteen-year-old girlfriend but thought nothing of it. He admitted this could not have taken place at home, but American social mores and pressures did not prevail in postwar Europe. What had not changed was white opinion about black men having German girlfriends. Ken Reed said "hard attitudes" existed about the blacks in his company "hooking up with German girls." For whatever reason, a short time later the black platoon was shipped out.[46]

• • •

Many units were saddled with the boring tasks of guarding POWs on work details and keeping DPs confined to camps in order to feed and process them. The refugee camps seethed with tension and hostility that sometimes erupted into violence between Poles and Russians. According to Thomas Woznicki, it "was a dog-eat-dog world," which the Americans seemed powerless to police. Russian ex-slave laborers proved especially difficult to contain. They frequently broke out and raided German homes for food and valuables; in Wildflicken a gang of Russians killed the *Bürgermeister* and his assistant after the two men complained to army officers about these raids. Ironically the Americans had to protect former enemies against wartime allies.[47]

All German POWs were forced to work, including SS soldiers, who received harsh treatment, including beatings. Fred Kampmier found guarding dirty, lice-infested German POWs at Ochsenfurt on the Main River, a particularly onerous and frustrating duty. After a time, the German POWs, if not connected to an atrocity or the Nazi establishment, were set free, while Kampmier could not leave. It galled him that the victors had to stay, and the defeated could go home.[48]

GIs generally disliked German POWs; bad feelings over the deaths of fellow soldiers and the language barrier made sympathy and communication difficult. The Germans harbored hostile opinions about the Russians, telling American soldiers they should be aware of the Soviet threat, which ran counter to American policy. Captain George Maertens felt like "slapping" German officers who suggested Americans join forces with them and attack the Russians, for he "only thought of Russians as our brothers-in-arms." A few months later, as America and the Soviet Union became Cold War enemies, Maertens realized he had been "pretty naïve" about this wartime ally, "while the Germans were better informed."[49]

Although relationships with German prisoners remained chilly, on occasion certain incidents revealed a sort of mutual connection. Joseph O'Neill had to take a group of POWs to pick up supplies from an overturned freight car a mile from the railroad station at Münnerstadt. He decided to make use of a flatcar and coast to the wreck. But O'Neill, who was standing, misjudged the drop in elevation and the flatcar began to pick up speed. Seeing him swaying, the prisoners crawled over and held his legs so he would not fly off: "I was amazed and impressed, for they could have just as easily pushed me off the car and run away."[50]

Another veteran recalled the behavior of a fellow platoon member who took pleasure in "depriving the conquered of any shred of dignity." At the prisoner camp an eight-hole latrine began to fill up, so a new one had to be dug. The bully began to shout orders at the POWs and wave his arms about in exasperation. This excitable outburst, however, caused him to lose his balance, and he slipped into the exposed hole of the old latrine where excrement reached his waist.

Despite his screams, none of the Germans would help him out, and
other GIs watched in amusement. After a few minutes, some platoon
members finally dragged him out, while the Germans jeered at him.
To the German and American onlookers alike, this messy, undignified
fall seemed just punishment.[51]

HOMEWARD BOUND

In May the U.S. Army adopted a point system as a method of determining which soldiers in Europe would first be allowed to return
to the United States, where they would be discharged. Individuals
accumulated points on the basis of several criteria: number of months
in service, number of months overseas, number of children, battle
stars, medals including Purple Hearts, and presidential unit cita-
tions. Initially the magic number was eighty-five points or more
(over time that total was reduced), and those men who had served
in veteran divisions became the first ones with high point totals.
Since many 99ers were inducted relatively late or were replacements
and therefore low-point men, they were transferred to other divisions,
while high point men came into the 99th. Don Perry happily recalled
that soldiers from the well-known 1st Infantry Division grumbled about
having to shift their Big Red One division patch to the right shoulder
while the identifying 99th's Checkerboard patch had to be sewn on the
left shoulder. So the 99th became a miscellany of strangers, and the old
platoons ceased to exist. In early September the reconstituted division
sailed for the United States, where it was deactivated, three years after it
had been created, its mission accomplished.[52]

Scattered to various POW camps and towns in Bavaria and elsewhere, the remaining 99ers spent their time in other outfits among
unfamiliar GIs. That summer some men signed up for another two-
year stint in the army to avoid participating in the expected invasion
of Japan; when the Japanese government surrendered in August,
they had to remain behind in Europe. Francis Chesnick almost signed
the papers because he wondered what work would be available when
he returned to the tiny village of Uniondale, Pennsylvania, where his
father had lost a dairy farm during the Depression. At the last moment
he handed the pen back to the captain without signing.[53]

In succeeding months, as fall stretched into winter, GIs left behind became increasingly frustrated because they knew others had reached home and families. One by one, 99ers finally accumulated enough points to be released from occupation duty. They hoisted themselves into 40-and-8 boxcars, enduring the incredibly slow and uncomfortable ride to U.S. Army "Cigarette Camps" (named after popular brands: Lucky Strike, Philip Morris, Chesterfield, etc.), huge tent cities near Le Havre, France, where thousands of impatient, bored GIs congregated and awaited a homeward-bound ship. Stuart Kline had adopted a dog and wanted to take him home. While on the train headed for Le Havre, he learned that no dogs would be allowed on a troopship. When the train pulled into a railroad station, Kline gave the dog to a Frenchman standing on the platform. Later when he reached the ship that would carry him across the Atlantic Ocean, he spotted a sign that read, "Pets Welcome."[54]

Standing on the fantail of a troop ship, James Larkey happily watched the French coastline recede in the setting sun. It was his twenty-first birthday, and he thought, "what a wonderful present." It had been three years since he quit the University of Pennsylvania and requested his draft board take him, so he might test his ability "to exist in difficult and dangerous circumstances." He had learned to live in a hole in the ground, eat monotonous, tasteless food, handle a "wide variety of personality types," and successfully perform the tough duties of a combat infantryman. He concluded these experiences gave him a greater understanding of his "capabilities and lack of them." Having survived intact and dealt with "fear and horror, I felt indebted to my army experiences."

Just before George Meloy scrambled up the gangplank of the *Rockhill Victory*, he decided to buy a one-pound can of Planters salted peanuts at the PX for the trip. Meloy began munching his peanuts on deck as the ship glided smoothly through the calm waters of the Le Havre harbor. But when the ship reached the open, choppy waters of the Atlantic, Meloy's peanut-filled stomach "roared" with displeasure. For the next several days Meloy filled his canteen cup with whatever his stomach did not want and carried the rejected material from his bunk to the toilet. While his trip home across the Atlantic proved much shorter than the initial crossing in 1944 because the ship no longer sailed in slow, zigzagging convoys, ocean travel continued to discomfit Meloy.[55]

For Warren Thomas and others stacked in hammocks from floor to ceiling deep in the troopship's bowels, the trip home resembled the earlier journey to Europe. The stormy Atlantic seas tossed the ship about unmercifully, and once again soldiers became seasick. Thomas recalled the latrine was wide open, and its foul contents spilled out onto the floors, ensuring the stench increased the nausea. After enduring infantry fighting for months, a final dose of misery beset the victorious GIs. But there was an important difference, namely, the destination.[56]

• • •

Every returning GI remembers the entrance into New York harbor. All soldiers on board inevitably rushed to the port side to gaze at the Statue of Liberty, the most important symbol of America for the troops. The sudden rush to the railing caused the ships to list several degrees toward the water, panicking ship captains, who asked all to return to their places—a plea always ignored, for this emotional moment of sheer joy and relief overshadowed any concern for safety. The worried captain on Maltie Anderson's hospital ship yelled out, "For God's sake, get back! Do you want to drown all these people after all they have been through?" William McMurdie recalled there "was not a dry eye aboard" because "we had thought we would never get back home." Thor Ronningen remembered, "A chill ran up my spine when I saw it, and I knew I was home." Ships sounding whistles and fireboats spraying water into the air hailed their triumphant return, as did a huge sign hanging from a hedge along the shore and another at the end of a pier that read: "Welcome Home—Well Done." On several occasions a dance band with attractive women on board a fancy yacht greeted the men with music, songs, and cheers. Civilians waved pillowcases from apartment windows and cars honked in honor of the returnees. Rex Whitehead happily observed the vivid outfits Americans wore: "We realized we had not seen clothes of any color in Europe, for even civilians wore drab clothes." They had escaped the dreary, devastated Old World of deadly wars and returned to the bright world of peaceful America. They were safe and eager to resume their former lives after a rather painful interlude.[57]

Even though there were no victory parades, Red Cross and Salvation Army women again appeared with donuts and coffee. T. J.

Cornett threw these offerings into the harbor as he bitterly recalled the Red Cross "charged us 5 cents for coffee and 10 cents for donuts overseas when we had no money." But most GIs felt appreciated, and one soldier remarked, "They really care what we went through"; Rex Whitehead said the reception made him and others feel "like heroes." Fred Verdecchi walked down the gangplank, kissed the ground, and gave silent thanks for the chance to see a son born while he fought in Europe. Hustled off to Fort Dix, Camp Shanks, or Camp Kilmer, not far from the docks of New York and New Jersey, the troops downed steak, potatoes, hamburgers, milk, and ice cream, all the foods so desperately missed in Europe.[58]

Some returnees had the opportunity to venture into Manhattan. Charles Swann hobbled into the city on crutches and enjoyed drinks bought by civilian patrons; however, somehow during the course of his alcoholic merriment he lost the crutches. Luke Brannon, who returned early to the U.S. because he had been wounded, discovered that others insisted on paying for his drinks and a sandwich, which made "you believe that maybe people really did appreciate some of the sacrifices that we made." Strolling along the city streets, Brannon encountered a prostitute who said to him, "I've got a room where we can have some fun. How about it?" Having never "known" a woman, he found her invitation as frightening as a German assault. Then she added, "I see you are wearing a Combat Infantryman's Badge. Come on, it won't cost you anything." Despite this generous, patriotic offer, Brannon declined.[59]

Usually civilians responded positively to returning servicemen, but on one occasion Francis Iglehart, wearing his uniform, Combat Infantryman Badge, and Honorable Service Emblem (the so-called Ruptured Duck) joined some of his former prep school friends at an upscale nightclub. A stranger, obviously a guy who had never served, spotted Iglehart and remarked sarcastically to his pals, "Here's one of our heroes now!" Having spent the winter on Elsenborn Ridge and wounded by a mortar shell, Iglehart had every reason to be incensed and angry. Heated words were exchanged but no blows ensued.[60]

• • •

The wonderful mess hall feasts offered to returning GIs, a reward for their service, failed to persuade most to remain in the Army.

Ronald Kraemer reached Fort Lewis near Tacoma, Washington, and discovered a huge pile of shoes, pants, and shirts that GIs had discarded, a final expression of their feelings about the army. When Warrant Officer Willis Botz arrived at Camp Beale in Marysville, California, a recruiting officer urged him to sign up for the army reserves. Botz responded, "No thanks! I couldn't drink myself through another war."[61]

The returnees boarded trains jammed with exuberant soldiers bound for various army camps to be discharged. (Men who had suffered serious wounds were shipped to hospitals, many undergoing additional operations and rehabilitation before they could be released to their families.) Then the men headed for hometowns and cities scattered throughout the country. In the years 1942–1944 they had left home individually, traveling to distant training camps, some attending ASTP schools, and then on to Camp Maxey where they joined together in squads and platoons. Transformed into combat soldiers, they set off on a dangerous mission in war-torn Europe, and in the process became a close-knit group of comrades. But combat produced severe losses (wounded, captured, sick, fatigued, killed) that caused the group to break apart. In the last stages of the war and the months that followed the German surrender, GIs returned home individually not collectively, and so this unusual group experience ended. In the years that followed, however, they did not forget what they had endured together and at division reunions rekindled that powerful sense of fellowship.

HOME

The long journey from an army camp to distant parts of the country required trains, busses, hitched rides, taxis, and walking, before each GI reached his final destination. Whether the reunion with family members took place in a train station or at the front door, that wonderful moment suddenly released a tremendous reservoir of pent-up emotion for the returning GI and his loved ones. Mothers, fathers, brothers, sisters, and wives had endured months of separation and apprehension about their soldier's fate. Weeks without incoming mail worried the folks at home, and telegrams announcing "wounded or missing in action" produced distress; those parents, siblings, and wives

informed of a death suffered a heartbreaking loss. When Rex Whitehead and others stepped off the train for a brief stop in Grand Island,
Nebraska, they found housewives distributing homemade cakes and
pies to returning GIs. At one point, a mother and father approached
Whitehead and his fellow travelers and inquired pleadingly, "Our
son is in Europe, and we just wondered if by chance some of you
boys know him." With several million American troops in Europe,
the question seemed incredibly naïve, but Whitehead realized how
desperate this couple was for any news about a deeply missed son.
Afterwards the group began to discuss the parents' situation; for
Whitehead it reaffirmed what most frontline GIs had known throughout their tour, namely, "that the war may have been harder on parents
than their sons."[62]

When Stanley Colby arrived at his home in Pontiac, Michigan, his
father tried to hold back his tears, but they flowed anyway. Ray Wenzel
stepped off the train in Wausau, Wisconsin, into his mother's arms:
"I never heard her sob so loud." Forbes Williams met his parents at
the Hotel Olympia in Portland, Oregon, and his father began to weep,
"the only time I ever saw my father cry." When T. J. Cornett arrived in
Beeville, Texas, tears ran down his father's face, causing T. J. to cry
as his dad hugged him. Luke Brannon's mother ran her hands up
and down his spine as she hugged him, checking to detect what
damage the artillery burst had done to her son. Harold Sporborg, a
former POW, whose family only knew he was missing in action, took
a train to Albany, New York, and then a trolley to South Manning
Boulevard. He had hoped to surprise his family, but a neighbor
spotted him walking along the street and called his mom. She was
waiting at the door when Sporborg arrived, and "of course, was crying."
During the ride from the train station to his home in Waterloo,
Iowa, Al Boeger's mother held on to him the whole way. Thomas
Woznicki wandered from room to room in the family house to convince himself he was really home. Richard Switzer wanted to surprise
his family, but his younger brother, who delivered papers for the
Cleveland Plain Dealer, saw Switzer standing in the vestibule between
cars and raced home to tell the folks. When Harry Hagstad's father,
who had a problem with alcohol, learned his son was missing, he
vowed not to take another drink until Harry returned safely, a vow
he kept.

Discharged on January 3, 1946, Merle Otto arrived home in Aurora, Nebraska, and happily discovered his parents had kept the Christmas tree up with presents under it. Similarly Warren Thomas's parents purchased a small, artificial tree that stood in the living room until their son arrived in early February. After a "Christmas dinner" prepared by his grandmother, Thomas went to bed and didn't awake until early evening of the following day. As Francis Chesnick stepped inside the family's home in Uniondale, Pennsylvania, his little beagle, Spud, sniffed him and then began running around barking joyfully at his owner's return. Charles Katlic caught the last B&A train south out of Baltimore, jumping off at Earleigh Heights Station soon after midnight. He decided to cut through the woods to shorten the distance, whistling while he walked. About one quarter of a mile from the house, his dog Brownie recognized the distinctive sound and began barking loudly while trying to tear the door down. The whole family woke up, including the six kids, so that all the lights were on as Katlic approached the house. Brownie nearly knocked him down with excitement as he stepped inside. Everyone kissed, hugged, cried, "gave thanks to God," drank coffee, and talked until daylight. After a long train ride on the Missouri Pacific, Roy Fish arrived home in Dumas, Arkansas, at 4:00 A.M. Since his parents were asleep, he decided not to disturb them. He settled into the front porch swing and napped until his parents woke up. Then his mom made him breakfast and called Lizzie Beeler, an eighty-year-old black woman and family friend, who came over and baked his favorite rolls.

In El Reno, Oklahoma, Virdin Royce married his seventeen-year-old sweetheart six days after he came home. Similarly Capt. Joseph Carnevale, who was engaged to Louise DePamphilis, refused to marry before leaving for Europe because he didn't want to leave his bride a young widow. Three weeks after his return they walked down the aisle in Mt. Vernon, New York. Anthony Pellegrino was given the opportunity to receive some much-needed dental work done after he arrived at Fort Dix, but he would have to remain in camp for three additional days. He decided that leaving the army was more important than the condition of his teeth and departed with his brother-in-law, who drove him the forty-six miles to Norristown, Pennsylvania. Along the way they stopped at a number of taverns, arriving home in high spirits. Frank

Garrett stepped off the train in Detroit and was surprised that his parents and two uncles were there to meet him. He asked, "Is everyone taking the day off for me? Why are you all here?" They explained that no one was working because it was May 8, V-E Day. After being discharged from Camp McCoy in Wisconsin, Robert Mitsch rode the train to St. Paul, Minnesota, singing quietly to himself the popular romantic song, "Sentimental Journey," that seemed to match the emotions of all returning GIs. Meeting his wife Alice at the station, they jumped into a waiting taxi and went to her parents' house where he saw his eight-month-old son Robert for the first time.[63]

Neighbors and friends received veterans with friendly greetings, but so many men trickled into towns and neighborhoods, returning service men became commonplace and few communities organized celebrations honoring them. However, when Tony Dodd, an ex-POW, arrived in his hometown of Broken Bow, Oklahoma, (population three thousand) he was the first GI to return from Europe. As he got off the bus and tried to walk across the street, a big crowd gathered around and hailed him as a war hero. Over night he became an object of interest to the town's young women, including his former girlfriend who had dumped him before he went overseas; wisely, he decided against taking up with her again. Soon a second GI appeared in town, and attention was directed at the new fellow, taking the pressure off Dodd.

After a long bus trip from Colorado Springs, where he was recovering from a serious hip fracture, Howard Bowers arrived in his tiny hometown of Riverton, Kansas, a dot on the map along Route 66. He walked to Mischler's gas station/diner and waited for his younger brother Lloyd to come by for his customary soda after school. Together they began walking north to the family's country home and garage where his father repaired farm machinery and cars. Along the way a truck stopped and gave them a ride. Stepping down off the back, Howard spotted his father sitting on a bench chatting with two neighbors, a scene that brought back memories of a peaceful world that once had been his. Only six months had passed since his departure from Camp Maxey, and yet a lifetime of unforgettable, painful experiences had been crammed into that short period.

When John McCoy arrived in Bensonville, Illinois, he found his brother home from the Pacific war. Together they joined the local

VFW and frequented the club for beer and conversation with other combat veterans. Subconsciously McCoy attempted to recapture that male comradeship he knew in the army. But McCoy's father, a hard working switchman, had little patience for idleness and soon secured John a job as a journal box oiler for the Milwaukee Road railroad.

William Galegar encountered a different reaction from his parents on the farm near Avant, Oklahoma. Worried that he might not be able to handle the transition to civilian life, they treated him with "kid gloves," and refused to let him help with the chores or the farm work. Gallegar admitted that initially everything seemed a bit strange, for he had been on the move so much and "under so much stress that doing nothing was almost unreal."[64]

Not all homecomings resulted in a happy reception. Homer Kissinger arrived in Ottawa, Kansas, in January 1946, when the "war was long over and nearly forgotten." Kissinger wore his uniform downtown the next morning, had a cup of coffee with an old high school pal, then went home, took off the uniform and never wore it again. Frank Hoffman made it to Mt. Vernon, Ohio, but his mother had remarried and lived in a house with her new husband some miles out of town. So Hoffman rented a room and resumed life on his own. He went back to his old job at the printing press, but his fellow workers, who hadn't served during the war, gave him no special recognition or consideration. Earl Faull came home to Butler, Pennsylvania, to find his mother, age sixty-eight, dying of colon cancer. James Larkey disembarked in New Jersey and rushed to Bayonne to see his dying uncle, who had vowed to stay alive until his favorite nephew returned. Then Larkey learned another guy, who avoided combat by going to dental school, had stolen his girlfriend. After Donald Wallace arrived in Park Ridge, Illinois, he called his girl-friend who had written him regularly while he was overseas. She confessed she was engaged to someone else, so it was a "bad time emotionally in the period after I left the 99th."[65]

First Sergeant David Spencer arrived in Sabina, Ohio, at night, and no one was there to greet him. He didn't even know where his wife lived and had to ask at the local drugstore where he might find her. He finally located the apartment and knocked. When a woman opened the door, he gave her a big hug, but it turned out to be his wife's sister. He met his two-year-old daughter for the first time, but she was frightened of him, and for months he could not touch her, a reaction that "bothered him a lot." Glenny Blanchard came home to Baton Rouge, Louisiana, in the fall only to learn his two-year-old daughter wanted him to leave. When Newman Smith left home he had a nine-month-old daughter, but when he returned to Barton, Georgia, in March 1946, his daughter objected if he entered their bedroom. "Man, come out of that room!" she called. Smith confessed that even later on "she never seemed to be close to me."[66]

Captain Harold Hill returned to his wife Mary in Goldendale, Washington, but no one "made a fuss over me," for the townspeople thought they "had done their bit" by going without luxuries and surpluses. Hill admitted, "I had a hell of a time adjusting to civilian life and wasn't going to take any more crap off anyone." And yet, he didn't want to make decisions about the farms he and his older brother worked, and he refused to serve on any county boards. Haunted by the deaths of some of his men, he wondered if he could have done better as their commander. When he paid a visit to the local American Legion hall, all he heard were complaints about officers. So instead of finding others with whom he could talk, Hill left and never returned.[67]

Thomas Woznicki also envied those who never served and was angered they held the jobs that should have gone to returning veterans. James Crafton was "resentful that not everyone had been in it," including football players at the University of Arkansas. His two college roommates never saw "a day of service" and yet didn't look up to him for going. Fred Gole, who had been drafted in November 1942, leaving a widowed mother and two younger brothers behind, came home to discover with some bitterness that his brother-in-law and others in Euclid, Ohio, never served; moreover, no one ever told him they appreciated what he had done.[68]

Many others had adjustment problems. When Albert Eckert arrived at home in Charleston, Illinois, nobody cared, "I was just another of those guys coming home." What bothered him were the cold and snow, which brought back painful memories of time spent on Elsenborn Ridge the previous winter. Eckert returned to Eastern Illinois State Teachers College but remained jumpy; he was careful passing doorways, ran up stairs, and always sat in the back corner of the classroom because he disliked having anyone behind him. Once he and his brother, also a combat veteran, went on a first date. When a fraternity brother arrived to pick them up, the Model T Ford backfired and both brothers instinctively jumped behind a hedge, accidentally knocking down the young women, who promptly asked to be taken home. James Larkey enrolled at the University of Pennsylvania but couldn't concentrate on his studies, for "everything seemed irrelevant after combat." The dormitory, with its lack of privacy, reminded him of army barracks when he wanted to be at home, which seemed "synonymous with security." He dropped out of college.[69]

Riding the train from Jersey City to Fort Dix, Fred Kampmier looked out to see people rushing into nice stores and along brightly lit city streets, seemingly oblivious to the destruction that Europeans had endured or the trials he had faced. Americans, he thought, had lived a sheltered existence, and he almost wished a bomb could drop on the street to give them a sense of what war involved. Despite the nation's appreciation of its fighting men, combat veterans felt somewhat detached from those who had not been on the battlefields. They had faced unforgettable horrors, including the death of comrades. No veteran wanted to retell or relive those experiences; besides, as Charles Swann said, "People really did not want to hear about it, and we didn't have the ability to explain it anyway." So the returning veterans often bottled up those emotions, trying to forget what would be the most searing experience of their lives. No matter how close their relationship to parents, wives, siblings, and children, a part of them would always remain closed off and unseen, except to those who had been in combat. The army pretty much ignored post combat psychological problems; besides, men of that generation were expected to keep personal issues to themselves and carry on silently. Those who broke down because of "combat fatigue," or failed in some manner, blamed themselves for not holding up under pressure and were plagued by a sense of personal failure they carried with them the rest of their lives.[70]

Most men successfully resumed their lives, returning to college or going to work and subsequently starting families. Unlike their younger counterparts, they were generally more serious, eager to make up for lost time. Everyone who participated, but particularly those who had fought on the front lines and survived, felt more confident and proud of what they had accomplished. Anthony Pellegrino, who was five feet three inches tall and had carried a chip on his shoulder before army service, came home less angry; his platoon had grown to respect him as a capable soldier, and he had proved it to himself. The better-educated ASTP men gained an appreciation for fellow GIs who came from impoverished or different backgrounds. James Larkey, by his own admission a "spoiled brat," discovered that guys who couldn't read or write were good soldiers, in fact, possessed superior abilities as combat infantrymen.[71]

Most veterans wanted to put the war behind them; as Robert Mitsch said, "I did my utmost to wipe out the traumatic events from my memory bank." Charles Katlic tried to forget but could not and would weep, wondering, "Why [do] humans kill each other?" Earle Slyder suffered from feelings of guilt, asking himself, "Why did they die and not me?" His solution was "drinking and general hell-raising." Those with permanent injuries could never repress wartime experiences, and GIs who had suffered frozen feet on the battlefield were reminded each winter by recurring discomfort. Henry Thomas commented bitterly: "How would you like to be a cripple the rest of your life?" The doctors had to fuse Thomas's right knee after a shell fragment struck him. Thomas spent more than two years in hospitals and, when finally discharged in June 1947, discovered, contrary to promises made when he left U.S. Steel in Gary, Indiana, his old job was no longer available. Instead he was assigned a "flunky" position at much lower pay, which prompted him to quit.[72]

For some men, erasing the past proved difficult, especially at night while sleeping, when horrible moments welled up from the subconscious. Bernave Aguillera, a former POW, was tormented by nightmares about riding in German boxcars. Byron Rawls remembered the Germans he had killed, and BAR gunner Joseph Thimm could not forget those he had shot "face-to-face and those whom I did not see but knew they were my victims." For years Howard Bowers suffered from a recurring dream in which a German soldier stood over him with a burp gun while "I lay wounded in the snow unable to move." In his scary dreams, Virdin Royce searched without luck for his rifle as German soldiers bore down on him. Robert Justice would yell out in his sleep, "Watch out! It's coming!" as he anticipated another artillery round. John Kuhn, an original member of the division, reflected, "Once you are in combat, you are never the same. Flashbacks of what you saw come back all the time." For twenty years Harry Hagstad suffered from nightmares about battle scenes with artillery shells falling and the Germans advancing with rifles. James Langford dreamed about events in the war, and when he tried to talk about them, "the dreams only got worse." William Galegar couldn't blot out scenes witnessed during combat, especially those involving men, women, and children who had lost body parts. In a letter to his parents, Carter Strong expressed the realization that normally he would not have been "in contact with so many things that have been unpleasant. I would have been able to enjoy a few more years of aloofness from many of the undesirable parts and people of the world." War and combat robbed GIs of their youth and innocence.[73]

• • •

These soldiers believed their cause had been just, and they had done their duty, defending the nation against evil forces threatening civilization. They paid a price, suffering physical and psychological hardships while experiencing destruction and death, including the loss of men they considered their buddies. Virdin Royce, like many others, had prayed in combat that he might be saved. But he could not say without tears: "God brought me home, but Smith and the others prayed, and they got killed." Royce and other survivors could not understand why they had lived. It was sadness and guilt that affected them emotionally, for they realized those dead GIs would never see their loved ones again nor have the chance to pursue a career, buy a house, or raise a family. While all were proud of their service, they had no desire to fight again. Unlike those who had never set foot on a battlefield, they knew what horrors war produced. William Galegar wrote, "Nothing will ever compensate for the memories of waste, brutality, and loss to the world of the finest manpower of both winning and losing nations."[74]

• • •

Growing up during the long, difficult Depression of the 1930s, this unlucky generation had been forced to participate in the mayhem of mass warfare. Many had witnessed unforgettable scenes of death and Nazi cruelty. Others experienced permanent injuries and disabilities they carried with them the rest of their lives. All suffered hidden psychic damage, including memories of young comrades who did not return. Years later, looking back on this period in their lives, they realized they had been connected in some small way to something much larger. Maybe there was "some consolation in what we did," Harry Arnold commented, "for we were an integral part of the leading edge in some of the most significant events of our time."[75] Wars have often been fought for reasons that offered little benefit to the participants. At least World War II veterans knew that in this instance much was at stake, the cause was worth fighting for, and they had triumphed.

99th Division Interviewees

393RD REGIMENT

1ST BATTALION

Bauer, Eugene
Bronson, Glenn
Hoffman, George
Legler, Matthew
McGilvray, John

A Company

Carnevale, Joseph
Cathey, Wendell
DeKoster, Edward
Gole, Frederick
Kennedy, Hershel
Richmond, Melvin
Swanner, Daulton
Waskiewicz, Joseph

B Company

Brommer, Donald
Johnson, Joseph
Pankop, Gerald
Stewart, Raymond

C Company

Boeger, Al
Burda, Bert
Costello, Paul
Heroman, W. J.
Lahr, Richard
Marmande, Henry
Morrisey, Patrick
Newsome, Richard
Rarick, John
Waddell, John

D Company

Adda, Lionel
Bruno, Lucas
Monsanto, William

E Company

Betts, Arthur
Bosetti, Andy
Carroll, Radford
Henson, Edgar
Schilling, Warren
Thompson, Lyell
Waldrep, Robert

F Company

Gianapoulos, Nicholas
Gorsline, Donald
Haudenschild, Harold
Jensen, James
Kagan, Joseph
Lehr, George
Malinowski, Walter
McCoy, John
McDaniel, Ernest

McIlroy, James
Spencer, David
Walker, Lathan

G Company

Barton, John
Hawn, Robert
Iglehart, Francis
Middleton, John
Speer, James

H Company

Doherty, Joseph

I Company

Beeman, Mark
Burke, E. Jay
Fish, Roy
Leseur, Leo
Maurer, Robert
Nelson, G. Allan

K Company

Baxter, Jack
Colby, Stanley
Crafton, James
Dodd, Tony
Fontenot, John
Grant, Robert
Harris, Howard
Mudra, William
Muis, Glen
Smollen, Frank
Sullivan, Edward
Thompson, David
Wilcoxson, Glenn
Wilkins, B. O.

L Company

Eimermann, Edward
Juhl, Kenneth
Meacham, William
Mesler, Robert
Moffitt, Jack
Ortalda, Robert
Prickett, Jack
Putnam, Roy
Walter, Robert C.

M Company

Wager, Elliot

394 REGIMENT

1ST BATTALION

Bishop, James
Burton, Robert
Cornett, Lewis
Lambert, Stanley
Mann, Harold
Smart, Earl

A Company

Dudley, George
Eubanks, Charles
Hitchcock, Stanley
Long, Lloyd
Jones, Arthur
Jones, David
McMurdie, William
Meehan, Richard
Mellin, John
Wiberg, Donald

B Company

Aguillera, Bernave
Carter, John
Cornett, T. J.
Davis, Robert
Davis, Teddy
Deal, Clarence
Gamber, Ralph
Hagstad, Harry
Henderson, B. C.
Jacksha, Richard
Knoblock, Richard
Perisin, Raymond
Selwood, Clifford
Tobin, John
Weeks, Max
Woods, Pendleton

C Company

Bentzel, Clair
Coulter, Jesse
Geller, Harry
Merritt, Reid
Otto, Merle
Perlman, David
Stein, Howard
Wenzel, Raymond
Wieleba, Emil

D Company

Bowers, Howard
Cornell, Robert
Kraemer, Ronald
Parks, Raymond
Pellegrene, Arthur
Stumpff, Delbert
Wagner, Leroy

E Company

Anderson, Maltie
Brooks, Charles
Bussen, James
Kallas, Steve
Kellogg, Walter
Oldroyd, Ralph
Spinato, Angelo
Weber, Harold
Wells, Cyrus
Whiteway, Curtis

F Company

Katlic, Charles
King, Richard

G Company

Etter, Hal
Hendricks, John
Langston, Jake
Loftus, John
Schaefer, Harold
Snyder, Marvin
Sporborg, Harold
Stottlemyer, Roger
Sullivan, H. C.
Tommey, Richard
Wachtman, Henry
White, William

H Company

Whitehead, Rex
Wolff, Haskell

3RD BATTALION

Roland, Charles
Kirkbride, William

I&R

Bouck, Lyle
Milosevich, Risto

I Company

Ankrom, Hank
Brechner, Saul
Cleveland, Wayne
Heisler, John
Jones, J. C.
Kampmier, Fred
Lake, William
Lamb, Jack
Lombardo, Sam
Langford, James
Larkey, James
Lehman, Max
Marcisin, John
Miller, George
Miller, Ralph
Moon, George
Oliverio, Sammy
Reagler, David
Roland, Peter
Rosen, Isadore

K Company

Boris, Lawrence
Hofmann, William
Kist, Harold
Marra, Joseph
Ralston, Richard
Render, Richard

Withers, Langhorne
Zonsius, Lawrence

L Company

Ansell, David
Bray, William
Brown, Neil
Danalfo, Louis
Engel, Eldon
Feigenoff, Fred
Grimm, Furman
Ingham, Allen
Kritzman, George
Linz, John
McDaniel, Cliff
Mitsch, Robert
Peloquin, Edwin
Peterson, Harry
Reburn, Byron
Shimko, Joseph
Suess, Howard
Swann, Charles
Thornburg, John
Wallace, Donald

M Company

Fickett, Robert
Paxson, Omar

N Company

Demone, Harold
Folmar, Richard
McElroy, Jack

S 394

Botz, Willis

S 924

Peters, Earl
Yager, Grant

395TH REGIMENT

1ST BATTALION

Jackson, Emmett
Hall, Carl

A Company

Chesnick, Francis
Custer, Herbert
Goss, William
Graeber, Mark
Hill, Ralph David
Jones, David
Lefevre, Leo
Martin, Richard
O'Neill, Joseph
Schneider, Cecil
Talbird, Raymond
Zuckerman, Norman

B Company

Burke, George
Pierce, Robert
Saffer Seymour
Weaver, Richard

C Company

Hineman, Joseph
Honey, Oakley
Hilkey, Charles
Payton, Wes

Rawls, Byron
Sawyers, Lindell
Shivone, Ralph
Smith, Newman
Stevens, Jack
Swanson, Vern
Whitmarsh, Bryon

D Company

Brannon, R. H.
Clark, Arthur
Davis, Albert
Sale, William

E Company

Gound, Edgar
Gregonis, Walter
Helms, J. P.
Hill, Double E
Hoffman, Frank
Jillson, Paul
Johnson, Jim
Justice, Robert
Koch, Robert
Nugent, Tim
Ratowsky, Fred
Reed, Ken
Wolf, Lynn

F Company

Amos, Dewey
Kawalek, Frank
Konda, Henry
Moody, Hubert
Norton, Reeve
Oakes, John
Piller, Robert

Pope, Fielding
Saalfeld, Robert
Slyder, Earle

G Company

Blanchard, Glenny
Brody, Bernard
Eckert, Albert
Eldredge, Eugene
Galegar, William
Hill, Harold
Kirkpatrick, Ken
McNish, Charles
Pellegrino, Anthony
Samuelson, Earl
Strong, Carter
Terry, Robert
Vasa, John
Williams, Forbes
Woznicki, Thomas

H Company

Dudman, Earl
Fischer, Stewart
Maclin, Robert
Norris, Max
Razzano, Rocco
St. Pierre, Leon
Sizemore, Floyd
Switzer, Richard

3RD BATTALION

Butler, McClernand

I Company

Herdina, Joseph
Lange, Harold

Nelson, Jay
Nothwang, George
Piersall, Thornton
Rogers, Leon
Ronningen, Thor
Royce, Virdin
Shaver, Gene
Shultz, Lambert
Simons, Homer
Tabb, John
Womble, Murray

K Company

Blasdell, William
Fischer, Stewart
Phillips, Horace
Maloff, Isadore
Ritchie, Robert
Shell, John
Thimm, Joseph
Thomas, Warren
Walter, Robert

L Company

Bloom, Estan
Neill, George
Pedrotti, Louis
Prager, George
Schnitzer, Alfred
Shipman, Duane
Tolmasov, James
Weinstein, Richard
Wickersham, Erskine
Williams, David
Wolffe, Peter

M Company

Faull, Earl
Kissinger, Homer
Lee, Marshall
Thomas, Henry
Thompson, Fred
Zioncheck, Edward

N 395

Stanger, Ken

A 371

Verdecchio, Fred

B 324

Sterling, Patten

B 370

Duren, Guy
Hightower, E. W.

E 324

Laisure, Jack
Weiss, Herman

P 099

Elinoff, Joe
Kline, Stuart

Q Med

Hojnowski, Edward
McCracken, Harry

S 371

Meyer, Otto

S 395

Perry, Donald

S 924

Goldstein, Alfred
Hartley, Burrell

Notes

INTRODUCTION

1. Eighty-seven divisions were organized and equipped for shipment overseas. Forty-two infantry divisions, plus four airborne divisions and sixteen armored divisions fought in northern Europe. Shelby Stanton, *World War II: Order of Battle*, 3; Michael Doubler, *Closing with the Enemy*, 236, cites 6,103 battle casualties and 5,884 non-battle casualties for an 85 percent turnover rate.

CHAPTER 1. THE COMING OF WAR

1. Warren Thomas, e-mail, December 8, 2005, April 11, 2006; Francis Iglehart, e-mail, December 8, 2005; James Larkey, e-mail, December 9, 2005.

2. Grant Yager, e-mail, December 11, 2003; Raymond Wenzel, e-mail, December 7, 2005; Robert Mitsch, e-mail, April 12, 2006; Joseph Thimm, e-mail, December 7, 2005; Robert Maclin, Memoir in "Some Uncommon Common Men," unpub. collection, ed. by Stewart and Myra Fischer, 2001.

3. Kenneth Reed, e-mail, December 9, 2005; Homer Kissinger, e-mail, December 12, 2005.

4. Howard Bowers, e-mail, December 11, 2005; William Galegar, e-mail, April 11, 2006; Charles Roland, e-mail, December 7, 2005.

5. B. O. Wilkins, interview, July 18, 2002; Samuel Lombardo, *O'er the Land of the Free*, 49; John Hendricks, e-mail, May 13, 2006; Samuel Stouffer, et al., *The American Soldier*, vol. 1, 432.

6. Glenn Bronson, interview, April 15, 2004; James Bussen, interview, November 21, 2002; James Larkey, interview, July 10, 2001; Rocco Razzano, interview, March 25, 2002; Nick Gianopoulous, interview, February 26, 2006; Edwin Stoch, interview, August 10, 2007; Lyell Thompson, interview, August 10, 2003; David Thompson, interview, December 10, 2001.

7. Frederick Feigenoff, interview, December 2, 2002.

8. Edgar Henson, interview, February 22, 2002; Thor Ronningen, "Memoir of a World War II WWII Infantryman," *Checkerboard,* no. 2 (2000), 15; J. C. Jones, interview, January 31, 2005; Francis Chesnick, interview, June 16, 2001; Joseph Hineman, interview, June 27, 2003; Radford Carroll, "Stories for my Grandchildren," unpub. memoir, 2001.

9. John Barton, interview, March 28, 2001; Earle Slyder, interview, August 31, 2001; Charles Swann, interview, June 2, 2001; Charles Katlic, interview, November 28, 2001; B. C. Henderson interview, August 23, 2001; Hubert Moody, interview, December 2, 2005.

10. Mel Richmond, interview, July 19, 2002; Howard Stein, interview, December 20, 2006; David Perlman, e-mail, May 23, 2005; Ralph Miller, interview, March 26, 2003; Radford Carroll, interview, July 17, 2002; James Langford, e-mail, December 8, 2005; Donald Wallace, e-mail, December 3, 2003.

11. Isadore Rosen, interview, June 27, 2001; Anthony Pellegrino, interview, February 18, 2006; Ralph Shivone, interview, August 11, 2001.

12. Robert Mitsch, e-mail, February 23, 2001; Louis Pedrotti, "Tales from the 99th Division," unpubl. memoir, 1–2; James McIlroy, memoir in "Some Uncommon Men"; Robert Maclin, memoir in "Some Uncommon Men."

13. Louis Pedrotti, interview, June 1, 2001.

14. Radford Carroll, e-mail, May 31, 2003.

15. Robert Palmer, et al., *Procurement and Training of Ground Combat Troops,* 434. Sixty-seven were infantry divisions; Jim Bishop, "A Call to Valor," unpub. history, 1998, 25–49.

16. Robert Mitsch, letter to Author, March 8, 2001; Radford Carroll, "War Stories," unpub. memoir, 7.

17. Joseph Thimm, interview, April 12, 2003; Jim Bishop, "A Call to Valor," 37–38; Samuel Stouffer, et al., *The American Soldier,* vol. 1, 411–12.

18. Robert Walter, e-mail, July 6, 2005.

19. Steward Fischer, e-mail, February 24, 2002; Robert Mitsch, interview, July 21, 2002; Howard Harris, interview, June 17, 2002.

20. John McCoy, interview, May 10, 2001; John McCoy, "Remembrance of Army Days, 1943–46," unpub. memoir, 2.; quoted in Gerald Linderman, *The World Within War,* 50; James William Gibson, *Warrior Dreams: Violence and Manhood in Post-Vietnam America,* 17–18.

21. McCoy, "Remembrance," 1; Joseph Thimm, interview, April 12, 2003.

22. David Kennedy, *Freedom from Fear: The American People in Depression and War, 1929–1945,* 710.

23. Ronald Kraemer, interview, November 16, 2001; Harold Mann, interview, April 28, 2003; Hershel Kennedy, interview, May 26, 2005; Joseph Thimm, interview, April 12, 2003.

24. Fred Ratowsky, interview, May 22, 2004; Anthony Pellegrino, interview, February 18, 2006.

25. Howard Bowers, "Memories of WWII," unpub. memoir, revised 2001, 4; Louis Pedrotti, "Tales from the 99th Division," part 1, unpub. memoir, 4; John McCoy, "Remembrance," 1.

26. Robert Mitsch, interview, March 22, 2002.

27. Joseph Thimm, interview, April 12, 2003.

28. Louis Pedrotti, "Tales from the 99th," unpubl. memoir, 6.

29. Fielding Pope, interview, May 1, 2001.

30. Joseph Thimm, interview, April 12, 2003; William Galegar, e-mail, June 14, 2004; Ernest McDaniel, e-mail, November 20, 2002.

31. Louis Keefer, *Scholars in Foxholes: The Story of the Army Specialized Training Program in World War II*, 51–78.

32. Stewart Fischer, e-mail, June 8, 2003.

33. Radford Carroll, "War Stories," 11; Robert Maclin, Memoir in "Some Uncommon Men"; James McIlroy, Memoir, in "Some Uncommon Men."

34. Joseph Thimm, interview, April 12, 2003; Risto Milosevich, interview, March 27, 2007; Rex Whitehead, e-mail, March 9, 2001.

35. Louis Pedrotti, "Tales from the 99th," unpubl. memoir, 4.

36. James McIlroy, interview, June 10, 2001.

37. Mel Richmond, interview, July 6, 2002 .

38. Thor Ronningen, "Thor's War" in *Checkerboard*, no. 2 (2000): 15, Louis Pedrotti, interview, June 1, 2002.

39. Richard King, "Teenagers at War," unpub. memoir.

CHAPTER 2. TRAINING FOR WAR

1. William Cavanagh, *Dauntless: A History of the 99th Infantry Division*, 9–31.

2. Matthew Legler, interview, July 19, 2002; Maltie Anderson, letter to author, July 2, 2001; Furman Grimm, interview, September 5, 2001; Willis Botz, interview, September 3, 2001.

3. Walter Lauer, *Battle Babies: The Story of the 99th Infantry Division in World War II*, 96; John Kuhn, interview, April 22, 2006.

4. Charles Roland, e-mail, May 8, 2006.

5. Louis Pedrotti, e-mail, June 5, 2003; Jay Nelson, letter, "Dear Mom," June 23, 1944 in Ruth Little, ed., *Love, and a Prayer*, 72.

6. "Camp Maxey," *The Paris News*, February 1, 1981,1.

7. Earle Slyder, interview, August 31, 2001; William McMurdie, letter, "Dear Mom and Dad, March 12, 1944 in *Hey, Mac*, 33–34; Angelo Spinato. "Recollections of One Soldier," unpubl. memoir, June 1, 2007; Albert Goldstein, "How I Won the War," unpub. memoir; George Neill, *Infantry Soldier*, 25.

8. Mel Richmond, interview, August 1, 2002; Carter Strong, "To Hellenbach," unpub. memoir, 1946, 28; Tim Nugent, interview, August 5, 2004.

9. William Meacham, interview, July 9, 2003; Robert Mesler, interview, May 21, 2004; Mel Richmond, interview, July 10, 2002; Richard Weaver, interview, July 19, 2002; Harold Schaefer, e-mail May 25, 2001; Leon Rogers, interview, September 22, 2001; John McCoy, interview, May 1, 2001.

10. Mel Richmond, interview, July 20, 2002.

11. Ronald Kraemer, interview, March 18, 2001; Donald Wallace, e-mail, April 24, 2006.

12. James Bussen, interview, November 21, 2002; Howard Barnes, interview, August 9, 2004; Forbes Williams, interview, March 25, 2003.

13. George Dudley, interview, November 27, 2002; Homer Simons, interview, December 26, 2004; William Hoffman, interview, June 8, 2006.

14. Hank Ankrom, interview, August 2, 2002; Rex Whitehead, e-mail, August 23, 2001.

15. Byron Whitmarsh, interview, August 15, 2001; Woodrow Hickey, interview, August 20, 2002; Louis Pedrotti, e-mail, February 22, 2001. Unfavorable attitudes toward officers were highest among better-educated privates. Stouffer, et al., *The American Soldier*, vol. 1, 364–68.

16. Leon Rogers, interview, September 22, 2001; Albert Davis, interview, October 23, 2005;

17. David Reagler, interview, September 30, 2001; Harry Hagstad, interview, April 26, 2006; Jack Prickett, interview, May 15, 2001.

18. Joseph Hineman, interview, July 7, 2001; John Vasa, interview, June 25, 2001, Byron Whitmarsh, interview, August 15, 2001.

19. Forbes Williams, interview, December 10, 2005; Arthur Pellegrene, interview, September 4, 2002; Howard Bowers, e-mail, December 15, 2001.

20. Mel Richmond, interview, April 6, 2002; Robert Walter, e-mail, July 18, 2005.

21. T. C., interview, August 20, 2002.

22. David Perlman, e-mail, July 8, 2005; Henri Atkins, "Recollections of WWII" unpubl. memoir, 14; Harold Lange, interview, November 15, 2002.

23. Byron Whitmarsh, interview, August 2, 2002; Ken Juhl, interview, March 23, 2002; Wayne Cleveland, interview, June 22, 2001; Ernest McDaniel, interviews, May 2, 2001, October 14, 2003.

24. Harold Hill, interview, July 20, 2002.

25. Robert Pierce, interview, April 3, 2003; David Jones, interview, June 26, 2001.

26. Ernest McDaniel, e-mail, July 5, 2003.

27. Harold Schaefer, e-mail, July 9, 2003.

28. Robert Walter, e-mail, July 6, 2005; William Bray, e-mail, December 7, 2001.

29. Byron Whitmarsh, interview, August 15, 2001; Harold Schaefer, e-mail, June 25, 2003; Richard King, "Teenagers at War," unpub. memoir; Louis Pedrotti, "Tales from the 99th," part 1, 6, and e-mail, December 8, 2001.

30. Francis Chesnick, interview, June 16, 2001.

31. B. O. Wilkins, e-mail, February 14, 2002.

32. B. O. Wilkins, interview, June 20, 2001; Radford Carroll, e-mail, May 7, 2002.

33. Louis Pedrotti, e-mail, April 25, 2002, April 28, 2003.

34. Louis Pedrotti, e-mail, December 19, 2001; Howard Harris, interview, June 17, 2003; John Thornburg, interview, November 23, 2002.

35. Fielding Pope, interview, May 1, 2001; William Blasdel, interview, October 3, 2001; Mel Richmond, interview, July 20, 2002.

36. Blasdel, interview, October 3, 2001.

37. Robert Mitsch, letter to author, November 24, 2002; Louis Pedrotti, e-mail, April 25, 2002 and April 26, 2002.

38. Leon Rogers, interview, September 22, 2001; Mel Richmond, interview, July 18, 2002; Louis Pedrotti, "Tales from the 99th," part 1, unpubl. memoir, 7–8.

39. Albert Goldstein, "How I Won the War"; Jay Nelson, letter, "Dear Mom," February 23, 1944, in *Love, and a Prayer*, 58.

40. Paul Jillson, interview, March 29, 2002 ; Ernest McDaniel, interview, February 15, 2002; Radford Carroll, interview, July 17, 2002; Robert Davis, e-mail, May 28, 2001.

41. Jay Nelson, letter, "Dear Mom," July 30, 1944, in *Love, and a Prayer*, 80–81.

42. Harold Kist, interview, May 10, 2006.

43. Joseph Thimm, interview, April 12, 2003.

44. Harold Kist, interview, May 10, 2006.

45. Jay Nelson, letter, "Dear Mom," September 5, 1944 in *Love, and a Prayer*, 83; Joseph Herdina, interview, November 8, 2002.

46. James Crafton, interview, August 19, 2001; Walter Kellogg, interview, December 7, 2001; Jack Prickett, interview, May 15, 2001; Al Boeger, interview, April 23, 2001; Allen Nelson, interview, January 6, 2006; Charles Roland, *My Odyssey through History*, 28; Tony Aiello, *Checkerboard* (May, 1990), 5.

47. Harold Kist, interview, June 8, 2006,

48. Rex Whitehead, "Alvin R. Whitehead," unpub. memoir; William McMurdie, *Hey, Mac!*, 48; John Baxter, interview, March 7, 2003; David Jones, interview, June 23, 2001.

49. Haskell Wolff, interview, March 9, 2003.

50. Milton May, unpub. memoir; William Bray, interview, June 23, 2001.

51. Walter Gregonis, interview, March 1, 2006; Joseph Herdina, interview, November 8, 2002; T. J. Cornett, interview, August 20, 2002; Harold Hill, interview, July 20, 2002; Jack Prickett, interview, November 7, 2002.

52. Harry Hagstad, interview, March 15, 2006; John McCoy, interview, July 6, 2006.

53. Paul Weesner, unpub. memoir, 1.

54. David Spenser, "Diary," *Checkerboard*, no. 6 (1997), 6.

55. Walter Kellogg, interview, December 7, 2001.

Chapter 3. Going to War

1. Richard Byers, "Battle of the Bulge," unpub. memoir, 9; Roger Stottlemyer, interview, June 1, 2007; Milton May, unpub. memoir, 19; Joseph Thimm, interview, April 12, 2003.

2. John McCoy, "Remembrance of Army Days," unpub. memoir, 5; Roy Putnam, interview. April 12, 2001.

3. Joseph Thimm, e-mail, October 19, 2003; Jim Bishop, "A Call to Valor," unpub. History, 110.

4. Jay Nelson, letter, "Dear Mom," October 31, 1944 in *Love, and a Prayer*, 91.

5. Harry Arnold, "Easy Memories: The Way it Was," unpub. memoir, 7.

6. Byers, "Battle," 9; Charles Roland, *My Odyssey Through History*, 43.

7. David Perlman, "Memories," *Checkerboard*, no. 6 (1996), 9.

8. Richard Byers, *Checkerboard* (December, 1988), 3, and Byers, "Battle," 10; John Thornburg, e-mail, November 19, 2001.

9. Harry Arnold, "Easy Memories," 8, 9–10.

10. Jim Bishop, "A Call to Valor," 122–23.

11. Harry Arnold, "Easy Memories," 11.

12. Milton May, unpub. memoir, 19.

13. Paul Weesner, unpub. memoir, 1945, 2; Charles Eubanks, interview, March 19, 2001; Richard Render, video, 1988, and interview, July 27, 2006; Harry Arnold, "Easy Memories," 11.

14. Jim Bishop, "A Call to Valor," 127.

15. David Reagler, interview, December 2, 2001; Harry Arnold, "Easy Memories," 12.

16. Jay Burke, e-mail, June 10, 2006; William McMurdie, *Hey, Mac!*, 59.

17. Milton May, unpub. memoir, 20; Richard Byers, *Checkerboard* (December 1988), 3; Harry Arnold, "Easy Memories," 12–13.

18. Jay Burke, interview, April 1, 2001.

19. William Bray, interview, June 23, 2001.

20. John Midkiff, "A Soldier's Memories, 1942–46," unpub. memoir; Francis Iglehart, *The Short Life of the ASTP*, 12.

21. Walter Lauer, quoted in "After Action Reports," (December 1944); Richard Byers, *Checkerboard* (December 1988), 3.

22. Raymond Perisin, interview, May 22, 2006.

23. Samuel Lombardo, *Land of the Free*, 79; David Reagler, interview, September 30, 2001.

24. Paul Putty quoted in Thor Ronningen, *Butler's Battlin' Blue Bastards*, 24; Joseph Thimm, quoted in J. C. Doherty, *The Shock of War*, vol. 1, 33–34.

25. Byron Reburn, typed notes; John Mellin, interview, March 15, 2001; Harry Arnold, "Easy Memories," 15; Radford Carroll, "War Stories," 29. Also, "Masculinity and the Role of the Combat Soldier," in Stouffer, *The American Soldier*, 131–35.

26. William McMurdie, letter, "Dear Mom and Dad," November 15, 1944 quoted in *Hey, Mac!*, 62.

27. Henri Atkins, "Recollections," 46; Stewart Fischer, e-mail, February 23, 2002; William Bray, e-mail, March 21, 2001.

28. *Cold Injury, Ground Type.* Washington,Office of the Surgeon General, (Dept. of the Army: Washington, D.C.,1958, 444; Steve Kallas, interview, June 28, 2001; John Mellin, interview, March 15, 2001; John McManus, *The Deadly Brotherhood: The American Combat Soldier in World War*, 30–33

29. David Reagler, e-mail, July 9, 2003.

30. Stuart Kline, interview, December 28, 2005; James Langford, e-mail, July 9, 2003.

31. Cliff McDaniel, unpub. memoir, 13; Jay Burke, interview, May 12, 2007; John McManus, *The Deadly Brotherhood*, 14–26.

32. Howard Bowers, "Memories of WWII," 13; William Bray, interview, June 23, 2001; Richard Byers, *Checkerboard* (December 1988), 3.

33. William Bray, interview, June 23, 2001; Lathan Walker, interview, May 21, 2001.

34. Stewart Fischer, e-mail, February 24, 2001; interview with Myra Fischer, September 1, 2007.

35. Louis Pedrotti, e-mail, November 5, 2003; Harry Arnold, "Easy Memories," 16.

36. Jack Prickett, interview, October 12, 2003; Bill LeFevre, unpub. memoir, 45; Henri Atkins, "Recollections," 49; John McCoy, "Remembrance of Army Days," 8.

37. William Bray, interview, June 23, 2001.

38. Byron Reburn, "Notes."

39. Stanley Hancock, interview, April 15, 2001; Joseph O'Neill, interview, November 21, 2005.

40. Jack Prickett, e-mail, January 5, 2002; William McMurdie, *Hey, Mac!*, 68.

41. James Larkey, interview, August 18, 2004; Earle Slyder, interview, August 31, 2001; Jack Prickett, interview, October 12, 2003.

42. Ernest McDaniel, interview, October 14, 2003, and "Memories of WWII," unpub. memoir, 1998, 30.

43. Frank Hoffman, interview, April 13, 2002.

44. George Lehr, interview, March 28, 2001; Joseph Thimm, interview, April 12, 2003; James Larkey, interview, January 26, 2005.

45. Francis Iglehart, interview, May 4, 2001; David Reagler, interview, October 29, 2003.

46. Byron Reburn, interview, March 10, 2001 and June 20, 2001; Howard Bowers, "Memories of World War II," 13; B. O. Wilkins, interview, June 20, 2001; Joseph Carnevale, interview, February 10, 2003.

47. Oakley Honey, interview, June 8, 2003.

48. B. O. Wilkins, interview, June 2, 2003; Henri Atkins, "Recollections," 36; Oakley Honey, interview, September 29, 2003; John Thornburg, interview, November 23, 2002; Francis Chesnick, interview, July 20, 2002; James Crafton, interview, August 17, 2001.

49. Jack Prickett, interview, May 15, 2001.

50. Oakley Honey, interview, June 1, 2002.

51. Jack Prickett, interview, May 15, 2001.

52. McClernand Butler, interview, October 1, 2001.

53. John Mellin, interview, March 15, 2001 and June 22, 2001; William Cavanagh, *Dauntless: A History,* 374–96; Stephen Ambrose, *Citizen Soldier,* 187

54. Charles MacDonald, *A Time for Trumpets: The Untold Story of the Battle of the Bulge,* 62–79; William Cavanagh, *Dauntless: A History,* 65–68; J. C. Doherty, *The Shock of War,* vol. 1, 39–65; Radford Carroll, "War Stories," 29; Swanson quote in Bill Warnock, *The Dead of Winter,* 15–26. Information on Beckwith, 113–18.

55. Paul Jillson, "Talk of War," printed note.

56. Paul Weesner, unpub. memoir, 4–5.

CHAPTER 4. THE BATTLE OF THE BULGE

1. Howard Bowers, "Memories of World War II," 16–17.

2. William McMurdie, *Hey, Mac!,* 75–76.

3. Harold Piovesan, letter, "Dear Cliff," August 13, 1995; Richard Byers, "Battle of the Bulge," 24.

4. Maltie Anderson, interview, June 15, 2001; John Mellin, interview, May 15, 2001.

5. David Perlman, unpub. memoir, 1946, 4; Perlman, e-mail, Feb. 7. 2007.

6. Richard King, "A Three Day Pass in December," unpub. memoir.

7. King, "A Three Day Pass"; Charles MacDonald, *A Time for Trumpets,* 203–204.

8. King, "A Three Day Pass."

9. Thor Ronningen, "Thor's War," *Checkerboard,* no. 5 (2000), 5; J. P. Speder, "The 99th Infantry Division in the Battle of the Bulge," unpublished essay, 21.

10. Hugh Cole, *The Ardennes: Battle of the Bulge,* 86–90; Will Cavanagh, *Dauntless,* 71; K.C. Jacobsen, "The Battle of the Bulge," *Military Lifestyle,* November 1994, 30–36, 53.

11. Charles MacDonald, *A Time for Trumpets,* 21–52.

12. J. C. Doherty, *Shock of War,* vol. 1, 27–35, 50; Cavanagh, *Dauntless,* 71.

13. Doherty, *Shock of War,* vol. 1.

14. Doherty, *Shock of War,* vol.1, 160–96; Roger Cirillo, *Ardennes-Alsace,* US Army Center of Military History, 11–12;

15. MacDonald, *A Time for Trumpets,* 179–80.

16. Doherty, *Shock of War,* vol. 1, 186–203; Matthew Legler, interview, July 19, 2002; Mark Beeman, "The Autobiography of I/393"; William Meacham, interview, July 8, 2003; James Larkey. interview, May 19, 2007.

17. James Langford, "Experiences of an Infantry Squad," *Checkerboard* no. 4 (2001), 6–7; James Larkey, "Combat," printed note.

18. Robert Corley, letter to Rex Whitehead, August 21, 1990; Harold Schaefer, "Retrograde Movement of the 2nd Battalion Infantry," unpub. memoir; John Hendricks, interview, December 31, 2007; Maltie Anderson, interview, June 15, 2001.

19. Rex Whitehead, "Alvin R. Whitehead," unpub. memoir.

20. Cavanagh, *Dauntless*, 100–105.

21. *Ardennes Alsace*, 21; MacDonald, *A Time for Trumpets*, 197–99; Doherty, *Shock of War*, vol. 1, 217–19; Cavanagh, *Dauntless*, 130–33; MacDonald, *Trumpets*, 374.

22. Doherty, *Shock of War*, vol. 1, 220–28; Cavanagh, *Dauntless*, Ibid.

23. Cavanagh, *Dauntless*, 105–108.

24. MacDonald, *Trumpets*, 198–204; Michael Reynolds, *The Devil's Adjutant: Jochen Peiper*, 37–42.

25. Richard Render, letter, "To Bill Meyer," August 13, 1987.

26. Richard Ralston, interview, June 8, 2006; Frederick Feigenoff, interview, December 2, 2002; Charles Roland, *My Odyssey Through History*, 49–50.

27. John Thornburg, "Wunflialdye!" [one fly, all die], unpub. memoir, August, 1945.

28. Ibid.

29. Ibid.

30. Charles Swann, interviews, June 13, 2006, September 11, 2002.

31. Jim Bishop, "A Call to Valor," 188–94; interview, September 9, 2002, November 1, 2002; Robert Gabriel, unpub. memoir.

32. MacDonald, *Trumpets*, 205–209; William Meyer, interview, May 31, 2006; Doherty, *Shock of War*, vol. 1, 258–62, 306–12.

33. MacDonald, Ibid, 459–65.

34. Doherty, *Shock of War*, vol. I, 331–32.

35. Ibid. 332–22.

36. Howard Bowers, "Memories of WWII," 20; Rex Whitehead, "Alvin R. Whitehead," unpub. memoir; Harry Arnold, "Easy Memories," 37; on importance of senior leadership, Peter Mansoor, *The GI Offensive in Europe: The Triumph of American Infantry Divisions, 1941–1945*, 22–23.

37. Howard Bowers, "Memories."

38. Doherty, *Shock of War*, vol. 2, 120–36.

39. John McCoy "Remembrance of Army Days," 9; David Spencer, interview, July 20, 2002; Harry Arnold, "Easy Memories," 42.

40. Doherty, *Shock of War*, vol. 2, 136, 162–64.

41. Brochure, "Elsenborn Camp," interview, Archivist Claude Schmetz. Camp Elsenborn, July 5, 2004.

42. Cavanagh, *Dauntless*, 181–86; Charles Biggio, "Role of the Field Artillery in the Battle of Elsenborn," *Checkerboard*, no. 5, 1998, 4–6.

43. Hugh Cole, *The Ardennes: Battle of the Bulge*, 123; Doherty, Shock of War, vol. 2, 254; Henry Thomas, interview, June 25, 2004.

44. Walter Lauer, *Battle Babies*, 69.

45. R. H. Brannon, letter, "To Bill Meyer" June 15, 1984; Cavanagh, *Dauntless*, 181–89; Doherty, *Shock of War*, vol. 2, 264–76; James McIlroy, *Checkerboard*, no. 1 (2000), 26.

46. William Galegar, interview, November 27, 2003; John McGilvray, interview, July 15, 2005.

47. Cliff McDaniel, memoir; Cliff Selwood, interview, September 4, 2001; Harry Arnold, "Easy Memories," 52, 68.

48. Samuel Lombardo, *O'er the Land*, 95; David Reagler, e-mail, June 30, 2003; William Bray, interview, June 23, 2001; Charles Swann, interview, September 17, 2003.

49. Francis Iglehart, *The Short Life of the ASTP*, 49–50.

50. Robert Waldrep, e-mail, Nov. 30, 2003; William Bray, e-mail, Nov. 22, 2003; Byron Reburn, note to author.

51. William McMurdie, *Hey, Mac!*, 103; William Bray, interview, June 23, 2001; J. R. McIlroy, "Foxhole Monotony," *Checkerboard* (September 1993), 5; Francis Iglehart, *Short Life*, 49; Paul Jillson, note, "Food to Go."

52. George Miller, interview. December 12, 2003.

53. Oakley Honey, interview, May 3, 2002.

54. Rex Whitehead, collection of interviews, edited by Ron and Robyn Daines.

55. Robert Walter, letter to author, Feb. 4, 2005; William McMurdie, *Hey, Mac!*, 103.

56. Stephen Ambrose, *Citizen Soldiers*, 260; John Ellis, *The Sharp End*, 184–85; *Cold Injury, Ground Type*, 444.

57. Louis Pedrotti, "Tales from the 99th," part 2, 2; Edwin Stoch, interview, August 9, 2008; audio memoir, Veterans History Project, Library of Congress.

58. Jack Laisure, interview, August 9, 2007; Laisure, audio memoir, Veterans History Project, Library of Congress; Jim Bishop, interview, September 9, 2002.

59. William Galegar, "One Man's Armageddon," memoir, 38; Rex Whitehead, collection of interviews, ed. by Ron and Robin Daines; William Meacham, interview, July 8, 2003; Jay Nelson, letter, "Dear Mom and Dad (Christmas Morning)" in *Love, and a Prayer*, 101; William McMurdie, *Hey, Mac!*, 93–94; Francis Chesnick, interview, July 20, 2002.

60. Paul Weesner, memoir, 7; Robert Koch, interview, August 3, 2004.

61. R. H. Brannon, letter, "To Bill Meyer," June 15, 1984, and *Checkerboard*, no. 4 (2004), 3.

62. Eldon Engle, interview, November 28, 2002.

63. Howard Bowers, "Memories," 23; George Meloy, "A Memorable Christmas Night," *Checkerboard*, no. 7 (1992), 2.

64. Ernest McDaniel, "Memories of WWII," 25.

65. William Galegar, "One Man's Armageddon," 38; Maltie Anderson, interview, June 15, 2001; Patrick Morrisey, "Personal Memories," memoir;

Lionel Adda, interview, December 2, 2003; Double E Hill, interview April 15, 2005; Jay Burke, memoir, 28.

66. William Galegar, "One Man's," 39.

67. George Moon, interview, December 10, 2003.

68. Richard King, "Teenagers at War," memoir.

69. Ernest McDaniel, interview, February 15, 2002; James Langford, interview, July 19, 2002; Robert Mitsch, e-mail, January 10, 2004; Al Boeger, interview, April 23, 2001.

70. John Vasa, interview, June 30, 2001; Robert Waldrep, e-mail, January 15, 2002; Fielding Pope, interview, May 1, 2001; George Miller, interview, December 23, 2003; Don Gorsline, interview, September 15, 2002; James Larkey, interview, August 18, 2004.

71. Harry Arnold, "Easy Memories," 53; William Galegar, "One Man's," 40.

72. David Reagler, e-mail, November 17, 2003.

73. Ernest McDaniel, "Memories," 29; J. R. McIlroy, "Foxhole Montony," *Checkerboard* (September 1992), 5; Maltie Anderson, interview, February 10, 2003.

74. John McCoy, "Remembrance of Army Days," 9; Peter Mansoor, *The GI Offensive in Europe: The Triumph of American Infantry Divisions, 1941–45*, 252.

75. Peter Wolffe, interview, February 18, 2004.

76. Double E Hill, interview, April 15, 2002, e-mail, November 25, 2003; Paul Jillson, interview March 25, 2002; Cliff McDaniel, memoir, 15.

77. Robert Ortalda, interview, March 22, 2002; James Crafton, interview, August 6, 2001; James Langford, interview, July 4, 2001.

78. Robert Waldrep, e-mail, June 5, 2003; Francis Chesnick, interview, July 20, 2002; Robert Mitsch, e-mail, November 26, 2003; Byron Whitmarsh, interview, August 2, 2002; Charles Swann, interview, September 17, 2003; David Reagler, e-mail, November 21, 2003.

79. Francis Chesnick, interview, July 20, 2002; John Vasa, interview, June 30, 2001; Ken Juhl, interview, September 10, 2002, Lionel Adda, interview, December 2, 2003; Charles Swann, interview , September 17, 2003.

80. Cliff Selwood, interview, August 27, 2001; Jack Stevens, interview, March 21, 2002; T. J. Cornett, interview, August 20, 2007; Jay Burke, interview, April 1, 2001.

81. Francis Iglehart, *Short Life*, 48.

82. William Galegar, e-mail, May 15, 2007; Cliff Selwood, interview, August 27, 2001.

83. Al Boeger, interview, April 22, 2001; Cliff McDaniel, memoir; William Bray, interview, June 23, 2001.

84. Ernest McDaniel, "Memories of WWII," 29–30.

85. Byron Reburn, note to author.

86. William McMurdie, *Hey, Mac!*, 101; Joseph Waskiewicz, interview, June 24, 2001; Fred Verdecchio, interview, September 20, 2003; Robert Waldrep, e-mail, November 30, 2003; George Dudley quoted in *Hey, Mac!*,

96. For a discussion about the importance of prayer for combat soldiers, see Samuel Stouffer, *The American Soldier,* vol . 2, 172–88.

87. William McMurdie, letter, 1945, quoted in *Hey, Mac!,* 95; John McCoy, "Remembrance of Army Days," 10; Cliff McDaniel, memoir, 12–13; Lathan Walker, interview, April 12, 2002; James Bussen, interview, November 21, 2002.

88. Thor Ronningen, "Thor's War," *Checkerboard,* no. 5 (2000), 5; Donald Wallace, *Checkerboard,* no. 1 (1998), 8.

89. David Reagler, e-mail, July 9, 2003; Lionel Adda, e-mail, December 24, 2003, Maltie Anderson, interview, June 18, 2001.

90. Harry Arnold, "Easy Memories," 56.

91. Rex Whithead, "The Soldier's Story," 41–42.

92. Ernest McDaniel, "Memories of WWII," 27–28.

93. Charles Roland, interview, November 20, 2002; James Larkey, interview, June 11, 2007.

94. James Langford, interview, August 4, 2002;

95. William Bray, interview, June 23, 2001; James Larkey, interview, June 11, 2007.

96. Cliff McDaniel, letter, "To Bob Cigoy, April 4, 1970, 97; B. C. Henderson, B. C. Henderson website, interview, August 27, 2001.

98. Harry Arnold, "Easy Memories," 78–85.

99. Radford Carroll, "War Stories," 52.

100. Francis Iglehart, *Short History,* 55–63.

101. Richard King, "Teenagers at War."

102. George Miller, interview, December 23, 2003; Ernest McDaniel, "Memories," 41–42.

CHAPTER 5. GOING ON THE OFFENSIVE

1. Ken Stanger, interview, May 25, 2004; Peter Womack, *Checkerboard,* no. 7 (1993), 12.

2. Oakley Honey, interview, August 6, 2003; B. C. Henderson, interview, August 23, 2001; William Bartow quoted in Thor Ronningen's, *Butler's Battlin',* 89.

3. Preston LeBreton, memoir in "The Autobiography of I/393."

4. Francis Haskins, "Ammo Train," *Checkerboard* 43, no. 5 (December, 1990), 10; interview, May 14, 2006.

5. Emmett Jackson, "Combat Diary" (1945), 22; Grady Arrington, *Infantryman at the Front ,* 98.

6. Samuel Lombardo, *O'er the Land of the Free,* 110; James Larkey, letter to author.

7. Harry Arnold, "Easy Memories," 98.

8. Ibid., 99.

9. Oakley Honey, quoted in Vern Swanson, *Upfront with Charlie Company*, 52–53; interview, September 29, 2002.

10. Jay Burke, interview, June 8, 2003, interview, July 5, 2004.

11. Thor Ronningen, "Thor's War," *Checkerboard*, no. 5 (2000), 5; Oakley Honey, interview June 8, 2003.

12. Ken Reed, interview (December 4, 2004); Jay Nelson, letter, "Dear Mom" (February 19, 1945) in *Love, and a Prayer*, 116.

13. Byron Whitmarsh, interview, August 15, 2001, July 20, 2002; Carter Strong, "To Hellenbach," 49.

14. Carter Strong, Ibid.; Harry Arnold, "Easy Memories," 116; Y. B. Johnson, letter, "Dear Folks," January 23, 1945; Samuel Lombardo, interview, July 9, 2001.

15. Thor Ronningen, "Thor's War"; Charles Swann, interview, September 11, 2002.

16. Jay Nelson, letter, "Dear Mom," February 21, 1945, in *Love, and a Prayer*, 117.

17. Maltie Anderson, interview, December 4, 2003; Oakley Honey, interview, June 8, 2003; B. C. Henderson, e-mail, November 27, 2003.

18. Robert Hawn, "In Retrospect: The Bridge at Remagen," memoir, 1; Ralph Oldroyd, interview, August 3, 2004; Fred Kampmier, interview, January 9, 2004; Edgar Henson, interview, February 22, 2002; Max Norris, e-mail, June 1, 2007.

19. Radford Carroll, "War Stories," 57; John McCoy, "Remembrance," 12.

20. Oakley Honey, interview, June 8, 2003; Carter Strong, "To Hellenbach," 51; Emmett Jackson, "Combat Diary," unpub. memoir, 22.

21. James Larkey, e-mail (May 16. 2006); Jay Nelson, letter, "Dear Mom," March 4, 1945, in *Love, and a Prayer*, 121.

22. Fred Kampmier, "Cologne Plain," unpub. memoir (1945); Robert Mitsch, "Lucking Out: A Recall of World War II, Survival and Observations," 17; interview, March 2, 2002; William McMurdie, *Hey, Mac!*, 119; Henry Thomas, interview, June 25, 2004.

23. Radford Carroll, "War Stories," 58; Hermann Knell, *To Destroy a City*, 165–268.

24. Fred Kampmier, "Cologne Plain," unpub. memoir.

25. Ken Reed, letter to author, December 4, 2004; Paul Weesner, memoir, 12.

26. Frank Hoffman, interview, March 15, 2005.

27. William McMurdie, *Hey, Mac!*, 116–17.

28. James Tolmasov, interview, April 1, 2004; B. W., interview, 2002.

29. Y. B. Johnson, letter, "Mother and Dad," March 8, 1945; Steve Kallas, "Dogface," memoir, interview, March 8, 2002; Byron Whitmarsch, interview, July 20, 2002.

30. James Larkey, e-mail, May 15, 2005.

31. Angelo Spinato, e-mail, June 12, 2007; Steve Kallas, audio tape interviews, June 28, 2001; Fred Kampmier, "Cologne Plain"; George Meloy, "Looters," memoir in "The Autobiography of I/393."

32. Fred Kampmier, Ibid.; Virdin Royce, interview, July 21, 2002; Leroy Wagner, interview, September 6, 2001; John McCoy, "Remembrance," 13; Joseph Thimm, interview, April 12, 2003. For the pleasures of destruction, Linderman, *The World Within War*, 244–46; J. Glenn Gray, *The Warriors*, 51–58.

33. Jay Nelson, letter, "Dear Mom," March 4, 1945, in *Love, and a Prayer*, 121; Willis Botz, interview, September 3, 2001; William Meyer, interview, May 31, 2006. Also J. Glenn Gray, *The Warriors*, 51–58.

34. Robert Hawn, interview, July 3, 2001.

35. Fred Kampmier, "Cologne Plain"; John McManus, *The Deadly Brotherhood*, 77–79.

36. Emmett Jackson, "Combat Diary," 40; Jay Nelson, letter, "Dear Mom," March 4, 1945, in *Love, and a Prayer*, 121.

37. Grady Arrington, *Infantryman at the Front*, 163; Robert Ortalda, interview, March 24, 2002; Fred Kampmier, interview,December 26, 2003; Robert Mitsch, "Lucking Out," memoir; Thomas Sams Bishop, "Diary," *Checkerboard*,no. 6 (1994), 20.

38. Y. B. Johnson, letter, March 5, 1945; Grady Arrington, *Infantryman*, 107–108; Richard Weaver, interview, July 18, 2002; Carter Strong, "To Hellenbach," 52.

39. Walter Lauer, *Battle Babies*, 164.

40. Leroy Wagner, interview, December 10, 2001; Robert Mitsch, "Lucking Out," 18; Francis Haskins, "Ammo Train," *Checkerboard* (December 1990), 10.

41. William McMurdie, *Hey, Mac!*, 116–17. John Scaglione, "The Cologne Plain," *Checkerboard*, no. 6 (1996), 11.

42. Fred Kampmier, memoir.

43. Robert Hawn, "In Retrospect."

44. Francis Chesnick, interview, July 20, 2002; John Marcisin, "Reminiscences of Your Local Friendly Medic," *Checkerboard*, no. 5 (1994), 2.

45. Carter Strong, "To Hellenbach," 52; B. C. Henderson, interview, August 27, 2001; James Larkey, interview, July 10, 2001.

46. Charles Roland, *My Odyssey Through History*, 74.

47. William Galegar, "One Man's Armageddon," 61; B. C. Henderson, website, "Crossing the Ludendorff Bridge at Remagen."

48. William Blasdel, interview, October 3, 2001; Francis Chesnick, interview, July 4, 2002.

49. Harold Hill, interview, July 5, 2002; William Galegar, "Armageddon," 61.

CHAPTER 6. CROSSING THE RHINE

1. Ken Hechler, *The Bridge at Remagen*, 41–75; Winston Ramsay, "Crossing the Rhine," *After the Battle*, no. 16 (Battle of Britain Prints, 1977); Henry G.

Phillips, *Remagen: Springboard to Victory*, Kurt Kleeman (archivist of Remagen), e-mail, February 15, 2005.

2. Kurt Kleeman, e-mail, February 17, 2005.

3. Hechler, *Bridge at Remagen*, 137–54; Dr. Walter Schaefer-Kehnert (battery commander at Erpel in 1945), interview, June 6, 2006.

4. Harold Schaefer, "Köln Plains," memoir, 8.

5. Maltie Anderson, interview, June 15, 2001; John Hendricks, interview, February 19, 2005; B. C. Henderson, "Henderson at the Ludendoff Bridge," Multimedia Data Base; William McMurdie, *Hey, Mac!*, 122.

6. Carter Strong, "To Hellenbach," 58–59; Charles Swann, interview, September 17, 2003.

7. James Langford, interview, July 19, 2002, e-mail, December 9, 2004.

8. Harold Schaefer, e-mail, December 20, 2004.

9. Guy Duren, memoir, 3.

10. William McMurdie, *Hey, Mac!*, 123; Richard Jacksha, interview, August 5, 2007; Cliff Selwood, e-mail, December 18, 2004; Byron Reburn, interview, March 9, 2001; B. C. Henderson, "B. C. at the Ludendorff," website; John Scaglione, "Over the Rhine," *Checkerboard*, no. 2 (1996), 6; Boyd McCune, interview, February 4, 2005.

11. B. C. Henderson, "Crossing the Ludendorff"; Harold Schaefer, interview, January 28, 2005; Charles Katlic, letter to author, December 10, 2004.

12. Katlic, Ibid.; Saul Brechner, interview, January 26, 2005.

13. Charles Roland, *My Odyssey through History*, 74.

14. Robert Mitsch, "Lucking Out," 21; Stanley Lambert, e-mail, March 2, 2005.

15. J.C. Jones, interview , January 31, 2005; David Reagler, e-mail, December 15, 2004.

16. Leroy Wagner, interview, September 6, 2002; James Larkey, interview, January 26, 2005, and note to author.

17. Robert Mitsch, "Lucking out," 22; Harold Schaefer, memoir, "You Ask For It," 9.

18. Cliff McDaniel, letter to Bob Cigoy, April 4, 1970.

19. Robert Hawn, memoir, "In Retrospect"; Harry Arnold, "Easy Memories," 119.

20. Robert Waldrep, e-mail, December 10, 2004; Frank Peck, memoir, in "The Autobiography of I/393"; Ken Juhl, interview, August 10, 2002; Radford Carroll, "War Stories," 61; Daulton Swanner, interview, October 1, 2003.

21. James Revell, "On Combat," *Checkerboard* (September 1992), 11; Guy Duren, memoir, 32; Steve Kallas, e-mail, January 19, 2005; Robert Hawn, "In Retrospect."

22. Guy Duren, memoir, 32; John McCoy, "Remembrance of Army Days," 14.

23. Harry Arnold, "Easy Company," 120–21.

24. Stuart Kline, e-mail, February 21, 2003, December 3, 2004.

25. John Scaglione, "Over the Rhine," *Checkerboard*, no. 2 (1996), 11.

26. Woodrow Hickey, interview, August 20, 2002; William Galegar, "Armageddon," 62–63; Carter Strong, "To Hellenbach," 60.

27. William Galegar, "Armageddon," 60; Harold Hill, interview, July 2, 2002.

28. Joseph Thimm, interview, April 13, 2003; unpub. memoir, "The Bridge at Remagen" (1995).

29. William Galegar, "Armageddon," 67, Galegar, e-mail September 1, 2004.

30. Bernard Brody, interview, March 7, 2004; Richard Gorby quoted in Ronningen, *Butler's Battlin'*, 113; John Scaglione, "Over the Rhine," *Checkerboard*, no. 2 (1996).

31. Francis Chesnick, letter to author, December 22, 2004; Byron Whitmarsh, interview, July 20, 2002, and e-mail, January 1, 2005; Carter Strong, "To Hellenbach," 60; Forbes Williams, interview, December 7, 2005; Lambert Shultz, e-mail, February 15, 2005.

32. William Galegar, "Armageddon," 64; "Crossing the Rhine," *After the Battle*, no. 16, 9.

33. James Crewdson, "Remagen," memoir, 14–31, 33.

34. Paul Weesner, Memoir, 14; Oakley Honey, interview, June 8, 2003.

35. Robert Fickett, interview, July 10, 2003; Warren Thomas, note to author, February 11, 2005.

36. Maltie Anderson, interviews, June 15, 2001, September 10, 2002.

37. Fred Kampmier, "Suicide Hill," memoir, 1.

38. Ibid., 2.

39. Ibid., 5.

40. Ibid., 5–7.

41. James Larkey, interview, July 10, 2001, e-mail, January 28, 2005.

42. John Marcisin, "Reminiscenses," *Checkerboard* no. 5 (1994), 5.

43. Fred Kampmier, "Suicide Hill," 9–10.

44. Ibid.

45. John Scaglione, "Honningen" *Checkerboard*, no. 2 (1994), 5.

46. Richard Ralston, interview, March 14, 2004; Arthur Betts, interview, February 23, 2007; Stanley Lambert, interview, February 28, 2005: James Strawder quoted in David Colley, *Blood for Dignity*, 100.

47. Colley, *Blood for Dignity*, 102.

48. Jack Lamb, e-mail, January 20, 2005.

49. Fred Kampmier, "Cognac Hill," memoir; John Heisler, interview, January 28, 2005.

50. Kampmier, Ibid.

51. Harry Arnold, "Easy Memories," 121; Robert Hawn, interview, August 5, 2004.

52. Arnold, Ibid., 124.

53. Jim Bowers, quoted in Arnold, "Easy Memories," 131, 136.

54. Radford Carroll, interview, July 17, 2002; Colley, *Blood for Dignity*, 100.

55. Allen Nelson, memoir, "Autobiography of I/393."

56. Robert Waldrep, e-mail, June 13, 2003.

57. Guy Duren, memoir, 35; e-mail, June 19, 2005.

58. Colley, *Blood for Dignity*, 101; Arthur Betts, interview, February 23, 2007; Radford Carroll, "War Stories," 65.

59. Carroll, Ibid.; Ernest McDaniel, "Memories of WWII," 55.

60. Oakley Honey, interview, June 8, 2003; Byron Whitmarsh, interview, August 2, 2002.

61. Harold Hill, interview, August 6, 2002.

62. William Galegar, "Armageddon," 68–69, e-mail, February 6, 2005.

63. Ibid., e-mail, January 4, 2004.

64. Ken Reed, e-mail, January 19, 2005, February 10, 2006; Harold Hill, interview, July 20, 2002.

65. Virdin Royce, interview, July 21, 2002.

66. Lambert Shultz, memoir, 6.

67. Lambert Shultz, Ibid., 7, e-mail, February 15, 2005.

68. Max Norris, *Checkerboard* (March, 1986), 8–9; interview, September 11, 2004.

69. Harry Arnold, "Easy Memories," 145; Ernest McDaniel, "Memories of WWII," 55, interview, October 14, 2003.

70. John Hendricks, interview, February 19, 2005.

71. Francis Chesnick, interview, July 18, 2002; letter to author, February 17, 2005.

CHAPTER 7. THE SOLDIER'S WORLD

1. George Dudley, interview, November 27, 2002; B. C. Henderson, e-mail, June 6, 2005.

2. Joseph Thimm, interview, February 12, 2003.

3. Virdin Royce, interview, July 5, 2002; Henri Atkins, "Recollections of WWII, unpub. memoir, 43; Francis Chesnick, interview, July 5, 2002; Albert Eckert, interview, October 1, 2001.

4. Rex Whitehead, e-mail, April 20, 2001; Joseph Herdina, interview, November 8, 2002.

5. Patrick Morrisey, interview, May 6, 2002, July 5, 2005, "Personal Memories of the Battle of Bulge," memoir.

6. William Galegar, e-mail, November 17, 2004; T. J. Cornett, interview, June 20, 2003; Joseph Hineman, interview, June 27, 2003; Tilden Head, *Checkerboard* no. 1 (2001), and memoir.

7. Paul Jillson, interview, March 25, 2002; Walter Kellogg, interview, December 7, 2001.

8. Rex Whitehead, e-mail, April 24, 2001; Harold Schaefer, e-mail, December 23, 2004; Eugene Eldridge, interview, May 26, 2004; Paul Jillson, interview, March 25, 2002.

9. William Galegar, e-mail, December 5, 2003; James Larkey, interview, August 18, 2004; e-mail, June 8, 2005.

10. Duane Shipman, letter to author, 2002; Robert Walter, e-mail, July 4, 2005.

11. Richard Martin, interview, April 12, 2001; Joseph Kagan, interview, May 5, 2001; Art Clark, interview, May 23, 2001; McClernand Butler, interview, August 19, 2001.

12. George Meloy, "The Autobiography of I/393."

13. James Langford, e-mail, December 12, 2001; Byron Whitmarsh, interview, August 2, 2002.

14. Joseph Herdina, interview, November 8, 2002.

15. William Huffman, quoted in Ronningen, *Butler's Battlin'*, 68.

16. Ronningen, ibid., 147; McClernand Butler, interview, August 19, 2001.

17. William Blasdel, quoted in Ronningen, *Butler's*, 146; Stan Lambert, e-mail, August 21, 2007, interview, August 22, 2007.

18. James Langford, e-mail, December 12, 2001; Radford Carroll, e-mail, December 11, 2001.

19. Ronningen, *Butler's*, 34; John Tabb, quoted in Ronningen, *Butler's*, 34; Lindell Sawyers, interview, March 20, 2002; Charles Swann, interview, January 12, 2004.

20. McClernand Butler, interview, August 19, 2001.

21. Leon Rogers, interview, September 22, 2001; Frank Hoffman, interview, April 10, 2002; Y. B. Johnson, letter to his parents, April 21, 1945; Emmett Jackson, "Combat Diary," 25.

22. Earl Slyder, interview, June 2, 2001; Charles Swann, interview, January 12, 2004; Peter Wolffe, e-mail, June 10, 2005.

23. William Galegar, e-mail, July 8, 2005; Horace Phillips, interview, June 4, 2001, Erskine Wickersham, interview, May 12, 2001; William Blasdel, interview, October 3, 2001.

24. T. J. Cornett, interview, August 20, 2002; Radford Carroll, Interview, July 5, 2002.

25. James Langford, e-mail, April 26, 2002.

26. Joseph Herdina, interview, November 8, 2002; Richard Weaver, interview, July 5, 2002; Robert Justice, interview, July 7, 2002.

27. B. C. Henderson, e-mail, May 4, 2004; William Galegar, e-mail, January 4, 2004; Fred Gole, interview, May 27, 2005.

28. Raymond Talbird, interview. May 10, 2001.

29. Paul Jillson, interview, March 25, 2002, and "Along the Danube," memoir.

30. Radford Carroll, "War Stories," 38, 71.

31. Leroy Wagner, interview, September 6, 2002.

32. Charles Swann, interview, June 2, 2001, Edgar Henson, interview, February 22, 2002; Jack Stevens, interview, March 21, 2002.

33. Robert Hawn, interview, July 21, 2002; James Bussen, interview, November 21, 2002; Fred Verdecchio, interview, October 10, 2002.

34. James Tomasov, interview, April 1, 2004.

35. Robert Story, memoir, in "Some Uncommon Common Men."

36. Cyrus Wells, interview, September 10, 2004; Alfred Schnitzer, quoted in Ronningen, *Butler's*, 117; William Galegar, e-mail, August 22, 2004.

37. Rex Whitehead, e-mail, April 24, 2001; Byron Reburn, note to author.

38. Reburn, Ibid.

39. Charles Roland, *My Odyssey*, 50; Wayne Cleveland, interview, June 22, 2001; Joseph Herdina, interview, November 8, 2002; Richard Gorby quoted in Ronningen, *Butler's*, 83.

40. Steve Kallas, e-mail, January 25, 2005, interview, April 13, 2002, memoir.

41. Lambert Shultz, e-mail, December 24, 2004, memoir, 8.

42. Albert Eckert, interview, October 1, 2001; Mel Richmond, interview, July 18, 2002; Hershel Kennedy, interview, May 26, 2005; Charles Swann, interview January 12, 2004; Stewart Fischer, interview, December 8, 2001; Jack Prickett, interview, June 12, 2001.

43. Don Wallace, e-mail, December 12, 2003; Joseph Herdina, interview, November 8, 2002; Walter Kellogg, interview, December 7, 2001; Byron Whitmarsh, interview, July 18, 2002.

44. Harold Schaefer, e-mail, August 17, 2005.

45. Jake Langston, interview, September 2, 2001; Jack Prickett, interview, June 12, 2001; Mel Richmond, interview, July 18, 2002.

46. Fred Feigenoff, interview, December 2, 2002; Charles Roland, *My Odyssey*, 72; George Meloy, memoir in "Autobiography of I/393"; Donald Wiberg, interview, by Mark Van Ells, Wisconsin Veterans Museum archives, September 7, 1995; Don Wiberg, interview, May 10, 2001; Y. O. Johnson, Letter, February 10, 1945; Horace Phillips, interview, June 4, 2001; Vern Swanson, interview, March 30, 2001.

47. Robert Story, Memoir, in "Some Uncommen Common Men," 21.

48. Ernest McDaniel, "Memories of WWII," 62–64.

CHAPTER 8. CLOSING THE RUHR POCKET

1. Grady Arrington, *Infantryman*, 175; Guy Duren, memoir, 42, e-mail June 21, 2005.

2. Emmett Jackson, "Combat Diary," 35; Max Norris, interview, September 11, 2004.

3. Paul Weesner, memoir (1945), 17; Harry Arnold, "Easy Memories," 157.

4. Fred Kampmier, "World War II Memories."

5. Carter Strong, "To Hellenbach," 80; interview, Karsten Porezag in Wetzlar, Germany, July 8, 2004.

6. Robert Hawn, interview, August 16, 2004.

7. Karsten Porezag, interview in Wetzlar, Germany; Radford Carroll, "War Stories," 62; *393rd Infantry in Review*, printed booklet.

8. Richard Gorby, quoted in Ronningen, *Butler's,* 137–38; Lindell Sawyers, quoted in Swanson, *Upfront with Charley Company,* 105.

9. Ralph Shivone, quoted in Swanson, Ibid., 106; Richard Tobias, *Checkerboard* 39, no. 3 (April 1986), 7.

10. Richard Switzer, interview, February 7, 2003; Oakley Honey, quoted in Swanson, Ibid., 106.

11. Charles MacDonald, *The Last Offensive,* 362–72.

12. Harold Hill, memoir, 98–99.

13. Robert Ritchie, interview, June 25, 2005.

14. Warren Thomas, e-mail, February 12, 2005.

15. Joseph Thimm, e-mail, December 6, 2002.

16. Fred Feigenoff, interview, December 2, 2002; Byron Reburn, note to author.

17. Harry Arnold, "Easy Memories," 163–65; Radford Carroll, "War Stories,"69; Thomas Sams Bishop, diary in *Checkerboard* no. 6 (1999), 20.

18. Fielding Pope, interview, October 10, 2001; Sammy Oliverio, interview, August 16, 2004; Joseph Thimm, e-mail, February 8, 2005.

19. James Larkey, Note; Charles Eubank, interview, March 19, 2001.

20. Tim Nugent, interview, August 9, 2004.

21. David Williams, interview, June 10, 2004; Charles Roland, *My Odyssey,* 82; Carter Strong, "Hellenbach," 90; Y. B. Johnson, letter, April 17, 1945; Fred Kampmier, memoir; Omar Paxson, interview, July 15, 2005.

22. Harry Arnold, "Easy Memories," 170.

23. Joseph Shimko, interview, August 11, 2007; audio tape, Veterans History Project, Library of Congress; George Maertens, memoir, "Autobiography of I/393"; Gunter Bischof and Stephen Ambrose, eds. *Eisenhower and the German POWs,* 92.

24. Maertens, Ibid.

25. Paul Weesner, memoir, 21.

26. Carter Strong, "Hellenbach," 95.

27. Harry Arnold, "Easy Memories," 182.

28. William Cavanagh, *Dauntless, History of the 99th,* 337.

29. Thomas Ebehard, (Hemer archivist), interview, July 12, 2004.

30. William Bartow, interview, August 11, 2004.

31. David Williams, "When I was a Soldier," memoir, (Library of Congress, November 2001), 36–37.

32. Bartow, Ibid.; Ronningen, *Butler's,* 156.

CHAPTER 9. PRISONERS OF WAR

1. Alfred Goldstein, "How I Won the War," memoir; interview, August 4, 2004; Earl Peters, interview, August 4, 2004.

2. Goldstein, "How I Won the War."

3. Burnett Hartley, letter to Lt. Larry Tabor, January 29, 1987; interview, August 3, 2004; Goldstein, "How I Won the War."

4. Robert Grant, "Biographical Background of My Military Years," memoir, 13; Howard Harris, interview, June 17, 2002; B. O. Wilkins, "Dec.16, 1944" *Checkerboard* no. 1 (1995), 14; Wilkins, e-mail, October 17, 2005.

5. Wendell Cathey, interview, August 1, 2004; Robert Grant, "Bio Background," 12.

6. David Thompson, interview, December 10, 2001; William Mudra, interview, July 26, 2005.

7. Harold Wagner, interview, June 18, 2005; Elton Kerbo, interview, July 21, 2005; Raymond Perisin, interview, May 22, 2006.

8. Jack McElroy, memoir.

9. Robert Gabriel, memoir.

10. Ibid.

11. William White, "POW Notes," memoir.

12. William Mudra, "Looking from the Inside Out," memoir, 1946.

13. Ibid.

14. Ibid.

15. Ibid.

16. Ibid.

17. Ibid.

18. Milton May, memoir, 24.

19. Ibid.; Jack McElroy, e-mail, December 27, 2002.

20. Furman Grimm, interview, September 5, 2001.

21. William White, interview, July 24, 2005.

22. Richard Render, video memoir, 1988; interview, June 9, 2006, July 27, 2006.

23. Clarence Deal, interview, January 2, 2006.

24. Pendleton Woods, "Joining the 99th," memoir, 8.

25. Stanley Colby, interview, August 8, 2005; Howard Harris, interview, October 1, 2005; Robert Grant, "Biographical Background," 14.

26. Marvin Synder, "My First Fifteen Months in the Infantry," memoir, 1945, 2; Dwight Bishop, e-mail, September, 20, 2005.

27. W. J. "Billy" Heroman, interview, July 25, 2005.

28. Robert Gabriel, memoir; Karel Margry, "The Hammelburg Raid," *After the Battle*, no. 91 (1996), 21–23; Dwight Bishop, interview, August 4, 2005.

29. Marvin Synder, "First Fifteen Months," 2.

30. Ariel Kochavi, *Confronting Captivity: Britain and U.S. and their POWS in Nazi Germany*, 1.

31. Emil Wieleba, interview, June 25, 2005.

32. Al Goldstein, "How I Won the War"; interview, August 4, 2004.

33. Raymond Wenzel, e-mail to author, August 12, 2005.

34. Kochavi, *Confronting Captivity*, 34; Earl Peters, interview, August 9, 2005.

35. Burrell Hartley, "letter," 7.

36. Frank Smollen, "Memories of Frank J. Smollen, Jr.," memoir.

37. Kochavi, *Confronting Captivity*, 34.

38. Robert Grant, "Biographical Background," 15; Herb Netter, interview, July 17, 2005.

39. Burrell Hartley, "letter," 6.

40. Pendleton Woods, "Joining the 99th,"10; Patrick Morris, "Prisoner of the Germans," 11; John Thornburg, interview, November 23, 2002; Harry Hagstad, interview, March 20, 2006.

41. Harry Peterson, Jr., *Our Days are a Shadow*, 98; Burrell Hartley, "letter," 7–8.

42. William Kirkbride, interviews, August 8, 2005, August 26, 2005.

43. Robert Gabriel, memoir.

44. Gabriel, Ibid.; William Kirkbride, interview, August 26, 2005.

45. Karel Margry, "The Hammelburg Raid," *After the Battle* no. 91 (1996), 3–36.

46. Ibid.

47. William Kirkbride, interview, August 8, 2005.

48. Robert Gabriel, Memoir.

49. William Kirkbride, interview, September 26, 2005.

50. Ibid.

51. Richard Knoblock, interview, October 10, 2005.

52. Al Goldstein, "How I Won the War."

53. Ibid.

54. Robert Grant, "Biographical," 17.

55. Al Goldstein, interview, September 9, 2005.

56. Al Goldstein, "How I Won the War"; Howard Harris, interview, October 1, 2005.

57. Howard Harris, Ibid.; Frank Smollen, "Memories."

58. Emil Wieleba, interview, October 7, 2005.

59. Harold Schaefer, "Moosburg," *Checkerboard* (1994, no. 2), 9.

60. Harry Hagstad, e-mail, May 29, 2005; Robert Davis, memoir; William White, interview, July 24, 2005.

61. Harold Wagner, interview, August 27, 2005; William Mudra, "Looking from the Inside."

62. Mudra, Ibid; John Thornburg, interview, July 25, 2005; Richard Folmar, interview, September 8, 2005.

63. John Thornburg, Ibid.

64. Harold Wagner, interview, August 27, 2005, July 14, 2007; Thornburg, Ibid.

65. William Mudra, "Looking"; Patrick Morris, "Prisoner of the Germans," memoir, 9–16; Harry Peterson Jr., *Our Days are a Shadow*, 119–28.

66. Harold Wagner, e-mail, July 1, 2007; William Mudra, "Looking."

67. Richard Folmar, e-mail, July 20, 2005; Jack McElroy, memoir; Milton May, memoir, 24–25.

68. B. O. Wilkins, e-mail, August 29, 2005; Harry Peterson, *Our Days,* 125; Harold Wagner, interview, August 27, 2005.

69. John Thornburg, interview, July 25, 2005.

70. George Aaron, *Farmer Soldier,* privately printed (1967), 160; interview, December 23, 2005.

71. John Thornburg, interview, October 3, 2002.

72. Richard Folmar, interview, October 10, 2005; Edward Soule and Harold Demone, "Our Last Days in Germany" (1946).

73. Richard Folmar, interview, July 20, 2005.

74. Harold Wagner, interview, October 12, 2005.

75. Ibid.

76. William Mudra, "Looking."

77. Ibid.; Herman Knell, *To Destroy a City,* 253–54.

78. Mudra, "Looking."

79. Patrick Morris, "Prisoner of the Germans,"17–18; Mudra, "Looking."

CHAPTER 10. THE WAR COMES TO AN END

1. Harold Atkins, quoted in *Dauntless,* 341.

2. William Galegar, "Armageddon," 86; Patrick Morrisey, interview, July 5, 2005.

3. Dewey Amos, interview, November 30, 2005; Jim Bowers, "Second Platoon," in Harry Arnold, "Easy Memories," 185.

4. Guy Duren, memoir, 50; Harold Hill, Memoir, 102; Herbert Orr, quoted in Ronningen, *Butler's Battlin',* 168.

5. Byron Reburn, interview, July 17, 2005, December 2, 2005.

6. Charles Eubanks, interview, July 3, 2001.

7. Jim Bowers, quoted in Arnold, "Easy Memories," 187.

8. Ken Reed, letter to author, February 2, 2006; Fred Kampmier, e-mail, December 12, 2005.

9. Ken Haas, "Frightening Panorama along the Rhine," on *Memories of War* website.

10. Harold Hill, memoir, 103–104.

11. Paul Weesner, memoir, 23; Frank Hoffman, e-mail, December 7, 2005; interview, March 3, 2006.

12. Harold Schaefer, interview, November 27, 2005.

13. Harold Atkins, memoir.

14. Harold Hill, memoir; interviews, September 28, 2005, November 27, 2005; e-mail, March 24, 2006. This forced crossing resembled a similar Patton operation across the Saar River on February 22, 1945, with disastrous results for the 94th Infantry Division. William Folley, *Visions from A Foxhole: A Rifleman in Patton's Ghost Corps,* 110–14.

15. Robert Piller, interviews. December 14, 2005, July 16, 2007; Alvin Cooper quoted in *Dauntless,* 351.

16. Robert Piller, Ibid.; Woodrow Hickey, interview, August 20, 2002.

17. Fielding Pope, interview, October 10, 2001, November 30, 2005, December 10, 2005.

18. Robert Piller, interview, December 14 and December 27, 2005, July 16, 2007.

19. John Oakes, interview, December 5, 2005, December 12, 2005.

20. Forbes Williams, interview, March 25, 2003, December 8, 2005.

21. Thomas Woznicki, interview, September 28, 2001, December 28, 2005; William Galegar, interview, November 26, 2003, September 1, 2004, e-mail November 29, 2005.

22. Harold Hill, Memoir, 66; Hill quoted in *Dauntless*, 352; Albert Eckert, interview, October 1, 2001; *Dauntless*, 353.

23. Ken Reed, memoir, 31; Paul Jillson, letter to author, December 27, 2005.

24. Ken Reed, memoir, 31, 34–35; Harold Hill, memoir, 66–67, interview, July 20, 2002.

25. Harold Hill, e-mail, November 29, 2005; Anthony Pellegrino, interview, February 18, 2006.

26. Harold Hill, Memoir, 66–67; interview, July 20, 2002; Charles McNish, interview, August 15, 2004.

27. Ken Reed, Memoir, 34–35; Robert Justice, interview, July 6, 2002, December 7, 2005.

28. Paul Jillian, "Along the Danube," and "On the Banks of the Danube," notes.

29. Paul Weener, memoir, 25; Walter Lauer, *Battle Babies*, 304.

30. Rex Whitehead, e-mail, May 8, 2001.

31. Ken Juhl, interview, September 10, 2002.

32. Oakley Honey, interview, September 4, 2002; Robert Stirling "Buck" Abraham (B-24 Pilot and POW), interview, October 15, 2002.

33. Cliff Selwood, e-mail, June 1, 2005, interview, September 4, 2001; Herbert Orr, Memoir, 109.

34. Selwood, Ibid.

35. Stewart Fischer, e-mail, February 5, 2006; Donald Wallace, e-mail, January 16, 2006; Richard Byers, *Checkerboard* (December, 1988), 8; Leon Rogers, interview, September 22, 2001; Homer Simons, interview, December 26, 2004; Peter Wolffe, interview, February 18, 2004.

36. Ken Reed, memoir, 37; J. C. Jones, interview, January 31, 2005; George Lehr, interview, March 28, 2001; Ernest McDaniel, e-mails, May 9, 2004, May 25, 2005; William Galegar, e-mail, May 10, 2005; T. J. Cornett, interview, August 20, 2002; Tony Pellegrino, interview, February 18, 2006.

37. Joseph Herdina, interview, November 8, 2002; Bill Meyer, interview, May 31, 2006; Guy Duren, e-mail, May 10, 2005; Cliff Selwood, interview, February 3, 2006.

38. Ken Reed, letter to author, February 2, 2006.

39. Harold Hill, Memoir, 109; Steve Kallas, "Dog Face," memoir.

40. Charles Eubanks, interview, July 3, 2001.'

41. William McMurdie, *Hey, Mac!*, 165; Fred Feigenoff, interview, January 13, 2006.

42. George Maertens, memoir, in "The Autobiography of I/393"; Allan Nelson, interview, January 6, 2006; Edward Eimermann, interview, March 10, 2006; Richard Tommey, interview, November 25, 2005; Robert Ritchie, interview, June 25, 2005.

43. Omar Paxson, letter to author, July 20, 2005.

44. Guy Duren, e-mail to author, June 16, 2005.

45. Robert Walter, e-mail to author, January 15, 2006.

46. Steve Kallas, interview, September 9, 2003; Anthony Aiello, *Checkerboard* 43, no. 2 (May 1990), 9; Fred Kampmier, interview, February 6, 2006; Ken Reed, letter to author, February 2, 2006.

47. Forbes Williams, interview, December 7, 2005; Tom Woznicki, interview, December 28, 2005.

48. Fred Kampmier, interview, February 6, 2006.

49. George Maertens, "The Autobiography of I/393."

50. Joseph O'Neill, interview, November 21, 2005.

51. Anonymous GI 394th, Letter to author February 13, 2005.

52. Donald Perry, interview, June 16, 2005.

53. Francis Chesnick, interview, January 14, 2006.

54. Stuart Kline, interview, December 28, 2005.

55. James Larkey, e-mail, June 10, 2007; George Meloy, memoir, "Autobiography of I/393."

56. Warren Thomas, e-mail, January 14, 2006.

57. Maltie Anderson, interview, February 10, 2003; William McMurdie, *Hey, Mac!*, 192: Thor Ronningen, "Thor's War, *Checkerboard* no. 2 (2001), 29; Rex Whitehead, Checkerboard no. 4 (2000), 8.

58. T. J. Cornett, interview, August 20, 2002, Rex Whitehead, Ibid.; Charles Swann, interview, February 10, 2003; Fred Verdecchi, interview, October 10, 2002.

59. Charles Swann, interview, February 10, 2003; Luke Brannon, letter to author, March 17, 2005.

60. Francis Iglehart, interviews, May 4, 2001, March 24, 2006.

61. Ronald Kraemer, interview, December 26, 2002; Willis Botz, interview, September 3, 2001.

62. Rex Whitehead, "War's End," *Checkerboard* no. 4 (2000), 8.

63. Stan Colby, e-mail, December 14, 2005; Raymond Wenzel, e-mail, May 9, 2005; Forbes Williams, interview, December 7, 2005; T. J. Cornett, interview, August 20, 2002; Luke Brannon, letter to author, March 17, 2005; Al Boeger, e-mail, April 25, 2001; Richard Switzer, interview, February 7, 2003; Harry Hagstad, interviews, August 10, 2001, March 10, 2005; Merle Otto, interview, January 8, 2005, and "Army Days," memoir; Warren Thomas,

e-mail, January 1, 2006; Francis Chesnick, letter to author, July 20, 2002; Charles Katlic, letter to author, January 17, 2006; Roy Fish, interview, February 6, 2004; Joseph Carnevale, interview, February 10, 2003; Anthony Pellegrino, interview, February 18, 2006; Frank Garrett, interview, August 11, 2005; Robert Mitsch, e-mail, February 27, 2006.

64. Tony Dodd, interview, August 3, 2005 and November 7, 2005; Howard Bowers, interview, June 7, 2007; William Galegar, interview, November 4, 2005.

65. Homer Kissinger, e-mail, November 14, 2005; Frank Hoffman, interview, April 10, 2002; Earl Faull, interviews, June 29, 2005, March 20, 2006; James Larkey, interview, August 18, 2004; Don Wallace, e-mail, February 18, 2006.

66. David Spencer, interviews, May 3, 2001, July 21, 2002; Glenny Blanchard, interview, February 9, 2005; Newman Smith, interview, July 6, 2002.

67. Harold Hill, interview, July 5, 2002.

68. Thomas Woznicki, interview, September 27, 2001, February 15, 2005; James Crafton, interview, August 6, 2001; Fred Gole, interview, May 27, 2005.

69. Al Eckert, interviews, September 31, 2001 and March 15, 2006; James Larkey, interview, August 18, 2004.

70. Fred Kampmier, interview, February 6, 2006; Charles Swann, interviews, February 10, 2003, January 23, 2006.

71. Anthony Pellegrino, interview, February 18, 2006; James Larkey, interview, November 7, 2005.

72. Robert Mitsch, e-mail, February 27, 2006; Charles Katlic, September 11, 2001; Earle Slyder, e-mail September 11, 2001; Henry Thomas, interviews, July 17, 2004 and March 11, 2006.

73. Bernave Aguillera, interview, May 31, 2006; Byron Rawls, interview, September 6, 2001; Joseph Thimm, e-mail, November 21, 2005; Howard Bowers, "Memories of WWII," 27; Virdin Royce, interview, July 5, 2002; Robert Justice, interview, July 6, 2002; John Kuhn, interview, April 22, 2006; Harry Hagstad, interview, March 11, 2006; James Langford, e-mail, January 1, 2002; William Galegar, interview, November 4, 2005; Carter Strong, letter, "Dear Mom and Dad," October 14, 1945.

74. Virdin Royce, interview, July 5, 2002; William Galegar, "Armageddon," 110.

75. Harry Arnold, "Easy Memories," 211.

Selected Bibliography

Books

Aaron, George V., *Farmer Soldier.* Self-published, 1967.

Adams, Michael. *The Best War Ever: America and World War II.* Baltimore: Johns Hopkins University Press, 1994.

Ambrose, Stephen. *Citizen Soldiers.* New York: Simon and Shuster, 1997.

Arnold, James. *Ardennes 1944: Hitler's Last Gamble in the West.* Oxford, G.B.: Osprey, 1990.

Arrington, Grady. *Infantryman at the Front.* New York: Vantage Press, 1959.

Astor, Gerald. *A Blood-Dimmed Tide: The Battle of the Bulge by the Men Who Fought it.* New York: Dell, 1992.

Bischof, Gunter and Stephen Ambrose, eds. *Eisenhower and the German POWS: Facts against Falsehood.* Baton Rouge: Louisiana State University Press, 1992.

Blumenson, Martin. *Patton: The Man Behind the Legend, 1885–1945.* New York: William Morrow, 1985.

Cavanagh, William. *Dauntless: A History of the 99th Infantry Division.* Dallas: Taylor, 1994.

———. *Krinkelt-Rocherath: The Battle for the Twin Villages.* Norwell, Mass.: Christopher, 1986.

Cole, Hugh. *The Ardennes: Battle of the Bulge.* Washington, D.C.: Dept of the Army, 1965.

Colley, David. *Blood for Dignity: The Story of the First Integrated Unit in the U.S. Army.* New York: St. Martin's Press, 2003.

Doherty, J. C. *The Shock of War.* Vols. 1 & 2. Alexandria, Va.: Vert Milon Press, 1997.

Doubler, Michael. *Closing with the Enemy: How GIs Fought the War in Europe, 1944–1945.* Lawrence: University Press of Kansas, 1994.

Ellis, John. *The Sharp End: The Fighting Man in World War II.* New York: Charles Scribner's Sons, 1980.

Farrar, Walton. *The Combat History of the 394th Infantry Regiment.* Privately published, 1946.

Folley, William Jr. *Visions from a Foxhole: A Rifleman in Patton's Ghost Corps.* Novato, Calif.: Presidio Press, 2003.

Gray, Jesse Glenn. *The Warriors: Reflections on Men in Battle.* New York: Harper Colophon Books, 1970.

Hechler, Ken. *The Bridge at Remagen: The Amazing Story of March 7, 1945— The Day the Rhine Was Crossed.* New York: Ballantine Books, 1978.

Iglehart, Francis. *The Short Life of the ASTP.* Baltimore, Md.: American Literary Press, 2000.

Keefer, Louis. *Scholars in Foxholes: The Story of the Army Specialized Training Program in World War II.* Jefferson, N.C.: McFarland and Co., 1988.

Kennedy, David. *Freedom from Fear: The American People in Depression and War.* New York: Oxford University Press, 1999.

Kennett, Lee. *G.I. The American Soldier in World War II.* New York: Charles Scribner's Sons, 1987.

———. *For the Duration: The United States Goes to War, Pearl Harbor—1942.* New York: Charles Scribner's Sons, 1985.

Kessler, Leo. *The Battle of the Ruhr Pocket: April 1945.* Chelsea, Maine: Scarborough House, 1989.

Kochavi, Ariel. *Confronting Captivity: Britain and the United States and Their POWS in Nazi Germany.* Chapel Hill, N.C.: University of North Carolina Press, 2005

Little, Ruth, ed. *Love, and a Prayer.* Stevensville, Mont.: Stoneydale Press, 1999.

Kindsvatter, Peter. *American Soldiers: Ground Combat in the World Wars, Korea, and Vietnam.* Lawrence: University Press of Kansas, 2003.

Knell, Hermann. *To Destroy A City: Strategic Bombing and Its Human Consequences in World War II.* Cambridge, Mass.: Da Capo Press, 2003.

Lauer, Walter, *Battle Babies: The Story of the 99th Infantry Division in WWII.* Nashville: Battery Press, 1950.

Linderman, Gerald. *The World Within War: America's Combat Experience in World War II.* Cambridge, Mass.: Harvard University Press, 1997.

Lombardo, Samuel. *O'er the Land of the Free.* Shippensburg, Penn.: Beidel Printing House, 2000.

MacDonald, Charles. *The Last Offensive.* Washington, D.C.: Office of the Chief of Military History, 1973.

MacDonald, Charles. *The Mighty Endeavor: The American War in Europe.* New York: William Morrow, 1988.

MacDonald, Charles. *The Siegfried Line Campaign* Washington, D.C.: Dept. of the Army, 1963.

MacDonald, Charles. *A Time for Trumpets: The Untold Story of the Battle of the Bulge.* New York: Bantam Books, 1985.

Mansoor, Peter. *The GI Offensive in Europe: The Triumph of American Infantry Division, 1941–1945.* Lawrence: University Press of Kansas, 1999.

McManus, John. *The Deadly Brotherhood: The American Combat Soldier in World War II*. Novato, Calif.: Presidio Press, 1998.

McMurdie, William. *Hey, Mac!* Gig Harbor, Washington: Red Apple Publishing, 2000.

Neill, George. *Infantry Soldier: Holding the Line at the Battle of the Bulge*. Norman: University of Oklahoma Press, 2000.

Niedermayer, Walter, *Into the Deep Misty Woods of the Ardennes*. Penn.: A. G. Halldin Pub. Co., 1990.

Pallud, Jean-Paul. *Battle of the Bulge: Then and Now*. London: Battle of Britain International Limited, 1986.

Palmer, Robert, et al. *The Procurement and Training of Ground Combat Troops*. Washington, D.C.: Dept. of the Army, 1948

Phillips, Henry Gerard. *Remagen: Springboard to Victory*. Penn Valley, Calif.: H.G. Phillips, 1995.

Peterson, Harry Jr. *Our Days are a Shadow*. Oak Park, Ill.: Lee Brooke, 2006.

Pyle, Ernie. *Brave Men*. New York: Henry Holt, 1946.

Ramsey, Winston. "Crossing the Rhine." *After the Battle* 16 (1977): 1–12.

Reynolds, Michael. *The Devil's Adjutant: Jochen Peiper, Panzer Leader*. Sarpedon, N.Y., 1995.

Roland, Charles. *My Odyssey through History: Memoirs of War and Academe*. Baton Rouge, La.: LSU Press, 2004.

Ronningen, Thor. *Butler's Battlin' Blue Bastards*. Lawrenceville, Va.: Brunswick Pub., 1993.

Rusiecki, Stephen. *The Key to the Bulge: The Battle for Losheimergraben*. Westport, Conn.: Praeger, 1996.

Schrijvers, Peter. *The Crash of Ruin: American Combat Soldiers During World War II*. New York: New York University Press, 2001.

———. *The Unknown Dead: Civilians in the Battle of the Bulge*. Lexington: University of Kentucky, 2005.

Stanton, Shelby. *World War II Order of Battle*. New York: Galahad Books, 1991.

Stouffer, Samuel, et al. *The American Soldier: Combat and Its Aftermath*. Princeton: Princeton University Press, 1949.

Swanson, Vern. *Upfront with Charlie Company: A Combat History of Company C, 395th Infantry Regiment, 99th Infantry Division*. North Royalton, Ohio: 1995.

Thompson, Harry. *Patton's Ill-Fated Raid*. Corinth, Texas: Historical Resources Press, 2002.

Warnock, Bill. *The Dead of Winter: How Battlefield Investigators, WWII Veterans and Forensic Scientists Solved the Mystery of the Bulge's Lost Soldiers*. New York: Chamberlain Bros., 2005.

Whiting, Charles. *The Battle for the German Frontier*. New York: Interlink Books, 2000.

———. *Battle of the Ruhr Pocket*. New York: Ballantine Books, 1970.

———. *48 Hours to Hammelburg*. New York: Jove Books, 1984.

Winters, Harold, et al., *Battling the Elements: Weather and Terrain in the Conduct of War.* Baltimore: Johns Hopkins University Press, 1998.
Zumbro, Derek. *Battle for the Ruhr: The German Army's Final Defeat in the West.* Lawrence: University Press of Kansas, 2006.

ARTICLES

Aiello, Tony. *Checkerboard* (May 1990): 5.
Byers, Richard. *Checkerboard* (December 1988).
Biggio, Charles. "Role of the Field Artillery in the Battle of Elsenborn." *Checkerboard*, no. 5 (1998): 4–6.
Bishop, Thomas Sams, "Diary." *Checkerboard*, no. 6 (1994):20.
Brech, Martin. "In Eisenhower's Death Camp: A U.S. Prison Guard's Story." *Journal of Historical Review* 10, no. 2:161–66.
Byers, Richard. *Checkerboard* (December 1988).
Fabianich, Keith, "The Defense of Höfen, Germany," *Infantry School Quarterly* 33 (July 1948): 43–58.
Haskins, Francis. "Ammo Train." *Checkerboard* (December 1990): 10.
Head, Tilden. *Checkerboard*, no. 1 (2001).
Langford, James. "Experienes of an Infantry Squad." *Checkerboard*, no. 4 (2001): 6–7.
Margry, Karel. "The Hammelburg Raid." *After the Battle*, no. 91 (1996): 3–36.
Marcisin, John. "Reminiscenses." *Checkerboard*, no. 5 (1994).
McIlroy, J. R. "Foxhole Monotony." *Checkerboard* (September 1993).
Meloy, George. "A Memorable Christmas Night." *Checkerboard*, no 7 (1992): 2.
Norris, Max. *Checkerboard.* (March 1986)
Revell, James. "On Combat." *Checkerboard* (September 1992).
Ronningen, Thor. "Memoir of a World War II Infantryman." *Checkerboard*, no. 2 (2000).
———. "Thor's War." *Checkerboard*, no. 5 (2000): 5.
Schaefer, Harold, "Moosburg: History of the POW Camp Stalag VII A, *Checkerboard* (second issue, 1994), 9.
———. Schaefer, Harold. ""2nd Bn 394 'Strategic Advance,'" *Checkerboard* (March 1991): 17–18.
Thimm, Joe. "Höfen—Winter of 1944–45." *Checkerboard.* (March 1991): 14–15.
Tobias, Richard. *Checkerboard* (April 1986): 7.
Wallace, Donald. "Overseas with the 99th Infantry Division." *Checkerboard*, no. 1 (1998): 8.
Whitehead, Rex. "War's End." *Checkerboard*, no. 4 (2000).

UNPUBLISHED MEMOIRS AND ESSAYS

Atkins, Henri. "Recollections of WWII." Memoir (1994).
Arnold, Harry. "Easy Memories: The Way It Was." Memoir (1985).

Bishop, Jim. "A Call to Valor." Memoir and history (1998).

Byers, Richard, "Battle of the Bulge." Memoir (1996).

Bowers, Howard. "Memories of World War II." Revised memoir (2001).

Carroll, Radford. "Stories for my Grandchildren." Memoir (1985; revised 2001).

Duren, Guy. "Personal Memoir" (1948).

Fischer, Stewart and Myra, eds. *Some Uncommon Common Men* (unpublished collection of essays, 2001).

Galegar, William. "One Man's Armageddon." Memoir (1991).

Goldstein, Al. "How I Won the War."

Hill, Harold. "Memoir."

Hawn, Robert. "Memoirs: 1943–1946" (2007).

Jackson, Emmet. "Combat Diary." (Memoir 1945; updated 1998).

Kampmier, Fred. "WWII Memoirs" (1945; updated 2006).

King, Richard. "Teenagers at War."

McCoy, John. "Remembrance of Army Days, 1943–46."

McDaniel, Ernest. "Memories of World War II" (1998).

Morris, Patrick. "Prisoner of the Germans."

Morrissey, Patrick. "Personal Memories of the Battle of the Bulge."

Mitsch, Robert. "Lucking Out: A Recall of World War II Survival and Observations" (1989).

Mudra, William. "Looking from the Inside Out." Memoir (1946).

Pedrotti, Louis. "Tales from the 99th Division."

Sawyers, Lindell. "Twelve Days to Christmas" (2001).

Schaefer, Harold. "You Asked For It." Memoir (2001).

Speder, J. P. "The 99th Infantry Division in the Battle of the Bulge."

Strong, Carter. "To Hellenbach" (1946).

Synder, Marvin. "My First Fifteen Months in the Infantry" (1945).

Thornburg, John. "Wunflialdye!" (August, 1945).

Weesner, Paul. "Memoir" (1945).

Williams, David. "When I Was a Soldier" (2001).

Index